EDUCATE, AGITATE, ORGANIZE

100 Years of Fabian Socialism

EDUCATE, AGITATE, ORGANIZE

100 YEARS OF FABIAN SOCIALISM

Patricia Pugh

METHUEN
London & New York

First published in 1984 by
Methuen & Co. Ltd
11 New Fetter Lane, London EC4P 4EE

Published in the USA by
Methuen & Co.
in association with Methuen, Inc.
733 Third Avenue, New York, NY 10017

Printed in Great Britain
at the University Press, Cambridge

British Library Cataloguing in Publication Data

Pugh, Patricia
Educate, agitate, organize:
100 years of Fabian Socialism.
1. Fabian Society – History
I. Title
355′.14   HX241.F3

ISBN 0–416–39080–3

Library of Congress Cataloging in Publication Data

Pugh, Patricia.
Educate, agitate, organize.
Bibliography: p.
Includes index.
1. Fabian Society (Great Britain) – History.
2. Socialism – Great Britain – History.   I. Title.
HX241.F333P84   1984   335′.14′09   84–19004

ISBN 0–416–39080–3

CONTENTS

LIST OF ILLUSTRATIONS

The illustrations appear between pages 178 and 179.

ACKNOWLEDGEMENTS

While writing is a lonely occupation, research can sometimes be quite the reverse. Working on this history has brought me so much friendship, goodwill, encouragement and help that it gives me the greatest pleasure to be able, here, to say 'thank you'.

My thanks are due in the first place to the Fabian Society itself for inviting me, a non-Fabian, to undertake such a fascinating study, leaving me completely free to tackle the subject in my own way. No constraint was placed upon what I wished to say or on the way in which I said it, nor was there any restriction on papers I wished to consult. Such trust and generosity is, indeed, greatly appreciated.

Next I wish to thank the Warden and Fellows of Nuffield College for, most unexpectedly, electing me an Associate Member of the college and allocating a carrel where I could work on manuscripts undisturbed. This gift of time and space immeasurably eased the long labour of consulting primary sources. The Fellows' interest and perceptive questions frequently cast a new light on facts and evidence and stimulated the growth of understanding. In particular, I would like to thank Dr A.F. Madden, who, long ago, placed my feet on the road that eventually led to the Fabian Society's papers, and to the Warden, Michael Brock, for most valuable advice over the last three years. To the college librarian, Christine Kennedy, and her staff I am unusually indebted, for they welcomed me back into the working body of which I was briefly a member in a manner that heartened me when the going was hard; they lightened the task more than they can possibly realize.

Without the varied labours of fellow-archivists who have shared the duty of conserving and reconstituting the true structure of Fabian archives in Rhodes House and Nuffield College and producing guides to their contents, this history could never have been produced. Very many students of Commonwealth history have reason, like me, to bless the 'ladies of the Hawksley Room', Patience Empson, Jean Cockayne and June Williams, for their admirable handlists of the Colonial Bureau papers. Students of political, economic and social development in Britain throughout the last century frequently give thanks, as I do, to Sally Mackesy and Eleanor Vallis, who toiled long but with unfailing cheerfulness and enthusiasm to complete the guide to the main series of the Fabian records. For help with other major sources of British Labour history I am grateful to Dr Angela Raspin of the British Library of Political and Economic Science, Richard Storey of the Centre for Modern Records at the University of Warwick, Marion Stewart of the Archives Centre, Churchill College, Cambridge, and the former and present librarians of the Labour Party.

It is never a simple matter for those at the centre of this country's political life, particularly Members of Parliament, to find time to answer the questions of a researcher, yet never has anyone refused either to grant me an interview or to reply to a series of written questions. Were I to name everyone who has patiently considered and answered my often naïve queries this passage would rival succeeding chapters in length. I would, however, specially like to record my indebtedness to the late Dame Margaret Cole and John Parker, MP, who, on visits to Nuffield College, recounted many hilarious anecdotes about the Society. All the Fabian General Secretaries have been most generous in helping me toward an understanding of the underlying significance of what is recorded in the Society's minutes. As well as John Parker, Lord Northfield of Telford (Donald Chapman), Andrew Filson, the Rt Hon. William Rodgers, the Rt Hon. Shirley Williams, Lord Ponsonby of Shulbrede (Tom Ponsonby), Dianne Hayter and Ian Martin have all endowed their particular sections of the Society's story with a vitiality that can rarely be derived from records alone. The late Dr Rita Hinden and Marjorie Nicholson both gave me a far more secure understanding of the Colonial Bureau than I could possibly have achieved otherwise. Elizabeth Durbin of New York, when a visiting fellow at Nuffield College, shared my enthusiasm for the New Fabian Research Bureau and allowed me to read in manuscript her study of its work. Carole Smith, a visiting student from Harvard, combed *Fabian News* for details of local societies, to which observations by Dorothy Fox and Sandra Melville, successive secretaries of the Local Societies Committee, gave perspective. I would have liked to

EDUCATE, AGITATE, ORGANIZE

have met and consulted many more Fabians than I did, but time did not permit.

From overseas I have received similarly bountiful assistance. In America, Canada, Australia, New Zealand and Japan politicians and academics have drawn on their memories and records to describe to me the impact of Fabianism in their parts of the world. George Cadbury of Ottawa put me in touch with a number of people who confirmed that in North America the influence of the Fabian Society was indirect. From Australia I received a constant flow of information from Race Matthews, who also invoked the help of Clyde Cameron and John Menadue. H.O. Roth of Auckland sent a draft paper on the history of the New Zealand Fabian Societies. Professor Naomi Maruo and Masata Oka, both of Yokohama, Japan, described in detail the foundation and work of the Fabian Institute of Tokyo.

The Society of Authors has most obligingly permitted quotations from the works of George Bernard Shaw. I am similarly indebted to the British Library of Political and Economic Science for permission to use extracts from manuscript material in its possession.

I am deeply obliged to Phillip Whitehead and Belinda Dearbergh for nursing this book through its final stage, and to Deirdre Terrins for help with the illustrations.

To my family are due apologies for the boredom so courteously concealed on being told constantly 'The Fabians said that years before'. As always, and in all things, my deepest debt of gratitude is to my husband who, throughout, has suffered neglect without complaint, nightly endured the pounding typewriter, provided continuous encouragement and given the most constructive criticism with tact and love.

Finally, I wish to state that none of the people from whom I have received help and information is in any way responsible for the views expressed here; they are those of the writer alone.

INTRODUCTION

Producing this history of the Fabian Society has been like reconstructing the story of a great, continuously occupied, and constantly modified Victorian house. Two major histories have already been written, both by people who spent a lifetime in the Society helping to direct its work. Edward Pease, whose *History of the Fabian Society* was first published in 1916, was one of its founders and served as General Secretary and Honorary Secretary from 1890 to 1919 and then for twenty years on the Executive Committee. Dame Margaret Cole wrote *The Story of Fabian Socialism* to mark the first seventy-five years of the Society's life. Her service took many different forms, culminating in eighteen years as its President. This centenary history is meant to complement their books, not supplant them.

The house has been extended several times and outbuildings added. Some of the extensions are still occupied by the family, some have been taken over by others and some are shuttered and locked because they are no longer used. Like all great houses it is costly to run, it sometimes looks shabby and periodically requires major repairs and reinforcements. Yet the influence of those who live there spreads far beyond its walls. The size of the family fluctuates. At times rebellious offspring storm out of the house; usually they return in a few years maturer and wiser, though some remain resentful and hostile and keep their distance. Occasionally there are additions to the family; then a great commotion of activity and productivity can be seen. Some members leave the house to work far from home, yet still keep in touch with what the others are doing. Always the shadow of the founders hangs over the house. The external appearance of the building may no longer be as they fashioned it, but the original design remains at its core.

The chronicle of a large family can rarely be unfolded a year at a time because the several stories of the different branches develop simultaneously. So it has been with the Fabian Society. Readers will have to be both tolerant and agile because they will often be asked to take a considerable leap backward in time in order to peer through another window into a different room. The significance of the first generation's actions at home and abroad is comparatively easy to discern because the family group was small and its story has a beginning, a middle and an end. The story of the second generation is more complicated because the family has grown and both internal relationships and those beyond its walls have become far more varied. Yet that story, too, has its beginning, middle and end and can be comprehended as a whole. For the third generation there is a beginning and a middle but no end to the story.

When the idea of producing a history of the Society in celebration of its centenary was first mooted there was no suspicion that the Society was about to enter a period of great stress resulting in fracture. Not until enough time has elapsed to reveal the lines of development of both the Fabian Society of today and the section which has recently broken away can a true understanding of recent Fabian history be achieved.

A single book, a single writer, cannot provide a definitive history of every aspect of a Society which has worked hard for a hundred years. When the Executive Committee invited me to undertake this centenary history it knew that, having spent several years sorting, listing and generally working on the Fabian records, I would base my research primarily on that archive, and there would be no attempt to produce a critical study of 'Fabianism'. In the past several writers have studied Fabianism in relation to British politics; others in the future will investigate the many facets of that philosophy. Bearing in mind Sidney Webb's maxim that the work of the Fabian Society is the sum of the work of individual Fabians, I have tried to describe the way the Society works, the distinctive contributions of individuals to that work, the structure they have built and the methods they have evolved to facilitate their labours. Fabians are of all kinds and have a variety of talents. Some are dedicated to shaping economic and social policies, speaking or writing about them and devising the political strategy by which they may be put into practice. Though these are the most easily distinguished Fabians, their ideas might vanish without the assistance of those good at organizing campaigns, recruiting members or raising funds, of those skilled in converting others and inspiring them to spread wide the ideas of the policy makers, or those who run the office, type the letters and despatch the literature. It would be ridiculous to pretend that all mention of what earlier writers have described could be avoided; such an exercise would provide a very distorted picture of the Society. Original material, now available for the first time has, fortunately, augmented those former descriptions and, in some cases, placed incidents in a new setting. Exploration of the archive has also revealed entirely fresh information and stories long forgotten, both of which add to our understanding. I trust, therefore, that what is written here will answer some questions for those curious about the Fabian Society and, in conjuction with the guides to the two Fabian archives in Oxford, will provide a tool for all those engaged in studies related to it.

I

FOUNDATION AND BASIS

'We had with considerable courage set out to reconstruct society,
and we frankly confessed that we did not know how to do it.'

Edward Pease, in his *History of the Fabian Society*, thus described the
intentions and feelings of its founders in 1884.[1]

Today, perhaps more easily than at other times, we can understand why
the Fabian Society began as and when it did, why the group of young men
and women who met in Edward Pease's lodgings in Osnaburgh Street in
London felt the need to create an organization to help reconstruct society
on more morally acceptable lines. The climate of opinion in Britain during
the 1960s and 1970s was very similar to theirs, with young people
becoming politically aware, dissatisfied with materialist attitudes, suspect-
ing the inventions of their expanding world were not being used for the
benefit of the many but for the enrichment of the few. Then, as now,
groups of young people dropped out to form communities in which they
tried to turn back to nature and live on the products of their own manual
labour. They pooled their resources and educated their children themselves. Then, as now, such communes constantly came to grief, lost
members and were revived by the few who remained. Then, as now, the
young sought spiritual leaders: in the 1870s some chose William Morris;
the more politically austere chose Karl Marx; others followed the teaching
of Henry George and believed that a single land-tax was the panacea for all
social ills; still others were attracted by the views of Thomas Davidson,
who returned from America to preach that a man must first reform himself
before he tried to reconstruct the world he lived in. The Tractarian
Movement, founded in Oxford, had been based on a related idea within
the context of the established Church; few of the young of the 1880s were
satisfied by liturgical reforms, though some took part in its work for the

poor in the London slums. On the whole, the Oxford Movement was felt to belong to the older generation. Darwin's theory of evolution had undermined paternalism and encouraged the idea that people had a right to expect continual improvement. Comte's organic interpretation of society supplemented this view. Man had only to give evolution a nudge in the social, economic and political spheres for the lot of all to be radically improved. Progress was the mantra of the time. The Fabian Society was founded in order to discover not only the answers to the moral questions raised by this revolution in thought but also practical solutions to the economic and social evils of the day.

The story has been told many times, with a little added in each telling, of how the young stockbroker, Edward Pease, invited some friends to meet in his rooms to discuss Davidson's ideas after hearing him lecture on his philosophy. They decided to create a Fellowship of the New Life to help them reshape their own lives and become a more valuable part of society. Pease, discontented with his work in the City, was already a dedicated joiner – or founder – of associations. At the very first meeting on 23 October were Pease's cousins, Emily and Isabella Ford, and their close friend Frank Podmore with whom he had founded the society for Psychical Research.[2]

Pease, though not entirely convinced by its manifesto, *Socialism Made Plain*, had already joined the Democratic Federation as well as the Progressive Association which advocated moral awakening as the foundation for social and political reform. He therefore invited the three Federation leaders, Henry Champion, J.L. Joynes and R.P.B. Frost to meet his Progressive friends, Podmore and Percival Chubb and discuss the New Life proposals.[3] Chubb brought along his cronies, Maurice Adams and Percival Pullen, and the Ford girls introduced a small family group consisting of an architect called Robins, his wife and daughter, together with a widow, Mrs Hinton, and a Miss Hadden. Fascinated by Davidson's ideas about free development of human faculties and education of children in a caring environment, they dreamed of a Utopian community.

Agreeing first to become better acquainted, the participants next decided both to read Davidson's paper on the New Life and consider a constitution for a fellowship. A tentative conclusion was reached that they would like to live in a community, but it would have to be urban, in which each would follow his or her own vocation but their combined efforts would be directed towards providing a worthy education for the young, and self-sufficiency. Although they were not aware of it, this project was essentially introspective. From the minutes it is not clear whether they sought to learn from the mistakes of others when they decided to ask Dale Owen, the daughter of Robert Owen, to address their next meeting on his experiments at New Harmony in America.

A fortnight later some of them met again, joined by the journalist Hubert Bland and Havelock Ellis, neither of whom had been able to accept the former invitation. In spite of objections to this formality, a draft constitution was presented, already much discussed and revised. Each clause was again dissected and discussed at such length that no vote was reached, but all agreed: 'That an association be formed whose ultimate aim should be the reconstruction of Society in accordance with the highest moral possibilities'.[4]

Obviously, no constitution could be drawn up by seventeen people, some of them nominally anarchists, all wanting their views incorporated in full. A group of five were detailed to redraft the second constitution defining the Fellowship's attitude towards a competitive economy, but all that could be agreed was that the Fellowship should recognize that the competitive system was not working and that society must be reconstructed morally. They decided a collection should be taken at their fortnightly meetings in lieu of any fixed subscription and the subject for discussion at the next announced. It was all very nebulous, but by the third meeting their numbers had doubled and thirty people crowded into Pease's rooms. The dichotomy between the practical men and the unworldly searchers for a new way of life now became evident. One side regarded the statement:

> The members of the Society assert that the Competitive System assures the happiness and comfort of the few at the expense of the many, and that Society must be reconstructed in such a manner as to secure the general welfare and happiness

as too materialistic. Their beliefs led to even more discussion and to the proposal that:

> The Society consist of those alone who are willing to devote themselves to the best of their abilities to the amelioration of the condition of Man, and who will work together for mutual benefit and help towards the eradication of selfishness and the introduction of the New Life.

Another section of the group was looking for more practical ways to set about reshaping society and put their ideals and aspirations to work. They agreed that the spirit of brotherly love, justice and equality was needed, but short of reviving the French Revolution, they also wanted something to *do*,

3

not just feel and think. Yet another committee was delegated to settle this point.

It met at the house of Dr Burns-Gibson, then leader of the more spiritual section. He declared that his group would not join the Fellowship if his own amendments to the disputed statement were not accepted. They tried to draft another resolution but when this and the resulting amendments were put to the meeting on 6 December all that could be decided was to reconsider the whole question at the next meeting. Most rejected the doctor's resolution because it expressed such idealistic and abstract aims that many generations could pass before society would be regenerated by living the simple life. It seemed as though the new movement might never be formed.

However, the new year brought new resolutions, this time framed by Frank Podmore and circulated before the meeting on Friday 4 January 1884, so that all could come with ideas clear and proposals well considered. Podmore suggested that they call themselves the Fabian Society after Quintus Fabius Cunctator, a Roman general of the third century BC who, he alleged, adopted the strategy in the war against Hannibal of undermining the enemy by mobile guerilla skirmishes, denying them the opportunity for a pitched battle and delaying full-scale confrontation long after his colleagues would have plunged into the fray, all in order to select the most effective moment for launching his own, fully prepared attack. After admitting that they could only hope to 'help on' the reconstruction of society, they were at last able to determine their first practical steps. Under Podmore's proposals, meetings for discussion and reading of papers were to be held, but Fabians were also to become deeply involved in the society they so greatly deplored, not merely indulge in pleasant cultural activity and mutual moral improvement. He proposed not just to set an example but to investigate those conditions which so repelled them and publish the results and conclusions. By ten votes to four the spiritually inclined were defeated and a pattern was set for the work of the Fabian Society which has continued, with timely modifications and expansions, for a hundred years. The new Society agreed that, as well as preparing and discussing papers, members should report to meetings what they had learned of social conditions. Some would then be delegated to attend meetings where those matters were being discussed, not only to learn and report back but also to disseminate Fabian views. Information on social needs and developments could be culled from newspapers and current literature to supplement their direct investigations. Those who balked at this down-to-earth design

4

withdrew to form their own Fellowship of the New Life. Some, like Chubb, became members of both societies for a while. The practical men remained and appointed Hubert Bland, Frederick Keddell and Frank Podmore as an executive committee for the first three months. After a collection was taken the Society was launched on 13/9d.

Fabians expected political measures and economic reforms to bring about their desired social reconstruction. Some went to a lecture by Henry George on land reforms, some to a conference of the Democratic Federation. At a members' meeting on 25 January 1884 they reported back on them and listened to J. Glade Stapleton's review of social conditions and means of reconstruction and development. In February, Podmore explained Fabian aims more fully and the Reverend W.A. Macdonald those of the Democratic Federation. After a hot debate the audience agreed with Bland that though the Federation seemed to be doing a good job, some phrases and statements in its literature were not at all acceptable. Obviously they would have to produce their own pamphlets and the infant Society acquired a committee to organize publication 'whenever occasion might arise'. Immediately it received a diatribe from the Society's sole working-class member, W.L. Phillips, a house-painter. It was unsuitable for publication so the whole Society worked over it sentence by sentence until it was fit to print as the first Fabian penny tract, *Why Are the Many Poor?*, of which 3000 copies were printed. Three were sent to each member for distribution, the rest sold like religious tracts. Meanwhile members were seeking out other groups and organizations interested in the same problems, wherever their professional concerns might take them. The pattern was established: observe, collect facts, discuss and publish.

People attracted by the Society wanted to know exactly what it stood for before joining. A printed card stating the Basis upon which they proposed to act was handed to all prospective members. Election to the Society entailed signed acceptance of the Basis. Since friends of Fabians in the provinces and overseas quickly became interested they agreed to allow persons known to existing members to become corresponding members if duly nominated and seconded. The first two elected thus were Dr David de Jong of Cologne and Norah Robertson who lived in Vienna. Strict rules of procedure at meetings were drawn up.

Before the year was out Tract No. 1 had to be reprinted. The publication committee, on which sat Edith Nesbit, the novelist wife of Hubert Bland, decided to print 5000 copies of their second tract, *A Manifesto*, by George Bernard Shaw. Supplies disappeared fast, as they were rashly generous. When the Scottish Land and Labour League asked for tracts to distribute at a rally it was sent 500 of each. But this was good publicity.

At most members' meetings papers were read which either tentatively examined the ways in which socialism could be introduced into Britain or reviewed current financial and economic theories. Already the Fabians had convinced themselves that they were socialists, although very few of them had read any socialist literature and fewer had any knowledge of economics. Rowland Estcourt must have bored everyone with two papers containing a mass of figures delivered at successive meetings, but no one would admit it. Bernard Shaw made his first appearance at the second of these meetings and so was in no position to show the speaker the error of his ways. This kind of Utopianism made its last appearance when Shaw mischievously introduced a Fifth Monarchy man into a meeting in summer 1886, by which time they had already abandoned all ideas of a commune in Chile or the Argentine.[5] Fabians were confident enough of having something worth revealing to the world that Bland's proposal to launch a series of autumn lectures in 1884 was enthusiastically adopted and volunteers to speak were many.

Shaw's imprint on the Society fast showed itself in the second tract which was imbued with his characteristic sentence rhythm and balance. The Society was indeed fortunate in attracting an active member who could epigramatically declare that: 'under existing circumstances, wealth cannot be enjoyed without dishonour, or foregone without misery', and that the state had been divided into hostile classes 'with large appetites and no dinners at one extreme, and large dinners and no appetites at the other'.

Even so, the society did not really know where it was going. Fabians were doing no more, in the first year, than look around, strike a few attitudes and declare half assimilated aspirations and intentions. Outsiders became interested when they advocated nationalization of land as a means of granting everyone an equal share in the wealth of the nation, for land then was synonymous with wealth, when they proposed state intervention in industry on a competitive but non-profit-making basis, direct taxation, provision of a liberal education for all, equal political rights for both sexes and the abolition of hereditary honours, and when they stated that they would rather face a civil war than another century of suffering such as that of the industrial revolution.[6] The suffering of industrial workers was the root of the Society's foundation. But the Society might have disintegrated if, in its second year, some members had not begun investigating the causes and effects of the pervading social misery.

Few of them were qualified for such work. They numbered no economists nor even practising politicians. The nearest they came to scientific observation of social problems was journalism, for several of them were struggling writers. Sidney Webb was still studying for an external law degree while working as a residential clerk at the Colonial Office. He had not even met Beatrice Potter, his future wife and collaborator. She, at least, had embarked on a study of social conditions, observing different social strata while doing voluntary work with the Charity Organization in Soho and staying incognito with distant members of her family engaged in the weaving trade in Bacup. Webb, however, knew Shaw, both being members of the Zetetical Society, a junior branch of the Dialectical Society. There they could discourse on political and economic theories, illustrating their points with what they knew of the social scene from precarious positions in the lower middle classes. Shaw had become a journalist and unsuccessful novelist after several years in humble, clerkly positions. Hubert Bland, who induced Shaw to join the Society, was also a journalist, relying on Shaw's introductions for contacts in the newspaper world.[7] Bland, the son of a self-made shipping merchant, had spent his childhood in more comfortable circumstances, but after losing his money through the defection of a business partner he experienced the same insecurity. For long periods his wife kept the family by writing children's books and by the genteel drudgery open to impecunious ladies. For these spinners of words socialism had to be approached through pamphlets and lectures, not revolutionary action. They all enjoyed converting others, but initially their socialism was a feeling, not a reasoned doctrine. In the words of Shaw they were 'communicative learners'.[8]

Marx died the year before the Fabian Society was founded. Towards the end of its first year the Executive Committee decided to learn something of his philosophy. An opportunity arose with the election of Mrs Charlotte Wilson, an ardent anarchist, to the Executive. She explained to the Fabians what anarchism meant to her and persuaded her friends to read together and analyse Marx's *Capital*, then available only in French or German. Years later, Shaw recounted vivid memories of her reading it aloud and the vigorous disputes that followed. Within weeks of her arrival Bland, in a paper on revolutionary prospects, maintained that revolution on the French pattern was improbable in Britain.

Members were getting to know each other but they realized they were still unsure of the facts underlying their arguments. There was no ready source of reference for those who wished to prove the need for reconstruction. Accordingly, Charlotte Wilson, who had time on her hands as the wife of the affluent stockbroker Rowland Estcourt, and a Miss Edwards were asked to study the working of the Poor Law. The pamphlet was never finished, but their labour was not wasted. Their material was used by an Executive subcommittee which produced a report, *The Government Organisation of Unemployed Labour*, in June 1886.[9] The first committee had lacked Webb's fantastic ability to drain the essence of a government paper and present facts and figures as matters for quick reference and easy digestion; Webb had only been elected to the Society two months after the original work began. It was at the next meeting after the report was commissioned that he was invited to read 'The way out', his first paper to a members' meeting. The Fabians instantly decided they wanted to hear more from this diligent young man. On 1 May he was elected to the Society.

The Fellowship of the New Life had stressed the need for social intercourse. The Executive decided at the beginning of May that a more social gathering was needed for all members and a conversazione was held at which they could introduce guests to the Society. No description of this particular event can be found; it probably followed much the same pattern as later social evenings which have been recorded, when the food served cost 6d a head, or 9d if fancy cakes were included; the beverage was tea. Entertainment consisted of musical contributions from those who could sing or play an instrument; there were always monologues and recitations of poems by William Morris or other friends whose verse was published in the socialist press. Such occasions helped the Fabians to understand each other and resolve their differences of opinion more equably.

The only tract published in 1885, *To Provident Landlords and Tenants*, warned that socialism in England would force all members of the upper class to work for their living; to forestall a revolution, they should hand over all undeveloped land to the peasants, who would then have a stake in the country and be diverted from revolution. The neat Shavian argument could certainly not have been expected to arouse more than a chuckle from ardent debaters of contemporary theories of land allocation. It could have made very little impression at meetings in working-men's clubs where Fabians lectured and sold their pamphlets. Radical and Liberal Associations which invited them to speak were probably amused, and induced to think a little about land distribution but even there the tract can only have enhanced the reputation of Fabians for being 'clever young men'. Its most appreciative audience was, undoubtedly, the Fabian Society itself.

As the Society approached its second birthday members thought some simple explanation of socialism should be produced. Having agonized over the dicta of Marx, Engels, the European socialist school and the Utopians, they now thought they knew roughly how socialist theories could be adapted to conditions in Britain. They needed something short and readable to sell at lectures and meetings to explain the difference between the two kinds of socialism preached in England, collectivism and anarchism. Engels was their first choice as author; he refused, probably deterred by the members' claiming the right to amend pamphlets before publication. Charlotte Wilson and others of the inner circle were not thus inhibited. As their expert on anarchism she wrote the major part of Tract No. 4, *What Socialism Is*, arguing that the English, though still dubious about socialism, all tended to be either collectivist or anarchist, a dichotomy leading to progress and stability. In explaining the collectivist point of view she drew heavily upon August Bebel's widely discussed theories. She distinguished between the two kinds of collectivist, those who introduced radical changes when the propitious moment was offered by evolution, and the opportunists who worked through the established institutions to bring about change gradually. Her anarchists were no bomb-throwing revolutionaries; they were individualists who proclaimed the maxim, 'To each according to his need, from each according to his ability', and believed that when people were freed from economic, political and social restraints crime would disappear and every man would be able to devote himself to his chosen work. Tempering idealism with a touch of realism she admitted that society might sink into mediocrity if all restraints were removed without compensatory cultivation of moral standards. Not until 1886 was this tract passed for printing and it was then greeted by the press as milk-and-water socialism and 'as silly as London socialism itself'.

An article in the *Morning Post* ridiculed the Fabians for holding their meetings not in the scruffy halls where dangerous socialists might be expected to gather, but in the affluent house of one of its members.[10] They arrived after dinner in their own carriages and handed their hats and coats to a liveried butler before taking refreshment in one of the ground-floor rooms. They then ascended to a luxuriously furnished room, to listen to a lecture on relief works for the unemployed. Pease is described sitting taking notes by a table-lamp; Annie Besant, the estranged wife of a clergyman who supported herself by journalism and publishing, as equally attentive, sitting surrounded by young girls who hung on her every word when she sprang to her feet to attack the speaker's views. Bland would then close the heated but inconclusive discussion by declaring that difference of opinion was the Fabian *raison d'être*. The house so described was in Cornwall Gardens, Kensington, the home of Walter Coffin, a dentist of

American extraction, also interested in psychical research.

The *Morning Star* ridiculed Phillips, calling him a 'fustian Fabian' whose report did not even make sense. It commented that if the Fabians wanted to illustrate the intelligence of the worker they had failed abysmally. Phillips had been delegated by the Executive to attend the Paris Commune Celebration at South Place Chapel, Finsbury, on 18 March 1886, organized by the Socialist League to mark the fifteenth anniversary of the commune's foundation.[11] Some visiting socialists from France, Germany and Italy had spoken in virtually unintelligible English.[12] Possibly that was why Phillips's report had made no sense to the reporter.

An earlier meeting at Cornwall Gardens, at which Edward Carpenter spoke on private property, drew the following gloss to the minutes from Shaw:

> Dreadfully dull meeting. Wilson yawning like anything. No wonder. Infernal draught from the window. Coffin fidgetting – putting coals on the fire, distributing ipecacuanha lozenges and so on. Miss Coffin sitting on the landing evidently bored. Culinda's [Annie Besant?] speech fetched her in. Somebody making a frightful noise like the winding of a rusty clock. Mrs Bland suspected of doing it with the handles of her fan. Wish she wouldn't. Two or three meetings like this would finish up any Society.[13]

Yet the Society grew. Soon no drawing-room could accommodate the meetings and so the Society moved to Willis's Rooms every other Friday. According to the Society's publisher, George Standring, these were just as comfortable as a private house. In his own paper, *The Radical*, he wrote:

> Figure to yourself a spacious and lofty apartment in the Westest end of London. The room is brilliantly lighted by a score of candles in handsome candelabra; the floor is thickly carpeted so that no footfall disturbs the solemn hush. About eight ladies and gentlemen are seated around on comfortable chairs, and a subdued hum of conversation fills the air. You might well imagine the scene to be laid in the Duchess of Brickbat's drawing-room and fancy the company to consist of Lady Fannys and Lord Arthurs, assembled to exchange the ghastly smalltalk of fashionable frivolity. But you would be wrong; for these are Willis's Rooms (or rather, one of them), and the company's almost exclusively composed of members of the Fabian Society – a Socialist body whose motto is: 'Don't be in a hurry; but when you *do* go it, go it thick!' (Of course, they don't express it in quite that way.)[14]

Since meetings were then attracting large audiences Annie Besant suggested extending the rules to allow the formation of local branches.[15] In London districts small groups could easily be organized to study socialist ideas and keep informed about socialist activities, and the intimate atmosphere of the early days could be revived. In the provinces there were friends who longed to study and hear lectures by noted socialists. On 19 February approval was given for groups of not less than ten persons to form Fabian societies in any town or district, to be virtually autonomous, controlling their own funds and drawing up their own rules provided these did not conflict with the Basis and aims of the main Society. Corresponding secretaries should keep the Executive informed of the members' names, addresses and activities and obtain literature and lecturers' names from the General Secretary. An annual general meeting would provide a link with the London Society and allow an opportunity for changes to be made in the general rules. All local society members might attend meetings of the London Society and play a full part in debate, but not vote on matters of business. Within three months a local society was founded in Edinburgh.

Establishing small local groups in London was more difficult. London members were nominated to a group in the constituency in which they lived, but, since they would still attend the main Society's meetings and contribute to its work, they retained their central membership. The London groups did not wish to be as independent as the provincial societies. Yet the Executive did not want to be responsible for activities by local groups which they were quite capable of organizing themselves. It was eventually agreed that a secretary and treasurer of each group should be, *ex officio*, full members of the central society, responsible for furnishing quarterly lists of members and notices of all group meetings to avoid programme clashes, and that a council of Executive members and group delegates could be summoned at short notice to deal with any emergency. This central organization of groups and local societies did not function effectively until about 1892.

In 1886 the Executive's preoccupation with organization made it lose sight of its real work. This was partly due to a rift between those who wished to engage in political propaganda and those who thought Fabians should confine themselves to long-range examination of the country's political, social and economic problems. A compromise was reached in the short-lived Parliamentary League proposed by Annie Besant. She moved that Fabians in favour of parliamentary action should establish a league with its own council and officers and separate publications financed by an independently raised fund.[16] This mild and eminently Fabian solution to an argument which had been raging for months effectively guillotined a move to transform it into an independent political party.

In September 1886, at the end of her lecture on socialism and political action, Annie Besant asked for a vote on whether socialists should form a political party to transfer control of land, the means of production and of the creation and distribution of wealth to the working community as a whole.[17] Many different opinions about formal political involvement were then expressed. William Morris, who had recently founded the Socialist League as a breakaway movement from the Social Democratic Federation, led those inclined to anarchism in opposing the motion. In his view, the compromises necessary in parliamentary government would blunt that clear vision of socialism that Fabians should present to the people. In the debate on his amendment Fabians hit hard and at each other. The parliamentary faction won this particular contest by a handsome margin, but since Webb manoeuvred Annie Besant into accepting a pressure group rather than a potential political party it was a philippic victory.

In the first flush of its existence the Fabian Parliamentary League prepared a tract which lacerated both the Liberal Radical Programme of October 1887 and Lord Randolph Churchill's extension of it.[18] It then outlined *The True Radical Programme*: adult suffrage, payment of annually elected Members of Parliament, a progressive system for taxing unearned income to the point of abolition, municipalization of land and reform of the workhouse system, state education with provision of school meals, nationalization of the railways and an eight-hour working day. The tract was obviously first drafted by one accustomed to street-corner oratory, probably Mrs Besant who, believing fervently in the workers' need for direct parliamentary representation, independent of either existing party, frequently addressed working women. Hubert Bland claimed that she probably knew the views of the working classes better than all the other leading socialists put together.[19] As a publisher she was a great asset to the Socialist League and the Fabians.

Her draft of the Parliamentary League's Manifesto, revised by Shaw, was printed in February 1887.[20] He produced a statement far more measured in tone than could have been expected from the League's enthusiastic founders. It opened with an oblique reference to the recently enlarged franchise, declared that the quickest way to realize socialism was by using the political power already possessed by the people and cited the progress achieved by socialists in the German Reichstag, the United States legislature and the Paris municipal council. He promised that the League would analyse the true implications of proposed legislation, support

measures advancing socialism and those candidates in local or parliamentary elections who most closely approximated to the League's ideals until
actual socialist candidates were available. Meanwhile it would not ally itself
with either of the political parties or suffer exploitation by them.
Anticipating that the League would soon be strong enough to run its own
candidates in local elections, the Manifesto urged members to be active in
their own districts and suggested ways of keeping watch on local
administration and learning about the management of social services. They
were advised to write to their MPs about pending legislation, putting the
socialist point of view. As a sequel the League published *Socialist
Criticisms on Some Bills now Before Parliament* on such matters as the
Truck Amendment Bill and leaseholders' enfranchisement.[21]

To discourage further splinters from the main body and to encourage
strong growth the Executive Committee, in 1887, sent a circular to every
member complaining of increasing apathy; after three years it was,
apparently, no longer dashing to be a Fabian.[22] Half the members were not
even attending meetings and they were certainly not recruiting their
friends. Income had dropped because only half the members had paid their
subscriptions that year and the recent Executive elections had been
uncontested. Members seemed to consider the Executive 'a mere Friday
evening entertainment committee'. Fabians were not honouring the pledge
made on joining to dedicate their political activity and social influence to
establishing socialism in Britain. The Executive begged members to review
their position and either resign or take those responsibilities seriously. To
help them decide a meeting on methods of work was called for 6 May. The
Executive warned that it would be very discouraged if attendance was
poor and discussion left to the officers. Radical proposals were promised
and members' ideas requested.

At the meeting eight ordinary members were picked to help the Executive
revise the Basis. On its behalf Annie Besant moved that alternate meetings
be devoted to carrying socialism to the unconverted in different parts of the
metropolis and that further attempts be made to form groups for local
propaganda. The eight chosen members knew their own districts well. For
instance, Thomas Bolas, representing the East End, believed strongly in
the influence of the press and had founded, with W.K. Burton, *The
Practical Socialist* (later *The Socialist*), which regularly reported Fabian
lectures and published topical articles by Bland and the other leaders.
This subcommittee decided a new members' list, arranged according to
locality, was needed, so that all those living in the same area could get to
know each other and work together. Each member would be asked to

13

report to the office on his area, describing the local socialist societies, working-men's clubs and political organizations, local newspapers, and naming all newsagents selling socialist literature and all halls available for monthly propaganda meetings. They were all expected to distribute socialist literature and persuade their local newsagents to sell it, advertise lectures in their areas and arrange for at least one of the local group to work for a branch of the Parliamentary League. To Fabian propaganda meetings, run by the group and supervised by a member of the Executive, they were expected to invite leading members of local organizations.

That summer and autumn, monthly meetings were devoted to lectures on propaganda and recruitment methods, though Shaw chose to speak on 'The illusions that blind us to socialism'. Webb had been writing notes in *The Practical Socialist* all summer on the subject, under the general title of 'Some economic errors of socialists and others'.[23]

The new-look Fabian Society was well publicized. Both Bolas and Annie Besant in *Our Corner* repeatedly printed the Parliamentary League Manifesto, the resolutions of the June meeting regarding local societies and groups and the revised Basis. This last had been circulated to members for consideration in May and was far more decisive than the previous one adorned by Walter Crane's three red-capped angels of Liberty, Equality and Fraternity.[24] Instead of declaring that the Fabian Society existed to promote the reconstruction of society so as to secure the general welfare, the new version stated baldly: 'The Fabian Society consists of Socialists.' Three years of talking had finally convinced Fabians that they were indeed socialists. The Basis now stated far more uncompromisingly that the Society was working for the extinction of private property in land and 'for the transfer to the community of such industrial Capital as can conveniently be managed socially'. Some of the arguments advanced in its tracts, such as that modern inventions were merely making the rich richer, and that elimination of private property led to equality of opportunity, were included. But even now, Fabians did not consider themselves revolutionaries; they still believed in the gradual spread of socialist opinions producing social and political change. The Parliamentary League's work was described in detail in the printed version of the Basis issued for the 1887–8 session; it presented itself as the practical side of the Society, predicting an expeditious and peaceful path to socialism through nationalization of the railways and municipal socialism and outlining the work of the groups. The following year the sections on the Parliamentary League and nationalization were discarded in favour of the bleak statement, 'The purely political work of the Society is in the hands of its Political

Committee', because the League no longer existed and the Committee needed to rethink policy. All three versions of the Basis produced so far had stated that the Society sought: 'recruits from all ranks, believing that not only those who suffer from the present system, but also many who are themselves enriched by it, recognize its evils and would welcome a remedy'.

The Fabians, themselves predominantly middle class, intended to draw politically powerful people into their orbit and persuade them to act in the interests of socialism even if they could not convert them wholly.

The Executive Committee had high handedly drafted the new Basis before the subcommittee selected by the annual general meeting met. There is no evidence of any recommendations from the rank and file other than 'Some suggestions towards a Basis' by the Committee of the Victoria Park Fabian Church,[25] which believed that there was more socialism around than men thought and that it was the duty of the Society to arouse latent socialists to action and to claim all humanity as a Brotherhood of Socialists. It wanted them to declare the study of philosophy and science to be but adjuncts to the major Fabian work of: 'Conduct; Politics; to get men to move together; to dare more to believe and hope in one another; to use and shape the world and its wealth for human ends and well-being', without bloodshed. The Executive, not surprisingly, decided to use its own draft for the Basis.

At the end of its first four years the Fabian Society had evolved a basic *modus operandi*, capable of considerable augmentation and modification in future years. Regular lecture meetings were held in London to educate and inspire. Ideas introduced there on socialism and how to make it work were further developed by the Society's nucleus of writers, who criticized and amended each other's work before it was printed. The principle had been adopted of promoting Fabian ideals through personal influence on receptive Members of Parliament and getting more such people into the House by calculated exploitation of the newly reformed electoral system. A system of local societies for disseminating Fabian views and methods throughout the country had been agreed but not yet created. Thus the first step towards regenerating society was taken.

2

PRACTICAL WORK
AND PROPAGANDA

The Fabian Society being designed for political action as well as research, discussion and instruction, some of the Executive did indeed become involved in bloodshed although they did not shed it.

Marches and demonstrations against growing unemployment were held in London during 1887, the focal point being Trafalgar Square. When bricks were thrown through windows in Pall Mall and Piccadilly, more and more regulations were passed to limit the right to hold public meetings and to free speech, more and more marchers were arrested and could lie forgotten in gaol unless people of sufficient standing and affluence bailed them out and forced a proper trial. Annie Besant persuaded a band of her friends to do this during the early autumn.[1]

One Sunday in November Shaw, William Morris and Annie Besant joined a march to Trafalgar Square organized by radical and socialist bodies to protest against the government's unemployment policy, Irish policy and the arrest of O'Brien. The Chief of Police had issued a writ forbidding meetings there and had ordered his men to block the roads leading to the square. As one of the intended speakers Annie marched at the front of one column and saw the police beat down with their truncheons the banner and those carrying it. She tried to rally those following by jumping on a cart and persuading the driver to thwart police entry into the square. Further back Shaw and the others were put to rout, but he struggled back to try and rescue her. Neither was injured or arrested, though many others were. Quiet was eventually restored by the more disciplined horsemanship of the Life Guards. That night Annie organized her friends into a more formal body to raise funds for bail and defence of those arrested. She and Eleanor Marx-Aveling stood bail for prisoners who were later defended by such eminent men as R.B. Haldane, soon to become a member of the Liberal Government and a close friend of Webb. Protesters planned to hold meetings in Trafalgar Square every Sunday until the writ was revoked. The more militant socialists prepared for a war of attrition, but the order was rescinded more quickly than expected, following the death of one demonstrator, Linnell. As a socialist martyr he was given a splendid funeral procession, for which William Morris wrote an elegy.

The editor of the *Pall Mall Gazette*, W.T. Stead, in response to the general indignation and with Annie Besant's help, founded another organization, the Law and Liberty League, designed to protect citizens against police persecution, reveal injustices and succour the downtrodden poor. With rather uncertain support from the Executive, Annie persuaded the January Fabian meeting to affiliate the Society to her League,[2] which was producing a weekly paper, *The Link*, and consisted of local groups who kept watch on local developments: twenty such groups formed a circle; an 'élite circle' at the top of this structure reported incidents to the leaders of the League. The incidents were reported in *The Link* and warnings issued publicly to wrongdoers. Such an institution was rife with danger and Fabians regarded it as an awful warning of what they should guard against in their own activities. Shaw had already been frightened off direct action by the Trafalgar Square incident. It is not known how many of the Society joined the League's groups in its early days, and there is only a solitary reference to it in the Fabian minutes. The Executive was, undoubtedly, relieved when Stead and Annie Besant withdrew their sponsorship on discovering that their League was being used as an outlet for personal and parochial spite.

One good thing came of the League, the publicity given by *The Link* to the strike of the match-girls at Bryant and May's factory which the Fabian Society did not hesitate to support. A collection of £7.7.8d was taken at one meeting in July 1888 to help provide strike pay for the 1200 or more girls. Shaw, Wallas, Olivier and Headlam were swept along to a hall in the Mile End Road by Annie Besant to give the girls the money raised by concerned bodies. After the strike ended in the capitulation of the employers she and Herbert Burrows organized a union for the girls and a meeting room furnished with ample reading matter, including a number of Fabian tracts and other literature selected by Webb and Shaw.

As the number of beggars haunting the West End grew the Society decided to tackle the London authorities about the treatment of the unemployed and to offer its own solution to the problem of relieving destitution during the hard winter of 1887–8. The year before it had instructed a subcommittee to draw up a practical scheme for national and municipal employment of labour.[3] Data were gathered from ministers of religion in the London parishes, from official documents and from anyone whom they thought able to give a balanced opinion. Some of the committee's conclusions shocked those who, just waking to the plight of the unemployed, willingly opened their purses in response to the Lord Mayor's appeal to alleviate distress. The committee judged such philanthropy to be the very cause of permanent unemployment in some sections of the community, declaring that 'indiscriminate charity ... made the donors feel good without really working for the true benefit of those to whom they gave their half-crowns.' The prevailing system of casual labour in the docks and migration from the depressed agricultural areas to the cities were more obvious causes of unemployment. The Fabians also advised the Government to check immigration of unskilled foreign labourers in some way, perhaps a poll tax, that would not prevent skilled workers being able to leave England and gain experience by work in Europe. To increase employment the committee advocated government sponsorship of tobacco-growing, cottage industries, industrial villages on the lines of the home settlement then favoured by Keir Hardie, acquisition of two distinct skills by those whose work was seasonal, and technical education for every child. These proposals may seem naïve, but when translated into today's jargon they show that ideas for reducing massive unemployment have progressed little in nearly a century. Universal conscription was mentioned by the committee, but more favoured proposals were reduction of the working day to eight hours in government departments, municipal control of liquor distribution, government organization of labour to prevent alternate gluts and shortages in jobs and products, and public works timed to coincide with predictable increases in the labour supply. National and municipal methods of relieving unemployed families were analysed and criticized, so too was private enterprise which discarded former employees once major projects such as road-building were completed.

In November 1887 Sydney Olivier, a colleague of Webb's at the Colonial Office, then secretary of the Society, having failed to persuade the President of the Local Government Board to receive a Fabian delegation presented him with a summary of their proposals augmented by practical suggestions such as local labour registries and small-scale public works.[4] Fabians could not claim that they achieved anything that winter, but they did obtain a hearing and many of them served on local distress committees. For the time being their proposals were shelved, to be revived later in several different guises, mainly by Beatrice Webb.

Olivier's enthusiasm for organization and efficiency suffused the Executive when he was acting secretary during Pease's absence in Newcastle-upon-Tyne. Stewart Headlam, the Liberal curate who founded the Guild of St Matthew, confined himself to speaking on Christian Socialism. Greater discipline in Fabian educational work being clearly needed the Executive selected two subcommittees to organize lecture courses and foster Fabianism in the universities.

Webb favoured a more regulated approach to lecturing. In August 1886 he had asked Wallas:

> What do you think of running a series of lectures in the Fabian this winter on 'The Mistakes of Socialists'? Just like the Fabian they would say. But we must have some new thing. The only other wild suggestion I have is to run a series of lectures *to* different classes.[5]

Webb was elected to the lecture committee and by 1889 the lecture list showed a large increase in the number and availability of lecturers and an even greater range of subjects. Fabian experience in London was growing apace yet hardly anyone in the provinces was prepared to lecture. A growing number of requests came from outside London for some of the big names on the Executive to come and speak.

By far the most important achievement of the lecture committee was the autumn series on the basis of socialism, each one explaining a different aspect of Fabian socialism.[6] It was first presented in Willis's Rooms in King Street, and was partially repeated during the Lent Term at King's College, Cambridge, at the invitation of the undergraduate political society, then again at Leicester.[7] The London course consisted of seven lectures entitled 'Socialism: Its basis and prospects'.

Webb opened with one on the historical basis of socialism, describing the decay of the medieval feudal system, the change wrought by the French Revolution and subsequent rule by the people. Postulating that a period of anarchy followed, he summarized the Utilitarian philosophy, the ensuing conflict between philosophic radicalism and *laissez-faire* policy, and the recent moral revolt against the resulting conditions.

Bernard Shaw dealt in the second lecture with the economic basis of socialism, a subject he had covered many times back in his Democratic Federation days. Following the economic theories of David Ricardo, he divided rent into three kinds, the profits to be obtained from land, investment of capital and the hiring of a man's ability. Nationalization of land was a question examined repeatedly. Profits from land had long been considered the only true products of a country, consequently landowners were charged with monopolizing wealth that was the due of all. Fabians had no difficulty in distinguishing between permissible and impermissible profits from use of capital, but felt less certain about the rent of a man's skill or ability. Examining the law of wages Shaw followed a well-trodden path, discussing the state of the proletariat (for whom he had no real sympathy), analysing the evils of competitive wages and discoursing on the evils of sweating then being revealed in the works of Charles Booth and his cousin, Beatrice Potter.[8] In speaking on the law of value Shaw drew on the theories of Galiani and Jevons as well as Ricardo. According to a printed synopsis, at Cambridge he concluded with a paradoxical attack on the apparent discrepancies between history and theory, socialism itself, pessimism, private property and the economic soundness of meliorism. As soon as university Fabian societies burgeoned he was in great demand and a strong recruiting and fund-raising attraction.

Sydney Olivier's London lecture on the moral aspect of socialism was not repeated at Cambridge. His thought processes were so complex that his lectures were difficult to follow. His theme, less controversial than either Webb's or Shaw's, dealt with motivation, collective tendencies and the growth of positive ethics. The subject was fascinating to philosophical Fabians but had little popular appeal.

William Clarke's lecture on the industrial aspect of socialism completed the first part of the London series. His thesis was that recent industrial development had increased greed, which contributed towards imperial expansion, exploitation of Africa and Asia and caused wars between the Great Powers. Greed also led to unemployment and the destruction of individual liberty. Clarke envisaged society's salvation as collective organization, which could only be reached by trial and error.

Annie Besant claimed to be utterly opposed to Utopianism in her lecture on industry under socialism. She dreamt of an organized society in which every anxiety over personal needs was swept away, the lure of wealth banished, condemnation by his peers becoming the ultimate sanction on a man's idleness – reinforced by the certainty of starvation. Graham Wallas more surely rejected the Utopian dreams of earlier socialists. His lecture recapitulated some of the other speakers' material, before examining the more abstruse question of property in ideas, copyright and patents.

Hubert Bland brought the series to a close with his views on the political outlook, the state of the existing parties, the virtual disappearance of the old Whiggism, the need to make politics more social and encourage the solidarity of the workers. Having proved so popular, five of the 1888 lecturers were booked for the 1889 autumn series on the theme of 'A century of social movements'. More importantly, the Executive Committee, containing all seven lecturers, decided to publish the lectures in book form, as *Fabian Essays in Socialism*.

Though Shaw, the effective editor, added a section on the transition to socialism which had not formed part of the original series, he did not unduly impose his own personality on the book. As he explained in the preface, the seven essayists, wearing their Executive Committee hats, made all the editorial decisions after considerable mutual criticism. Yet each essay presents not a consensus but the individual's thought. In fact, the essayists disagreed quite vigorously over some points; Bland's views differed markedly from those of the others. Shaw aimed to present each chapter of the book in the form in which a speaker with only an hour at his disposal could deliver the subject matter to his audience. Some left their lectures virtually untouched, for example William Clarke and Annie Besant, both journalists with little patience for rewriting. Olivier, more accustomed to redrafting Colonial Office minutes, and Wallas, who constantly reshaped his lectures for audiences of different intellectual capabilities and was constitutionally reluctant to release anything he had written as fit for publication, completely rewrote their contributions. Bland compromised by adding a large section to his. Criticism from Fabian membership was invited after publication. In the preface, the writers' divergent views were presented as a virtue preventing exclusive dogmatism. Shaw introduced them not as authorities or teachers but as 'communicative learners'. A certain wistfulness in a reference to provincial readers may well have inspired a Derbyshire solicitor, Henry Hutchinson, to supply funds for personal appearances by the essayists outside London in 1890, and for paid lecturers to visit political, co-operative, ethical or Christian Democrat organizations in the north and west of England.

With their ablest writer editing the *Essays* and Annie Besant made responsible for publication, publicity and sales, the rest of the Executive was free to return to other, preferred activities in the Society. The lecture committee was dissolved after this single, outstandingly successful year, but both Wallas and Webb undertook heavy lecturing commitments. Wallas recounted the history of social agitation, the Chartist and co-operative movements, and the French Revolution. Throughout the winter and spring Webb lectured at the City of London College, in Moorfields, on political economy as it could be studied in the pages of *The Times*.[9] It was a novel idea and a summary of the lectures preserved in the Fabian archive provides an insight into his lifelong habit of gathering facts and forming conclusions no matter what he was reading. He used each section of the newspaper in turn to demonstrate how, by intelligent reading, he might learn from the situations vacant columns much about the current wage levels and economic relations, or by studying the money market articles he could understand the causes of market fluctuations, the principle of discount and reasons for paying interest. Skilfully Webb interwove these lectures with much in the *Essays*. By the end of his course he turned to more frivolous aspects of the news and pointed out how even the entertainment sections could elucidate the economics of social development, the value of sunshine in providing opportunity for recreation and leisure facilities, and how much these increased the standard of life. As in the *Essays*, the value of ideas, artistic production, invention and their safeguards of copyright and patents were discussed. The course ended with an explanation of the relationship between individual and social economics and between social evolution and economic change.

The first printing of the *Essays* sold like hot cakes, but heralded a breach in the ranks of the Executive Committee. Most of them were piece workers, as Shaw termed it, in the production of words and were accustomed to haggle over their sale. Pease, back from Newcastle where his monetary transfusions had failed to keep the furniture co-operative alive, and Annie Besant began to disagree over terms for the *Essays*: 1000 copies, priced at 6 shillings, had been sold in a month. When the Publishing Committee realized it had a potential best-seller and the Society's finances could be put on a sounder footing by the royalties relinquished by the writers, it decided to employ a canvasser to push the second thousand. Unfortunately, by the time Annie Besant was told she had already sold some of the second printing to booksellers at the ordinary trade rate. Immersed in Theosophy now, she was making a last stand as a business-woman and publisher and resented any cut in her profits. In March 1890 she wrote to Pease:

> If we are to continue to publish for the Fabian Society, it must be on a business footing, and not in the amateurish, happy-go-lucky way that was harmless enough when a few penny tracts were concerned but which is really injurious to our reputation as publishers with a book like the 'Fabian Essays'.[10]

The Publishing Committee apparently backed down at first over the canvasser, Pease noting that its decision was only effective if Mrs Besant agreed. Within a couple of months, however, she was writing to it herself with details of the conditions under which Simpkin and Marshall were willing to instruct their travelling salesmen to push the book all over the country.[11] Agreement was short-lived; two months later she sent Pease a most indignant letter complaining that a message had been left with one of her employees, pressing her for an account of the book's sales. The true source of her annoyance was that another firm had been given the right to publish the cheap edition of the book. She decided to close the Fabian account on the next quarter day and return all unsold stock, but could not resist telling the Publishing Committee that it would not get as good terms from the new publisher as she would have given it if her firm had been allowed to tender for the cheap edition.[12] With her final royalty cheque she also sent her resignation from the Society. Pease decided to ignore this and continued to send her notices of meetings until the Fabian Society reluctantly recorded in the minutes of a meeting in November 1890 that Annie Besant was 'Gone to theosophy'.[13] Her Freethought Press had come to an end the previous month and, as a result, every horizontal surface in Edward Pease's flat was covered with unsold Fabian publications.

The Executive elected in April 1890 and indistinguishable from the previous one realized that the Society needed a more professional attitude. Edward Pease, now a married man, was appointed General Secretary at an annual salary of £50. Executive Committee minutes were at last kept in a systematic manner and a general reorganization was announced at the annual meeting of members. In future the Executive Committee would meet only once a month, leaving routine matters to be dealt with by subcommittees. Royalties from the *Essays* began to provide an income other than members' subscriptions and the trickle from penny tract sales, and income and membership matters became the business of a Finance and General Purposes Committee, including Pease and Bland. The Political and Lecture Committee, containing both Webb and Shaw, dealt with the growing demand for lectures, of which 1000 were given in this session alone, and initiated and co-ordinated Fabian political activities. Olivier, Clarke and Wallas guided the work of the Literature and Publishing Committee. Alice Hoatson, the third member of the Bland household, acted as its general factotum. No Executive member might then sit on more than one subcommittee, each of which reported monthly to the Executive.

The Society achieved more in this year than ever before. A list of the eighty-six members was printed with Londoners divided into eight groups, each covering a number of electoral constituencies. A card index of members was begun, recording dates of election to the Society and the amounts of subscriptions. Recruitment now became so rapid that the 1891 list had to be interleaved with blank pages for additional names. On printing it recorded nearly 400 names, but the office copy acquired about 120 more in the next eighteen months; only eight were excised. That was the first list to register local societies and their membership. In 1890 there had been a single section for all provincial members, each of whom was recorded as living in a separate town. Members scattered as far afield as America, Australia, British Guiana, Egypt and Japan. Among those in America were Percival Chubb and, temporarily, Henry Hutchinson.[14]

The restructured administration tried to assess what kind of people had become Fabians in the first six years. Members were asked for details of their qualifications for political work and Pease analysed the replies. Unfortunately, no record of his analysis survives. Earlier he had appealed to provincial Fabians to launch vigorous propaganda campaigns,[15] maintaining that Fabians must create a spirit of political activism in the provinces comparable to that in his beloved London. A little help might come from the London Society: 'For altho' we have not a farthing to spare, we might at a pinch pay the travelling expenses of the Lecturers, or at least part of them, and try to recoup ourselves by the sale of tracts at the meeting.' He also appealed for any information that might help London Fabians understand the provinces.

The differences between rural and metropolitan views seem to have been a major preoccupation during this very important year. The Political Committee wanted Fabians to help prepare a political programme for the provinces to guide voters in all kinds of elections, a programme similar to one recently drafted by Webb for London.[16] Graham Wallas was responsible for correlating suggestions and identifying the kinds of reform most desired. Fabians were encouraged to prepare pamphlets on reforms needed in their own towns, taking as their pattern Tract No. 9, *The Eight Hours Bill*. Edward Carpenter's leaflet, *Our Parish*, was recommended as a template for the rural areas.

The Executive was not prepared to leave the spread of Fabianism outside London entirely to members actually living there. A Rural Committee, including Ramsay MacDonald, was directed to formulate a scheme for the purpose. The Rural Committee's proposal that Wallas and Clarke prepare a scheme of lectures to be given in Manchester in September was approved in July 1891. Hutchinson offered £100 or even £200 for propaganda in country centres.[17] From that moment the plot to inundate Manchester and the surrounding district with lectures on the Fabian brand of socialism was assured. By mid-August the Fabians could contemplate sending 1000 circulars offering lectures to political bodies in Lancashire and 2000 to co-operative societies and appointing a local organizer. The core of the campaign was a series of four lectures delivered in a really large hall in Manchester.[18]

The Lancashire campaign ran from 20 September, when Webb opened with a lecture to the Rochdale Social Democratic Federation branch on 'The new Reform Bill', to 27 October when Edith Bland addressed the Houghton Women's Liberal Association. Biographical sketches of the lecturers appeared in advance in the *Oldham Advertiser* and the *Manchester Examiner and Times*. Sidney Webb's first lecture was described in the *Manchester Guardian* as lengthy. He had painstakingly reviewed all the legislation governing the franchise, explaining that since there were 160 Acts involved the work of the reformer was very difficult – hardly the inflammatory socialist propaganda expected by his audience. He ended with a plea for socialist measures such as reduction in the periods of electoral registration, payment of Members of Parliament and shorter Parliaments in general – a foretaste of the Liberal Newcastle programme inspired by him the following year. The popular notion of 'mending or ending the House of Lords' was mentioned only as a matter demanding a separate Act of Parliament. When Hubert Bland spoke at the Longsight Liberal Club on 3 October he used Webb's text, as the report in the *Manchester Guardian* the following day proves.

After Webb's lecture the newspaper had claimed that: 'The Fabians are the gentlest and most pacific of socialists and their subject will probably remain an affair of gentle and debatable "legislative tendencies".' Not all its readers thought so. The Oldham weavers who knew of Fabian support for the Eight Hour Bill, which they abhorred, were antagonistic towards the 'bright young man from London', being convinced that if the working day were so restricted they would be unable to compete with other countries for the world trade in cotton piece goods.[19] Webb greeted his audience there by saying he wanted to find out what Lancashire was thinking about the Eight Hour Bill. He did, in no uncertain manner! As the editor of the *Oldham Advertiser* wrote the next day, the cotton operatives of Oldham and Lancashire knew the Bill threatened trade and their jobs and:

What Mr Webb and his colleagues must clearly understand is that Lancashire will tolerate no interference .... We are eminently practical and when brought face to face with practical problems we may possibly teach the Fabian lecturers something in return for the knowledge they impart.

Shaw carried an audience with him far more easily than did Webb. Reports of his lectures are often sprinkled with descriptions of the laughter of the audience or their approving 'hear, hears'. Webb analysed and chronicled his subjects, explaining legislation, its consequences and the general trend of necessary reforms. Shaw related his points to the experience and aspirations of the people he was addressing. In talking of levelling down or levelling up on the economic scale he would make his point by naming a notoriously wealthy man, such as the Duke of Westminster, saying he had too much and that it should be redistributed to the likes of them. He goaded his audience one minute, shocked it the next, then resolved his whole argument in a gust of laughter. What he said left its mark and those who heard him realized afterwards that what he had been saying was really very different from what they had thought at first.

Annie Besant was a controversial figure from her connection with Charles Bradlaugh and her pamphlet on birth control. Consequently her lecture was overcrowded and large numbers had to be turned away. In dealing with distribution of wealth, she drew her statistics from Tract No. 5, *Facts for Socialists*, but prefaced her argument with heart-rending accounts of poverty in the crowded cities. Her barbed comments on Ministers of the Crown and their work were as much appreciated by her provincial audiences as in London. Stewart Headlam presented his one lecture on Christian Socialism, linked with nationalization of the land. Most Fabians involved in the campaign travelled from place to place, lecturing each day for a week or so; the heaviest burden fell, naturally, on Webb and Shaw.

When Pease came to issue the lecturers' report on the campaign in November it appeared that they were delighted with the onslaught made 'on the stronghold of Old Unionism and the new Toryism'.[20] They were eager to repeat the experiment. A strain of Liberal support not attracted by open-air meetings and recruitment tactics of the Social Democratic Federation had been tapped. Their least successful meetings had been held under the auspices of the Co-operative Societies, which Fabians considered had become merely a form of joint-stock company, without Robert Owen's original socialist inspiration. Young socialists in the congregations of Unitarian ministers were accorded the highest praise. The report's conclusions on the industrial situation in Lancashire were later found to be not based on authenticated facts but on what Fabians had been told by discontented workers. Lecturers were smug about the number of individual members they had enrolled and the crop of local Fabian societies being formed as a result of their efforts, especially in the Birmingham area where the local society could soon boast a larger membership than the London one. They therefore concluded that: 'At this moment, therefore, the provincial work of the Society is probably of even greater importance than our London propaganda, and it should, we believe, be developed to the utmost limits which time and funds will allow.'

Although Webb had been the most fiercely attacked of the Fabians, he could write to Beatrice Potter:

> I do not grudge the time and money: Whatever influence the Fabian Society has gained is due largely to our constant willingness to do small jobs – to be as cordially willing to convert one man as a hundred – and to be ready to start off and lecture even to a handful. I like to think of ourselves as the 'Society of Jesus' of Socialism – without, I hope, the mental subjection which the Protestants accuse the Jesuits of, and also without their moral shiftiness (which I believe is also a libel).
>
> But it does sometimes seem much work for small results – compared with others.[21]

Henry Hutchinson was extremely pleased at the outcome of his investment. The following summer he told Shaw that he was willing to finance a second autumn campaign as: 'I am clearly of the opinion that my last year's contribution was, and is, no mistake'.[22]

3

SUBURBS
AND THE PROVINCES

At the beginning of 1891 Webb and Wallas opened the Society's eyes to the need to organize and control the mushroom growth of local societies and a resurgence of energy in the small groups in London. Over the Christmas holiday in 1890 Webb, who was convalescing from scarlet fever, discussed the society with Wallas. They agreed that it had already outgrown, in income, reputation and numbers, its organization.[1]

1890 had seen the *Essays'* signal success but succeeding lectures had not been considered worth publishing. Only two tracts were published that year. Webb was bothered that the Society had virtually disregarded local elections for vestry members and guardians of the poor. Most of the Executive's energy had been spent on personal appearances in the provinces, and on defining the work of its new subcommittees. Since in 1891 the society needed to profit from the change in status by becoming more businesslike, the two friends produced a memorandum on how the Society's structure and work could be improved for presentation to the very next meeting of the Executive Committee.

First Webb and Wallas proposed to publish twelve tracts that year, advising the Executive to get the London Groups to prepare first drafts. They proposed a well-publicized schedule of summer meetings at which members could discuss them. Public autumn lectures could be arranged with a second book of essays in view, on applied socialism to complement the theoretical approach of the first volume. In 1892 the Society might have fun in the spring lectures attacking the opposition to socialism. Two courses had already been arranged for spring 1891, on 'Applications of socialist theory', and 'The industrial problems of the day from the socialist point of view'.[2] They were not quite what the two men had in mind but might pave the way for the autumn course.

Wallas devised a scheme whereby London Group members should list local bodies ripe for indoctrination, should help to prepare new tracts and should be consistently supervised by Executive members' attendance at their social meetings. Webb, in a review of provincial work, proposed regulated communication between the General Secretary and the officers of local societies, and preparation of analyses of local economic and social conditions, as Bristol had already done, to be vetted before publication by the main Publishing Committee. In return, local societies would be given the opportunity to comment on proofs of the Society's tracts before publication and asked to contribute new ideas. Once a quarter a member of the Executive should speak to each society on the latest ideas on socialism. Bland's earlier idea of a monthly circular to keep the local societies aware of developments within the Society was incorporated in Webb's scheme.

With all these new activities to organize Pease would need an office and office boy. While Sydney Olivier had acted as secretary the Fabian records were kept on a table in the Colonial Office.[3] When Pease became part-time General Secretary, Fabian papers still took up very little room in the flat he and his wife, Marjory, occupied in Hyde Park Mansions. But ever since the closure of the Free Thought Press, piles of old Fabian publications and parcels of new ones awaiting distribution filled every nook and cranny. As the memorandum pointed out:

> We might propose to Pease that his dining-room should be furnished with a high stool, and that he should regard the office boy as another addition to his family! But he is not likely to see it in that light and some changes may *have* to be made before the summer,

a covert reference to the imminent birth of the Peases' first son. In April Pease's post was acknowledged to be full time and his salary doubled to £100. D'Arcy Reeve generously installed him in a rent-free office at 276 The Strand. Members were invited to inspect it whenever they happened to be in the vicinity and so began the habit of dropping in at the office. E.J. Howells answered an advertisement for a 'sharp boy' at 10 shillings a week. He was to remain in Fabian employ until 1939, and continued to act as a scrutineer for the Executive elections for many years after.

Shaw expressed general approval of the scheme, commenting, not quite fairly, that the Society had been dead for a number of years except for a 'rather mechanical external activity'.[4] Bland's novel idea that provincial members should have their own department and secretary had to wait fifty years for implementation. Most of the memorandum's propositions were approved and put in hand. Even to those not in the inner Fabian ring it soon became obvious that great changes were taking place and they enthusiastically endorsed what the officers were trying to do. *Fabian News* was the first innovation to impress the members. D'Arcy Reeve donated £500 for its publication which began on 1 March 1891. It provided each member with a summary of the London Society's meetings, notices of lectures and courses, accounts of its political work, reports from the provincial and foreign societies, reviews and notices of books worth reading, facts for socialists, general instructions and draft resolutions with which to bombard MPs, councillors, school boards and boards of guardians. Pease, as co-editor with Bland, revelled in this means of abolishing the multitude of individual notices he had previously had to circulate.

The London Groups received a boost at this time. The Executive refused to accept Pease's statement in the annual report for 1889 that the group scheme had failed completely and directed him to work out a new one based on Wallas's proposals. Pease suggested that each group secretary ask his members to list all political societies to which they belonged and try to get elected on to their committees. A press secretary in each group should monitor the local newspapers and obtain publicity for lectures and tracts in them. The group secretary should report the actions of vestries and boards of guardians to the General Secretary and nominate group members for election to local school boards. They were to be encouraged to arrange meetings and study and discuss economic and socialist books. Members of the Executive promised regular visits; Shaw and Webb were most assiduous in keeping this promise and became enormously popular. Pease took a census of the London Groups, listed the constituencies each covered and then waited to see what would happen.

The East London Group, with only six members to cover fourteen constituencies, was the first to respond and caught the proselytizing fever by mid-July. A minute book was opened to record a meeting at which Harry Lowerison announced that he had been affiliated to the main Society.[5] Lowerison was a most ardent lecturer, George Samuel an enthusiastic secretary and Tom Mann the most influential member. With three others they set out to spread socialist ideas in thirteen East End constituencies. They asked Pease to print a list of books on economics and socialism which ought to be in public libraries, so that Fabians could persuade their local library committees to buy them. Lowerison, with a heavy lecture schedule himself, persuaded Pease and other leading members to lecture in the East End. As membership rose weekly, so work increased. Lowerison and Samuel tried to get every Group represented on the Executive Committee. Other groups were not interested and so the East London Group contented itself with nominating Lowerison for the next Executive election. At his suggestion, attendance records were published in *Fabian News* each year before the Executive elections from this time.

The Group's first annual general meeting was held in Poplar Town Hall. Tom Mann spoke on municipal workshops with great ardour, then Shaw poured cold water on the whole idea. Webb took the opportunity to announce that: 'although he did not know whether he should enter Parliament, he would be ready to do so if he received an invitation from an East End constituency.'[6]

The meeting was widely reported in the East End press. The Group distributed 500 copies of the secretary's report and each member undertook to pay sixpence a month into the funds. Average attendance at business meetings then was only eight, yet the Group organized five courses of local lectures in the winter, Samuel had been a Fabian delegate to the Legal Eight Hours Demonstration Committee, William Crooks had been elected to the executive of the London Trades Council and Tom Mann had been working for the Dockers' Union. Membership had increased fourfold and, once the report was distributed, attendance at meetings doubled, though the Social Democratic Federation derided the Group's claim to be converting the East End to socialism. Lowerison and H.W. Massingham, editor of the *Star* for which Shaw was the music critic, were both elected to the Fabian Executive. The Group's fame spread and in April 1891 the Oldham Fabian Society was asking it for guidance on local society work.[7] For the Eight Hours Bill demonstration in Hyde Park in May the Fabian Society was allowed to nominate eighteen speakers; four came from the East End Group, Mann, Lowerison, Crooks and a new member, Ben Tillett.

Open-air lectures in Victoria Park on Sunday afternoons were run by the Group that summer and it was asked to provide speakers when the dockers began organizing educational meetings, sometimes attended by 1000 people, outside the dock gates on Sunday mornings. The group distributed Tracts No. 10 and No. 11 with the annual report free to each East End MP and managed to respond to any appeal from the main Society for information and statistics. By October 1891 the workload had grown too heavy for the joint secretaries, and so it was decided to split into a Hackney and a Poplar Group, with Lowerison as one chairman and Crooks the other, although they still combined for the annual general meeting.

The Hackney Group did a great deal of serious work during the next couple of years. Members wrote to the newspapers and appealed to the Home Secretary concerning the dispute over the right to free speech at the World's End public house in Chelsea. They assumed responsibility for the Victoria Park meetings until the Poplar Group challenged their right. Their prime concern, though, was the high rate of local unemployment, even some of their own officers were jobless, and they struggled to alleviate destitution.

The second annual meeting, in 1892, was an even greater success than the first, with Webb and Shaw joined by Wallas. Poplar Town Hall was packed. A joint annual report was presented announcing the creation of a Labour Party in Tower Hamlets. Will Crooks and W.C. Steadman from the Poplar Group had been elected as Progressive representatives of the East End on the new London County Council and Ben Tillett had become an alderman. Webb, who had masterminded the London local election campaign, congratulated them warmly in his speech as president of the meeting. The Fabian Society had distributed 700,000 leaflets of Webb's own *London Program* [sic], Tracts Nos 30–37, before the local elections and he credited it with the Progressive victory. A resolution by Crooks advocating public control of water, gas, tramways, markets, docks, cemeteries and all public funds administered by the City Guilds and Corporation received rapturous support. So, too, did Shaw's demand for the rapid extension of democratic institutions to ensure full public control over the land and all other instruments of production.[8]

Shaw, who often used meetings in the East End to try out his new ideas, roundly condemned a number of front-bench Liberals for their reactionary policies. Similarly, he opened his campaign for monetary support of parliamentary candidates by the workers themselves at a Victoria Park lecture.

George Samuel and another member of the Hackney Group had been appointed to the London Electoral Council for Hackney, Shoreditch and Bethnal Green, which supported the unsuccessful Radical candidate, Fyfe Stewart, in the general election, canvassing having been too thinly spread. They later formed the South Hackney Labour Party and exhorted Group members to join the revived Hackney Parliament, where they succeeded in establishing a Socialist Party.

Meanwhile the Poplar Group was permeating the East End in quite different ways. W.C. Steadman induced the Mile End Vestry to raise the wages of its employees and allow them the Saturday half holiday. Will

Crooks persuaded the Public Library Commissioners to purchase for a temporary, experimental reading-room the complete list of books recommended by Graham Wallas in *What to Read*, Tract No. 29. Dock gate lectures were as popular as ever. Poplar was one of the Groups to urge the Fabian Executive to press for public meetings on unemployment, as it rose ever steeper. Fabians had been represented on the Unemployment Organization Committee from its formation by the combined socialist bodies in London. An enlarged version of the 1886 Trafalgar Square Demonstration Committee, it was resuscitated in this second slump to regulate demonstrations by the unemployed, lobby MPs and organize propaganda and publicity. In December the Executive, and some other organizations, withdrew their delegates, on the grounds that some stewards hired for the marches were over-provocative. Group secretaries obeyed but were annoyed. The Hackney Group angrily delegated two of its members to organize the unemployed locally and contributed 3/6d to a demonstration in Trafalgar Square; but its mild rebellion soon subsided into more constitutional action. Its members stood for Board of Guardians and vestry elections, in the autumn it sent a large deputation to the Board to discuss winter relief for the poor, published *Facts for Hackney* and *In Darkest Hackney and the Way Out*, a leaflet to persuade rate-payers of the need for a public library.

Few Groups were as politically active as those in the East End. The North-Western Group seems to have been most concerned with the social aspect of Fabian activity. The South-Western Group, whose first secretary was Graham Wallas, submitted the text for Tract No. 20, *Questions for Guardians*, very shortly after its formation and vociferously supported the campaign for free speech at the World's End. Hampstead made toys for Board School children and appealed to other Groups for volunteers to assist. The Woolwich Group, within whose territory Bland dwelt, combined with the Tenants' Defence League to attack the power of landlords and conducted missions in the summer months to convert Erith and Dartford.

The Working Men's College formed its own Group, earnestly working under the direction of Frank Galton, the engraver's apprentice who became a research assistant to the Webbs for their book on the history of trade unionism and eventually General Secretary of the Fabian Society. During its first summer members asked for direction from the Society on how to run open-air meetings. Autumn, however, brought difficulties, as it was unable to persuade the college authorities to start an official course on economics though it did get them to add some of the standard works listed by Wallas to the college library. The Group studied economics independently, shared books, provided lectures for the East End Groups and reported to Pease a fair record of practical work.[9]

William Clarke, Harold Cox, Stewart Headlam, Ramsay MacDonald and Bernard Shaw were all members of the Central Group. Wallas was persuaded to transfer from the South-Western Group to ginger it up as secretary. Membership doubled in the two months after his move. One of its first acts was to study Beatrice Potter's book on co-operation.[10] Its agitation for free libraries in Holborn and Bloomsbury brought rapid results.

Not all London Groups gave as little trouble to the Executive. The Southern Group, covering fourteen constituencies from North Lambeth to Wimbledon, boasted as members J. Brailsford Bright, William de Mattos, Rowland Estcourt, Joseph Fels (a friend of Webb and Shaw since Zetetical Society days who later became a wealthy soap-merchant in America), W.L. Phillips (who had had to resign from the main Executive because the times of committee meetings clashed with his working hours), H.W. Massingham and the Reverend Percy Dearmer. In May 1891 John F. Runciman replaced the first two secretaries, Phillips and de Mattos, and launched a series of lectures with such aggressive titles as 'The elimination of the parson'.

In November Runciman, an intolerant character, launched an attack on Webb, who had declined at a members' meeting to read out a resolution by Olaf Bloch and his sister Harriet, both of the Southern Group, condemning the Aerated Bread Company for underpaying its employees and demanding that the Society boycott it.[11] Bloch might have been placated by a straightforward explanation of the rules of procedure at meetings had not Runciman, who later married Harriet, lost his temper and intervened. In a printed letter sent to all London Group members he accused Webb of dishonourable conduct in preventing the resolution being put to the vote. Recipients of the letter deplored the attack, discounted the charge against Webb but pointed out to Pease that the Executive was not immune from errors in judgement. Most group secretaries recommended turning a blind eye to the quarrel but, as Runciman sent increasingly acrimonious letters to the Executive, members were summoned to two meetings to pass judgement on the affair. Some members demanded Runciman's expulsion, which caused him to circulate a grudging apology to Webb for accusing him of trickery and of having a financial interest in sweating the ABC's employees.

Neither Runciman, specifically invited, nor Webb could be present at the special members' meeting to hear the Society's opinion. As a demonstration of loyalty to its secretary the Southern Group called its own annual meeting for that day. Webb was booked to lecture in South Wales that night and would not break the engagement.[12] On the train he drafted a statement for Pease to read on his behalf, explaining the point of procedure which had caused him to shelve the Blochs' resolution. He begged the Fabians to be patient and charitable and eschew the common failing of revolutionaries, attributing an improper motive to any act of which some individual happened to disapprove. Confident that the meeting would vote in his favour he had written to his fiancée, Beatrice Potter:

> The Fabian Society is getting so much influence that we must try to save it and guide it; and there is a very large section, perhaps a majority, who are fully on our side. The enclosed notice of a meeting will help us, as the very foolish accusation against me therein cannot fail to rebound. I shall not be at the meeting: and there is sure to be a huge majority against the offender, and so virtually for me. It is the new members, who have not been under the 'influence' long, and have not caught our missionary and educational spirit who are rebellious, not those who know me best – and this is something.[13]

Shaw chaired the meeting, stated the Executive's position, read the correspondence and the apology. Members duly censured the Southern Group for supporting Runciman and calling a rival meeting. Finally, to avoid all possibility of the Aerated Bread Company bringing a libel suit, Pete Curran prevented a vote on the Blochs' resolution by moving the next business.

This storm in a teacup was, in fact, the manifestation of a deep unease felt by the Fabian rank and file at the Executive's policy of working through the Liberals instead of adopting a more radical means for converting England to socialism. Ordinary Fabians had completely lost faith in the Liberals' ability or even desire to improve the lot of the working man. Webb, as the chief advocate of permeation, became the scapegoat and was accused of selling the Society 'into the hateful bondage of the Liberal Party'.[14] When he undertook to stand as a Progressive for election to the London County Council, the Southern Group encouraged its secretary to defy an Executive ruling on the circulation of documents, and when other Groups massed behind the Society's officers, the Southern Group closed ranks behind its own secretary. Runciman was not expelled from the secretaryship then, or from the Society, but relinquished the post a few months later to one whom he called a 'dilute man' and continued to be a most uncomfortable member of the Society, complaining frequently to the General Secretary about the behaviour of other Fabians.

Of course, Webb had a personal interest in encouraging the Groups and keeping relations with the central Society sweet. In 1891 they were his main agents for rallying the electorate in local elections and pushing Fabian Progressives on to the London County Council. His eight leaflets of the *London Municipal Program*, distributed free during the campaign, proved so popular and instructive that, bound in a single red cover, they sold well later. Canvassers used them to spread Fabian theories on unearned income, redeployment of the City Guilds' income to alleviate poverty in the city, the virtues of municipal control of public utilities, docks and markets, and a labour policy for local authorities.

Group secretaries' quarterly meetings with the Executive to discuss policy and methods of work began in February 1892 with a conference on the Webb-Wallas memorandum.[15] The conference drafted a model agenda for Group meetings, agreed members might canvass for public libraries, wash houses and public swimming baths and inspired the East London Group to raise money for two bronze shields (designed by the Mile End Road Guild and School of Handicraft) as annual swimming trophies for the boys and girls of London's Board Schools. Once Fabians' concern for the welfare and amenities of their own neighbourhoods was recognized they were readily accepted on local boards and councils. At the Poplar Town Hall Webb could, therefore, be very smug about the local election results.

February 1891 brought changes in local society organization. Pease opened a register of the names and addresses of each society's secretary, the date of its establishment, the number of members and, later, the number of copies of *Fabian News* required by each.[16] The average life of the ninety local groups founded before 1895 was under two years. Pease and Howells were expected to handle all provincial matters and no more was said about a Local Societies Committee.

Until June 1890 only four areas outside London could boast three or more Fabians: Birmingham, Cornwall, Edinburgh and Oxford.[17] Chipping Norton, Bristol and Tunbridge Wells had two members each, as did America. In Adelaide, South Australia, the Reverend C.L. Marson spread Fabianism as did H.W. Utley in Europe. There was a nine-member society in Bombay founded by Mrs Sarah Gostling, her husband and daughter. After a course of lectures on socialism for Europeans, four lectures 'for educated natives' was organized in the Framji Cowasji Hall on 'The history, doctrine, fallacies and adaptability of socialism to Indian life'. This Bombay Society encouraged agitation by the Anti-Usury League, believing the money-lender to be the greatest social enemy of the Indians.

With two controversial lectures in September 1890, just before the Lancashire campaign, Shaw confirmed the foundation of the Birmingham Society. At the height of its popularity it reached 135, with an average attendance at lectures of 170. For five years it was extremely active, preparing *Facts for Birmingham* and publishing its own newspaper, *The Hesperus*. The Tyneside Fabian Society was founded by some of Pease's friends from the carpenters' co-operative and the trade union he had helped to organize. In its first six months it could boast of six lecturers and three members of school boards on its roll. After two years it merged with members from a wider area, became the Newcastle-on-Tyne Society with a membership of between sixty and seventy and survived several of its contemporaries.

At first the Manchester and District Fabian Society was considered the outstanding success of the Lancashire campaign. By the time it was reported moribund in December 1892 the Executive was glad to disavow it. Dr Pankhurst, its first president, made a good start, with *Facts for Manchester* soon under way, and a system for the distribution of tracts from its lending library to every house within each member's district. A weekly paper was launched, the *Manchester Citizen*. When membership exceeded 120 the society divided into four independent groups, East and South Manchester, South and West Salford. Thomas Harris, the Social Democrat editor of the *Sunday Clarion*, published in Manchester, was persuaded by the society to stand as a Socialist candidate for the South Salford Division by 1000 signatures collected as proof of support, and it nominated an unsuccessful Socialist city council candidate for the election in December 1891. The London Fabian Society arranged a series of lectures in Manchester by members of the Executive the following February. However, at its first annual general meeting a resolution was passed that no members of the Conservative, Liberal, Liberal Unionist or National League Parties should become or remain a member. There was then no official Labour Party and some Fabians had reservations about the Social Democratic Federation. When the main Manchester Society foundered through inflexibility a new one with fifty members sprang from the wreck, based on Harpurhey and North Manchester. The Executive, still intent on exploiting the Liberal Party, censured the Manchester Society in *Fabian News* for the exclusion clause in its constitution.

The *News* was the chief nexus for local societies. If local branches had remained at the three English and one Indian of 1890, liaison would have been a simple matter, but now the office was flooded with letters. During the Lancashire campaign Henry Hutchinson had offered to finance a

Fabian socialist people's press. After much discussion the Executive refused the offer because it felt unequal to the responsibility, adding, however, that it was prepared at any time to receive money.[18] He responded by sending £100 for a New Year lecture tour in the north of England, organized from Manchester by Bland and de Mattos and repeated in the west country.

The birth of each new society was announced at the London meetings. One red-letter week three were recorded – at Bristol, Wolverhampton and Plymouth, two the direct result of Bland's tour, Bristol being a transformation of the former Bristol and Clifton Christian Socialist Society.[19] The score had risen to twenty-seven by the end of 1891, mainly in the industrial Midlands. An affluent branch in South Australia under Marson's influence sold an impressive number of *Essays* and was granted leave to reprint Fabian Tracts and adapt No. 13, Shaw's version of *What Socialism Is*, to Australian conditions.

If Shaw was the most popular initiator, de Mattos was the Executive's most active promoter of local societies. For £2 a week and expenses, he was sent out to consolidate the gains of the Lancashire campaign by organizing lecture courses in the provinces, sound out local aspirants to Westminster on their policies by using Tract No. 24, *Questions to Parliamentary Candidates*, and collect information on their sponsors and funds. De Mattos became convinced that with more time and money, a Fabian society could be set up in each major northern town. Unfortunately, he caused the Society considerable embarrassment,[20] through his belief in 'free love' which he discussed with his hosts during lecture tours though never in his lectures. In May 1892 complaints reached the Fabian office that de Mattos was greatly harming the Society by his moral position and by gossip involving a female lecturer whose tours he organized.

Katherine St John Conway, who had read classics at Girton College, Cambridge, was converted to socialism while teaching at Redlands High School for Girls in Bristol by witnessing the processions of striking cotton-workers into the city's churches during Sunday services.[21] She resigned her post in order to teach in a board school and lodge with the working-class Irving family. Dan Irving, who later played a considerable part in the founding of the National Independent Labour Party at Bradford, was a member of the Bristol Socialist Society. De Mattos arranged lecture tours for Kate, feeling he was saving her from too heavy a burden of work. She soon drew large audiences wherever she was billed to appear, and Webb and Beatrice Potter used their influence to obtain work for her as a free-lance journalist. But she precipitately abandoned her engagements and rushed back to Bristol on receiving a letter from Irving reproaching her for making his invalid wife delirious by her defection.

In Bristol, Kate's friends, Enid and Paul Stacy, very active local Fabians, encouraged her to tell the General Secretary that she could no longer work with de Mattos, of whose character they were highly critical, because of the rumours coupling their names. Pease was not convinced by the evidence against de Mattos who was, after all, a friend and fellow-member of the Executive who maintained that he had done for Kate no more than he would have done for any other Fabian woman in need. After a prolonged altercation, the Executive decided to ignore the whole affair. Provincial lectures were suspended for the summer and de Mattos was so far reinstated that the following year he was named in Hutchinson's will as a trustee for the Trust. Enid Stacy became a popular Fabian lecturer in the north of England, often touring with Ramsay MacDonald, who became an organizer after being hired as a temporary secretary during Pease's convalescence; she later married Percy Dearmer, a Christian Socialist. Clifton and Bristol Fabian Society (formerly Socialist Society) pursued a stormy career. It dissolved in 1894 when, like so many other local societies, it decided to merge with the ILP.

During summer 1892 the Fabians' other benefactor, D'Arcy Reeve, offered £500 for a winter campaign in the provinces. The Executive thought £300 would be sufficient to cover 80 to 100 towns. Courses were prepared for Newcastle, Lancashire and the Halifax district where new societies were springing up. Members of the original Manchester Society set up branches which soon became full-scale societies. W.H. Utley, who had succeeded MacDonald as assistant secretary during Pease's long convalescence, was appointed Lancashire organizer for the autumn and Pease was instructed to engage a typist and a temporary assistant to deal with all the extra work.

A Leicester Society failed, according to its secretary, because it attracted only working-class socialists and lacked the middle-class members who always did the organizational work in a Fabian society then. A society in Jarrow aimed at being an educational centre to assist the local Independent Labour Party, which already had 800 members. The Liverpool Society rose to over 100 members in six months and remained for many years the most active local society. A manifesto, drawn up in conjunction with the local Trades Council and Mersey Labour Federation, was produced in its first month, and was followed by *Facts for Liverpool: Liverpool Wealthy and Poor* and *Strike or Legislate? An Appeal to Trade Unionists*. It issued a monthly circular on the lines of *Fabian News*. It also wrote articles for

Labour Pulpit and started a bureau for the unemployed in 1893. The local authority soon proposed taking it over as a municipal labour department. Liverpool was the only local society to take seriously the duty of training young people. Within a few weeks of its own birth the Liverpool Fabian Society even instructed its secretary to found another at Birkenhead.

During the autumn of 1893 signs appeared that many of the new local societies were withdrawing from the Fabian Society. Some died when the first glow of enthusiasm faded with the tedium of listening to dull papers by local speakers who lacked the glamour and skill of London lecturers. Others discovered that their concept of socialism would best be met not by permeation but by merging with the local ILP or SDF branches.

Little was lost to the socialist movement by the demise of most local Fabian societies in 1893 and 1894. Their former members continued to read Fabian literature to acquire reliable facts and stimulation for work within the local branches of the new political parties. Provincial Fabians contributed much to the foundation of the National Independent Labour Party at Bradford in January 1893 and helped dilute extremism with rationalism in its further development throughout the country. Their subsequent disappearance as strictly Fabian bodies is understandable because they were a great deal closer in spirit to a political party than to the London Fabian Society.

Although the Fabian administration in London favoured the principle of local societies as a means of converting Britain to socialism, it was not powerful enough to exert the necessary central control and had no real desire to do so. The result was great diversity in development and a certain diversity in aims, though not necessarily in ideals. If the administration had paid more attention to the provinces, its grasp of developments in central politics would have slackened and it would have neglected its specific task of refining and expanding socialist ideas and working out practical modes of implementation. Policy was the Fabian Society's sphere, not management of a country-wide network of political cells. Thus there was no sense of failure when the great majority of this first generation of local societies disaffiliated in favour of the local political branches. The official stance was that if a local Fabian society thought that in the cause of socialism it could operate more effectively as an ILP or SDF branch it should do so.

4

PLANNING THE CAMPAIGN FOR LABOUR

To crown the Fabian Society's first decade of work a manifesto was published entitled 'To your tents, O Israel!'. It appeared first as an article in the *Fortnightly Review*, on 1 November 1893, and caused a great stir. An enlarged version was issued two months later as Tract No. 49, *A Plan of Campaign for Labour*.

Tract No. 49 had had a long gestation period. Its conception occurred on 13–14 January 1893 when Shaw and de Mattos attended the Bradford conference, which established the National Independent Labour Party. The Executive had been invited to send them with the proviso that 'The Fabian Society, as a society for the propagation of Socialism, is and must remain independent of all political parties at present existing or likely to be formed in the future'.[1] The two Fabians arrived in Bradford determined to persuade the other delegates to work through the Liberal Party. But when Shaw called a meeting in his room the evening before the conference, they discovered that provincial Fabians supported the demand by the trade unions and other socialist bodies for an independent Labour Party presenting its own candidates at the next election.

London Fabians believed the workers were still not ready to choose and support parliamentary candidates from their own ranks. Twelve months before, when James Bartley had urged the formation of a working man's party, both Shaw and Pease had rejected the idea. Pease had reminded Bartley that socialist attempts at action independent of the two established political parties had failed disastrously.[2] Shaw's reaction was a scathing indictment of the workers' lack of initiative and drive. Mere enthusiasm was no foundation upon which to build a political party; party organization and a policy for Labour required 'a vital faith in human equality'.[3] Still, Bartley proceeded to found the Bradford and District Labour Union, and in May 1891 the provisional administrative committee asked Ben Tillett to stand as its first parliamentary candidate. Tillett refused on the grounds that a Labour candidate would have no chance of success; so did Tom Mann.

The Bradford committee next offered Shaw the candidacy. He refused on the ground that although he worked for his living, he was one of those who were still classed gentlemen and that, until the workers stopped running after top hats and frock coats and learned to trust their own kind, they would never have a genuine Labour Party in Parliament. If it could not find a working man, it would do better to choose someone who could pay his way. His final self-disqualification was that: 'seats in Parliament ought not to be made the prizes of fluent speakers and smart writers'.

The Bradford committee ignored that advice and chose Robert Blatchford, a fluent speaker and journalist, and the author of *Merrie England*. Blatchford's condition that 1000 signatures to a requisition should be obtained before he formally agreed to be their candidate was met. There could now be no retreat for the committee even though within a few months Blatchford withdrew his candidacy on becoming editor of the *Clarion*. Ben Tillett then agreed to take Blatchford's place as candidate, though he warned the selection committee that it would have to find funds for him. He was defeated at the general election, but achieved a respectable poll. However, Keir Hardie's success heartened the local Independent Labour Parties and put them in the right frame of mind to plan a combined line of action for future contests.

John Burgess, the prime instigator of the Bradford conference and editor of the *Workman's Times*, had joined the Fabian Society in London before his paper moved north. He claimed to have raised the case for independent Labour representation repeatedly at Fabian meetings, though the Society's minutes contain no record of this. London Fabians were uninterested in a new political party in 1892; they believed they knew how to manipulate the two-party system and did not need a third. However, the February conference of local society and group delegates passed a resolution, seconded by Webb, which welcomed formation of an independent party.[4] Organizations for promoting independent Labour representation were invited from every Parliamentary constituency to send one delegate for every 500 members to Bradford. The conference resolution qualified the Fabian Society for representation there, but the London membership hardly warranted two delegates. In Shaw's view, a national party thrust upon the workers by Burgess and his friends would be an imposture, and therefore wrote to him:

> Just imagine your feelings, dear Autolycus, if the Fabian Society were suddenly to call itself the 'Independent Labour Party'. You know very well that you would simply damn our impudence. And you would be quite right: but then imagine *our* feelings when you and your friends, without half our numbers, our hard-earned reputation, or our resources, set yourselves up under that same high-sounding title! What can we do but laugh good-humouredly at your folly? It may annoy you to see us posing as superior persons at this rate, but as long as the Fabian [sic] keeps its head level and the rest of you don't, the Fabian will have a superior air in spite of all its efforts to look modest.[5]

When the organizers, including Dan Irving, heard of Shaw's private meeting of all Fabian participants before the conference, they suspected him of trying to sabotage it. On the opening day an objection was raised to the credentials of Shaw, de Mattos and even to Dr Edward Aveling, a marginal Fabian who was representing the International Labour League. Aveling also represented the Bloomsbury Socialist Society, against which no objection could possibly be made, and so he was allowed to join the delegates in the body of the hall. Shaw and de Mattos were banished to the gallery, where they could not take part in the discussion, while a vote was taken on whether they should be admitted. This gave them time to think and, in view of what he had learned the night before, Shaw concluded that the Executive had seriously underestimated the strength of feeling throughout the country. The moment had already come to strike and strike hard. By the time the delegates decided, by 49 votes to 47, that they would admit the two Fabians, Shaw had abandoned his original intention of making a speech defending permeation of the two existing parties and was prepared to help draft the constitution for a new, nation-wide, political party. Later he ridiculed the delegates' response to the 'great Fabian terror', but at the time he was angry and dismayed that representatives of the working classes should reject the Fabian contribution to the new political movement. He had to exercise Fabian patience in order to achieve a voice in the construction of the new party; he was rewarded when he was invited to help draft its constitution.

Shaw did not, however, precipitately abandon the policy of permeation; Webb's dedication to that strategy prevented him. Some Fabians supported a move to incorporate the fourth clause of the Manchester and Salford Independent Labour Party's constitution in that of the new national body; this prohibited support of Liberal or Conservative candidates in constituencies where there was no Labour nominee, even though they might stand for the policies Labour members advocated. Their resolutions were frustrated by typically Fabian amendments. Shaw exulted that the 'freedom to nobble the Liberals whenever that is the right policy' was secured at the conference, together with the right 'to vote Liberal or Tory if necessary, or to play the true Fabian game of capturing the Liberal vote by forcing their candidate upon the Liberal Party – Battersea Fashion'.[6]

An attempt to frame qualification for attendance in such a way as to exclude the Fabian Society from the next Independent Labour Party conference was blocked by Shaw Maxwell, who realized that the new party might some time be grateful for Fabian help. Shaw believed Fabian virtues had already made the constitution and immediate programme tauter. Yet federation with the new party was not possible for the Fabian Society; therefore it could not, of right, have seats upon its executive. If it was to retain its peculiar utility for Labour – performing the necessary research, taking the long view, developing socialist thought – then it had to eschew political responsibilities. Individual Fabians might shoulder the burden of political obligations, not the Society as a whole.

The Socialist Democratic Federation may have foundered but it was not sunk. Ten days after the Bradford conference, William Morris chaired a meeting of the Fabian and Hammersmith Societies which agreed to form a joint committee with the Federation to explore ways for socialists to act in concert.[7] No action could be pledged by the Fabian representatives without prior consultation by the whole Executive, but discussion was welcome.[8] For a trial period of three months Shaw, de Mattos, Utley, Olivier and Pease represented the Fabians on this experimental Socialist Alliance Joint Committee. It delegated Morris, Shaw and Hyndman, one from each organization, to draft its manifesto. A Fabian members' meeting discussed their completed draft and authorized the Executive to make all necessary verbal alterations before the Society's representative signed it. *The Manifesto of English Socialists* did not become a numbered tract, but was issued in 'an exquisite red cover' for sale in Hyde Park on Labour Day at an Eight Hours Bill demonstration. It had to be reprinted within a month.[9]

At the end of its trial period the Joint Committee directed Pease, Dobson its joint secretary, Shaw and Webb to prepare a report on the British socialist movement for the Socialist Congress in Zurich. The Fabian Executive had already agreed to spend £13.3s on sending Shaw and

Olivier to Zurich, accompanied by Utley the assistant secretary 'on half pay if necessary'.[10] The draft report survives in the Fabian archive, bearing corrections by both Shaw and Webb.[11] It was never presented or published because the Joint Committee came to grief over its electoral policy and terms for admission of the New Fellowship, formerly the Fellowship of the New Life. Fabian predilections dominate the text of the report. The section describing the Society insistently contrasts the smallness and exclusiveness of its membership with the amount and quality of work done by it. The Fabian aim was defined as education of itself and the public on the practical measures for socialism, its political formula as permeation. The writers cast doubt upon the Independent Labour Party's ability to become a great political force in the state because the trade unions were not committed to it and might take an independent route to Parliament.

A couple of months later all Fabian enthusiasm for collaboration had evaporated. The Executive decided to withdraw its representatives from the Joint Committee, explaining in the *News* that they had found it impossible to make the more enthusiastic members of the other bodies observe proper procedure and restrict their activities to matters agreed by all three organizations.[12] Federation and Fabian policies were, in any case, incompatible, but as a sign of goodwill the Fabians, on resigning, tentatively promised support for any future, practicable joint action. Olivier and some of the more impetuous members questioned the Executive's decision but the majority of members either approved or were indifferent to the withdrawal.[13] Thus the uneasy partnership ended.

Ever loath to waste any effort spent on a failed project, the Fabians determined to issue their own statement on a practical socialist policy. The Executive asked Shaw in September 1893 to write a Fabian Manifesto for publication in the *Fortnightly Review*, then edited by Frank Harris.[14] By mid-October 'To your tents, O Israel!' was completed. Discussed and amended, first by the rest of the Executive and then in a long and heated debate by the members, it was passed for publication in just two days.[15]

When the article's contents were leaked to the press, a storm broke. The *Weekly Times* proclaimed that Fabians favoured splitting the vote and were encouraging Radicals to smash the Liberal leaders who barred the way to progress.[16] The *Cheshire Evening News* announced that the Society had become implacably hostile to the Liberal Party.[17] One or two newspapers suggested that the statement might close the rift between the Fabian Society and the rest of the socialist movement; that speculation soon died.

Within a week the Society was stricken with dissension. H.W. Massingham, political editor of the *Chronicle*, who had been abroad during discussion of the draft, was the first to raise objections.[18] He informed Edward Pease that he felt he could no longer remain a member of a society which had publicly gone back on its wisest teaching. Professor D.G. Ritchie, a firm Liberal, resigned promptly, deploring both the fatuity of urging revolt against the Liberals just when some reforms had been obtained, and its indecent attitude towards Gladstone and Morley. Several more resigned in the next few days, staunch Liberals who felt their attempt to bring about reforms by constitutional means as the Society had hitherto advocated, had been debased by this statement. Some of the more radical Liberal politicians who were not Fabians were similarly alienated because they felt they had been unjustly condemned for failing to introduce reforms before they had any chance of success.[19]

'To your tents, O Israel!' opened with a declaration that the Fabian Society had come to the end of its patience with the Liberal government. (The *Pall Mall Gazette* commented that having come to the end of its patience, the Society had blandly come to the end of its Fabianism.[20]) Shaw next accused the Gladstone government of rejecting the Newcastle Programme 'which had vanished on the morrow of the General Election, having served its turn'. He named Webb as the programme's progenitor because he had outlined its points in a privately, though widely, circulated pamphlet of 1888 entitled *Wanted a Programme*,[21] and claimed that he himself had helped foist it on the Liberal Party.[22] Of course he was exaggerating Webb's role. In any case, few, if any, of the proposals were novel. Indeed, nowhere has it been claimed that Webb was the sole propagator of the ideas put forward in its programme. In the Fabian Manifesto's review of the Liberal press the several sources and development of these ideas are indicated. The Newcastle Conference's Manifesto cannibalized the programmes presented to the most recent Liberal conferences, all of which had been supported by the Liberal press and by the Fabians at one time or another; it also added to that material some of the political measures advocated in Fabian tracts. With the cry of 'We are all socialists now' it was adopted by the fourteenth conference as official Liberal policy for the 1892 general election.

Tract No. 49, *A Plan of Campaign for Labour* printed the Newcastle Programme in full as proof that the Liberals had promised such devolutionary measures as Home Rule for Ireland, disestablishment of the Anglican Church in Scotland and Wales, and full municipal powers, including control of public services, for the London County Council and all other municipalities. The series of land reforms proposed came very close indeed to those advocated in early Fabian lectures and publications, including the *Essays*. Promises had been made of more democratic election procedures, reform or abolition of the Lords, and recognition of the need to pay MPs so that workers might be adequately represented. Promised reform of the Factory Acts and of taxation in order to provide the 'free breakfast table' concluded the Newcastle programme. With such bounty proffered by the Liberal Party, the workers thought they had no need to form their own and gave the Liberals their votes. Shaw claimed that their social reform programme had returned the Liberals to power, not the Irish Home Rule policy.

Shaw castigated the government for allowing sixteen months to pass without implementing their promises. The excuse of Tory obstruction was summarily dismissed since many reforms, being administrative, could have been introduced without legislation. Time had been deplorably wasted. Wages and working hours in government departments were as bad as they had ever been, but Fabian criticisms on this head were unfair since the eight-hour day and the living wage had not been planks in the Liberal platform. In a review of the several Ministers' post-election activities only Acland, Mundella, Asquith, Haldane and Buxton emerged with any credit; the last three were all familiar guests at the Webbs' dinner-table.[23] Gladstone, completely absorbed with Home Rule, was accused of having blocked their initiative. The broken promise to reform London's administrative machinery had angered the Fabians, many of whom either served on local administrative bodies or were trying to gain seats.

Shaw was now edging away from trying to indoctrinate the Liberal front bench; Webb was not yet ready to do so. As he had done in the *Fabian Election Manifesto of 1892*, Tract No. 40, Shaw now, in Tract No. 49, reproached the working classes for letting yet another election find them unprepared and still trusting a government out of touch with their aspirations. Conveniently ignoring the founding of the National Independent Labour Party he scolded them for having done nothing to improve their lot over the last two years and advised them to make the best of the Liberal programme which was, at least, 'better than the no programme at all' of the Conservatives. In place of the Liberals, the trade union movement had become his target for permeation. The Webbs were then in the last stages of preparing for publication their great work on the history of trade unionism and were extremely impressed by the movement's potential. Shaw believed the recent appointment of a Parliamentary Committee by the TUC indicated that that body was moving in a Fabian direction. Political power was available if the unions would seize it. Shaw tried to persuade them that they were far more advanced and effective in their organization than any other body and their ability to cope with parliamentary elections was, therefore, unrivalled. He argued that if every union member gave a penny a week, £300,000 could be raised in a year. If one-tenth of that sum were levied the combined unions could easily support an initial fifty Labour MPs while learning Parliamentary ways. Labour's political organizations could not do this for they were small by comparison and could not levy from members more than £2000 – enough to provide the union leaders with propaganda for convincing their huge membership but no more.

Before Tract No. 49 was issued the Fabian Society had to face the press reviews of 'To your tents, O Israel!'. The *Scotsman* said that though the Fabians were bluffing and their former utterances had been hollow, impudent and pretentious, it might be unwise to disregard them as a voice in politics.[24] The *Daily Chronicle* declared that the Fabian Manifesto had no socialism in it and that Shaw and his friends were 'only at their fun'.[25] Socialist newspapers tended to be the most derogatory, accusing the Fabians of playing into the hands of the Tories.

The *Pall Mall Gazette* and *St James's Gazette* gave Shaw an opportunity to answer his critics in alleged interviews on 31 October. Since he was then employed by the former, he possibly wrote that 'interview' himself, extending his original points and insisting that his article had been written in deadly earnest. In the 'interview' he accused the Labour movement of having tricked the Liberals into promoting the Newcastle programme before the election by false claims to strength and then producing only three extra Labour MPs. He said the government was perfectly justified in dropping a programme which patently had little support from the people. In the *St James's Gazette* interview he pointed out that, far from trying to switch the vote of the working man from Liberals to Tories, the Manifesto was attempting to persuade Fabians and their sympathizers to boycott the next election. Alliance with the Liberals might be at an end because Fabians felt they had been betrayed after they had converted many working-class Radicals to Liberal views. That did not mean they would join the Conservatives or even undertake independent action for which the Society was not strong enough. Fabian policy, he declared, was to support an Independent Labour or trade unionist party, but he gave no definitive guidance on the use of workers' votes.

Shaw may have been clear in his own mind about proper Fabian attitudes at the next election; his supple twists and turns in argument masked that clarity from his reader. He certainly gave no real guidance on how the workers should use their votes in constituencies where no Labour candidate would be standing. He at once urged them to abstain and to vote for any candidate whose answers to Fabian *Questions to Candidates* were acceptable.[26]

Webb, too, was interviewed by the *Pall Mall Gazette* and the *Sun*.[27] Though he followed much the same line he still preached permeation of the Liberal Party, and claimed that publication of 'To your tents, O Israel!' had been timed to give the Liberals a further opportunity to fulfil their promises. He declared there was no proposal in it which could not be carried out within the next two months. His reluctance to abandon the Newcastle programme caused the *Daily Chronicle* to observe that all the Fabian Society had intended by the Manifesto was to 'warn Mr Gladstone in time to save him, keep the Newcastle program [sic] going and wake up the Old Gang'.[28]

Puzzlement continued inside and outside the Society. The Reverend Stewart Headlam, a Fabian Liberal, blamed Shaw and Webb for deserting their position as leaders on the extreme left of Radicalism. He protested:

> To advocate the introduction of working-men, as such, into Parliament, as the Fabians seem now to be doing, is utterly absurd: as honest, unbribable, advanced socialist politicians, certainly the more the merrier: but simply as workmen who will merely try to raise the wages in their own trade, or even of Government workmen generally, a thousand times no.[29]

In reply, *The Plan of Campaign for Labour* explained that opposition between socialists and Radicals was out of date: the ranting kind of campaigner and candidate no longer had a place in the constituencies. A Labour candidate who had made his reputation by agitation could so easily antagonize his own colleagues and supporters; it was a waste of time to run him as a candidate because he could not win a seat. He now needed:

> pleasant manners, high personal character, a level head, and a tight grip of the fact that the issue at the General Election will lie, not between the present dispensation and the millennium, but between Parliament as it is today and Parliament with an energetic Collectivist minority acting as a separate party in the interests of Labor [sic].

The general Labour movement believed that fifty candidates could not be found and groomed in time for the next election. John Burgess attacked the Manifesto fiercely. As Autolycus of the *Workman's Times* he wrote:

The average Fabian doesn't care so much what he is doing – if he is only doing something. Fussy by nature, philanthropic in temperament, frightened lest he may be overlooked, furious if he be not heard to the bitter end, the Fabian is constantly on the prowl, poking with his penknife at every popular movement, contented if he can scratch the initials of the Fabian Society on its surface. At the last general election the Liberal party was the victim of its vandalism. Mr Gladstone was popping up and the Fabian Society cannot afford to be on the unpopular side .... The movement in favour of Independent Labour representation owes nothing to the Fabian Society, and now that it is growing so rapidly the Fabian Society, who have hitherto always discouraged it, cannot be permitted to usurp the place of power on the strength of such an unsound piece of special pleading as is contained in this precious manifesto.[30]

'To your tents, O Israel!' may have startled the political world, but the Fabian Society had a tough assignment ahead of it if it were to guide the Labour movement into the path of parliamentary government.

Webb took over Shaw's customary publication chores for the Society in November 1893 and instructed Pease to let him concentrate on transforming an article designed to attract readers of half-crown magazines into a penny tract for rapid reference by speakers to clubs and unions, to be distributed to the Labour movement through the ninety local Fabian societies. In December Webb told Pease that he had been through the draft himself and 'by excising all Shaw's most objectionable efforts, reduced it to 32 pages! We can't print more, so please resist additions or restorations'.[31] Webb's ministrations were intended to prevent it from antagonizing the National Liberal Federation. Some Liberals might be induced to submit resolutions to their annual conference in January on payment of MPs and election expenses, financial relief to London and adoption of the eight-hour day in government workshops.[32] At Webb's behest Pease sent a circular to all the Fabians in the National Liberal Federation, asking them to use their influence to get such resolutions passed in their local branches.

The career of one Liberal Minister, Sir Charles Russell, was greatly affected by 'To your tents, O Israel!' When he tried to defend the government against the Fabian charges at a meeting of the London Liberal and Radical Union, Shaw replied that one either had to pat the Liberal government on the back or kick it and he preferred to do the latter. Press reports of this confrontation generated such excitement that Russell resigned his chairmanship of the Union saying he felt that, as a Minister, he could no longer represent the London Radicals. Recounting the incident in *The Plan of Campaign for Labour* Shaw triumphantly claimed that Russell had thus confirmed the incontrovertibility of the Fabian arguments. Publication of the tract allowed Shaw to answer many of his critics, such as Michael Davitt who, in the *Nineteenth Century*, had accused the Fabian Society of injustice and misrepresentation of the Liberal record in office.[33] *The Plan of Campaign for Labour* thus became a very different document from the original Manifesto and kept the issue boiling for some time.

Shaw had warned that Gladstone could rally Labour to his side only by ensuring that his next budget was a radical one; this he could not do without splitting the party. Within a couple of months the Webbs' more radical Liberal friends divulged that the first crack had appeared within the party and it was not long before Chamberlain's Liberal Unionists joined forces with the Conservatives.

Since *The Plan of Campaign for Labour* was designed to stir the whole Labour movement into concerted effort it challenged the ILP to declare at its conference in Manchester the number of candidates it would field at the next election, insisting that there were plenty of good, able men in the trade unions ready to stand and that the unions were perfectly able to finance them. Among a host of instructions on how to conduct an election campaign he issued the warning that the unions had to leave the election in the hands of the constituencies and not expect candidates to represent only union interests, and that adequate funds were essential. Candidates should not have to pay a single farthing of their own and when successful should be adequately supported by funds from the local parties and trade unions until legislation provided salaries for MPs. The candidate was instructed to have a definite, practical, up-to-date programme because the work of an MP was to make laws. A general declaration of loyalty to the principle of collective ownership of the means of production and distribution was useless as an election policy statement because any man with common sense realized that the next Parliament would not be in a position to legislate for such things. It warned against demanding a complete ministerial programme at this stage. Shaw's final growl was that if Labour again allowed itself to be caught unprepared at the next election it would not have another chance in the nineteenth century.

Much of the advice and guidance proffered by the Society to the Labour movement at this most critical period in its development was uncongenial to the politically aroused common man. Fabian advice was clever, clear-sighted about the possible traps for the movement for direct representation of workers' interests, and perceptive about its weaknesses. Unfortunately it was also patronizing. No eager, new political movement welcomes into its planning structure an advisory body which constantly says that it is going about things in the wrong way, however accurate that warning might be. Radicals inevitably resent being told that the indirect approach will achieve more than a straightforward onslaught on social evils. Some leaders of the Labour movement appreciated that the Fabians had a certain value to them and were prepared to make use of them just as far as it suited their purpose. Belief in gradualism and permeation made this attitude perfectly acceptable to the Fabians. As long as there was a chink into which they could insert the thin end of the wedge they were happy. Nevertheless, every now and then exasperation was bound to break out on one side or the other.

5
THE HUTCHINSON TRUST

Had Henry Hutchinson not committed suicide in August 1894 the Fabian Society might well have ended in its second decade. It wanted to do more to help set the Independent Labour Party on a firm foundation and spread socialism throughout Britain but was frustrated by lack of money.

The year opened with the Executive adopting a sterner attitude towards the society's activities. There should be no 'conference, soirée, conversazione, party or other frivolity' that session.[1] The focus of attention was to be education of the public in how to select parliamentary candidates and of the successful MPs in what to fight for. Lecture courses were arranged for Fred Hammill in Newcastle, where he was Labour candidate in the imminent by-election, for W. Slingsby Godfrey at Gosport, and for Hubert Bland in the north, where, for a few weeks, an organizer whom the Social Democratic Federation could no longer afford was hired to make the arrangements.[2] D'Arcy Reeve yet again contributed a small sum and MacDonald was sent up to speak a few times.[3]

In London even greater attention was now paid to parliamentary affairs and political developments.[4] Money was raised for the Newcastle by-election, *The Plan of Campaign for Labour* was sent to all MPs and Ministers in the Lords, to the secretaries of all trades councils, trade unions and branches of the SDF and ILP and even to the leaders of the German Social Democratic Party. Briefly collaboration with the National League for the Abolition of the House of Lords was contemplated. Pease was elected to its committee but, after a couple of months, he condemned it as indecisive, and so resigned. The Fabian Society did not actively campaign for the abolition of the Upper House for another forty years.

The Gladstone Club at Southampton and the Fabian society at York both asked the Executive to pick a parliamentary candidate for them. Ramsay MacDonald's nomination for Southampton was unpopular with the local Fabian society, which disaffiliated and merged with the Social Democratic branch. York would have been delighted to have him but the Executive had chosen Hugh Bellot. MacDonald was also much in demand at Attercliffe to help with Frank Smith's speculative campaign. None of the candidates won his by-election, but the Executive was pleased with the proportion of the vote its nominees polled.

These activities aggravated the dire financial straits which necessitated a major investigation into office expenditure and methods that autumn. Hutchinson's death at this juncture was providential. By a will made a few months before his death, after certain family bequests, the residue of the estate was left to the Fabian Society, to be spent within ten years on furthering its propaganda, objects and socialism in any way it deemed advisable.[5] Sidney Webb, as one of the executors named in the will, was informed of this bequest at the beginning of August and discussed its disposal with his wife; his immediate reaction was that it would cause great trouble.[6] Pease was informed but enjoined to secrecy because Webb thought there might be 'huge claims' on Hutchinson's fortune and that the will might well be disputed. His co-executor, Hutchinson's younger daughter Constance, also thought that her mother and brothers might contest it, claiming that her father had not been of sound mind at the time he made the will since the widow had been left an annuity of only £100. Webb did not want Fabian expectations raised in vain, certainly not before he had determined how the legacy should be used, although Pease, also a trustee, dreamed of spending it on publishing tracts then in preparation. The executors had been instructed to spend £100 on hiring a literate person to examine Hutchinson's own writings in case any were worth publishing; if so, they were to spend a further £500 on publishing them under the Fabian imprint. Pease, who was allocated this task, decided that in all Hutchinson's writings there was nothing of value to the socialist cause and the money could be put to other uses.

Most of the legacy was in 3 per cent Derby stock and amounted to a little over £10,000. Webb was president and administrator of the trust, William Clarke, de Mattos, Pease and Constance Hutchinson the trustees. The two sons did not question their own or their sisters' meagre legacies, but they did question their mother's. Webb discussed this with them and persuaded the other Fabian trustees to waive all Fabian claim to the widow's furniture, double her annuity and grant an additional £200. He asked the Executive to endorse this action although its consent was not necessary. Nothing was revealed of the legacy until plans for its use were consolidated because Webb feared that if members thought the Society was sufficiently endowed from an outside source they might disavow all financial responsibility for – and consequently emotional commitment to – the work already in hand.

During their summer holiday the Webbs had been discussing how to 'attract the clever young economists to the working out of collectivism, and thus get some research done'. They knew how precarious was the Society's future and that of socialism generally, and they longed to set up a school for the study of economics as had been done in Stuttgart. Now they saw their chance. For safety's sake they consulted their barrister friend Haldane on whether the Trust could be used to found a school. Pease had no doubt that whatever Webb chose to do was right, but some of the other officers, particularly Bland and MacDonald, considered he was bending the terms to suit his own convenience. Bland was won over; MacDonald was never convinced and carried on a quarrel with Webb for several years as a result.

Haldane dismissed the Webbs' qualms. In his view the Trust could certainly be considered a charitable one and:

> the expressions 'propaganda and other purposes of the said Society and its Socialism' do not confine the Trust to the precise Basis and Rules of the Society as these exist now, but that, so long as the propaganda of the Society are Socialistic, any objects within the Basis and Rules for the time being, or even within its practice, if that is not directly contrary to these rules, will be proper Trust purposes.[7]

The trustees need not put the funds at the disposal of the Fabian Executive, as MacDonald had maintained. They were themselves the proper administrators. Only if they committed a breach of the Trust could the Executive intervene. Haldane judged that payment of MPs' salaries was not within the trustees' competence, but the funds could certainly be used for research into problems connected with socialism and for instruction in economic and political science, funding lectures, scholarships or new educational centres. All that was just as legitimate as the publication and free distribution of books and pamphlets, payment of lecturers in the provinces and suburbs and the other means of disseminating Fabian propaganda which Hutchinson had paid for in his lifetime. However, Webb was adamant that the Society ought not to rely on it as a regular part of its income. If *ad hoc* grants for particular projects were made, at least half the legacy could be set aside for founding an institution for economic research and teaching in London. That place was the London School of Economics and Political Science.

Much has been written about the way in which the Webbs launched and navigated the School until it eventually became self-supporting and an integral part of the University of London.[8] There is therefore no need here to describe in detail how they economized on the cost of the premises by persuading Charlotte Payne Townshend, later Mrs Bernard Shaw, to rent a flat over the School; how they started the British Library of Economics and Political Science by culling excess volumes from their own and their friends' collections; how they cajoled lecturers already making a reputation elsewhere to give individual lectures or short courses at the School; how they encouraged Bertrand Russell to endow the first scholarship with the stipend from his Trinity Hall Fellowship and themselves employed some of the research students for short-term projects of their own so that the School might be saved the cost of bursaries. The history of the LSE is undeniably linked with that of the Fabian Society. Many eminent Fabians were educated there, many have taught there, publications of both institutions have often been related and Fabian studies have frequently been shaped by the researches carried out in the School. This history is concerned only with that portion of the fund in which the Hutchinson trustees and the Fabian Executive Committee employed for direct Fabian work.

It was logical that a considerable portion of the money should be spent on those objects the donor himself had supported. A demand for Fabian lectures certainly existed in country areas. MacDonald was one of the first to benefit from the Hutchison Trust, being hired to lecture in the south of England on the political history of the nineteenth century in winter 1895–6.[9] As some of his lectures were delivered in the Southampton area he was able to nurse his constituency at the same time. Enid Stacy was engaged to give two courses on the same subject in the north. Frederick Whelen, an Executive member who worked in the Bank of England and was an authority on the London Progressive Party, lectured in his spare time on municipal socialism in the industrial Midlands.[10]

During his first lecture season Ramsay MacDonald realized the scheme's potential for extending socialist enclaves throughout the country, incidentally consolidating his own reputation within the Independent Labour Party. Back in London, he challenged the way the trustees had allocated the Hutchinson funds for the next year; the reservation of £1500 to endow the library attached to the school made him particularly angry. He believed Webb to have specifically promised a good sum for promoting

Fabian aims; he now heard that only one tenth of that sum was intended annually for the Society.[11] He decided to make a bid to get that administration more firmly into the hands of the Society by bringing a motion before the members' meeting to force the trustees to account for their actions.[12] Webb felt constrained thereafter to make an annual report to the Society's annual general meeting on how the money was being spent.

Pease lost patience with MacDonald's insinuations and told him to present a definite scheme of work to the Executive costing less than the trustees were already committed to spend on the Clare Market library building. MacDonald's sole proposal was to finance a Fabian tour in Australia by Carolyn Martin, a very popular young lecturer who was joining the Fabian team. Unfortunately she died soon after the proposal was made. Beatrice Webb thought MacDonald was opposing the trustees out of spite at not being appointed a lecturer at the LSE.[13] He was more probably disappointed at seeing funds which might have been devoted to his particular plans slipping from the Society's grasp. He explained to Pease, in April 1896, that his scheme for Fabian use of the Trust Fund 'will not only contribute to an immediate practical end, but will improve the human material with which we as Socialists will have to deal within our own ranks'.[14]

By June the Executive was seriously considering his second proposal to spend £700 on advertising the Fabian Society in the press, paying for six provincial lecture courses and hiring a travelling organizer who would spend one week in every four on research and the rest on propaganda to increase the Society's influence in branches of the Social Democratic Federation and Independent Labour Party throughout the country. Fabians would thus find themselves preaching to the unconverted. Some of this programme attracted the Executive, so his proposals were pared down to reduce expenditure and adopted for the next session.

The Hutchinson lecturers would have to be well endowed with factually-based material; each would be paid £10 a month to study and prepare. Enid Stacy was selected to lecture on social reform in the Midlands in October and repeat the four, weekly lectures during November and December, speaking in Liverpool on Mondays, Burnley on Tuesdays, Bolton on Wednesdays, Rochdale on Thursdays and Oldham on Fridays – all for £2 a week. Hamilton worked equally hard around Birmingham, where Fabian local society membership was rapidly increasing; his subject was English labour and the causes of poverty. In January and February Joseph Clayton, who had been given an extra period of study to bring his lectures to university extra-mural course standard, was sent to

Oxford and the Norwich area to lecture on 'The making of modern England'.[15] Harry Snell, part-time secretary and student at the LSE, joined the team in the New Year, to cover Darlington, Middlesbrough, Stockton and Waterhouses, while Hamilton attacked Brighton and Tunbridge Wells.

Snell's were the most revealing of the lecturers' monthly reports in the *News*. He preferred provincial to London audiences, considering them less childish in their comments and more prepared to criticize the lecturer's thesis by advancing their own opinions. Organization by local groups was still poor and so Snell advised far more central management. Despite local hitches, the small band managed to deliver about 180 lectures in fifty different towns, speaking to Fabian groups, Liberal Associations and clubs, ILP and SDF branches, unions and co-operative societies. This cost the Hutchinson Trust £300.

Apart from these courses, Executive members also lectured in Aberystwyth, Cambridge, Oxford, Reading, Tunbridge Wells and several other towns.

Two successful series of Trust lectures made the Executive determined to colonize the provinces and focus attention on Fabian socialism and the Labour Party. It announced: 'Our Society, like the Chartered Company in Africa, will capture the hearts of the natives, and control them, as the Chartered Company does, for its profit and their own good at the same time'.[16] It thus embarked on the 1897–8 'intensive culture campaign'. Snell was despatched to Scotland, where he found little trade unionism but sympathy towards socialism if patently successful. His tour ended in South Wales where audiences were less inclined to serious thinking.[17] He lectured five nights a week, often twice on Sundays throughout the winter, giving 140 lectures in all, occasionally holding a debate with a locally well-known anti-socialist. Nevertheless, September 1898 found him prepared to set out on three, separate monthly tours in the north of England. By December his health had broken down and S.D. Shallard completed his course and then became the permanent Trust lecturer.

Several attempts were made to convert the Irish to socialism. On their honeymoon in 1892 the Webbs had visited trade unionists in Ireland and spread word of Fabianism, though Beatrice took rather a dim view of its chances.[18] Now Shallard and Bruce Glasier were sent on a two-month campaign to central and southern Ireland to encourage and educate the new Labour Party.[19] The civic authorities welcomed this offer of political education and many lectures were given in town halls with the mayor presiding, although there was some opposition at first from the Church.

Bruce Glasier sent back such glowing accounts of the brass band reception he was given, that the trustees made a supplementary grant to extend his work there. Before the campaign opened they had paid for the hurried publication of two special tracts, Nos 98 and 99, on *State Railways for Ireland* and *Local Government in Ireland*, so that the two lecturers might leave behind some tangible proof of English socialist interest in the country. The tracts were given green covers, not red, and a selection of others with some relevance to Irish problems were bound up with them as presentation copies for leading local people.

Shallard's second tour had an unpropitious beginning when he was shadowed by the police as a dangerous man. Nevertheless, he managed to persuade some MPs and influential townsmen to take the chair at his lectures and they were excellently attended. To build on this foundation, he was sent out for a third tour in the autumn. But it had to be abandoned when he nearly died of appendicitis, complicated by delayed and poor treatment. The Society and the Trust supported him throughout, sending his brother and even paying his doctors' bills.[20] On his return to England, he insisted on fulfilling the engagements booked before his illness, then agreed to accept the less demanding post of secretary to the Socialist Centre in Birmingham where he was also on the ILP National Administrative Council.

Shallard had proved a great success as a lecturer. As Fabian lectures were fully reported in the local press he was convinced that they influenced local affairs more than any other socialist activity,[21] and he warmly praised Harry Snell's groundwork. After his departure Webb considered asking Philip Snowden to take over but decided against it, not wishing the scheme to become more the mouthpiece of the ILP than of the Fabian Society.

Contraction became necessary as the Trust's stipulated ten years drew to a close. When W. Stephen Sanders offered to lecture on a part-time basis for the next session, the Executive gladly accepted. Sanders took over the London suburbs, the Home Counties and East Anglia; socialism had been widely disseminated in this area by the early Fabians, but it was growing apathetic and needed re-education. The northern and Welsh towns, however, had reached saturation point. There the local ILP branches were absorbing socialist energy and running their own educational campaigns though they relied on the Fabian Society to supply literature and some speakers.

Even after the Hutchinson Trust was officially wound up, the Executive managed to continue the lectures on a small scale under the same name. At its first committee meeting of 1896 it was announced that Constance

Hutchinson had died, leaving virtually the whole of her estate to the Fabian Society and naming Webb, Pease and Clarke as trustees with very wide powers of application. Her bequest of just over £1000 was treated as a supplement to her father's trust and administered as part of it until 1904. Then, finding that more than £3000 remained, the trustees reconstituted the whole of her capital and placed it in a separate Fabian account known as Number 2. They also bestowed an additional £477 directly on the indigent Fabian Society. From the Number 2 Account lectures and book-boxes continued to be financed until the Trust was finally wound up in 1924. The remaining funds were swallowed up in 1904 by projects concerning the LSE.

R.H. Tawney was asked in 1908 to take over as Hutchinson lecturer, but journalism tied him to London and he had to refuse.[22] Two years later Henry H. Schloesser was recruited to give a few lectures within reach of London.[23] By that time Webb and Shaw seemed to be the only regular lecturers in the provinces, being much in demand by the University societies, and, of course, drawing no salary from the fund. Webb was an enthusiastic lecturer;[24] Shaw refused to take more than one country lecture a month.[25]

When the original Hutchinson Trust was wound up on 24 June 1904 the trustees accounted to the Society for their trusteeship. Constance Hutchinson, de Mattos and Clarke had been replaced by Charlotte Shaw, Bland and Frederick Whelen. They justified Webb's original decision not to finance directly the work of the Society and make 'a present of their trust funds to the individual members of the Society'.[26] They claimed that by promoting 'solid educational work' rather than mere political agitation and street-corner oratory, they had attempted to fulfil the donor's unexpressed intent. Correspondence in the Fabian archive clearly shows that the attitude adopted towards the use of the Trust funds was inspired by Webb.[27] Beatrice was less convinced that he was right. He therefore allowed some leeway, providing subsidies for the Fabian book-box scheme introduced in 1892, an essential aspect of follow-up work after the lectures.

In 1894 the Society had six boxes of books, culled from Executive members' personal collections, for lending to local societies, and the general membership was asked to provide by subscriptions others at a cost of £4 each.[28] Within two years, ninety-six organizations were participating in the scheme. Not all the organizations requesting boxes were Fabian groups, as the scheme was well-advertised in the trade union and Labour press, and co-operative societies, ILP branches, working-men's clubs and mutual improvement societies were sent circulars each year. Books were selected according to the applicants' particular needs. The peak demand came in 1903, after which it subsided gradually until the scheme was wound up in June 1939. The latest publications on social and economic subjects were bought for the boxes. Webb designed the boxes with a hinged back so that they opened up to form a small, standing case for use in a club-room.

By 1904 the Trust had given £1030 to the scheme. London members might borrow books during the slack summer season, after which the Executive held a 'sorting-bee' to select and repack the contents of the boxes.[29] Some boxes were chosen with Ruskin Hall correspondence courses in mind, others according to the current Hutchinson Trust lecture themes. Books that had become out of date were replaced and sold off cheaply to members who could also make proposals for new purchases.

Before Ruskin Hall introduced correspondence courses the Fabians experimented with their own, charging members a shilling and non-members half a crown.[30] In 1893 Professor D.G. Ritchie of Oxford acted as tutor for a course on the British constitution, and the following year Webb supervised one on trade union history.[31] Students were warned that not less than six hours of study a week was necessary and that an elementary knowledge of economic theory was a prerequisite for Webb's course. With an ordinary working day of over eight hours, few people finished a course though many started. While McKillop, the librarian of the LSE, was running the course, it was a success, but the work became too heavy for him and Webb, who took over in 1899, was a self-confessed failure, being too busy with local government duties.[32] With relief, the courses were dropped when Ruskin Hall courses began to overlap. Though viewed as an extension of the Hutchinson Lectures, the correspondence courses were self-supporting.

Conversion of the middle classes to socialism was the chief concern of the Fabian Executive at the turn of the century and entailed more publications. Since part of Henry Hutchinson's money was earmarked for *ad hoc* socialist propaganda, the trustees willingly listened to schemes for distributing free Fabian tracts and leaflets. Lawyers were deluged with them when legislation on certain matters was contemplated, doctors when there were plans for reorganizing the public health services, university graduates when Fabians wished to recruit more 'people of influence, belonging either to the centre or to the non-political class'.[33] Pease would have liked to combine such campaigns with a plea for funds; this Webb at first firmly discouraged.[34] Reprints of existing tracts and publication of new ones were paid for by the Trust. It subsidized, for example, Webb's

Tract, *Twentieth Century Politics*. Shaw's Tract No. 107, *Socialism for Millionaires*, was not felt to need a subsidy, however.[35] A reprint of Tract No. 101 was linked with the Housing Conference in London, also subsidized by the Trust, when reform of metropolitan slums was under review by the County Council.[36] The trustees thought the results of such campaigns were inconclusive and were glad they had only spent £316.6.8d on them.

Had the whole legacy been spent on *ad hoc* propaganda campaigns there would be little now to show for the generosity of Henry Hutchinson and the restraint of his wife and family. The lecture courses and the book-box scheme established the Fabian Society outside London as a purveyor of rational socialism, but it was the founding of the London School of Economics that was most important in the long run. At the winding up of the Trust the widow wrote to Webb of the trustees: 'I think that Mr Hutchinson would have been quite satisfied with what has been done with the money left in their care. I am glad the foundations of something has been laid with it'.[37]

6

LABOUR REPRESENTATION

Had Britain possessed in the 1890s two strong internally united parties, the Labour movement would have had little chance of creating a new one to represent the workers' interests. But the Conservatives could not offer a completely unified front while the Liberal Party was revealing a number of serious flaws. Gladstone was following his own line over Irish Home Rule; an inconsistent foreign policy had resulted in disasters in Afghanistan and the Sudan, a challenge to British control of West Africa by the Germans and a dangerous discontent among the Boers over the Transvaal independence settlement. All this led to dissension within the party while Britain's prestige diminished in a Europe fast catching up in industrial development. At home there was a visible split between the *laissez-faire* and the radical reform factions. In the face of Liberal impotence the Labour movement could grasp the opportunity to create its own representative party and the Fabian Society thereupon evolved its related political role.

The challenge issued to workers in the *Plan of Campaign for Labour* to choose and pay their own parliamentary candidates morally committed the Fabians to contribute to electoral expenses. For the 1894 general election £80 was raised and seven candidates named as warranting Fabian support. MacDonald was defeated in Dover, so was Fred Hammill at Newcastle although he could attract crowds of up to 6000 when he spoke.[1] Frank Smith suffered the same fate at the Attercliffe by-election soon after. Tom Mann and Ben Tillett also lost by-election contests. None of them had been notably short of campaign funds or support: some other defect was obviously preventing Labour candidates from winning elections.

Determined to solve this problem before the next general election the Fabians examined it on the domestic scale and discovered that the electoral rolls urgently needed updating. Many Labour supporters eligible to vote on the extended householder and tenant franchise created by the 1888 County Councils Act had not been registered in time to use their vote. Fabians, therefore, canvassed from door to door throughout the London wards to persude everyone to register. They also discovered that workers' representatives were few because they needed financial compensation for missed hours of work. Earnings sacrificed by Will Crooks, Poplar's representative, while attending council meetings were being refunded by the local Labour Electoral League to the tune of £200 a year. All three Fabians standing as Progressives in the 1895 LCC elections, Webb, Crooks and W.C. Steadman, topped the poll, despite a general decline in that party's popularity. Though Crooks and Steadman had received grants from a Fabian campaign fund, the Executive turned down a proposal to create another to pay the latter's wage as a councillor. An *ad hoc* fund at election time was feasible; continuous financial support was quite out of the question. It also refused an ILP request for a £50 loan to Hammill, maintaining that his welfare between elections was the responsibility of the people in the constituency.[2]

In July 1895 the Executive appealed for contributions towards MacDonald's and Hamill's expenses in the general election but issued no fresh manifesto, merely redistributing the *Plan of Campaign for Labour*. Since the ILP had done nothing to implement its recommendations, an editorial in *Fabian News* declared sanctimoniously that the Labour movement, through apathy and disregard of warnings, had once again found itself out of the fight: if twenty socialists and trade unionists were elected it would be surprising. Despite the TUC's resolutions there was still no official electoral fund and the ILP was warned that it could hope only for the return of a very small group who would 'represent discontent with other parties rather than voice the constructive demands of organised Labor [sic]'.[3]

Of thirty-eight socialists, only John Burns succeeded, standing as a Liberal, and Keir Hardie lost his seat. In constituencies without a Labour candidate Fabians voted for whichever candidate came nearest to Fabian policies thus giving Liberals a little extra support. MacDonald managed to collect 866 votes where formerly Labour could command none. In many other constituencies poor organization contributed to the defeat of socialist candidates in spite of Tract No. 64, *How to Lose and How to Win an Election*.

When Parliament opened in the autumn the socialist bodies took stock. Unless its numbers in the House of Commons increased in five years' time the ILP cause would be lost. The Society was invited to send three representatives to a conference of Labour leaders to consider a United Socialist Party. Macrosty, J.W. Martin and George Standring were sent along with instructions to vote against any proposal to create a new party other than a federation of Labour Leagues.[4] Any new party would destroy the toehold already gained and condemn the whole movement for not knowing its own mind. The suggestion that a band of propagandists called Socialist Scouts might distribute literature, handbills and notices in London was given restrained approval by the Executive as a harmless ploy to ginger up the existing movement, as long as it was not considered in any way a Fabian body. After the first conference failed in its objective, the ILP in spring 1896 invited the Fabian Society to combine with it in calling a Joint English Socialist and Trade Union Congress. The Executive agreed, stipulating that all the other socialist bodies should be asked to participate on equal terms for it had no intentions of being inveigled into becoming part of a faction ranged against the SDF and other socialist groups. Not until many years later was a true Joint Standing Committee of the two bodies formed, although attempts were made whenever the ILP felt so in need of Fabian talents that it could tolerate the differences in outlook between the Society and the rest of the movement.

Such differences proved too much in 1897 when the ILP summoned a meeting of a Joint Socialist Committee to work out a procedure for settling disputes between rival parties wanting to nominate socialist parliamentary candidates in the same constituency. The Fabian delegation was expected by its hosts to favour a court of appeal for disputed nominations whose decisions the executive committees of all the socialist bodies would be bound to accept unconditionally. Bland, Pease and Shaw refused to make this pledge because Fabians were prepared to accept nomination and support from any party prepared to accept them and their views.[5] After this stand the SDF increasingly resented the presence of Fabians on the Committee and, though the ILP struggled to keep the Society within the fold, when the Federation delegates finally refused to remain at the July meeting if Fabians were present, the ILP preferred to retain the Federation's goodwill and allowed the Society's delegates to withdraw.[6] Thus it seemed as though the Society had been rejected by the wider movement; yet by reverting to fund-raising and supporting general election campaigns and waiting for the right moment, the Executive managed to keep it in touch with the developing political party. Though there was no permanent Fabian parliamentary fund, *ad hoc* appeals were sent out to Fabians in 1896 and 1897 when Keir Hardie stood for Bradford, Pete Curran for Barnsley and Tom Mann for Halifax.[7] MacDonald was always sent to speak in any constituency where a candidate was favoured by the Society. As the next general election approached a Political Elections Committee was appointed to supervise nomination of Fabians as candidates.[8]

Thus lines of communication remained open and the ILP and the Fabians could make yet another attempt to present a united front in 1899 at the Conference of Labour Elected Members to Public Bodies held at Easter in Leeds in conjunction with the ILP's annual conference. A large number of Fabians attended, as Fabian women were frequently elected to school boards. Trade unionists, land reformers, co-operators were all there but the SDF held aloof from such non-socialist representatives of the Labour movement. At the conference an association was inaugurated for which all members of local administration were eligible provided they could claim to be some kind of socialist. It would give help and guidance on legislation affecting members' work and powers, information on administrative developments in different parts of the country, suggestions on how to present a collective stand.

Elated by this success Webb, as conference chairman, suggested that a joint committee of the ILP and Fabians might be formed to take over and expand the work on local government already being done by Edward Pease in the Fabian office.[9] From this proposal was born the Local Government Bureau which held the two organizations together for some years. The ILP helped finance its publications and was expected to take over complete responsibility for running it after a couple of years, but the Fabian Society initiated all its work and the transfer was delayed from year to year.

Webb, who could never encounter a group of people without wanting to organize them into a useful working force, now planned 'to build up this Confer[en]ce as an Annual affair and to give it tone, and set it on practical and worthy lines, it *would* be worth doing'.[10] Another conference was called in Glasgow the next year. A smaller number attended, perhaps because Webb himself was not booked to speak, but by then the association had proved its worth. Fabian and ILP literature on municipal and rural administration was distributed free to councillors. Tracts on local government and municipal socialism, on allotments, a health service, school administration and provision of labourers' cottages were now reaching a much wider and more immediately concerned readership.[11] The Local Government Bureau organized the third conference. From the beginning the Bureau's main object was to report on Bills before Parliament, and soon it was consulted by anyone in local government, regardless of political affinities, managing to survive on £15 a year.

On 6 December 1899 the TUC Parliamentary Committee, the Fabians and the ILP and SDF executives met once more to discuss financial support for candidates. As secretary of the ILP, MacDonald had already suggested to Pease that each of these bodies ought to run two candidates at the next election with a joint political committee acting for all.[12] Already the TUC Parliamentary Committee had invited the Fabians to discuss ways of increasing Labour representation in the next Parliament.[13] The next general election promised to be crucial to the future of Labour representation. Scepticism about the effectiveness of work through the Liberals was growing in all but one or two of the Fabian leaders. Shaw certainly had doubts and he was the obvious choice as delegate to the joint conference. He and Pease were invited to sit on the organizing committee and advise on how to enmesh the political parties. In the event, Pease was the sole official Fabian representative, though several Fabians were serving as individuals on the ILP National Administrative Council and their moderate views enabled Keir Hardie successfully to oppose the exclusionist Manchester Clause Four. The SDF's move for a distinct party was defeated by those who appreciated the political weakness of the Labour movement. The moderates agreed with Hardie that a distinct Labour group in Parliament should co-operate with any party promoting legislation beneficial to labour and that they themselves should support any candidate sympathetic to the movement, provided he was approved by some part of the Labour Representation Committee created at that conference. It was absolutely essential for the Fabian Society to be officially on that committee from the very beginning. Pease therefore nominated himself the Fabian representative.[14] Shaw and Pease saw the Labour Representation Committee as the perfect agent to secure financial support for Labour MPs. Pease's first task was to help prepare an official list of approved candidates, with the aid of the Fabian Political Elections Committee formed earlier that year. The Executive thought that, for the time being, the Labour Representation Committee should concentrate on the political part of its task and leave financial schemes to the Society.

In August 1900 Pease reproduced in *Fabian News* the Society's circular already sent to all leading trade unionists and socialists, elaborating a plan for the maintenance of Labour MPs of any denomination. Each candidate was likely to cost £200 a year for the duration of the Parliament. The Fabians proposed that a joint finance committee should ask for a guaranteed

£2000 a year to provide for ten MPs and only claim in proportion to the actual number elected (tacitly admitting that Shaw's ideal of fifty Labour MPs had been over-ambitious). The Labour Representation Committee on the whole disapproved of this plan, but agreed to discuss it at its first annual general meeting since the Fabians had received a good proportion of favourable replies to its circular from the labour organizations.

Many requests for financial aid were received before the general election in October, but the Executive Committee vetoed an election fund, offering instead free Fabian literature to candidates; *Questions for Parliamentary Candidates* was revised and reissued.[15] It wished to emphasize the dire need for a fund raised by the whole Labour movement (and the fact that the Fabian Society did not run its own candidates). But it did appeal to members to assist Steadman's campaign because he was facing a particularly hard fight in Stepney.[16] Shallard, then lecturing for the Hutchinson Trust, was given leave of absence to help Keir Hardie in his campaign in Merthyr Tydfil.

At the Labour Representation Committee's first annual conference, S.G. Hobson, the Fabian delegate since Pease was there *ex officio* as a member of the Committee, proposed adoption of the scheme for financial support. Considerable opposition came from the trade union representatives who claimed that the unions were already supporting their own nominees, and from Bruce Glasier of the ILP who argued that the majority of Labour supporters would suspect certain factions of paying to get their own men into Parliament. Unexpectedly the SDF supported the Fabian scheme, but in the end the Fabians were told that if they wanted something done they must do it themselves.

Because a resolution was passed rejecting all collaboration with either of the established political parties in Parliament, this conference was described by the Fabian delegates as 'one of the most momentous political events of the century'.[17] Much intrigued, the Old Gang waited to see what would happen to this mood of rebellion. Opinion in the Party Conference that year had been more favourable towards a fund because the Gas Workers' Union, not the Fabians, had demanded one. Suspicion of the bright, but no longer young, men of the Society was still rife in the Labour movement. A subcommittee was at last appointed to devise a method for paying a quarter of the returning officers' expenses and a salary of £200 for every approved candidate. It sent a draft scheme for raising a penny per member for comment to every trade union regardless of whether they were affiliated to the Conference. In 1904, when the Conference was held in Bradford, the scheme was adopted by all but a few unions. Immediately after the 1903 Conference Edward Pease had been named as a prospective trustee for a Parliamentary Fund. He now pointed out to the unions that a Labour Member of Parliament must represent the whole of the Labour movement, not just a section of it, and that a common Parliamentary Fund was the best way of ensuring the movement's solidarity. The Fabian Society then had a membership of under 800 and so its capitation fee was £3.4.7d. Contributions to the fund, made by about half the affiliated bodies, came to £2277.10.6d in its first operative year. Since only subscribing bodies might apply for financial aid for their nominated candidates, by the following year the amount received had doubled. Pease's constant pressure at every executive meeting of the Committee had gradually worn away opposition to the working man paying for his representative in Parliament.

Meanwhile Labour candidates were finding it much easier to obtain nomination for by-elections under the new understanding between the ILP and SDF. Hobson, for instance, was nominated by both to stand for Rochdale in 1902, and all sections of the Labour and Socialist movements supported Will Crooks when he fought and won by a large majority the Woolwich by-election in 1903. The Fabian Society enthusiastically supported Crooks, billing him as the only Poor Law schoolboy who had achieved a national reputation by presiding as chairman of the Schools Board. According to Beatrice Webb, the TUC had been captured by the ILP and was determined to sponsor a large number of candidates at the next election.[18]

At the Liverpool Representation Conference in 1905 an attempt was made by the rank and file to exclude Fabians from its executive and its deliberations. Members of the political organizations were beginning to think they could manage without Fabian help and resented the fact that, though the Society repeatedly denounced the Liberal Party's actions, it had not abandoned the tactic of getting Liberals to pass socialist measures. The Society weathered the storm and continued to pay its affiliation fee and subscribe to the Parliamentary Fund, while Pease remained on the executive of the Committee. Nevertheless, the Fabian Executive realized that clarification of its position on the Liberals was imperative or the Society might be expelled from the next Conference and lose its voice in shaping the emerging Labour Party.

A Fabian election manifesto was therefore published in the form of a letter purportedly from the Liberal leader Campbell-Bannerman to members of his next government. Webb had actually been nursing this format for a tract for a year but had to wait for the 'right moment' to employ it.[19] 'The Liberal cabinet: An intercepted letter' was read to members at a meeting in the Essex Hall on 6 January 1905 and published with their consent in the *National Review*. Reprints were circulated to all the Society and to anyone else the Publishing Committee thought might benefit. The editor of the *National Review* was instructed to state that the Society had given no explanation of how the 'intercepted letter' had come into its hands, but no one could doubt its provenance. Ornamented with numerous in-jokes and oblique references to general complaints and political gossip, it offered, as future Liberal policy, measures presented in all Fabian manifestos since *Wanted a Policy!*, thus implying that the Liberal Party would be forced by the expected balance of seats in the House to adopt all the social reforms and economic changes advocated by Fabians for more than a decade. The 'Letter' was patently directed to those familiar with current political gossip and previous stages in the struggle with and within the Liberal Party. No longer was the working man reproached for apathy and irresponsibility. The Fabians now cast out their lures for the middle classes.

Thirteen Fabians contested seats in the general election in January 1906; of the seven elected, two had stood as Liberals (including Percy Alden, a member of the Executive), one as a Progressive and Labour nominee and the other four as straightforward Labour. Subscriptions to the Fabian Parliamentary Fund brought in less than £40. This made nonsense of the Representation Committee's refusal to recognize the Fabian nominee for North Lambeth, Dadabhai Naoroji, because 'they interpreted the provision for promotion by an affiliated association to mean substantial financial support'.[20] Naoroji was not elected and returned to India later in 1906 as chairman elect of the Indian National Congress.[21]

Pease thought poorly of the Labour Representation Committee as an authority on Labour's aims, purposes and requirements. A review in *Fabian News* of Conrad Noel's book, *The Labour Party, What It Is and What It Wants*, reveals his true opinion:

> This is an excellent account of the Labor [sic] Party, its history and constitution, and, above all, its ideas, not because the writer displays profound knowledge or philosophical insight, but because he is scrappy, haphazard and somewhat superficial, and this is precisely what the Labor Party is itself.[22]

A week after the election results were announced the Executive decided that a committee consisting of Bland, Chesterton, Hobson, Macrosty, Pease, Sanders, Shaw and Taylor should produce a tract describing a socialist policy for the Labour Party in Parliament.[23] Determined that the workers should not rest on their laurels but start building a bigger parliamentary group for the next election, when sharp reaction against the large Liberal majority seemed inevitable, the committee called vociferously for a convincing and distinctive Labour Party programme. Only a clear policy would hold the new party together. Tactics, strategy and political attack were what the Society believed it could teach the Labour Party. The subcommittee produced a tract which instructed the party to direct all its hostility against capitalism, aim to form the Empire into a great, democratic commonwealth, and abandon the idea that its members represented sectional interests. The Labour Party should seize every opportunity to air its views regarding the right to work, rural decay, the drink problem, the need to feed as well as teach children in schools, the trade unions, industrial legislation and the wage structure. While Liberal leaders were still patting Labour MPs on the back they should strike hard for the economic revolution which alone would bring about the social changes they desired. Though Labour MPs would be outvoted in the House, the real power of the party would grow in the constituencies and prepare the way for a massive gain in numbers and power at the next general election.

Thus, in the decade spanning the turn of the century, the Fabian Society played a characteristic part in the creation of the third political party, destined to be recognized as the official opposition less than a generation after its conception. The Fabian contribution was seldom welcomed by the other party makers. Lack of the common touch combined with a tendency to preach irritated Labour's rank and file and even alienated some of its leaders. Confident of their own rightness, their peculiar indispensability to the Labour movement, and fortified by the accepted legend of their namesake, the Fabians sat out this unpopularity and persisted in helping in their own way.

7
EXTENDING THE HORIZON

At this stage British socialists nurtured an essentially parochial philosophy. Lip-service was paid to international brotherhood, but even this only applied to fellow Europeans, in particular to members of the International. The new political movement in Britain interpreted socialism as relevant only to the industrialized masses and peasants of western civilization. Conceivably Indians might adopt socialism in the not too distant future, but it was not regarded as a possible way of life for Africans, West Indians Chinese or Japanese. Most British socialists concentrated on policies which would bring domestic benefits and thought of foreign policy as a means of achieving a favourable balance of trade to pay for them while averting the wasteful distraction of capitalist wars in Europe. In the mid-1890s, before the Boer War shattered this complacent view, Fabians also concentrated on an exclusively domestic reorganization of their Society.

Webb's insistence that the Hutchinson Trust Fund should not be swallowed up by the routine activities of the Society made some members realize just how run-of-the-mill those had become. In March 1895 they hopefully instructed a Fresh Activities Committee to increase the Society's effectiveness, expecting it to scintillate with original schemes.[1] MacDonald had just presided at the inauguration of the Oxford University Fabian Society, whose members were individually affiliated to the main Society in the hope that they would remain Fabians after they left the university. He then proposed a campaign to extend university societies. Some far from original proposals to proselytize in rural areas, foster church debating societies and scrutinize legislation were made while *Fabian News* was restyled into a more lively, even gossipy, monthly, bearing much-abbreviated reports of lectures, brief notes of individual Fabians' activities and considerably more book reviews. Lantern slides of diagrams and tables were produced to illustrate four courses of lectures on how the poor lived and the benefits of municipal socialism, photographic slides depicting 'typical workers' were begged from members and a prize offered for the best one sent in.

After an Executive attempt to produce a new series of books was scotched by lack of material, MacDonald, irritated at this failure, revived his squabble with Webb over the Trust Fund and made yet another appeal to the Executive to produce something more than 'pottering little penny-worths of boiled down law'.[2] Either to mollify him or to teach him a lesson it invited him to act as editor of a second volume of Fabian essays. The first was still popular enough for the Fabian leaders to distribute free on request to public libraries and to send it, unsolicited, to teachers' training colleges in the hope of indoctrinating a new generation with Fabian economic theories. Between 1895 and 1897 an edition was printed in America and permission granted for a German translation.[3] All hoped that a second edition would be equally influential and profitable. Webb, the first choice as editor, had given up after six months in which only four essays had been produced: an excellent one by MacDonald, two needing enlargement and one impossible. MacDonald jumped at the opportunity to make his name as prominent as Shaw's in socialist literary as well as political circles.[4] Within a month he produced a work schedule; Bland, Sidney Ball, Shaw and Olivier were asked to produce essays and the publication date was set for March 1899. However, this passed without a sign of the volume and the scheme seemed to have been forgotten until, in June, Shaw, who had been out of action for some time with a poisoned foot, declared that he was fit to resume work on his contribution and a progress report from the editor was eagerly awaited. None arrived and no more was heard of MacDonald's volume of essays.

As a last venture Grant Richards who had succeeded Scott as Fabian publisher revived the idea of a Fabian Series, with Frederick Whelen as general editor for the Society but reserving to himself the right to the final word on the contents of each volume. MacDonald wanted greater control by the Executive but the rest were content with the arrangement and in the end Grant Richards produced three longer works for them: *Labour in the Longest Reign* by Webb, a reprint of Tract No. 75; *The Report on Municipal Tramways* by Alderman Thompson; and Shaw's third manifesto, *Fabianism and the Empire*. This last book is all that now remains of a crisis in the Society at the end of the century which threatened to destroy it.

In 1899 the Executive decided to devote the autumn lectures to foreign policy in the hope of evolving some guiding Fabian principles, as foreign affairs had suddenly captured everyone's attention. Earlier mild attempts to raise an interest in the subject among members had failed. On 13 October 1899 Arthur Halliday, a London member, submitted as an urgent motion for debate at that evening's meeting:

> That this meeting expresses its deep indignation at the success of the infamous conspiracy against the independence of the Transvaal, which has resulted in the present wanton and unjustifiable war, tenders its heartiest sympathies to the gallant people whose sole crime is that they love too well their liberty and independence, and trusts that it may yet be possible to secure a cessation of hostilities while leaving the Boers in possession of liberties guaranteed to them by the 1884 convention.[5]

At the Executive Committee meeting preceding the members' meeting there was long discussion of the motion.[6] Frederick Whelen, who was scheduled to lecture on the Mediterranean, argued that the Society was not sufficiently well informed to tackle the subject of the Transvaal. MacDonald fluently disagreed, deploring any attempt by the Executive to evade or postpone the issue. Pease, who had already signed a petition against the war, declared that the subject was outside the concerns of the Society but agreed in the end to announce the Executive's majority recommendation to reject Halliday's motion without revealing the closeness of the vote, 7 to 5. Debate at the members' meeting was even more prolonged; eventually the remnant who stayed the course defeated the motion by 26 to 19.

Few were content to let this important matter rest there. Olivier was horrified that the Executive had refused to give members a lead in advocating debate. Often he had sided with MacDonald, though they reached the same conclusions by different routes. Now he reiterated previous warnings that if the Society did not commit itself it would become a mere agent of the Hutchinson Trust, producing increasingly statistical tracts and abandoning political criticism.[7] Olivier dashed off a leaflet on the relevance of the Transvaal war to socialism, read it to the next Executive meeting and demanded that it and an expanded, tract-length version be published, at once. As with so many of Olivier's schemes, the ideas were far too numerous for a single tract and so the leaflet was relegated for detailed consideration by the Publications Committee. First he wanted to examine the justifiability of empire; the committee decreed that since Britain had an empire it had to bear the consequences and responsibilities. (This remained Fabian policy until most of the Empire had become independent within the commonwealth and responsibility to the Third World took its place.) His second proposal, a study of imperial defence, was so specialized that it warranted a separate tract. Moral questions of imperial expansion and militarism were indeed of immediate concern and the committee advocated a tract by Whelen, not Olivier, with examples drawn from the current sitation and a consideration of whether autonomy in domestic matters, with equal rights for all whites, was feasible in the Transvaal and Orange Free State. In less than a month the problem had expanded to include home rule for the gold district independent of the Transvaal, the position of the Governor General, possible confederation with South Africa, retention of imperial forces to protect European rights, curbs on capitalist domination and making the gold mines defray the costs of the war. But the political situation moved so fast that the project was abandoned and Olivier contented himself with a proposal that a tract might be issued at some future date.

Bland supported Pease in his desire to keep the Society running along its accustomed track, observing that Olivier had:

> always been the 'terrible infant' of the Society, subject to sudden and feverish outbursts, the result doubtless of compulsory restraint 'in another place'. However, he has never before had an attack so fraught with mischief to the Society as this. It looks as though you and I and the remnant of the old gang (of which Olivier has never been at heart a member) would have to make one more fight to secure the Society's usefulness in the future.[8]

He warned that if they failed to prevent the Society joining the radicals of the Liberal Party he would resign. No one heeded him. Bland was always threatening to resign, especially when Fabian agreement with Liberal views offended his Tory heart. (Yet he managed to remain treasurer, unopposed, for twenty-six years.)

Shaw, holidaying on the *Lusitania*, also believed the Society might be destroyed if it issued a statement on 'a non-socialist point of policy' and that 'To wreck ourselves on the Transvaal after weathering Home Rule would be too silly. Our sole business is to work out a practical scheme for securing the mines when we "resume" the Transvaal.'[9] He supported the view that holding the Society together was the most important issue. According to Beatrice Webb,

> Shaw, Wallas and Whelen [were] almost in favour of war, J.R. MacDonald and Sydney Olivier desperately against it, while Sidney

occupies a middle position – thinks better management might have prevented it but that now it has begun recrimination is useless and that we must face the fact that the Transvaal and the Orange Free State must be within the British Empire.[10]

Olivier discovered an ally in S.G. Hobson who was likewise disgruntled about the Society playing a flat second fiddle to the Hutchinson Trust. Sharing Olivier's indignation over the publication fiasco he confided to him that, though he felt hurt by the Society's refusal to discuss the Transvaal business, he deplored even more its lost *diablerie*. He believed Fabians had 'ceased to be feared and are only regarded as amiable and harmless students of certain restricted social phenomena'.[11] He blamed Webb for this narrow vision. Hobson suggested that they should attack this lack of policy, using the Transvaal as an example, and that he should make a requisition for a discussion meeting. Olivier, who held an official position at the Colonial Office, could not initiate a public debate on a colonial policy.[12] But on 8 December members met to consider a controversial resolution by Hobson and an Executive amendment presented by Shaw. Both texts appeared in that month's *Fabian News* and Shaw asked Pease to sound out any Fabian coming into the office on support for the amendment.[13] Claiming that the British desire to gain supremacy from the Cape to the Zambezi had caused the war, not the Outlanders' franchise question, Hobson had demanded Fabian dissociation from capitalist imperialism and vainglorious nationalism and the members' pledge 'to support the expansion of the Empire only in so far as that may be compatible with the expansion of that higher social organisation which the Society was founded to promote'.[14] He asked them to increase their attack on commercialism and to refrain from criticizing the Boers' political claims. Hobson particularly resented the way involvement in the war had diverted attention and resources from reforms at home, and had strengthened the power of the financiers backing the military power of the country.

Shaw's amendment introduced a number of new and indigestible ideas. After declaring that the right to vote was no longer worth fighting for, he argued that the government should not only protect public rights over the country's resources from speculators, whether public or private, but also workers' health and safety by legislation. Consequently, if Britain won the war the people had a right to expect the government either to nationalize the Rand mines or exact royalties to their full economic rent, first to pay for the war and later to spend on public works (whether in Africa or Britain was not specified). At the same time a stringent Mines

Regulation Act should be enforced by the British government for the miners' protection. The government would thus avoid waging a sordidly commerical war in the name of public-spirited imperialism. To counter the popular misconception that the war was being fought to protect the Outlanders' voting rights, Shaw called on the press and politicians to demand greater liberalization and better government in South Africa.

Participants were interested by the argument but had no intention of being railroaded into immediate endorsement of Shaw's colonial policy. A vote on the main motion was avoided and so the subject was left open for further discussion. A tremendously interesting problem remained for Fabians to unravel and, as Shaw foretold, the fun was only just beginning.[15]

Olivier accused his opponents of making unfair use of Shaw, who could command a large vote from sycophants.[16] His demand that the whole Society be balloted by postal vote was rejected by the Executive as unconstitutional. A few days later Olivier resigned from the Executive, not on account of this dispute, but because he had been appointed Colonial Secretary in Jamaica. Amidst all this wrangle a farewell dinner was held at which most of the Executive spoke of him with affection. His lecture on the 'Psychology of race' was read after his departure by Lawson Dodd who, nominated by him and seconded by Hobson, was co-opted on to the Executive in his place.

MacDonald henceforth was Hobson's champion. At the first Executive Committee meeting of 1900 he presented a draft referendum to discover whether Fabians wanted an official pronouncement by the Society on imperialism and the war.[17] If so, further questions would elicit whether they wanted the Society to declare itself opposed to the national wave of imperial sentiment, whether they wanted, like Shaw, to apply socialistic ideas to the terms of the post-war settlement, or whether they wanted to seek a compromise of some kind. The answers could then be taken as the basis for an entirely new Executive statement. After a long haggle he obtained his referendum, restricted, however, to the simple question of whether the Society wanted a statement.[18]

Cases for and against a formal statement were briefly presented in *Fabian News*. To the arguments against were now added the points that it was too late to pass resolutions on the causes of war and too soon to pontificate on its effects, that a statement could not influence the public in the current inflamed atmosphere and might well split the Society. Members responded well, and those who asked to reverse their signed replies after posting them were allowed to do so. The result was a vote of

259 to 217 against any Executive statement. The closeness of the decision prevented the Society from splitting in two because each side chose to remain and try to convince the other.

On the night the result was announced Shaw delivered a lecture on imperialism which led directly to the manifesto *Fabianism and the Empire*. His theme was that Fabians had invented imperialism in the best sense in that they believed 'that the most governed state over the largest area is preferable to a number of warring units with undisciplined ideals',[19] and that by divorcing socialism from class warfare they had reconciled it with imperialism.[20] He argued that imperial expansion was impossible to halt and that neighbouring small states had to come within the borders of the large ones willingly or be 'crushed out of existence'. Disregarding Sydney Olivier's justified opinion that Britain's ability to govern South Africa was an illusion and that it would develop without her assistance, Shaw declared that since capitalism prevailed there, it was far better for it to do so under the control of the British government than under Dutch farmers.[21] He envisaged a federal imperial system which, though created by aggression, would end war within its own borders and bring general peace by alliance with similar federations. He was edging towards the concept of a league of great powers. After summarizing four conflicting views of the war, ranging from the pro-Boer to the ardently patriotic, he claimed that each was a perfectly valid position for a Fabian to adopt; all Fabians were of necessity imperialists and should declare themselves as such. This lecture was his usual *tour de force*, designed to make people think. *Fabian News* reported this meeting as the largest on record in Clifford's Inn.

No matter how confidently dogmatic Shaw might appear on the platform he was perfectly well aware that nothing had been resolved. Writing to his actor friend Charrington, he observed:

> At present the Fabian is troubled in its soul, because it knows that both the vulgar party sides about the war are wrong, and yet [it] cannot find the right line, being unable to unravel the confusion between the social destiny of the world and the blunders and bad blood of the statesmen.[22]

At the annual election of the Executive, which for once promised to be fiercely contested, Shaw was prepared to push Hobson's candidature and vote for him. He foresaw that MacDonald would resign, commenting 'he is genuinely disaffected to the Society in a way which I could only describe by going into psychology'.[23] The strong pro-Boer group would then be faced by three 'dangerous Imperialists' – Bland, Oakeshott and himself – with a considerable number in the middle.

MacDonald did resign in April, taking with him his wife Margaret, Pete Curran his own close political supporter, Halliday, Walter Crane the artist, a young member of the Colonial Office named J. Frederick N. Green, and a dozen others – just over 2 per cent of the whole membership. The disturbance was less than expected and the Old Gang congratulated itself that the Society had lost only a few, most opinionated members who could not conceive that anyone disagreeing with them could possibly be a socialist.[24]

Frank Lawson Dodd decided to outflank the imperialists on the Executive by urging the 800 members to vote only for the eight candidates who guaranteed to bring the Society closer to the general socialist movement and pledged to oppose the national aggressive policy. Having earlier been defeated by the Old Gang, these eight did not now try to revive the issue of imperialism.[25] Webb and Shaw issued a 'counter-appeal' to all those who had voted 'no' or abstained in the referendum, addressing the envelopes themselves, for which they were well rewarded by the ballot result.[26] Three of Dodd's friends were defeated, leaving his faction with one-third of the fifteen seats, just enough to keep the imperialism dispute ticking over. The Society knew that it would have to make up its mind about the Boer War and Jingoism at the next general election.

That election was not far off. During the summer England had fared far from well in South Africa and Webb correctly anticipated that Parliament would be dissolved at the end of September. In August he persuaded Shaw to seek agreement with Hobson over the line the Society should take in its manifesto for the election.[27] Less than three weeks later the first draft of *Fabianism and the Empire* had been written by Shaw, read and emended by Webb and sent to Wherry Anderson of the opposing faction for criticism. It then made a virtually complete round of the Executive, and apart from minor quibbles even Hobson approved it.[28] Though no longer than the normal tract it was first printed as a shilling book to cater for more affluent readers and because books were reviewed in the monthly journals whereas Fabian tracts only occasionally caught the eye of the press.

Every word of the book bears Shaw's imprint, yet it is very rightly introduced as edited by him. Knowing that members would be very annoyed if they were prevented from criticizing the disturbing text, Webb had overruled Pease's wish to avoid further controversy by omitting the usual circulation of proofs before printing. Members' response was unprecedented and 134 proofs were returned bearing pencilled comments, with covering letters, all of which Shaw considered before redrafting. Without Wallas's criticism, for instance, there would have been no reference to the non-white races in the analysis of the South African situation, nor to the defence of Britain's bureaucratic rule in Africa as preferable to government by the white traders.[29]

The second major point in the manifesto dominated official Labour colonial policy for a great many years: socialists needed to face the fact that Britain possessed an Empire whether they liked it or not, therefore they had to do their best for it. Because the Empire had to be administered, a constitutional policy was needed, for mismanagement was a greater danger than attack from without. As Shaw wrote:

> The British Empire, wisely governed, is invincible. The British Empire, handled as we handled Ireland and the American colonies, and as we may handle South Africa if we are not careful, will fall to pieces without the firing of a foreign shot.[30]

He warned that if Britain treated the people of India like children they would rebel. He also foretold that in South Africa Britain would not be able to hold the white colonies permanently against the will of the white inhabitants even though she might be 'governing in the interests of civilization as a whole'. Membership of the Empire should be seen as a privilege, and expulsion from it as an ultimate sanction. Shaw insisted the ideal way of governing dependent territories was by a world federation, with the great powers using their military forces as an international police force. Meanwhile responsible imperial federations would have to act as surrogates. Constitutions framed for the colonies would have to be more liberal than the existing British or American constitutions, with provision made for freedom of speech, freedom of the press, freedom of combination, and with responsible governments in the colonies themselves answerable to a representative imperial council in permanent session in London.

Of more immediate interest to those interested in Fabian policy on South Africa specifically was Shaw's half recantation of the view that the war should be paid for by the gold mines. He regarded reparations raised by an imperial tax as the ideal solution; since Britain had no such tax, some other way would have to be found which avoided bleeding the white provinces after incorporating them into the British Empire. At the same time the natives in the mines and factories would have to be protected by colonial officers administering laws enacted by Parliament with built-in safeguards to protect them from any interference by the local government. He had no fears that such measures would generate hostility between the two races because this existed already and needed curbing.

Although *Fabianism and the Empire* was the first exposition of Fabian colonial policy, half of it dealt with home affairs: the drink problem, the education muddle, the need for labour legislation and a minimum wage – familiar Fabian themes. It was, after all, an election manifesto. Only in the last section, where the 'moral of it all' was stressed, was a new idea introduced: the claim that Britain needed experts at the head of government departments, not political amateurs. Webb had propagated the idea some time before, with special reference to local government. Now, for the first time it was advanced as official, Fabian national policy to substitute a meritocracy for the aristocracy which, admittedly, was 'ready to die for its country, but not to live for it; to do any quantity of tedious duty under orders, but not to earn the right to be intrusted [sic] with that duty by learning and thinking about it'.[31]

At a meeting on 25 September, reported as 'pleasantly notable for absence of bitter feeling', the manifesto and Shaw's own amendments were approved by a 90 per cent vote.[32] It was published on 2 October and within three days 1000 copies had been sold.[33] But sales fell off as soon as the election was over and the tract was remaindered. The general public was just not interested in colonial responsibilities, and could not be made to take an interest for another generation.

As a statement of policy the manifesto could not even be claimed as the unanimous opinion of the Society. In 1902 Pease was forced to deny that the Society officially supported government policy in South Africa, on the grounds that 'Every shade of opinion in relation to the war is represented among the members', and that *Fabianism and the Empire*, though representing the general views of the Society was not binding on any member.[34] Nevertheless the fundamental principles of responsibility towards colonial peoples, defence of indigenous peoples against exploitation of settlers, accountability in some form to other world powers for administration of dependent territories, abstention from economic exploitation of other members of the colonial empire, and the confederation of empire being used as an instrument of world peace were all stated in this first colonial policy declaration.

8

MR WELLS AND REFORM

In a rather slapdash way H.G. Wells wrote in his *Experiment in Autobiography*, 'by the time I came to London Fabianism was Socialism, so far as the exposition of views and policy went. There was no other Socialist propaganda in England worth considering'.[1] When he was a student at the Normal School in Kensington, in 1885, he attended meetings at Morris's house and then spent several years observing Fabian socialism before actually becoming a member of the Society in February 1903, a year after meeting the Webbs and being shamed by their industry for his 'indolence and mental dissipation'.[2]

Fabians were just as interested in Wells as he was in them. Haden Guest reviewed *Anticipations* for the Society.[3] In this book Wells gives the Webbs' theory of experts and Olivier's league of sane men a scientific setting, in which scientific discoveries and technical inventions create, if not a Utopia, a New Republic. He had not then met Olivier or heard his views.[4] Scientists, technicians, managers of nationalized industries and government authorities perform the work in the New Republic; lacking cohesion, the shareholder and the common labourer become redundant and impotent. Fabians questioned many of his premises. The Webbs and Shaw regarded the trade unions as a great institution for organizing the workers into a social force. But this young man could obviously provide a peculiarly Fabian, Friday evening entertainment, as an alternative to Shaw. Accordingly he was persuaded to lecture to the Society and to join it. While Shaw talked and wrote about the new imperialism and a world federation, Wells was writing about a world state of the future. The Society wanted to hear more, although Mr Wells was no orator.

He was booked to speak in March 1903 on 'The question of scientific administrative areas in relation to municipal undertakings'. Contrary to Webb's views, Wells declared that the unit upon which municipal socialism was then based was too small to be efficient or to compete economically with national-scale private enterprises. Recognizing that the age of the commuter had already arrived, he foretold that within a century administrative regions with a hundred-mile radius would evolve, serviced by 'quasi-public companies'. Efficiency ought to be the sole criterion for determining whether entrepreneurs or the state operated a particular utility or means of production. Thus his lecture advocated a mixed economy with regional control of public services. It was published, with permission, as an appendix to his next book.[5]

Wells was the last man to subordinate his opinions to a consensus. Autumn lectures in his first year on the biological aspect of socialism irritated him, a science graduate, because Fabians with no scientific training had uttered great nonsense in debates. He also objected to the Society's pronouncements on fiscal matters, study of which had absorbed members all winter. *Fabianism and the Fiscal Problem*, Tract No. 116, edited by Shaw, caused him to send in his resignation.[6] The Executive persuaded him to remain by pointing out that it was not essential for Fabians to agree with the contents of every tract produced. Ungraciously he consented, maintaining that he strongly disapproved of the Society.[7] To pacify him he was asked a couple of months later to sit on the Fabian committee for studying areas and functions of local government and its relation to central authority.[8] It was one of several committees created to contrive constructive policies on electricity, transport and the feeding of schoolchildren and to draft Bills suitable for immediate introduction by Labour MPs.

Positive action was needed to bring Fabians in line with the new attitudes developing in the Labour movement under the tutelage of the Labour Representation Committee. More Labour MPs were a distinct possibility; they required something to do, but the Society then seemed unable to provide the Parliamentary Labour Group with ammunition, as it had done for London councillors during the municipal reform campaign. New members resulting from the changes in the Labour movement needed something to get their teeth into, otherwise they would quickly disperse.[9] Shaw, sensing that the wind was blowing to the left, saw how difficult it was to explain to new socialists what the Fabian Society actually did and told Pease in June 1905:

If you and Webb were to make out the best case you could for the old policy and the old gang, and Wells, Guest and [Cecil] Chesterton were to do all they could to explode us, we should get something that would really give us an overhauling. Our methods are substantially what they were 15 years ago; and they and we must be getting rather stale.... All I want is a stir up and a stock-taking to make Fabianism interesting again. I have no far-reaching design, not any very definite intention beyond a general desire to reflect on our past life.[10]

Pease, ever resistant to proposals to change the Society, procrastinated for some weeks, but the die had been cast.

Wells set to work to undermine the General Secretary's stodginess, offering to lecture to the Society on propaganda provided Pease attended. As the first lecture of 1906 Wells read an article already published in the *Independent Review* entitled 'This misery of boots'; a month later, he presented to a members' meeting a second paper, 'Faults of the Fabian', with a resolution proposing a committee to consider measures to increase the scope, influence, income and activity of the Society and another to delay election of the next Executive until after that committee had reported.

'Faults of the Fabian' began with a plea for more visually pleasing tracts. The Publishing Committee tried with a reprint of *This Misery of Boots*, giving it an eye-catching cover by Arthur Watts. It bore a sketch of a misshapen boot with men in shoddy suits clinging to it and clawing their way up it, against a background of dark, satanic mills. Its format was so unlike the usual tract that it was not included in the numbered series and the tracts themselves continued to look much the same as always. (When Edward Pease was asked to write a note on the history of tracts some seventeen years later, he was able to boast that no other organization had produced so many publications to the same format.) Like Webb's *Intercepted Letter*, *This Misery of Boots* benefited the Society financially: immediately because Wells donated his fee from the *Independent Review* to the Fabian funds, and in the long term because it remained a best-seller for years, being a most vivid presentation of moderate socialism.

This Misery of Boots illustrated brilliantly the kind of propaganda Wells thought the Fabian Society should produce. In a parable about ill-fitting boots Wells presented socialism as a way of life in which:

Nobody dreams of a time when everyone will have exactly as good boots as everyone else; [he was] not preaching any such childish and impossible equality. But it is a long way from recognizing that there must be a certain picturesque and interesting variety in this matter of footwear, to the admission that a large majority of people can never hope for more than to be shod in a manner that is frequently painful, uncomfortable, unhealthy or unsightly.... There is enough good leather in the world to make good and sightly boots for all who need them, enough men at leisure and enough power and machinery to do all the work required, enough unemployed intelligence to organise the shoe-making and shoe distribution for everybody.[11]

Middlemen and property owners of all kinds who drew profits obstructed his kind of socialism, designed to bring about a complete revolution by gradual change. Yet gradualism was not, for him, 'some odd little jobbing about municipal gas and water ... and backstairs intervention between Conservative and Liberal'.[12] Webb's methods, he believed, could never produce the millennium; on the contrary, 'You might as well call a gas-jet in the lobby of a meeting-house the glory of God in Heaven!'.[13]

'Faults of the Fabian' sharply attacked the Society's lethargy and lack of imagination. It said that everything but the Society had changed in the last twenty years. Its old-fashioned methods were preventing it from selling socialist theory to the intelligentsia and applying its principles to the existing social institutions. It blamed the Society for nearly destroying itself by involvement in issues on which Fabians might legitimately hold opposing views, such as the Boer War. Associating too closely with the Labour Party prevented the Society from fulfilling its proper function of converting to socialism the educated middle class. Despite all the talent at its command the Society had dissipated its strength and wasted opportunities. Wells saw no virtue in Fabian exclusiveness, in always courting financial disaster, in overworking the staff in dreary, cramped quarters. He scolded Fabians for leaving so many good projects unfinished, for just playing at political and sociological research, for compiling lists of lecturers who never lectured, for being suspicious of admitting vigorous young people as members, for antagonizing newcomers with the Fabian giggle and joke, and for toadying to Shaw. He certainly overstated the case but there was a lot of truth in what he said. His ridicule of the accepted interpretation of the legend of Fabius and the treasured strategy of permeation was salutary. Several leading Fabians also felt that the Society ought to concentrate on its real task of making socialists. Accordingly the Executive was extremely helpful when Wells presented his plans for reform, a fact he scrupulously acknowledged.

Membership in 1905 had dropped to little more than 700; Wells blamed the stringent election procedure for that. He had so far had a good deal of support, but he made a tactical error when he began proposing constructive measures to remedy the faults. When recommending a new set of educational tracts to recruit new members he offered to draft them himself, a natural and generous offer for a writer to make. Immediately Fabian hackles rose at the thought of their revered Shaw being supplanted by this newcomer. Pease was affronted when Wells declared that the secretarial staff must be enlarged and the size and appearance of the office improved. Overworked as he was, he protested against the unflattering comparison drawn between his room in the semi-basement in Clement's Inn where he worked then and the bright offices of capitalist firms in the Strand. Wells made no attempt to disguise the fact that he thought Pease a dry old stick with antediluvian ideas. When he proposed an additional, income-related, voluntary tax on members to raise funds for expansion, many people condemned it as ungentlemanly and savouring of the draper's shop. They traditionally thought small where their own money was concerned, except for rare spirits like Hutchinson and D'Arcy Reeve. Wells proposed to seek talent among young people just down from the university, prospective journalists and politicians, and draw them into the Fabian orbit first as voluntary help. Such tiros in socialism were to be encouraged to speak, first in the university societies which needed active development, then in the main London society where older members would have to be encouraged to stay on at the end of meetings to listen to them, not drift away when the well-known figures had had their say.

Those sitting in the packed Clifford's Inn hall on that February night in 1906, listening to Wells enumerate the faults of the Society, must have been incensed by these criticisms. Yet they acknowledged their justice and voted unanimously to allow him a special committee to consider drastic reforms. Since none of the Executive wanted changes made without airing his views fully, they all volunteered to serve on it and suggested that an equal number of ordinary members should be nominated, bringing the number up to thirty. Wells hated cumbersome committees; later he resigned from all the Fabian subcommittees to which he had been appointed because they were too large and wasted too much time.[14] Now he insisted that ten would be quite enough to do the job and the Executive gave way when he refused to consider any other plan but his own.[15] Mrs Shaw, unlike her husband, favoured the small committee and was nominated one of the three Executive representatives on it, Stewart Headlam and G.R.S. Taylor being the others. Wisely the Executive decided that Pease ought not to serve on the Special Committee even though Wells invited him; this spared him much distress. Sydney Olivier was appointed chairman and Jane Wells the committee secretary. Wells was quite content to leave matters in their hands and departed for an American lecture tour immediately on setting things in motion.

Wells had demanded a full reprint of his paper in *Fabian News* followed by his own report of the ensuing debate; an abbreviated, bowdlerized version was sent to members. The Executive was reluctant to make even this compromise because it was hard enough to conceal from the press what went on in private members' meetings and Wells was asking the Society to blaze abroad its weaknesses. The parts particularly hurtful to the General Secretary were excised and he was instructed to use his discretion about what to say to the reporters besieging his office.

Bland sought to profit from this publicity and recommended setting up a new order of associates declaring themselves in general sympathy with Fabian objects; he probably wished to retain the traditional blackballing of undesirable candidates for full membership. At this first sign of positive change the Special Committee took fright and declared the move premature. Disregarding all objections the Executive amended the rules to provide for admission of associates at a half-guinea subscription and gave Bland's daughter, Rosamund, permission to form a junior branch of the Society called the Nursery.[16] The Special Committee concentrated on drafting a more inspiring and less dogmatic and materialistic version of the Basis and preparing its report. Though its enthusiasm remained high that of Wells had faded by the time he returned from America. The press was then forecasting a split in the Society. Shaw warned Wells that if he turned out the Old Gang he would have to run it himself, and advised him to serve on the Executive for a couple of years to learn committee manners before taking the plunge. Probably he would not be able to make the Fabian any more effective than the Old Gang had, but he might learn how to exploit it and thus become 'something more than a man with a grievance'.[17]

The report of the Special Committee turned out to be far less revolutionary than expected. The essence of Wells's original criticism remained, but greater stress was laid on the Society's vocation to convert the middle classes. Socialist newspapers were directed at the working classes; Fabian pamphlets ought therefore to seek a different readership. Young people should be drawn into the university societies, the Nursery and new-style provincial groups. All the methods of recruitment recommended had been tried many times before and the proposed role for local societies varied little from that formerly pursued and earlier condemned by Wells. Recommendations were made for inclusion of clauses in the Basis supporting the emancipation of women and the protection of children from the abuse and even whim of parents, while the use of economic jargon in it was utterly deplored. The report proposed creation of two small, powerful committees, one to control local societies and groups, the other to make Fabian publications more professional. Wells wanted to pare down the Executive Committee to three members, advised by a monthly General Council. His hostility towards the General Secretary was very thinly veiled in the draft report and though offending passages were deleted before it reached the printers Pease certainly knew of them.[18] Blame for the decline in Fabian energy and fortune was laid at his door. Not only did the Special Committee wish to supplant him, it even wanted to discard the name Fabian in favour of British Socialist.

Far from destroying the Society the internal wrangling brought new members flooding in. Wells's opening lecture in the autumn series on 'Socialism and the middle classes' attracted the largest audience ever to Exeter Hall.[19] Membership increased to about 1100 by the December meeting to discuss the report.[20] As usual, Shaw drafted the Executive's reply containing counter-proposals to increase its number by six instead of contracting to a very active triumvirate and passive council. The council, weekly publication of the *News* and changing the Society's name were all rejected outright, but much was conceded and promises were given that, when numbers and income increased sufficiently to justify the move, larger offices would be hired. Most of the Executive preferred not to tamper with the Basis, at least until a great deal more thought had been devoted to it. The Old Gang recalled the long struggle over a former revision and in the end its views prevailed. The Special Committee was granted the customary time to submit amendments to the Executive's comments for discussion at the second December meeting and all members were sent copies of the report and comments in that month's *Fabian News*. Four meetings were needed to discuss the report.

Some coercion took place in the meantime. For example, certain Fabian women, led by Maud Pember Reeves, threatened to vote for the Special Committee Report unless a clause advocating equal citizenship for men and women were inserted in the aims of the Basis. The Executive gave way without a struggle but in a manner implying that the women were a little silly to insist because in the Society equality had always been taken for granted: a complete misinterpretation of the women's demand for active advocacy of equality.

At the first discussion meeting on 7 December Wells was allowed to discourse on the council-cum-triumvirate scheme and his belief that the

Society's political activities should be kept distinct from, though parallel to those of the ILP. He called the Executive's political proposals irritating, irresponsible and a stupendous piece of bluff. Webb retaliated that the Special Committee had been entirely chosen by Wells and was, therefore, not a representative body and yet it was proposing to jettison all the Fabian Society had been and done in the past in order to transform it into something entirely alien. Again he defended permeation and castigated Wells for pursuing quantity, not quality.

The *Daily News* published and dissected the two reports and was immediately forced to apologize to the Society for unauthorized publication of private documents. That brought the Society to its senses. Several of its leaders suddenly realized that if the Special Committee won, the Society would fall apart. They now begged for a compromise. Wells attempted to make the sitting Executive resign in favour of a new one before any decision on action was taken. This was blocked by Shaw who pointed out that it would amount to dimissal without honour of the Old Gang; he begged members to show loyalty to the officers they had elected, or at least not opposed, for so many years. Completely undermined, Wells withdrew his amendment and the audience cheered the Society's reprieve. However, when he read the report of the second meeting in *Fabian News*, he wrote to protest that he had been most unfairly represented and that he had been manoeuvred into withdrawing his amendment. His letter was published, as requested, in the *News* with an editorial gloss attributing to him an 'apparently incurable delusion that the ordinary procedure at public meetings is chicanery, and that the Executive Committee is a conspiracy of rogues to thwart and annoy him'.[21]

Wells was accused of obstructing the true business of the December meetings by presenting his amendment. Yet Wells was right in his ultimate assessment that 'in the end it will be the spirit and purport of the Report of the Special Committee that will become the spirit and purport of the rejuvenescent Society'.[22]

Mrs Reeves's new clause on sexual equality pre-empted the first business meeting of 1907. The Executive's amendments to the Basis and Rules had to be dealt with in February at the annual general meeting and a new Executive elected. By now the Fabians were definitely beginning to flag. When Olivier proposed at the end of a third night of debate that meetings should continue from week to week until settlement was reached, the prospect was sufficiently daunting to make everyone more amenable.

Charlotte Shaw, certainly tired of the long proceedings which were whittling away Fabian confidence and faith in the future of socialism, produced a list of activities beginning with lectures on 'The faith I hold' by eminent Fabians who would each interpret socialism, describe what socialists could achieve when finally in power, and relate that to their personal faith. She also wanted simple tracts, a new version of *What to Read*, and a quarterly magazine on more discursive lines than the *News*. Groups to study specific subjects seemed to her a far better proposition than local groups in London. She persuaded the Executive to experiment with all these ideas.

A fourth and final debate on the report tackled the Society's relationship with the Parliamentary Labour Party. The more socialist Fabians wished to remain aloof from the practical politics of parliamentary representation, the rest wanted amalgamation with the new party. The Executive moved that the newly elected body should appoint another special committee to seek the best means of setting up local societies of the Fabian type to increase socialist representation in Parliament, independent though co-operating with the Labour Party. Shaw explained that while the working classes were gaining entrée into Parliament, middle-class political and economic independence was waning and therefore it was 'the mission of the Fabian Society to succor [sic] the middle class'.[23] Nevertheless, the audience was puzzled by the Old Gang's eagerness to sponsor local societies. Only six new provincial societies had been successfully launched that century, all but four of the older ones had died and Fabians had transferred to the apparently thriving ILP and SDF local branches. Once more the meeting ended inconclusively.

The annual general meeting on 22 February proved surprisingly smooth. The much overdue report for the year ending the previous March had passed without question. Executive proposals for changing the rules were adopted without debate or division. Mrs Reeves's amendment to the Basis was merely referred for ratification in six months' time to comply with the constitution. Candidates for election to the Executive were told they might send out election addresses with the ballot papers, at the Society's expense. The controversial clause in the Basis sanctioning compensation for property taken over by the State was allowed to stand and members instructed the next Executive Committee to prepare a revised statement of both Basis and Rules for their future consideration.

The Society had proved far from moribund. New members were joining, mainly young and middle class, though with a considerable number of women from all classes.[24] Election addresses were needed to explain where each of the thirty-seven Executive candidates stood on reform: Sidney Ball, Maud Pember Reeves, R. Mudie Smith and H.G.

Wells issued a joint manifesto, ten others presented individual addresses, including Edward Pease. His statement was characteristically blunt and colourless, merely recording that he, the chief official of the Society, wanted to carry on with his work and that, though not neutral over the recent controversy, he was not associated with any faction nor was he promulgating a personal line of policy.[25]

All but one of the retiring members who stood again were elected, Wells coming fourth to Webb, Pease and Shaw. Twice the usual number of members had voted, 78.25 per cent. Fabians congratulated themselves that the new, enlarged Executive fairly represented the views of the whole membership and, with relief, left it in peace to carry out its instructions.

It immediately instructed one-third of its number, finely balanced between old and new members and between the two factions, to select five new subcommittees and draft their terms of reference. Besides the Political Committee, promised earlier, they chose one to direct propaganda and membership, a Publications Committee, a Finance and General Purposes Committee and a special one to revise the Basis. Wells refused an invitation to chair the Publications Committee: not normally given to considering the feelings of the Society he may, on this occasion, have realized that to stand down in favour of Shaw was tactically sound. However, he accepted appointment to all the others and tried to make them all answerable to the Finance and General Purposes Committee. The Executive refused to concede this point. Nor would it let him rush through a new rule and other amendments to the Basis while his enthusiasm for reform was still intensified by his success in the election. But in May it asked him to produce a syllabus for the elementary tracts he had proposed and to edit a series of Utopian texts from Plato to the present day, with introductions by suitable Fabians. Wells was not enthusiastic and the series was dropped. But the publisher Fifield, who had his own ideas of what a saleable Fabian series should be, arranged to produce reprints of selected Fabian tracts, six to a volume.[26] Seven such volumes materialized in the next two years while the Society benefited financially from repeated reprints of *This Misery of Boots*. The idea of a quarterly magazine was readily abandoned when A.R. Orage and Holbrook Jackson took over *The New Age* to run on Fabian lines with Fabian contributors.[27]

Non-literary means of teaching and converting to socialism were the realm of the Propaganda and Membership Committee. It was responsible for lectures, recruiting members and vetting any joint action proposed by the ILP. Machinery for propaganda even within the Society was far from adequate. The few remaining London groups were developing in a very ramshackle way because of the differences in area and community covered by each. Methods of work and procedure suited to provincial societies continued to be quite useless for metropolitan groups with a much closer relationship with the parent society. After an impractical scheme to establish countrywide cells for propaganda and political activity had been rejected by the Executive, an entirely new subcommittee was told to construct a plan to give existing local societies a greater degree of autonomy in electing officers, managing funds and deciding whether to be bound by any resolution passed by the main society.

Converting the middle classes and redesigning family structure had both been done to death in lectures of the two previous years. Fresh subjects were essential and the Propaganda Committee's choice fell on imperial and foreign policy, requisitioning the remainder of the Hutchinson Trust Funds, the No. 2 Account, to finance them. Consistent with the general desire for a more professional approach, W. Stephen Sanders was appointed organizing secretary, at a salary of £100 plus lecture fees, to supervise the formation and administration of local societies and groups from the office, attend their meetings whenever necessary and act as secretary to this committee. It was proposed that he tour Scotland and the northern counties in the autumn to found new groups and lecture, provided the local societies paid his expenses.

This scheme had first to win members' approval. Two representatives from each local, university or subject group were invited to a conference in London on 6 July to discuss the new scheme. It was the first national meeting of Fabians since 1892 and forty-eight delegates attended. The scheme was approved and the delegates convinced that a new, dynamic Fabian era had begun in which each of them had a part to play. In fact, the scheme differed little from the original organization of local societies; it was just a little more centralized. Associate members of local societies still had no voting rights in the main Society. By the end of the year there were sixteen local and five university societies, fledgeling societies were being announced at every members' meeting and total membership was over 2000.[28]

Because Wells did not attend Executive Committee meetings for some months and no one wished to antagonize him by acting in his absence, the promised Political Committee was not appointed until midsummer.[29] By then much of the task originally assigned to it was already being performed by the Propaganda Committee. However, one important duty remained: to define both the extent of the Society's involvement as a corporate body in the political activity of the Labour movement and the principles upon which political guidance to individuals should be based. On the premise that while the ILP and the Society were socialist institutions, the Labour Party was not because it was responsible for representing trade union members even if they were not socialists, the Political Committee concluded that the Society ought to exercise greater influence at elections and nominate candidates provided they were acceptable to the National Executive of the party. Since Labour circles were likely to suspect Fabians of foisting their own men on the Party, the Political Committee stipulated that the Society should contribute to Labour's Parliamentary Fund £1100 for each successful nominee to support him for the life of the Parliament. This would not necessarily allay suspicion; it was proposed merely as an interim measure because the committee was uneasy about Fabian candidates having to rely on any party for financial support. Fabians still hoped that a measure for paying MPs might be passed during the current Parliament, so the Political Committee vaguely recommended the Society to seek other ways for socialists to enter Parliament. Its report for January 1908 insisted that local Fabian societies should appeal to the middle class and leave the workers for the ILP branches.[30]

Standing committees entailed a great deal more work for the office staff which, in July 1907, had numbered four. Yet another subcommittee was asked to investigate this situation and recommend improvements. The only increase in staff it advised was a junior clerk and the most revolutionary innovation was that both the office and Standring, their printer, would have telephones installed. Three months later, the Finance Committee reported that though the cost of running the office had doubled, members' subscriptions had tripled, also sales of tracts. A better suite of offices in the same building was then secured and the staff was able to deal with the current boom in comfort.[31] After profiting for ten years from the runaway sales of Tract No. 82 on *The Workman's Compensation Act*, the Fabian Society finally insured its employees under its terms.[32]

93

9

THE NURSERY
AND THE GROUPS

Possibly the most interesting development from the Wells controversy was the Fabian Nursery. Young Fabian members were seldom called on to speak in debates, but without their participation and consequent political education, the Society would be in danger of sinking into old age. Therefore, encouraged by Wells, Rosamund Bland and her friends prevailed upon the Executive to permit them to create their own branch of the Fabian Society, to be known as the Nursery. Twenty young people, who met in the Fabian office on 11 April 1906, agreed that it should be a purely educational group for those aged under 28.[1] A small grant from the Society enabled them to hire halls for meetings and they embarked on analysis of the popular misconceptions of socialism, and organized a course of lectures of their own for the next session on the economics of socialism, a conscious echo of the way the early Fabians had begun their investigations twenty years before.[2]

The Nursery was an offshoot, not a rebellion. The Executive was consulted about a suitable reading list, Shaw was invited to lecture on the law of rent and, with an eye to the main Society's programme, debates were organized on *Fabian Essays in Socialism*, imperialism, internationalism, communism and state socialism and their philosophic aspects.[3] Senior Fabians proved very willing to spend an evening talking to the Nursery, but it was Wells, forecasting a science-dominated future and describing the 'new woman', who really captured their imagination and allegiance.[4] Lessons on public speaking were arranged, Fabian tracts systematically analysed, experience gained by inviting other political organizations to provide speakers to take part in debates. Requests for the Old Gang to lecture decreased, although, whenever Nursery funds were low Shaw or Wells would speak at well-advertised public meetings. Occasionally the better speakers of the Nursery were invited to speak at Fabian members' meetings and the young people were constantly roped in to canvass at elections and help with addressing and dispatching chores.[5] To keep in touch with the Fabian societies at Oxford and Cambridge, some members helped to create the University Socialist Union to arrange socialist lectures in provincial universities, found new societies and encourage exchange of ideas by inter-university debates.[6]

The Nursery also entailed a great deal of fun, with country rambles, socials, dances and cabarets. Fabian Schools, Christmas and New Year parties and summer outings were much enlivened by the nurslings' dramatics, ukuleles and gramophones.[7]

The Arts and Philosophy Group, founded in March 1907 by Orage, Holbrook Jackson and Eric Gill, attracted novelists, playwrights and playgoers, also a large proportion of the Nursery. This group studied the relationship between crafts and industry, the difference between unions and craft guilds and the limits of collectivism. Guild individualism was more sympathetic to it than trade union collectivism. Yet they were attracted by Wells's Samurai theory – the fruit, as he explained later, of a 'transitory and never entirely harmonious marriage of minds' with the Webbs.[8] Despite its high entertainment value it disintegrated after a couple of years.

A Biology Group, with membership restricted to those who had some knowledge of the subject, chiefly doctors, lasted about twice as long. It studied and compared Darwin's and Mendel's theories of natural selection and heredity, attempted to observe the effect of environment on human development in London and to decide whether socialism could be justified from a biological point of view. A course of study of standard biology textbooks literally bored the Group to death in 1911. A proposal to found a Medical Group, made by one of its members, resulted in the foundation of the Socialist Medical League, independent of the Fabian Society.[9] Webb suggested a Fabian Law Group in June 1909, to attract lawyers to socialism, but the independent Haldane Society was not formed until 1930.[10]

The interests of the Lyceum and the Education Groups overlapped. The former was set up by Fabian women who found the newly created Lyceum Club for Women a convenient meeting place in which to discuss the training of children and what could be done to improve elementary education. When the Club prohibited political meetings on the premises, the group transferred to the Fabian Women's Group but continued to meet once a month for tea at the Club.[11] The Education Group investigated children's health, welfare and schooling, ran conferences and summer schools, and regularly published précis of its lectures in *Fabian News*. Its activities virtually ceased at the outbreak of war in 1914, as its members, being teachers, university lecturers or local government education committeemen, were co-opted on to local distress committees and similar bodies. But in January 1917 some members reconvened the group to plan post-war campaigns for raising the school-leaving age to 16 and extending compulsory, part-time education to all young people up to the age of 18. The 1918 Education Bill was greeted by the group as a useful first step.[12]

A small, earnest group was set up to resume the work of the 1904 Local Government Committee which had produced the four tracts in the New Heptarchy Series to advocate public control of electricity and transport, the revival of agriculture, provincial or regional organization and the abolition of the Poor Law Guardians.[13] It discussed the problems of expanding urban areas, liquor licensing, local taxation, housing and town planning. Throughout 1909 it scrutinized the Poor Law Reports in order to criticize rationally the Royal Commission on the Reform of the Poor Law's legislative proposals. Later Mabel Atkinson, a member of the group and author of a book on Scottish Local Government, pioneered a fascinating study of local organization of labour according to occupations, the varying terms governing apprenticeships and the range of limitations imposed on certain professions. Membership more than doubled while this was under way, but no more was heard of the Local Government Group after 1911.[14]

Meanwhile, the Nursery built up its confidence and powers of self-expression. To that end Frederick Osborne began producing 'The Nursling' in 1910, a single copy magazine containing handwritten or badly typed articles and verses, in green board covers literally nailed together.[15] Each person to whom it was circulated could keep it for forty-eight hours. At first its stilted little articles on socialist themes were mere reproductions of what the writers had read or heard at lectures, but soon discussion evolved, the writers' views were challenged, and their style relaxed. Verses by St John Ervine, then a writer of unperformed plays, and R.C.K. Ensor, later the eminent historian, filled the odd page. Parodies of nursery rhymes became an instrument of satire, leading Fabian personalities were lampooned and in-jokes abounded. A review of Tract No. 159, *The Necessary Basis of Socialism*, accused Webb of knowing little about democracy although he persistently crammed it down Fabian throats. *The*

New Machiavelli by Wells had done much to colour the Nursery view of the Webbs. Shaw, however, was constantly quoted; he made them laugh, squirm and search their consciences, consequently they held him in affection. The young people were bored and unconvinced by Beatrice Webb's *Minority Report on the Poor Law* and her National Committee for the Prevention of Destitution's mode of operating. The Webbs might be crowd-catchers in Oxford and Cambridge but the Nursery viewed Sidney's statistics and Beatrice's committees with scepticism and disrespect. Eager to recall the socialist movement to its early principles, to abolish poverty completely rather than counter the evils of destitution, they accused their elders of 'wanting to run the poor for the fun of it'.

'The Nursling' died of financial starvation, but the Nursery itself flourished and within five years its committee was boasting that its lecture list was better than that of the main Society. Meetings had become so popular, drawing audiences of fifty to a hundred every other week, that, when the Society invited collaboration with the ILP, arrangements were made to run a joint ILP–Nursery lecture course with a historical theme and the speakers all drawn from the Nursery. Lecturing on the Earl of Shaftesbury, Sidney Herbert insisted that socialists paid too much attention to economics and too little to history. Clement Attlee lectured on Cabinet Government under Walpole, while H.H. Schloesser, who was to become the first Labour government's solicitor-general, spoke on Chatham and the freeing of public opinion. The Nursery's most ardent speaker, Jack Gibson, dealt with Cobden and the triumph of individualism. Old Gang collectivism received very short shrift.[16]

Wells ceased to thrash about in the Fabian pool in September 1908. Though he still believed that the Basis needed to be changed, that Fabians should sponsor a campaign for every child to be supported by the state independently of its parents and that the Society should completely redirect its political aims, he was not prepared to bring all this about. He was discouraged by the rate of recruitment. While the Labour Party had gained half a million members in two years, Fabian membership was less than 3000; his target had been 7000.[17] After being scolded by the Executive for trying to persuade electors to vote for a Liberal in the North Manchester by-election, against Dan Irving the Labour candidate, Wells began opposing Fabian allegiance to the Party and its Parliamentary Fund.[18] S.G. Hobson and F.W. Galton, who later became General Secretary, supported him on the Executive, but, throughout 1908, every proposal he made was defeated in committee and so he lost heart and withdrew.[19] At first he became a non-voting subscriber, keeping in touch with the Nursery and the Arts and Philosophy Group which, he said, evinced a new concept of socialism and a fresh attitude towards life. After Jane Wells resigned from the Executive in 1910 the excuse of Wells's subscription being five months overdue was used to purge him from the Society and Shaw and Wells ceased squabbling.[20]

The ripples left by Wells had still not subsided when the Society completed its first quarter century and the compulsion for reform stirred again. In 1909 a Constitution Amendments Committee was set up, on which the Nursery was well represented and the recently formed local societies had a voice.[21] It aimed principally at bringing the new societies, which had sprung up as a direct Fabian response to the formation of the Labour Party in 1906, closer to each other and to the local structure of the party. It gave the local societies a larger voice in the affairs of the Society through an annual conference and closer contact with the central office, in return for a capitation fee for administration costs. Associates of local societies, as opposed to full members, were still not allowed a vote in any policy decision affecting the national body.[22] Unfortunately, these local societies were not long lasting. Sanders, the Organizing Secretary, and his temporary assistants tried to nurture them with frequent, intensive lecture courses. A special effort was made in autumn 1913 to boost membership in the provinces, but in vain. Most local societies needed to be tied to political stakes and by the outbreak of war had again amalgamated with the local ILP branches.

Hobson and Galton soon followed Wells, both objecting to the Executive's change in policy over Parliamentary elections since the formation of the Labour Party.[23] Galton, a Liberal, resigned when the Society acceded to the Party's request to help it sponsor Frank Smith, a Fabian member of the LCC, as a Labour candidate in the Taunton by-election, traditionally a safe Conservative seat. Shaw, Pease and Sanders, as Fabians, helped Smith draft his election address and several prominent members canvassed in the constituency, with Keir Hardie, Ramsay MacDonald and Arthur Henderson from the Labour Party Executive, and two Fabian Liberal MPs, Josiah Wedgwood and Chiozza Money. After a hurried campaign, Smith gained a third of the vote in an area where Labour had never stood before. The Executive and candidate were both well pleased, the latter exulting that he had 'been privileged to carry the Fabian banner in its first fight'.[24] The Taunton Labour Representation Committee asked the Fabians to repeat their sponsorship of Smith at the general election in January 1910 but the Executive refused because it knew the seat could not be won and a second defeat would do more harm than good to the socialist cause there.[25] After an initial refusal to renew support for Harry Snell in Huddersfield the Fabians gave way. Stephen Sanders, who had been supported by the Parliamentary Fund in Southampton in January, but had abandoned it as a forlorn hope, went to help Snell in Huddersfield later that year. The Parliamentary Fund also subsidized Crooks in Woolwich when this second election in less than a year found the local Labour association out of funds.

The Fabian reputation for being slippery with regard to elections was made worse by the Haggerston incident, when H.G. Chancellor, a far from active Fabian, stood as a Liberal against an SDF candidate. Blamed for not declaring him in the *Fabian News* pre-election list of candidates, the compilers had been unaware that he was still a Fabian and surprised when he traded on it. Afterwards it was duly claimed as a Fabian/Liberal victory with the Executive justifying its position by stating that 'objection in principle cannot be taken to a member of the Society standing in opposition to another Socialist candidate when there is a genuine division in policy or principle between them'.[26] This left the Labour Party and many Fabians very unhappy.

When the demand for a clear-cut policy had been made in 1909 Shaw was asked to produce a manifesto urging members to vote for a Liberal where no Labour candidate was nominated.[27] Since the vital issue of the 1910 elections proved to be the frequent reversal by the House of Lords of legislation passed in the Commons, a modification was introduced into Shaw's 'Special advice to members on the political crisis' advising Fabians to vote for the candidate opposing the House of Lords. Nevertheless members insisted in April 1910 that the consent of the whole Society should be obtained for any new election manifesto and that an investigation must take place into 'the advisability of limiting by rule the liberty of members to support, or stand as candidates of, political parties or organizations other than Labour or Socialist'.[28]

R.C.K. Ensor, after reviewing the complete history of Fabian toleration of political variations, maintained that the Society could not impose a rule forbidding Fabians from standing against socialist candidates, though it had become 'improper' to oppose well-known ones.[29] Since members were free to refuse subscriptions to the Parliamentary Fund they could, with clear consciences, remain active members of the Society even though objecting to it running Labour candidates. Because the study and development of socialist ideas were as important as winning parliamentary seats, and only the Fabians appeared to be performing this service, tolerance towards all strands of socialist thought, tempered with common sense, was an essential Fabian requirement. The members were content to accept Ensor's ruling for the immediate future because he allowed that current practice could not be taken as the final word.

His report was presented just before the election in December 1910, for which the Executive advised support for the Liberal government where there was a straight fight with the Conservatives, but for Labour or socialist candidates in the minority of constituencies where they were standing. Thus, with each election Fabian policy and advice to members on allegiance shifted its position a little. A mere footnote to this election manifesto dealt with the other election issues: state payment of MP's salaries and election expenses, enfranchisement of women, the controversial Osborne judgement and the proposals in Beatrice Webb's Minority Report for the Abolition of Destitution. All this tedious finessing left in the air vibrations audible still in 1981.

In 1911 some of the Old Gang thought it was time they retired and allowed younger members to take over control of the Society. Webb feared that if they stood down *en bloc* members would suspect some ulterior motive or quarrel. He therefore proposed that long-serving Executive members should, of right, become consultants without voting powers for a further three-year stint.[30] Shaw agreed that the Old Gang had become a sort of House of Lords (a pejorative term just then) and were keeping younger men out of Fabian counsels. In a senatorial role (a term Webb deplored), with no vote on matters of policy, they might still give the benefit of their experience by advice and persuasion. This senate should be so framed as to provide a model for the solution of the second chamber problem, then much on their minds in relation to the larger political scene. He observed that, 'Men desire the counsel and conversation (if not at too great length) of the wise and clever; but they have a mortal dread of being in their power'.[31] The weakness of the scheme, he admitted, was that it did not prevent the Old Gang from 'sitting on the heads of the younger members with the dead weight of their presences as Panjandrums. But at all events, the younger ones will be there to be sat upon, whereas now they have not even that melancholy privilege'.[32]

Bland certainly wanted to retire; Webb had a fundamental need to hover as an *éminence grise*. Shaw was sincere in his wish to hand over formal responsibilities although he could not forebear lashing, goading, shaming or teasing Fabians into action. They were all disappointed that the Executive had not attracted more new blood since 1906.

When a combination of Shaw's and Webb's schemes was presented formally to members, the Nursery objected that it was perniciously undemocratic.[33] They did not want the Old Gang officially breathing down their necks when they eventually took control of the Executive. Their elders were deeply offended at their reaction. For various reasons Bland, Ensor, Headlam, Shaw and Standring declined to stand for the next Executive election and were replaced by five former Nursery representatives. They came at the bottom of the poll but the Nursery hailed their return as a great victory and, led by Henry Schloesser, embarked on realignment of the Society with the Labour Party.[34] But at the annual conference of local society delegates, a Nursery resolution to restrict Fabian membership to supporters of the Labour Party was defeated by 41 votes to 6, mainly because members of the SDF would thereby be excluded. But delegates passed with acclaim a motion to permit alteration of the rules and by-laws only by a conference of all the Fabian societies.[35] From this time the Conference had to be summoned every year in June to discuss the annual report and any resolutions duly notified in advance. It had the right to pass resolutions on general policy, though the Executive reserved the right to hold a postal referendum on the decision. With a two-third majority it could amend the rules, provided three months' notice was given; with a three-quarter majority it could even change the Basis. No longer could London members expect to rule the roost.

The Parliamentary Labour Party how numbered forty-two, enough for its vote to matter, and second generation Fabians were determined to influence it. Schloesser, Clifford Allen, Dr Marion Phillips, St John Ervine and one or two others dubbed themselves a Reform Committee dedicated to end permeation of the Liberal Party and ensure that Fabians taking part in politics supported the Labour Party exclusively.[36] They believed Fabians were in danger of becoming 'superior Socialists', that the trade unions were weakening the Parliamentary Labour Party, and that Fabians should become reconciled to the expediencies of politics. By recruiting from the middle classes, the Labour Party might be able to discard its image as the expression of workers' discontent, and use its voting power to put Labour candidates into Parliament instead of just to keep Conservatives out. Above all the Reform Committee wanted integration with the Labour Party so that it could convert unionists to socialism. It demanded joint committees with the ILP wherever feasible and offered to send speakers to local branches to explain the committee's policy. Its manifesto, produced in November 1911, stringently asserted that: 'The old idea that a Fabian must be one who stood for the policy of "getting something done *somehow*" through any party in power must give way to the policy of "getting something done *properly*" through the Labour Party.'

The committee sent out its manifesto bearing the office address. Local societies and individuals thought it was an official Fabian policy statement about which they had not been consulted. Excerpts were published in the press under the same misapprehension, which led to a short, sharp battle between the Executive and the Reform Committee, waged partly in the pages of the *Labour Leader*.

The Nursery now raised its age-limit to 30 because the cream of the group, those in the Reform Committee, would otherwise soon have to transfer to the, in their view, verbose and inactive senior Society. A précis of the Reform Manifesto was linked in the *Labour Leader* with the Cambridge Labour Party's motion, about to be submitted by Clifford Allen, the Reform Committee's secretary, to the Labour Party Conference in Birmingham. The motion urged that: 'any socialist organization affiliated to the Labour Party should make every effort to secure that its members support that party and no other'.[37]

The Nursery itself split, the more moderate deserting the reformers, and the militants accusing the Old Gang of being 'amiable idiots and wire-pullers' plotting to destroy the group.[38] The Executive was naturally irritated by this charge and by being forced to defend its actions in the Labour papers. Schloesser had forced the issue by publishing the Reform Manifesto instead of presenting it as a report to the Executive.[39] The chairman and both secretaries of the Fabian/ILP Joint Committee also protested because, though one of its members, he had not seen fit to tell them about his committee's existence, much less what his manifesto said.[40] The *Labour Leader* was rebuked by Pease for printing the manifesto and by many of its working-class readers who protested that the Reform Committee consisted of 'superior Socialists'. In the end Clifford Allen discreetly made a formal apology to the ILP for not telling its Joint Committee members about the background to the manifesto.[41] Alban Gordon of Manchester University, who had just completed a long series of articles in the *Labour Leader* on socialism and the middle classes, restated in its pages the case for permeation:

> If the Fabian Society were to shut off wilfully all those channels by which it makes its influence felt at Westminster, it would be sacrificing a far greater advantage to Labour than would be gained by its merging its present identity in the ranks of the Labour Party or ILP.[42]

St John Ervine replied that the Reform Committee merely wanted the Fabian Society, having allied itself with the Labour Party, to be loyal to it.[43] A specially appointed Fabian committee, on which Schloesser but none of the Old Gang sat, devoted three months to resolving the dispute and eventually disowned both the Reform Committee and its manifesto.[44] Clifford Allen, recently appointed secretary to Labour Newspapers Limited, a company formed to produce the *Daily Citizen*, was in a quandary. The company's board, including MacDonald, fearing it might be held responsible for any statements concerning the relations between the various organizations within the Labour movement on which Allen's name appeared, asked him to resign from his secretaryship of the Reform Committee without insisting on complete severance from it.[45] After agreeing, Allen had second thoughts when the Fabian Society claimed that Ramsay MacDonald, by making this request, had declared himself opposed to the action of the Reform Committee.[46] Schloesser published Keir Hardie's reply approving the manifesto's main contention on the grounds that if Fabians were allowed to support other than Labour candidates, all organizations affiliated to the party could claim the same right and chaos would ensue.[47] He demanded the right to place before the Executive MacDonald's statement that he had never authorized it to say that he opposed the Reform Committee's policy.[48] At this point, with Pease still belligerent, Shaw intervened and delivered his long promised lecture on the Reform Committee's proposals to the Nursery.[49]

Attempting reconciliation in his customary unplacatory manner he told them flatly that the Labour Party as well as the Fabians were annoyed by the manifesto's proposals. After sketching the history of the Society he proceeded to debunk their illusion that socialism could be established by enlisting the whole of society and that all reforms must come through the Labour Party. The Society's function was, he said, to recommend socialist solutions to problems, secure direct representation of the workers by a Labour Party and establish in Parliament a socialist party completely independent of Liberal, Unionist and even the Labour Parties, because it had become increasingly obvious that the Labour Party would not be a socialist party. Fabians should, therefore, get into Parliament under whatever colours they could and then form a socialist party.

Although Schloesser was ostentatiously given a hearing, being allowed to ask a members' meeting to vote on the exclusion of Liberal and Conservative MPs from the Fabian Executive, he was effectively silenced by an overwhelming vote in favour of the Executive's case for continued tolerance. It argued that though the Society had never given a single penny to any other party and had supported the constitutional Labour movement ever since 1890, it should still reserve the right to elect its governing body from the whole Fabian membership, whether Labour Party members or not. Members were obviously content to persist in this traditional, ambiguous line which disregarded the wishes of the Labour Party and naturally excited its suspicion.

The Nursery remaining obstreperous, the Organizing and Propaganda Committee elected to investigate its administration. Considerable laxity over admission to membership came to light, with some who were over age being recruited, some under the limit being refused admission and associates being allowed to vote like full members. This could no longer continue because the Nursery's direct representation on the Executive gave it a voice in national Fabian policy. Surprisingly, after receiving a sharp admonition to regulate its affairs, the Nursery revised its rules and decided to cool the fervour for political action, meet less often and revert to an educational role.

The officers of the Reform Committee again stood for election to the main Executive. St John Ervine lost his seat and the others received a noticeably smaller vote in April 1912. Marion Phillips and Schloesser then stood for election to the LCC and retired from the Fabian Executive in 1914, believing that their work for reform had accomplished as much as it ever would. Clifford Allen created the Inter-University Socialist Federation at the April meeting in Manchester of the university Fabian societies. On its executive committee it offered to have a representative of the Fabian Executive to act in an advisory capacity; in return the Society agreed to make occasional grants of £10, to help with printing and secretarial needs in emergencies and to give advice on request.[50] Beatrice Webb invited one member of the Federation to attend the summer school as her guest.

H.D. Harben was the Fabian liaison officer with the Federation; he devoted much time, energy and tolerance to forging sound relations between the two after a rather stormy beginning.[51] In June 1912 he called for a twelve-month truce in the wrangle over admission of Liberals to membership, to be followed by a full-scale debate upon the subject when the 'pin-pricking and bitterness' had subsided. A Liberal himself, he believed that only questions of method divided Liberal socialists from Labour. Most Fabians were then tired of the introspection and wrangling. A continuous mild rumbling about the need for change was heard during the next two or three years, but nothing to compare with the thunder throughout 1906 and 1911.

Edward Pease sometimes appeared curmudgeonly and antagonized those wishing to introduce new ideas, but there can be no doubt of his devotion to the Society. When its very shaky financial position was revealed at the end of 1913 he resigned the secretaryship, saying that he had received a substantial legacy and could best serve the interests of the Society by making way for a younger man.[52] Pease assumed that Sanders would step into his shoes and the post of organizing secretary be abolished. Sanders had too great a regard for Pease's feelings to supplant him completely. He therefore suggested acting as General Secretary provided Pease remained honorary secretary to advise him. This arrangement worked extremely well; it even allowed Sanders to volunteer for active service during the war while the Society supplemented his officer's pay and Pease resumed his former duties, unpaid except for expenses. Thus, indirectly subsidized by Pease's inheritance, unearned income, the Fabian Society was able to weather a very hazardous financial period up to 1919.

The dispute between the Fabian founders and the young socialists at the beginning of the century may seem dead history now, yet the stance adopted by each side is still relevant to the recent traumatic decision to refuse full participation in the Society to members of the Social Democratic Party. The attitudes, motives and reasons that were being worked out then still have force today.

10

THE WOMAN QUESTION

Ramsay MacDonald blamed the conservatism of the Old Gang for failure to come to grips with the problem of women's rights.[1] In the mid-1890s the Society attempted to produce a tract stating the claims of all women to share the civil and political rights then enjoyed by men but abandoned the project in despair.[2] Beatrice Webb and Shaw salvaged something by writing *Women and the Factory Acts* and *Women as Councillors*.[3] Fabians repeatedly agreed that equal citizenship would be a good idea, then hastily let the matter drop. During the Wells controversy Maud Pember Reeves, with the antipodean forthrightness natural to the wife of the New Zealand government's former representative in London, virtually blackmailed the Executive into including equal citizenship for women in the aims of the Basis, hoping that male members would then feel compelled to press for women's suffrage. Large numbers of women now joined the Society, but nothing really changed. Admittedly Sidney Olivier once persuaded a members' meeting in November 1906 to congratulate the Women's Political and Social Union, in particular those in gaol, on its success in drawing attention to women's citizenship claims.[4] Though many Fabian women were members of other organizations in the suffrage movement, the Society as a whole continued to ignore it.

When, in March 1908, the women's suffrage movement was encountering bitter opposition, Mrs Reeves made up her mind that the Fabians would have to do a lot more. She persuaded a few friends to branch out and create the Fabian Women's Group to work on those problems they had hoped the Society itself would tackle.[5] Though undeniably a part of the general movement, from its foundation the Group had wider aims and so became very different from other organizations crying 'Votes for Women!' which believed once the vote was gained all would be well. It knew that women who had always been politically powerless had to be equipped to exercise the rights they were demanding. Middle-class girls, such as Mrs Pember Reeves's own daughters, saw themselves as the 'new women' of modern novels and plays.[6] With the improvement in female education a greater number were qualifying as teachers or doctors and were obtaining degrees or the equivalent in the arts and sciences. A handful at the LSE were doing research and even lecturing on economic and historical subjects. But most young women, even the educated, were destined to be absorbed into the traditional environment of the home, without independently exploiting their newly acquired skills. They had to be inspired to apply them in their lives and to seize opportunities to improve the social life of the country, particularly the lot of the working-class woman. Her life was hard in the extreme because no one had ever considered her needs. Aunts and mothers of the 'new women' would also receive the right to vote. Many would need guidance in exercising that right if any change were to be wrought in the political life of the country, if their votes were to mean any more than automatic endorsement of their male relatives' choice.

The aims of the new Group were to compel the Society to make equal citizenship a major part of its propaganda, to study women's economic position and to discover how their obtaining financial independence would fit into socialist theory. Economic dependence being the most recognizable symbol of women's general social subjugation, they chose 'Equal opportunities for men and women' as their motto. To equip themselves to play a part in public affairs the Group schooled itself in debate, studied how to present evidence to official bodies, and set about obtaining a proper proportion of women on the Fabian Executive Committee. As soon as the Group's own executive committee was selected it appealed to its 150 members to name suitable candidates from their own number for local authority elections. This committee comprised Maud Pember Reeves, Charlotte Shaw the chairman and Charlotte Wilson the secretary, and five others.

Charlotte Shaw, who had been on the Fabian executive since 1898, and was contemptuous of its voluble inaction, wanted to see other Fabian women acting as reasoning and energetic Fabian members. Mrs Reeves joined her on the Exective in March 1907, having been a Fabian for only one year, during which she had been appointed to the Select Committee for the revision of the rules and, being a revolutionary in the Wells pattern, was eager for change throughout the Society. Charlotte Wilson was also re-elected to the Fabian Executive, after some years greater devotion to anarchism, as was Millicent Murby, treasurer of the Fabian Women's Group, a civil servant who in 1906 had presented evidence on behalf of first-class women clerks to the government's Select Committee on Wages and Conditions of Employment in the Civil Service. The other new female Executive member, Beatrice Hutchins, after having been taught by Beatrice Webb at the LSE had become a lecturer there and a writer on the Factory Acts. Despite their strong personalities, these four women found they made little impression on the governing body of the Fabian Society. (Shaw had predicted as much in a letter to Wells.) They now decided not to wait for the main Society to act but to carry out the required educational, investigative and propaganda work on women's social and political rights without the help of the men.

At first the Group was neither proficient nor impressive. In Millicent Murby's first lecture to the whole Society on 'The woman question' statistics were muddled, illustrations trite and the argument, based on ill-founded though common assumptions, was inconclusive. The first exclusively Group lecture, on 'The disabilities of women' by Edith Bland, took the line that women were: 'predominantly creatures of sex, whose paramount need is a mate and children', and that to satisfy this natural urge the state should endow maternity or recognize some form of polygamy, and women should be prepared to accept short-term mating and motherhood in preference to life-long marriage and family life.[7] This entailed training every woman to be self-supporting. Those of her audience familiar with the Bland household easily recognized this lecture as a rationalization of her own situation. Nevertheless, their hackles rose when she of all people argued first that the world would lose little if all the output of women were obliterated, secondly that great women were either barren or unmotherly, that cultivation of the intellect led to sterility, and finally that there was no reason why all professions should not be thrown open to women.

The Group formed a Board of Studies which, in its first formal course of lectures, investigated women's presumed physiological and mental disabilities, destroying a number of old wives' tales in the process. Charlotte Wilson drew up the scheme of study for discovering how women could make themselves economically independent and defining their consequent responsibilities and duties. Young clerks and teachers were exhorted, on joining, to undertake special enquiries and their skills in shorthand were employed in recording the Group's meetings. Their reports, with abstracts of the lectures, were edited by Millicent Murby and Charlotte Shaw, printed at the latter's expense and distributed to members as a permanent record of each lecture course.

In the first three years woman doctors, teachers and sanitary inspectors attempted to determine which mental and physical weaknesses attributed to women were natural and inevitable, which the consequence of social conditions and which merely imaginary. A conference was summoned on Bastille Day, 1910, to discuss the Group's findings with the Associations of Headmistresses and of Women Sanitary Inspectors, the Salvation Army, the Women's Labour League and other marginally interested groups. No great revelations were made, but the Group was encouraged to proceed with the second part of its programme, examining the role of women as producers as well as consumers of the country's wealth, from which emerged the Group's first book, a collection of essays on *Women in Seven Professions*.[8] The Group assumed that the secret resentment of the 'non-working' woman was the real motive force behind the women's movement. This implied that paid employment could liberate the woman without small children from domestic drudgery, provided that she paid another woman to do her housework for her, but that mothers deserved economic aid from the state because they were performing a service for it by producing children.[9] Nevertheless, the Group was not blind to the difference between the dependence of the middle-class woman and that of the working-class wife. In Lambeth Dr Ethel Bentham and Maud Pember Reeves carried out an experiment of supplementing the diet of thirty-two poor but respectable pregnant women, to find out if the health of the child benefited. They studied the families' weekly budgets to discover how parents and up to eight children managed to live on the men's low wage. A tract, *Family Life on a Pound a Week*, and a very popular book, *Round About a Pound a Week*, by Maud Pember Reeves, gave their findings.[10] They thus demonstrated that not only paupers but even among the respectable poor, women deprived of independence suffered moral subjection.

Another, Citizenship, committee concentrated on making sure that women qualified to vote in local elections were registered and that London's 100,000 women electors and prospective candidates were fully informed on their new rights and powers. Membership of the Group was not permitted to conflict with members' accepted role in the family. When able, members distributed the Women's Local Government Society's pamphlets on voting qualifications, helped to set up branches of that Society and the Women's Labour League in their neighbourhoods, and persuaded Fabians to lecture on local government to drawing-room gatherings. In October 1908 one active woman from each London electoral district was co-opted on to the Citizenship Committee to exchange local knowledge, personal experiences and to co-ordinate action during elections.[11] Many volunteers were encouraged to infiltrate, as secretaries, the Borough Distress Committees which were then investigating the local education authorities' deficiencies in feeding schoolchildren.

Mabel Atkinson, Mrs Miall-Smith and Maud Pember Reeves, having been assured by a group of Fabian barristers that any woman whose name appeared on the electoral roll was eligible to stand as a candidate in the London County Council election, determined to contest seats in 1910. With the support of the Women's Labour League, Dr Ethel Bentham had already been adopted as a candidate in North Kensington. At her first public meeting Graham Wallas took the chair and Shaw spoke. But Mabel Atkinson, who had hoped to stand on the Progressive ticket at Bow, withdrew on finding that canvassing would consume more time than she could spare. Mrs Reeves could not find an amenable constituency while Mrs Miall-Smith could find no suitable, Progressive partner for the dual seat of North Hackney and so withdrew. All available funds, about £120, and all the Citizenship Committee's energies were therefore devoted to getting Dr Bentham elected. Unhappily she came bottom of the poll, though with a gratifying 2724 votes. The Group persuaded her to keep a foot in the door by getting herself appointed a school manager there. Mrs Miall-Smith procured election to the Board of Guardians of the Poor in North Islington for the same reason.

As confidence increased with experience, the Citizenship Committee selected the demand for a pure milk supply for mothers and babies as the Group candidates' platform in the succeeding borough and urban district council elections. Study of family diets in Lambeth had demonstrated how necessary this was, the demand was immediately comprehensible and designed to attract women's votes and, indeed, brought success to Ethel Bentham and Marion Phillips in 1912. With that achievement behind it the Citizenship section decided to leave guidance and support of women voters and candidates to the main Fabian Society, the ILP and the Women's Labour League, to concentrate on the national elections and merge with the suffrage section of the Group. The marked change in attitude towards women in local government owed much to the work of the Fabian Women's Group.

Women's suffrage was, naturally, a burning question. As opinion among the Fabian women ranged from militancy to moderation, the Group was very cautious about making policy statements or sponsoring the action of any other body. Yet it wanted to participate visibly in the campaign for votes for women. In December 1908 their financial accounts showed that their largest expense was a banner designed by William Morris's daughter, May, and stitched by members.[12] It was first carried in a suffrage demonstration on 13 June, at which, the Group claimed, it had made the Fabian Society the very first socialist body to support the suffrage agitation.

Eleven Group members were imprisoned in 1908 and the following year Miss Wallace-Dunlop was reported in *Fabian News* as having fasted for ninety-one hours in prison, in protest at being refused recognition as a political prisoner.[13] The new assistant secretary, Ellen Smith, suffered frequent bouts of illness as a consequence of her imprisonment. Others, led by Mabel Atkinson, refused to pay their taxes on the 'no taxation without representation' plea and had distraints placed on their goods for pitifully small sums. Apart from sending protests against treatment of the prisoners to the Home Secretary and the press in November 1909, the Group was active at an individual, rather then collective level.

The Fabian Executive asked it for a pamphlet on the conditions of woman in prisons. Tract No. 163 was compiled in 1913 by Helen Blagg and Charlotte Wilson from a fine collection of letters from experienced members. It was far from being an emotional work. Much serious research into prison reports and histories of criminology and penal theory was done by the assisting committee. Whereas prisoners granted political status, in the first division, were allowed to supplement the regulation food with the help of their friends, ordinary prisoners received a daily ration of plain suet pudding and gruel – a great hardship for middle-class Fabians. Congenital mental deficiency, aggravated by economic hardship, appeared to the writers to be the chief cause of crime among women, though they also recognized that intellectual deprivation could subvert the intelligent. Recent reforms, chiefly the Borstal system, won their acclaim. They recommended better training for prison officers, but what they really longed for was a prison version of Florence Nightingale to prove that the work of a wardress was as important, and could be as uplifting, as that of a nurse. They were the first to make a plea for appointment of women on the medical staff of all prisons housing women, as governors in women's prisons, in the police force and on the magistrates' bench, arguing that women were supremely anxious to participate officially in the judicial procedure and administration of the penal system. This tract was possibly the most valuable result of the Group's suffrage interest before the First World War.

The Fabian banner was carried in five demonstrations in London in 1910, the first being the great Women's Social and Political Union rally at the Albert Hall on 28 May. Marching from the Embankment, the Group was present in force and zealously sold Fabian literature to the other suffragists. At the end of the demonstration on 9 July Mrs Shaw held an emergency executive meeting in Trafalgar Square to consider the WSPU's invitation to join the Hyde Park Rally a fortnight later and 'woman' a platform there; she persuaded the others to rope in some Fabian men to speak to them. Those who participated spoke of this particular rally with nostalgia, recalling the white dresses and green and purple sashes of stewards and speakers, the attentiveness of the crowd, and the friendly collaboration of the police who removed railings from part of the park to allow free movement to the demonstrators.

In 1911 the Fabians were outraged by a gratuitous snub by the WSPU to a socialist group.[14] The Kensington ILP branch, loyal supporters of Ethel Bentham, after being specifically invited to join in a march, was ordered by stewards to remove its banner. Written protests by the Fabians to Christabel Pankhurst were persistently ignored and the group angrily refused to take part in the Union's demonstrations. Marion Phillips continued to speak at rallies as an individal but she soon resigned from the Fabian Women's Group because she found its policy insufficiently militant.[15]

Eight members of the Group were by that time on the main Fabian Executive. It could therefore advocate constitutional action and bring the whole weight of the Society to its aid. Mabel Atkinson inspired the creation of a Suffrage Section to persuade Labour MPs to support the Conciliation Bill as the only currently available means of securing political rights for women, and to work in future for full adult suffrage for both sexes. The Suffrage Section drafted a manifesto of which 7000 copies were distributed, pointing out that, though the government had promised a Reform Bill for men, with the possibility that by a non-party vote on an amendment women might be included, the reliability of the offer was in doubt. It urged all who believed in true adult suffrage to make sure that the new Bill included both men and women on the widest possible basis. All women were exhorted to offer to back Labour in the constituencies if the PLP moved an amendment enfranchising women.

After the Suffrage Section had waged a vigorous campaign in the provinces in favour of the new Reform Bill, there was great consternation when Asquith announced the withdrawal of the Conciliation Bill and its ultimate replacement by one introducing manhood suffrage. Three of the group's executive joined the main Fabian delegation lobbying the Labour Group in the House of Commons to vote against the Third Reading of the Franchise and Registration Bill if women were not included in its provisions. Individual Members, such as Lloyd George, were pressed to make a public declaration of personal support for female suffrage.[16] Mabel Atkinson induced the Fabian membership to pass a resolution of support and enlisted H.D. Harben to use his influence with MacDonald to improve the *Daily Citizen's* editorial attitude towards suffrage.

As a moderate influence in the women's suffrage movement the Group was repeatedly invited in 1913 to send representatives to other committees. Support for Chrystal Macmillan's proposed Suffrage Information Bureau was refused, even though it was the kind of enterprise to appeal to Fabians, because it might prove too costly. The £50 received by the Fabian Women's Group as its share of the collection of jewellery at the Albert Hall rally, had been spent long ago. The Fabian Society's response to appeals did not even cover the secretary's wages, for which a separate fund was set up by about twenty of the most prosperous Group members, supplemented by Mrs Shaw whenever necessary. After Mrs Pethick-Lawrence was banished by the Pankhursts from the WSPU Mabel Atkinson and Marian Berry were instructed to attend meetings of her Women's Freedom League. Mrs Harben represented the Group at the International Suffrage Congress, while Mabel Atkinson sat on both the Parliamentary Action and Joint Suffrage Committees, where she successfully combated a resolution to condemn all those who indulged in militant action, thus demonstrating Fabian neutrality.[17]

Although the Pankhursts' manipulations and developments in the more strident suffrage bodies troubled the Fabians, Mrs Cavendish-Bentinck represented them at the WSPU meeting protesting against Government treatment of the Regent Street window-breakers in 1913. After the Society's own formal protest at the discriminatory administration of the law against conspiracy and incitement to violence, under which men might be released after two days' imprisonment, while women suffered from the cat-and-mouse system, the suffrage section faded gently away. Individuals continued to lecture sporadically on the franchise to branches of the ILP and Women's Labour League while Mabel Atkinson's energies were channelled into vice-chairmanship of the Federal Council of Women's Suffrage Societies and reporting on the international movement to the Fabians. However not until 25 January 1917 was the section officially dissolved.

Meanwhile, the Group's educational role was not forgotten. Women knew so very little about their legal and industrial rights, their economic position, their opportunities for education, or even what support could be required of institutions such as trade unions or local health authorities. Until mid-1912 Beatrice Webb kept the Group busy supplementing her work on trade unionism and industrial democracy by investigating women's place in the unions, the obstacles preventing their full contribution to the national economy and proposing remedial legislative measures. Several interesting tracts emerged from this study. Using information culled from the Webb's *Minority Report of the Poor Law Commission*, from official publications and reports of philanthropic institutions, Beatrice Hutchins showed in *The Working Life of Women* that paid employment was a vital necessity to a third of the female population who were not only tending physically but also supporting financially their homes and families.[18] Mrs Townsend, in another tract, attacked a philanthropic body for obstructing social improvement.[19] While the whole Fabian Society was simmering over Lloyd George's National Insurance Bill, the Group published two pamphlets criticizing its provisions and describing its damaging effect on women's interests.[20] Beatrice Webb helped construct these two tracts at the same time as preparing her own counter-blast, *The Prevention of Destitution*.[21]

Like all middle-class women then, Fabian women were much exercised by the servant problem. They wanted to be fully extended intellectually while reserving the right to have children. Acknowledging that the emancipated, middle-class woman would have to delegate care of house and children to employees, the more Utopian members envisaged transforming housework into an attractive professional occupation.[22] The Group therefore petitioned the LCC Education Committee to expand technical education for girls to cover all branches of domestic service. A new Domestic Relief Committee began looking for ways to set women free to choose their occupations and eliminate all class distinctions between mistress and servant.[23] It sent a questionnaire to all Fabian women to discover the average time spent on specific household tasks and to collect suggestions on how to redesign a house in order to simplify work. Replies were few and surprisingly conservative. Though many household hints on how to reduce brass-cleaning, black-leading and hearth-stoning were produced, Fabian wives were not enthusiastic about labour-saving devices such as the early washing-machine. They rejected outright schemes for co-operation between households. This response was considered very feeble and individualist by the more radical reformers on the subcommittee, who redirected their energies towards setting up trade schools and employment

agencies for domestics. Both ideas failed, partly because the year was 1915
and likely candidates for such schools were then being trained in the
polytechnic colleges for war work in munition factories, employers were
reducing their staff and the whole pattern of service was indeed changing.

Two problems concerning female employment dominated the Group's
agenda for some years. A fair wage for a man was estimated as the amount
necessary for him to support a wife and the average number of children; for
a woman doing equivalent work, that which would support her alone.
Since one eighth of the female workforce was widowed, supporting a young
family, that was patently unjust. When the Fabians realized this and that a
demand for equal pay would price women out of the labour market, their
original aim that a woman 'should receive her individual share of social
wealth to consume as she desires'[24] was scrapped as irrelevant and the far
more complex problem tackled. A watch was kept on wage rates, the
occasional Question tabled in Parliament at their behest and the Group
affiliated to the National Federation of Women Teachers, which was also
trying to do something about it. In reality, there was little they could do to
solve the problem, merely elucidate its true nature. Immediate and long-
term effects of the war on female employment posed the other question. At
first, women suffered much distress through unemployment when their
traditional occupations were restricted or abolished, but soon they were
encouraged to fill what were normally considered to be men's former jobs
in factories, on the land and in offices. The Women's Group studied the
effect of this on the labour market and wages and defined the lasting
implications in *The War: Women: and Unemployment*. They recognized
that women's position in the trade unions was in a state of flux. The
Executive in 1915 advised amalgamation between the Fabian Research
Department, guild socialists who were studying trade unions, and the
Fabian Women's Group, which would concentrate on the women's angle
comparing contributions, benefits and votings powers of men and women
in the unions, committee membership and the advantages and disadvan-
tages of mixed unions rather than separate branches.[25] That work
completed, the Group's attention turned to post-war reconstruction issues,
clarifying them to assist Beatrice Webb in her work for several government advisory committees on labour matters and demobilization.

After the armistice the Group's work reverted to familiar matters, such
as the effect of different occupations on women in childbirth and on the
health of their children. It kept an eye on the legislation involved in
creating the Ministry of Health and seized every opportunity to influence
the government and local authorities on children's education, nurture and

welfare, the vocational training of adolescents, working-class housing and protective legislation in industry.

In 1918, having served on the executive committee of the Group for ten years, Charlotte Shaw, Charlotte Wilson and Ethel Snowden resigned, aware of the need for a change of management and for a fresh approach to the unresolved problems in the very different, post-war setting.

The unique role of the Group in the fight to gain recognition of a woman's right to be treated by the state as equal to a man had been to seek the truth about her existing status, dispel many false illusions about her incapacity to fulfil a position equal – though not necessarily identical – to a man's, investigate her true economic, physical and intellectual needs and those of her family, educate her about these and give her the confidence to claim them. By publicizing all this, as well as supporting the franchise campaign with moderation, by demonstrating how women could use the constitutional means already available to achieve the status they desired, the Fabian Women's Group was able to build a firmer and far more reasonable foundation for the liberation of women than the suffrage movement could ever have achieved unaided.

11

THE FABIAN HOLIDAY

The first Fabian summer school took place in 1907. Mabel Atkinson, after attending a German summer school, wrote to Pease suggesting he hire a hall in some pleasant country town for Fabian lectures and invite members to find their own accommodation in the neighbourhood.[1] At about the same time, Frank Lawson Dodd produced a scheme for hiring a house large enough for a group of Fabians to live in during their holidays and pursue a programme of education and recreation. Pease told them to pool their ideas and they produced a joint design. Shaw immediately prophesied that management of the school would be seized by the less reputable members of the Society and disaster would ensue.[2]

The rest of the Executive were charmed by the plan and asked its instigators to look for a house and draw up a programme for the first school. Since the Society was unwilling and unable to finance the project, a group of enthusiasts formed a management committee to run it and pledged their own money in ten-year loans at 5 per cent interest. Under Lawson Dodd's chairmanship there were twelve members, including both the Shaws, Beatrice Webb and Wells.

Lawson Dodd discovered at Llanbedr, in Snowdonia, an unfurnished house called Penn-yr-Allt and handled all the domestic administration. Mabel Atkinson, a lecturer at Armstrong College, Newcastle-upon-Tyne, laid down a general educational programme which lasted for decades: lectures on Monday, Tuesday, Thursday and Friday mornings and two or three evenings, a day excursion to some place of interest on Wednesday, with other afternoons left free for walks, bathing, sports or sight-seeing. A gymnastics teacher, Mary Hankinson, was hired to give instruction in

Swedish drill and contributed a great deal more, including a country-dancing course. Lawson Dodd installed furniture and got the house ready, a piano was hired, Beatrice Hutchins lent music and the Society provided two book-boxes. Fees were fixed at 35 shillings a week with an extra half-crown for Swedish drill. The gardener, Owen, was retained as odd-job man, a cook and housekeeper were hired, undergraduates enlisted to clean and wait at table and the school was ready to open in August 1907 'for the study of social science and to afford students, whether avowed socialists or not, an opportunity for meeting and social intercourse'.[3] Its popularity was ensured because it provided young professional women with an unexceptionable and pleasant means of spending a week or two with interesting companions.[4] Attendance was so good that the first school was able to run for a month, with most people staying for a fortnight.

Shaw, appeased by his wife with a promise of puritanical management and clearly defined rules, attended this first school and helped make it memorable by getting lost during a Sunday ramble, and, after walking many miles, spending the night at Tan-y-Croes Hotel. Penn-yr-Allt had no telephone and so the rest of the school spent much of the night searching for him. When he eventually returned to base the next morning he professed himself astounded that they should have worried about him.[5] Apart from the impact on the neighbourhood of this event, the school caused quite a stir by its oddities, which even warranted reports in the press. Swedish drill classes shocked some because the women agreed to adopt the convenience of bloomers topped by a tunic in which to brave the morning dew on the lawn. Locals, who suspected that this strange exercise performed by socialists was in preparation for a revolutionary uprising, were much puzzled by that most unmilitary garb. The ladies, on the other hand, were so charmed by their new costumes they often did not change out of them until the evening, even though the main meal was served in the middle of the day as a conscious blow for social liberty. The habit of sleeping in the open air also shocked the chapel-going Welsh. As Mabel Palmer recounted:

> During the later weeks of the School there was a craze among the younger set for sleeping out of doors, and I have always wondered whether the young woman who, when it was pointed out to her that this was a dangerous practice, said to the Executive Committee: 'Oh, but I was quite safe – Mr Ashley Dukes was just on the other side of the tree!', was completely innocent or was doing a mild leg-pull of the Executive Committee.[6]

At the end Webb pronounced the school a great success and gave it his blessing.[7] Financially it had certainly proved so, producing a profit of £200 over the running costs.

Arrangements were made to hire an additional house, Carmeddyg, the following summer and, for the overflow, owners of tents were invited to erect them in the grounds and in an adjacent field. A director was nominated for each fortnight, to administer the school and report on his term of office. Directors' log-books are still to be found in the Fabian archive and provide most entertaining reading. Students as labour proved too costly and so, for succeeding schools, local help was hired to work under the direction of the housekeeper of the LSE. Mary Hankinson was invited to act as general manager under the director, assisted by an undergraduate who dealt with the day-to-day paperwork. Year after year she performed this role, much loved by the early students. Her birthday in August was always celebrated with a cake, a present and a birthday ode.

Swiftly the schools achieved a distinctive character. Each Sunday morning the director welcomed the students and read the rules governing meals and lecture times, lights out, noise after hours, times when musical instruments, including the phonograph, might be played. Consumption of alcohol on the premises was strictly forbidden. Many Fabians were enthusiastic walkers and the slopes of Snowdon were thoroughly explored. On 10 August 1910 an excursion was made to Beddgelert in a brake, but one member of the party 'not content with cycling to Beddgelert and ascending Snowdon with the others, afterwards rode on to Cader, ascended the mountain, saw the sunrise from its summit and was back in time to attend Thursday morning conference'.[8]

Fancy dress was contrived for some of the evening gatherings, such as the mock trial in 1908 when Arnold Maude was indicted and convicted of having led a simple life. Lectures were delivered whenever possible in the open air. Some prominent Fabians held propaganda meetings in the villages or on the sands. On more frivolous evenings, revues were presented in which the idiosyncrasies of residents and the contents of lectures were burlesqued, or less creative scholars might resort to performing Shaw's *Press Cuttings*.

In 1910 the lease for Penn-yr-Allt came to an end and, though the committee was able to get it extended until the following spring to accommodate a Fabian Easter school on medicine and socialism, it was clear that another house would have to be found. It was decided to abandon north Wales, which was palling, for some other hilly area. Partly because Easter schools and short Christmas gatherings had become popular, partly because of judicious subletting, the Management Committee had over £350 in hand and owned considerable assets by way of furniture. It therefore paid off the guarantors' loans and offered the school to the Executive, to benefit the Society. About 2000 people had attended the schools in four years and with an initial capital outlay of £350 it had achieved a turnover of well over £3000. A little reluctantly the Executive accepted the responsibility in order to keep the school on Fabian lines.[9]

The Webbs were now eager to draw young university men and women into their net and summer schools offered an attractive bait. In 1910 all male university Fabians had been sent a school prospectus bearing no external indication that it came from the Fabian Society.[10] Now representatives from the Oxford and Cambridge University Fabian Societies and the Nursery were invited to join local society and group delegates on a new Schools Committee.[11] The Executive merely reserved the right to appoint directors and approve the general scheme of lectures. Advertisements for a new house brought a disappointing response and so the new committee chose Hotel Monte Moro at Saas Grund in the Swiss Alps for the first overseas school in 1911.[12] The entire hotel was booked for six weeks and the proprietor and his wife did all they could to make the Fabians welcome. After the advertisement appeared in *Fabian News* eighty bookings were accepted. Badges procured for wear at all times, maps and handbook on alpine flowers were added to the regulation book-boxes with three dozen *Songs for Socialists*, a new song-book compiled by a small Fabian committee.[13] It included the 'Marseillaise', the 'Red Flag' and the 'Internationale', together with non-political favourites. The book claimed to be: 'a representative collection of songs that have been sung during the past hundred years or more by revolutionists of many schools both in Europe and America', and thus included some of William Morris's best-known chants for workers, also William Blake's 'Holy Thursday' and 'To mercy, pity, peace and love' (though not 'Jerusalem' which might have been welcomed by the Christian socialists), Shelley's poems addressed to Men of England, with Swinburne's 'Star from far to star speaks' and 'We mix from many lands'. Some contemporary members placed their poems at the committee's disposal: Dr Ethel Smyth, Edward Carpenter, Edith Bland and R.C.K. Ensor.

An overseas school every year was then too ambitious for the Society and too expensive for some young Fabians. A bursary scheme was introduced to pay part of the fees for one or two needy students, but considered an exception rather than a rule because charity was abhorred. Moreover, at home the Society had about £250 worth of furniture, a distinct asset in keeping down expenses. Accordingly, at the beginning of 1912 Lawson Dodd discovered Barrow House, near Keswick, which could cater for sixty guests. By Whitsun Barrow House was open for a short conference.[14]

Fabians were divided between those who wished the school to be predominantly holiday and those who favoured more education. As a compromise two weeks each summer were reserved for concentrated study of practical socialism; for the rest of the time, lectures on philosophical and artistic subjects were interspersed with day-trips, tennis tournaments, bathing and similar entertainments. Often the educational weeks were organized in collaboration with the ILP, trade union and co-operative movements. Occasional sublets helped to defray the cost of running Barrow House and the various subject groups were encouraged to hold conferences there. The Fabian Research Department hired the house in 1913 and 1914, after which the first objection was lodged against Mary Hankinson's 'early to bed, early to rise' rule. It was rumoured that G.D.H. Cole's resignation from the Society the following year was sparked off by her rigid regime, under which everyone was sent to bed promptly at 11 o'clock, the time when discussion was reaching its height. The following year an hour's extension was permitted in one particular room, on condition that the director for the week applied the guillotine strictly.

In the Lake District the School continued to hold open-air evening meetings in the town, advertised by a cohort of ladies who would spend the previous afternoon chalking notices of the meetings on the Keswick pavements (to which the police turned a blind eye).[15] Hubert Humphreys, a Birmingham engineer who as Lord Mayor of the city refused to wear the official top hat, attended the school every year until the 1960s. By standing on a wooden box and declaiming Morris's 'Come hither' he could draw a crowd of 500 to hear a summary of the latest series of autumn lectures.

At the beginning of the 1914 school, telegrams of excuse were sent by many lecturers and students, who felt they could not attend because of the threat of war. Edward Pease came to the rescue, substituting lectures with readings from his history of the Society and speaking on the control of drink as a municipal duty. No one was inclined to devise sketches for the customary Friday evening entertainment and so Hubert Humphreys volunteered to read *The Devil's Disciple*.[16] The following year, the last at Barrow House, attendance revived a little with Fabians reverting to familiar holiday habits. Reading Shaw's latest play became an established evening ritual, Shaw being persuaded to read himself when present.

More ardent spirits, who considered the population of Keswick had been permeated to saturation point with Fabian ideas, welcomed their landlord's refusal to renew the lease of Barrow House. Balliol Girls' School, at Sedburgh in Yorkshire, in 1916, proved popular and a financial success, producing a balance of £834. The main theme was drama and music; a farce of 'a tearful and screaming nature' was produced in which Dr Laetitia Fairfield played the title role of 'Little Orphant Hankie', while her sister, Rebecca West, one of the lecturers, portrayed Mrs Humphry Ward in another sketch with 'just the right touch of hauteur'.[17] Sedburgh was, however, deemed suitable for one year only, as opportunities for outings were very limited. Another school was sought, for girls rather than one for boys because female establishments tended to have a higher proportion of bathrooms. The next location was therefore Priorsfield School, at Godalming in Surrey, where weekly attendance averaged eighty-five in 1917. Roger Fry and Lowes Dickinson were enticed into spending a day at the school to hear Shaw lecture on drama and contributed vigorously to the discussion. Difficulties occurred at Priorsfield over shortages of staff and sugar, but members buckled down to making their own beds, and clearing the tables. Years later one old member wrote to the General Secretary recalling, with proud nostalgia, sharing the washing-up with the great man himself.

For 1918 and 1919 the Schools Committee had to search for yet another site because Priorsfield was closed for repairs. The choice of Penlee, a vegetarian establishment at Dartmouth, which housed only thirty but provided a great variety of scenery, good walking and places to visit, was not popular because of the food and distance from London. After two rather uncomfortable summers it was abandoned.

In view of all the annual crises, survival of the Fabian summer school after the First World War might appear a triumph of hope over experience. On the contrary, the summer school survived because it was much more than a Fabian holiday with a few more or less interesting lectures thrown in. For one month a year it fulfilled one of the first principles of the founders, that socialists of their ilk should live in a community and work out co-operatively their social, economic and political philosophy. Ordinary members mixing with leading Fabians identified more completely with the work and aims of the Society. Each year the theories and political developments uppermost in the minds of the lecturers, pamphlet writers and governing body in London were analysed over the breakfast cups, tea-time scones or evening cups of cocoa; the country member and novice were both able to put forward their own ideas in a manner uninhibited by the formality of London meetings. Some who would never open their mouths in the autumn lecture debates would, on an afternoon walk, challenge points made by Webb, Shaw or one of the other lecturers and get them to elucidate further. Young people, licensed to burlesque their elders, in the process learnt the art of making points with humour and accepting ridicule with style. The more exalted benefited from meeting the criticisms and hearing the reservations of the less well-known, bringing them down to earth. They were able to pick out the most promising young people and foster their political or literary ambitions. In short, the annual Fabian holiday provided opportunity for elucidation of socialist philosophy, development of ideas on its practical application, recognition and patronage of talent and cultivation of a friendly democracy within the Society.

12

THE FABIAN
RESEARCH DEPARTMENT

Soon after *Reflections on Violence* by Georges Sorel appeared in 1908 young socialists in the universities began discussing syndicalism, workers' control over industries achieved through trade union action, strikes and even more violent means. Fabians lecturing to the university societies learned of this interest and by summer 1912 concluded that the Society should define its policy on syndicalism.[1] The Webbs wrote a long article on its history for *The Crusade*, the organ of the National Committee for the Prevention of Destitution.[2] But the Fabian Society had not evaluated what systems, apart from socialism and capitalism, existed for the control of industry. Problems concerning land and rural development also needed urgent attention. Accordingly, two committees of inquiry were appointed, one on the control of industry directed by Beatrice Webb and the smaller, less prestigious committee on rural affairs chaired by H.D. Harben.

In three months or so Beatrice Webb collected ninety members and allocated work to every one. Availing itself of the research material collected by the Prevention of Destitution Committee, her new project appealed for funds and embarked on a year's study of alternatives to the control of industry by capitalists. Its objective was:

> to work out in intelligible detail the main lines on which the widest measure of personal freedom and initiative can be combined with the maximum of democratic control and management of Commerce and Industry, obtaining the largest national product with the most equal distribution of services and goods among the people.[3]

Until the Webbs applied their talent for subdividing and controlling the subject, socialist thought on it had been chaotic, with too much faith placed in one form of unionism after another as the sole route to industrial democracy.

The ninety volunteers were taught how to gather information from witnesses, original documents and government publications and how to record their own, personal observations of industry using uniform note-paper and a rigid classification system, devised by Beatrice. She assured her Committee that only by fragmentation of the subject and an elaborate collection and registration of facts could it arrive at a new truth.

The research was split into three separate investigations: associations of wage-earners, covering syndicalism proper; the associations of producers, dealing with self-governing workshops, profit-sharing and co-partnership; associations of consumers, including co-operative and wholesale societies and public services run by the state or municipality. Each subcommittee was armed with a bibliography of reference works which included her study of *The Co-operative Movement in Great Britain* and *Industrial Democracy Part I* written with her husband.[4] She estimated that the work of the committee would cost £1000 in office rent, wages for the secretary (Julius West at first and then William Mellor) and the research materials. Contributions to the research fund came to only half that amount but the committee managed to complete its first scheme of investigation on even less.

One problem thought worthy of attention was whether the block vote of the trade unions gave rise to sheep-like docility or reckless militancy and whether it really did represent the views of those assumed to be represented. Fabians believed they had to find the answer to this question before a revolution in the control of industry took place, since either the 'reckless militant minority' or the 'majority of incompetent voters' might produce unwelcome results in supervising nationalized mines, railways or banks. In an attempt to discover how far it was advisable to associate trade unions with management a subcommittee investigated the possibility of federating unions concerned with the mining and building industries.

A Board of Trade report on co-partnership and profit sharing was the focus of a second subcommittee's work, and involved the study of syndicalism in England, France, America and Italy. G.D.H. Cole wrote an assessment of the validity of syndicalism based on the findings. W. Stephen Sanders, who had personal links with German trade unionists, was sent to Germany to observe and report on their system. C. Mostyn Lloyd studied the French and Belgian unions' organization. As far as possible co-operative systems were surveyed in the same regions and considerable attention was paid to the Co-operative Wholesale Society in Britain. Monographs and memoranda were produced on industries run as municipal concerns; joint stock banks were studied for comparison.[5]

Before holding a summer school at Barrow House to compare the notes and views of all the investigators, the Committee on Industrial Control prefixed Fabian Research Department to its title.[6] The Webbs summoned to Keswick the chairmen, secretaries and nearly all the most active members of the Department's four working committees, with their expert advisers from the co-operative movement and industry, to discuss the research already completed on the control of industry and to map out their future programme.[7] Beatrice Webb opened the school with a talk on the spheres of science and religion in social reconstruction and an interim report on their work. Mornings were spent on discussions of each of the subcommittees' work, afternoons on committee meetings followed by walks, for which nailed boots had been recommended, swimming, boating or playing games. On the last day everyone interested was invited to help the officers draw up a schedule for completing the control of industry inquiry during the autumn and winter, after which the Webbs would combine all the materials and conclusions in a voluminous report to be published the following July. Because the initial scheme of research had worked so well they encouraged the committee to embark on an enormous, independent study of industrial insurance when the Government announced that it was introducing a new, more restrictive Insurance Bill.[8] Seven subcommittees were thought necessary merely to tackle Part I of this Act, the section dealing with sickness benefit, and the Fabian Women's Group was asked to make a special study of the implications for women.[9] Once again an appeal for £1000 was made to support this work over the next two years. Shaw enthusiastically earmarked his large annual subscription to the Fabian Society for publications by the Research Department. When the Executive insisted that year on the Department's advisory committee being formally elected instead of self-perpetuating, some resentment was caused, but Shaw was chosen as chairman, Cole as vice-chairman, G.P. Blizard as secretary and all was well again.[10]

Despite Shaw's generosity the Research Department would have had difficulty in publishing its reports if its chief begetters had not provided it with a sibling, the *New Statesman*. Launched in the winter of 1912–13 by the Statesman Publishing Company – formed by the Webbs and Shaw, with E. Whitley and H.D. Harben co-opted for their monetary support to the board of directors – it was designed to provide means for continuous expression of collectivist theory and a policy of social organization independent of party politics. It, too, was housed in the office of the Destitution Committee at an annual rent of £10.

Clifford Sharp, son-in-law of Hubert Bland and a very active member of the Nursery, was chosen as editor of the new paper.[11] His flair for typography had earlier won him the editorship of *The Crusade* and he thus became one of Beatrice Webb's protégés. The Fabian office junior, Julius Rapoport, who was the son of a Russian emigré, was swept up by Beatrice to become her committee's first secretary, from where he moved on to secretaryship of the *New Statesman*, changing his name to West in the process.[12] Foreign and imperial affairs, which then received very poor coverage in the British press, were to be examined weekly in a special article by C. Mostyn Lloyd, one of the Department's most prominent members. Hubert Bland, who died a year later, was engaged to review new novels, Emil Davies provided a City page and Dr Saleeby was appointed to provide a regular column on health and medical matters, including social problems.

Like most of the Webbs' creations, the *New Statesman* had the most exiguous financial basis. They contributed £300 to its foundation, each of the other directors guaranteed £1000; a general appeal to Fabians for subscriptions and a personal appeal by Sidney, Beatrice and GBS to friends in the universities, the theatre and the arts raised the additional £700 needed for the first issue to appear. The Board intended to produce regular literary supplements, occasional supplements on specific subjects and, three or four times a year, analyses of government legislation and proposals to be known as the Blue Book Supplements. These last were compiled most impressively by Frederick Keeling who, like so many Research Department volunteers and members of the Nursery, was soon to die in battle. A few years later, when the Webbs relaxed their grip on, but not their interest in, the paper, regular supplements on financial affairs and compendiums of publishers' lists replaced the Blue Book and subject supplements.

The first topical supplement published was a group of articles, under the general direction of Shaw, reviewing the situation in Ireland. The second was the report produced by Harben's assiduous but unspectacular Committee on Rural Reform. Originally the Fabian Executive had planned to publish it in book form in autumn 1913, but its hand was forced by the inquiry into rural conditions set up by the government in May. Pease persuaded Sharp to publish the report in August, just when public interest was first caught by the official inquiry.[13]

Catch-penny promises made in the directors' appeals that Webb and

Shaw would be regular contributors were kept though the editor decreed that articles should not be signed. However, when Shaw's idiosyncratic contributions came to be regarded as the policy of the paper, Sharp decided to identify them as Shaw's personal views by the addition of his name. They quarrelled and, after a number of tetchy communications, Shaw withdrew his literary, though not financial, support in 1916. By then the *New Statesman* was well established and other writers had built up their own following of readers: though running at a loss, it could survive without Shaw's provocative items. More entertaining features were added; reviews of the arts, poems by Rupert Brooke, Walter de la Mare and James Elroy Flecker, criticism by T.S. Eliot, and an occasional short story by Leonard Woolf. For twenty-two weeks it carried a series by the Webbs on 'What is socialism?' and until it was four years old it presented the reader with the first fruits of the Fabian Research Department. Arthur Creech Jones, a conscientious objector, asked his fiancée to have the supplements bound for him in one volume so that they might count as a single item in his allocation of personal books during his very long prison sentence and he later volunteered to work in the Research Department on his release in 1919, while he was seeking a post in the trade union movement.[14]

A rift within the Research Department became evident at the very well-attended summer school in 1914 when Cole, supported by a strong contingent from Oxford, battled with Webb over guild socialism.[15] Webb fiercely defended the principle of collectivism and a wild and woolly debate ensued. Shaw defused the conflict by insisting that, though guild socialism derived from idealization of the Middle Ages and collectivism from a hatred of the Bible in the 1880s, there was really very little difference between the two. Although the young people accepted his authority in the summer-school ambience, once again the gauntlet had been flung at the feet of the Old Gang.

Declaration of war in 1914 curbed the ambitions of the Research Department for a while, though its leaders worked as hard as ever. Plans to publish books on trade unionism by Cole, Lloyd, Sanders, Mellor and Gillespie, and a Labour and Socialist Annual had to be shelved until the market improved.[16] The Fabian Society had moved into new premises in Tothill Street and to help pay the rent the Research Department occupied two second-floor rooms, leaving more space for the *New Statesman* in its former office. Many fact collectors had to join the fighting forces and the work changed considerably as a result. At the autumn general meeting in November, when R. Page Arnot was appointed secretary, Beatrice Webb laid down as the next year's work the investigation of professional organizations. The staff had begun to prepare the 700-page Labour Year

Book, in consultation with the TUC Parliamentary Committee and the Labour Party Executive. The Research Department now had 250 subscribing members and it seemed possible to manage on an income of £500 a year and an occasional appeal to Shaw for funds when printing costs were heavy.[17]

Joseph Rowntree used to send £100 to the Destitution Committee every year. When its work came to an end, Beatrice Webb persuaded him in 1915 to transfer his gift to the Research Department. A Quaker, he stipulated that it should be used to discover the ideal terms for a peace settlement and so Leonard Woolf, already employed by Beatrice, was asked to prepare a report on this for half the grant.[18] Woolf's synopsis was ready within a month and submitted for the Webbs' detailed and thought-provoking criticism.[19] With their advice on how to handle both his material and the Society's International Agreements Committee to which the finished work would have to be presented, he set to work for three months. When the committee read his draft report it disagreed strongly with some of his independent and controversial ideas and so a second Barrow House conference was called to resolve the differences. The Bryce Committee, set up by Lowes Dickinson and also studying international organization, was invited. An elaborate scheme was drawn up for an International High Court empowered to circumvent war by arbitration on all disputes between sovereign states, backed by an International Council with policing capabilities to ensure that its decisions were observed. After long and vigorous debates, Woolf convinced the conference of his proposals' validity. The report in *Fabian News* claimed that:

> Most people left the Barrow House conference with a ray of hope that it was possible to devise some scheme which might be inserted in terms of peace whereby the likelihood of future wars would at any rate be considerably diminished.[20]

Woolf wrote two articles outlining his theories (modified to some extent by the conference) of what a League of Nations and an International Court of Justice should do to establish world peace. They were published in July 1915 as two *New Statesman* supplements: 'Suggestions for the prevention of war', and 'Articles suggested for adoption by an international conference at the termination of the war'. The ideal of international control of colonies, proposed in *Fabianism and the Empire*, was transformed to international self-discipline through voluntary submission to a supra-national arbitration tribunal. Woolf, however, was sceptical about the possibility, this century:

of the British Empire and Russia entering an international system in which the future position of Indians, Irishmen and Finns in the respective Empires is to be decided at some sort of international conference. The possibility seems to be remote, and that undoubtedly means that the possibility of any pacific settlement of differences involving nationality is also remote.

He stated that it was:

absolutely essential that the question of whether or not a particular question is to be referred to a conference must never be allowed to be the subject of negotiation, otherwise the free discussion by representatives becomes itself only a pawn in the diplomatic game, and the conference is either used as a threat with which to extort a concession or as a committee of diplomatic gentlemen called together to reduce an agreement to writing and ambiguity.[21]

In 1916 the International Socialist Bureau asked the British Section for a statement on peace terms and a conference was proposed by the British Socialist Party for the purpose of drawing up a combined report. The Fabian Society agreed to attend the conference but had no intention of signing a joint statement. Webb, who was then writing *How to Pay for the War*, a study of post-war reconstruction, was instructed by the Executive to draft an independent report and submit it to the International Socialist Bureau himself.[22] Read to the Executive Committee on 28 July 1916, the report included all Woolf's recommendations for an international council and high court, a cooling-off period for aggressive states and a commitment by all states in a league to combine against an aggressor. Webb also proposed an international fund to restore to prosperity any nation ravaged by war, with reparations to be paid to the common man as well as to wealthy industrialists. He recommended an open-door policy towards nations without colonies, so as to remove all pretext for future wars, and active discouragement of that natural reaction to war, the desire for national self-sufficiency. Unemployment being the greatest post-war danger, he exhorted all governments to undertake schemes of public works, so organized as to keep the labour demand and supply stable, thus preventing unemployment – a Fabian dogma dating from winter 1886.[23]

Woolf next investigated the way existing international organizations, such as the postal service, functioned. This enabled him to expand the *New Statesman* supplements into the book *International Government*.[24] Interest in his ideas spread rapidly and the Fabian Society found itself arranging for

American, French and Swiss (German language) editions of the book.[25] Nevertheless the Society still had more to say on the subject. Under Mabel Atkinson's chairmanship the International Agreements Committee continued to meet and J.A. Hobson presented an economist's view of the conditions essential for creating an effective international peace-keeping organization to the annual general meeting of the Research Department in November 1916. Shaw had derided the possibility of a political association of nations on Woolf's lines, proposing that the British Empire should become a world peace force. The Executive therefore invited him to select and chair a committee to report on a new imperial constitution.[26] The report was undertaken by H. Duncan Hall and eventually appeared under his name as *The British Commonwealth of Nations* in 1920.[27] Meanwhile Woolf began research on international trade, financed by profits from a very popular autumn lecture series on 'The world in chains', and the Fabians undertook to supervise his book's publication.[28] However, Woolf's energies were diverted by having to produce *Co-operation and the Future of Industry* in 1918.[29] By the time the other work was ready for publication as two complementary volumes, *Empire and Commerce in Africa: A Study in Economic Imperialism* (1919) and *Economic Imperialism* (1920), the Fabian Society had relinquished control of the Research Department.[30] Renamed the Labour Research Department, it was transferred to the Labour Party headquarters and inherited responsibility for getting Woolf's work published. His prime allegiance then went to the party, on whose Imperial and International Advisory Committees he served as a devoted and effective secretary for most of his life. Yet as a member of the Fabian Society and eventually as chairman of its Internationl Bureau he contributed uniquely to its international policies.

Beatrice Webb was to a large extent responsible for the Research Department's transformation. She had continued to supervise the work of committees on trade unions and professional associations, directing that each profession be examined in turn to see whether organization was extant or possible, and committing the Women's Group to observe the effect of the war on women in industry. She regarded the study and investigation into trade unionism and industrial control as more important than a Fabian monopoly of that work. When, in 1916, she wanted trade unionists and other useful socialists to collaborate in the work of the Research Department, especially Cole who had recently resigned from the Society over the guild socialism issue, she decided it needed a longer leash. She got the rules amended to allow non-Fabians full membership and participation – over a hundred trade unionists were already associates – and in return renounced the Department's right to send delegates to the Fabian Annual Conference and to be represented on the Schools Committee.[31] The Research Department gradually edged closer to the trade unions and Labour Party.[32] It had abandoned the study of industrial insurance because of the uncertain state of legislation at that time. The Munitions Act and the vastly increased employment of women in factories had demanded immediate investigation of the position of women in industry. Collaboration with the Fabian Women's Group, the Women's Industrial Council and the British Association in an investigation revealed the danger of the trade unions losing sight of where they were going. The Research Department decided that this must be prevented at all costs. In 1916, therefore, it embarked on a comprehensive survey of trade union organization and activity in Britain, to help the Labour movement to solve its problems after the war.[33]

Beatrice Webb, Cole and some other members of the Department met in March 1917 to discuss ways in which it might be weaned from the Society and made more of an asset to the Labour Party and trade union movement.[34] Preparations were made for the change, money was raised and there was a vast influx of members and associates when an anonymous member offered a subsidy if numbers and funds were doubled within six weeks. A decision to allow affiliation by labour organizations resulted in fifty-five unions, trade councils and local Labour Parties supporting the work on the survey by September 1917. The Research Department was patently no longer a Fabian institution.

13
EVOLUTION
NOT REVOLUTION

More volatile socialists talked a great deal of nonsense about the Russian Revolution early in 1917. Fabians were soon checked by reports from two Executive members, former staff, who visited Petrograd. Captain Sanders's duties involved much travel for military intelligence, but occasionally he was able to lecture to the Society at fairly short notice. In spring 1917 he was sent on a mission to Russia to observe developments in the army. The very day he returned to England he lectured to a large audience on his experiences.[1]

The first shock he delivered was the news that though socialists in and out of Russia had been preparing for revolution for many years, when it actually happened the revolution was an accident and not controlled by the planners at all. Sanders described the confusion following the Tsar's abdication, the inexperience and lack of authority and direction of the Workmen's and Soldiers' Committee which found itself in charge of the country for want of anyone else. He told of the extremists' dismay on finding themselves forced to become members of a bourgeois government under Kerensky in order to carry on the war from which Russia could not be extricated. No picture of a brave new world emerged but one of confusion, incompetence and loss of direction. Yet he thought the Russian soldiers were magnificent and believed that once their disorganization was resolved they would fight for revolutionary ideals.

Just as he returned to England the Fabian Society received an invitation from the Workmen's and Soldiers' Committee to send a delegation to Petrograd to discuss with them arrangements for holding an international socialist conference in Stockholm. A delegation was out of the question,

but the majority of the Executive overruled objections by Webb and
Sanders that there was no need to send anyone and agreed that the Society
could spare £100 to send Julius West, then secretary to the *New Statesman*,
to report on the situation in Russia and among the socialist parties in
Europe.[2] They were also eager to send as many representatives of Fabian
socialism to the Stockholm conference as possible, to present the case for
moderation, and appealed for money to send the Webbs, Shaw, Pease,
Susan Lawrence and West.[3] First they needed to test the temperature of
the water in both places and, since West was of Russian origin, they felt he
was the best man to do that.

An ILP delegation was to have travelled with West, but was turned back
when the crew of the SS *Vulture* refused to let Ramsay MacDonald
embark because of his pacifist views. West tried to change their minds but
in vain, so continued his journey alone. He confided later to Pease that he
suspected the militant Mrs Pankhurst, whose daughter was also on the
boat, was partly responsible for the crew's hostility towards MacDonald.[4]
West arrived in Stockholm 14 June 1917. He had talks with Hjalmar
Branting and Camille Huysmans, the Congress secretary, who seemed very
anti-British.[5]

Despite being unsupported and representing only a very small fraction
of the British Section, West was expected to discuss with the Scandinavian
and Dutch representatives not only international labour legislation but also
the peace terms acceptable to the British Labour movement. He stipulated
that their discussions should be off the record and told Pease he intended to
give as his personal opinion 'the usual thing, plus the "Supernational"
proposals, plus no economic war after the war'.

While waiting to hear from Arthur Henderson who, as secretary of the
Labour Party was *ex officio* secretary of the British Section, whether he
should continue his journey without the rest of the British party, West
presented a memorandum to the Dutch-Scandinavian Committee. In it he
refused on behalf of the British to take part in any conference at which
German delegates might be present and stated that the British Section had
no wish to send delegates to discuss the basis of peace terms proposed by
that Committee because they had been drawn up entirely from the German
point of view and included the future of such territories as Persia,
Morocco, Tripoli, Egypt and Malta as semi-colonies. Branting assured him
that those countries would not be discussed and recommended the Fabian
Society to produce a pamphlet of its 'peace-and-war utterances' for the
information of the conference, just as the two German socialist factions had
already done. West thought this a good idea and suggested it might contain

the memorandum by Webb on Peace aims published by the International Socialist Bureau, extracts from Shaw's *Fabianism and the Empire*, his 'Commonsense about the war', the other *New Statesman* supplements and some other articles written for the paper by Fabians.[6]

With Henderson's permission, West continued his journey and joined him in Petrograd, staying three weeks. There they agreed that unless the Russian delegates came to an Allied Socialist Conference first, there would be no point in holding the Stockholm conference, whether Branting's Committee were running it or the Russian delegates who were hoping to take control. An Allied Socialist Conference in London was planned for 8 and 9 August. Webb, Shaw and Pease were to represent the Fabian Society and go afterwards to Stockholm.[7] Under protest four Russian delegates came to London, Pease organizing their visit through a Labour committee.

West wrote an account of his visit to Petrograd for the August number of *Fabian News*. He described Petrograd as 'the city of utter incoherence, of rumour and depression. It is a scene of magnificent episodes and some fine striving, but its total effect is appalling'.[8] By then he had visited Paris with Henderson and found out what the French and Belgian Sections felt about this new initiative of the Second International. They doubted it would achieve anything but West still believed there was considerable reason to attend a conference called jointly by the Dutch-Scandinavian Committee and the Russians if only because British war aims were totally misunderstood in Russia and 'nothing is so likely to throw Russian Democracy into the outstretched arms of the German Majority Socialists as a refusal on the part of the British and French Socialists to defend their positions.'[9]

Before returning to Russia in autumn 1917, West presented to the Executive a paper originally intended as a report for the Labour Party but which it had refused to publish. It was rushed out as a Fabian tract, No. 184, *The Russian Revolution and British Democracy*, edited by Pease, and incorporating some of Henderson's amendments. It is a rather scrappy attempt to explain the attitudes of Russian workers to the British middle class, the evolution of the Workmen's and Soldiers' Committee, the relationships between the various Russian socialist parties and groups, Lenin's position, Russian industrial and agricultural organization, the way in which the zematvos had taken over the country's administration during the war and, finally, the economic situation in Russia. West saw a gloomy outlook for Russia because of lack of discipline and the revolutionaries' predilection for 'innumerable unenlightened disussions on an extraordinary number of purely theoretical matters.' He had noticed that deserters from the army tended to reel off a set speech picked up from Leninist orators about not caring whether the German capitalists replaced the British and French capitalists who then ruled over them, but they could not say who those Allied capitalists were. Predicting anarchy for any people dominated by a purely materialistic view of life, he warned that Germany and the rest of Europe would be laid wide open to a reactionary takeover by disciplinarians – to Fascism. Salvation for Russia depended on continuing contact with the western Allies. West prophesied also that:

> The future peace of the world will depend very largely upon the relations of the great democracies to one another when the common cause of war has ceased to hold them together. Britain is united with the USA by ties of blood, and with France by a common tradition and a great memory. If these three nations conclude a people's pact with the Russia which will surely arise from the present disorders, the world will be able to afford to laugh at the lessening menace of the few remaining autocracies.[10]

From his second visit to Petrograd West produced two lively accounts for the *New Stateman* of the meeting in the Smolny Institute when Lenin brought the endlessly discursive and fractious proceedings to heel with a twenty-minute speech on peace proposals and Kamonev abolished private property to unanimous acclaim before amendments were introduced to modify his scheme almost out of recognition. At the two meetings of the Conference of the Soviets attended by West the formation of a new government was declared, the Council of National Commissars, with Lenin as premier and Trotsky in charge of foreign affairs, and 'those present believed that the fate of Russia was in their hands'.[11] Even though four separate armies were rumoured to be closing in on Petrograd, there was general chaos and strikes multiplied, and the people turned against Kerensky and Kornilov. West, therefore, saw no reason to rescind his earlier prognostications.

In the event, the Stockholm conference fell through, but West's efforts were not wasted. The coverage given to his views in Fabian and quasi-Fabian publications helped convince the last of the British revolutionaries that evolution was the only course for the British Labour movement. Neither Sidney Webb nor Henderson, who were already collaborating over a new constitution for the Labour Party, thought Britain was naturally inclined to revolution even though the post-war situation would bring great unrest.

With Arnold Freeman, Webb had written a study guide for the Workers' Educational Association called *Great Britain after the War*, which warned of the probable industrial situation after hostilities ceased.[12] Their predictions were based on the work of the Fabian Society and Research Department during the previous three years. They warned that widespread unemployment was likely on demobilization of the 6 million in the fighting forces and the factories devoted to war production. Estimating that loss of life might be half a million men of employable age, they asserted that productivity could easily be restored by each man working an extra hour a week. Shortage of capital was perhaps the greatest obstacle to recovery, but they believed that the country now being better organized, prosperity could be restored quickly by the application of science, intelligence, hard work and adaptability. The government's wartime demands for abandonment of workshop customs, union regulations and demarcation lines between skilled and unskilled labour in the interests of greater productivity in certain industries would leave the trade unions debilitated. Webb believed that the way was clear for a clean sweep and the establishment of a rational, and therefore powerful, new union system, disregarding the workers' probable desire for old, familiar ways after the war. For him, prosperity could only be re-established through the hard work and willingness of the workers to adapt to the new demands of industry and he argued:

> It is, indeed, as plain to the man-in-the-street as to the economist in his study, that only by constantly producing more commodities and better, at a steadily diminishing 'real cost of production', can the people progressively adapt their economic environment to their ever increasing needs.[13]

A prosperous, fully employed Britain could only be obtained and preserved through peace. Webb demonstrated how this could be achieved in his *Memorandum on War Aims*, written in August 1917 and accepted as a policy statement by the Special Labour Conference in December.[14] The Labour Party was to insist on the abandonment of imperialism, secret diplomacy and profitable armament firms and impose arms limitation; foreign policy should be entrusted to a democratic legislature and disputes between states settled by arbitration through a League of Nations and an International High Court. Incentives for war should be removed by abandoning international economic competition, accepting international industrial legislation and provision of unemployment relief, controlling food supplies to prevent famine and controlling post-war reparations by an international organization.

In *Labour and the New Social Order*, also by Webb and adopted as the party manifesto, traces can be found of all the Fabian Society's former campaigns to improve the lot of the worker and his family: the balance of the labour supply by controlled public works, municipal control of the milk supply, workers' housing, the gas and electricity industries, and public transport, and the nationalization of land, railways and mines.[15] Economic theories which the Society had been elaborating since the 1880s were represented as a revolution in national finance. A Council of Ministers from the Dominions and other British dependencies, and the League of Nations with an International High Court were proposed as the core of imperial and international policy (a fusion of Shaw's and Woolf's recommendations). In fact, just about every long-held proposition of the Society was offered to the Labour Party as acceptable policy and received from it serious consideration if not acceptance in all cases. Henderson cannibalized Webb's *Memorandum on War Aims* and *Labour and the New Social Order* for his work, *The Aims of Labour*, to which they were attached as appendices.[16] This lent them the authority of accepted party policy, one far more socialist than it would previously have contemplated.

Henderson then had to design a party structure to make possible Labour's accession to power. He knew this could be achieved only by rejecting both the party's class interest basis and guild socialism,[17] building a strong national organization, based on the constituencies and opening membership to individuals as well as to those able to affiliate through their trade unions. Henderson wanted 'a national party, rooted ... in democracy'.[18] He wanted a Labour candidate standing in every constituency and new members properly represented on the policy-making bodies. By dint of Webb's outstanding drafting skill the new party constitution adopted in February met all these conditions and advocated broadly similar home, foreign and colonial political aims as Fabian publications. Among these aims was the future bone of contention:

> To secure for the producers by hand or by brain the full fruits of their industry, and the most equitable distribution thereof that may be possible, upon the basis of the common ownership of the means of production and the best obtainable system of popular administration and control of each industry or service.

As an overt sign of support for the reorganized party the Executive appealed to all Fabians, as the 'brainworkers' of the party, either to stand as Labour candidates at the next election or to help with money, canvassing or other propaganda work.[19] Three lectures were arranged in the King's Hall, in which Henderson, Shaw and Webb discoursed on the new structure, programme and possibilities of the party. Although the Society was short of funds, the proceeds from the lectures were donated to 'the Labour Party's Department of Information and Research on Economic, Social and Political Problems', in other words the Labour Research Department.

Just before the war ended the No Conscription Fellowship appealed to its members, most of whom were also ILP members, and many of whom were still in prison, to write to the ILP National Committee about the kind of world they wanted.[20] The Webbs' nephew, Stephen Hobhouse, Fenner Brockway and Arthur Creech Jones, one of the Nursery, were three who responded to the appeal. Clifford Allen, the former president of the University Socialist Federation and an active member of the Fabian Research Department, who was to play a major role in the new Labour movement, had already been released from prison because his health had broken down. He persuaded the other three, on release, to write a book under the auspices of the Labour Research Department on the state of the prison service, compiling evidence from their own and their fellow objectors' experiences just as the Women's Group had done.[21] When Allen was made treasurer of the ILP he gathered these and other like-minded young men around him to help revitalize ILP policy. The No Conscription Fellowship disbanded itself to avoid competing with the ILP, but its members still wanted to work for peace, disarmament and international socialism. A large part of ILP funds came from Quakers who sponsored this aim. They and the Fellowship group were bitterly disappointed when the first Labour government did not carry through a disarmament policy.

Parallel with this peace movement ran a campaign to improve the lot of the common man. One of the outstanding manifestos of this time, which formed part of the 'Socialism in our time' programme launched by the ILP on the demise of the first Labour government, was *The Living Wage*.[22] Written by H.N. Brailsford, J.A. Hobson, Frank Wise and Creech Jones, it embodied Hobson's underconsumption theory, a version of the national minimum policy put forward by the Fabians and the ILP before the war, and proposed a version of family allowance, another idea favoured by Fabians. Much of *Socialism in Our Time* in 1926 was an extrapolation of theories adumbrated more than ten years earlier in Fabian literature.

The Fabian Publishing Committee did not meet at all between May 1917 and October 1919 while more important fruits of Fabian work were being published by the Research Department. The only tract produced in 1919 was Webb's *National Finance and a Levy on Capital*.[23] Then came a resurgence of interest in publication. Local government was the obvious area for study. Great changes had taken place in administration and powers, and in the electorate. In response to public demands for information, the Fabian General Purposes Committee decided to engage an expert on local government to collect data, answer questions and prepare tracts on the subject.[24] The National Committee for the Reform of Local Government was willing to subsidize publication and so, in 1920, C. Mostyn Lloyd, an LSE lecturer, produced three pamphlets on urban district councils, housing and the Poor Law, Clement Attlee, a new Executive member, produced another two on borough and metropolitan borough councils,[25] though both undertook to give courses of lectures to local Labour parties and W.A. Robson, then a student at the LSE, was hired as local government adviser.[26]

Since the Labour Party was intent on building up the membership of constituency branches, the Society determined to concentrate on education. In July 1919, it appealed for volunteers to join Attlee and Mostyn in a lecture campaign directed at the constituencies. These Hutchinson Trust type lectures dealt with the history, aims and policy of the Labour Party. A tutorial course on the same theme proved very popular. The autumn lectures were on new phases of socialism but no second volume of essays ensued. Purchases at the Fabian bookshop showed a heartening rise and all seemed set for a new Fabian boom.

To symbolize the new spirit in the Society, Webb decided that the Basis should be revised yet again. A more subtle interpretation of the way in which Fabians were to tackle the problem of ownership of land and capital industries, the redistribution of wealth, and the control of production and resources was offered to the annual general meeting in a new draft and approved after due consideration. There was no question of private property being abolished at a stroke, as the Soviet delegates had done in Petrograd, or of instant nationalization of all industries, for the Basis laid down that:

> the Society ... works for the extinction of private propety in land, with equitable consideration of established expectations, and due provision as to the tenure of the home and homestead; for the transfer to the community, by constitutional methods, of all such industries as can be conducted socially; and for the establishment, as the governing consideration in the regulation of production, distribution and service of the common good instead of private profit.[27]

This, of course, is quite a long way from what is now known as Clause Four Socialism. The Basis defined the relationship of the Society to the Labour Party in such a manner that ample leeway was allowed for Fabians to work for the constitutional attainment of their kind of socialism through any organization it chose for the purpose. It modified the declaration that the Society was a constituent part of both the Labour Party and the International Socialist Congress by a clear indication that it intended to retain its independence of action, stating that 'it takes part freely in all constitutional movements, social, economic and political, which can be guided towards its own objects'. Nor were those who were not members of the Labour Party to be excluded from the Society, for in the light of its belief in equal citizenship it was 'open to persons irrespective of sex, race or creed, who commit themselves to its aims and purposes, as stated above, and undertake to promote its work'. The scope and pattern of that work was to remain the same:

(a) the propaganda of Socialism in its application to current problems;
(b) investigation and discovery in social, industrial, political and economic relations;
(c) the working out of Socialist principles in legislation and administrative reconstruction;
(d) the publication of the results of its investigations and their practical lessons.

Although Webb persuaded the annual meeting that he was presenting more accurate and precise statements of principles, method and aims, critics would have perceived very little in this rewording to convince them that the Society had become less devious. In December 1919 the new Basis was ratified and the Society continued on its way undisturbed by any startling ideological revision.

Public interest in *Fabian Essays in Socialism* again revived. Half the 1920 reprint of 3000 was quickly sold and more ordered from the printer. Demand for the book-boxes was also soaring as men settled back into civilian life and the Society looked forward to a new surge of activity. Stephen Sanders returned to the office after demobilization and released Pease from his three-year war-service. However, Sanders soon accepted a post in the International Labour Office in Geneva. Of forty-nine applicants for the post of General Secretary, F.W. Galton was chosen.[28] Since his resignation from the Society in 1909 Galton, the son of a London saddler like Sanders, had worked as secretary to the Progressive Party in the LCC, under the Webbs' patronage, where he was, apparently, not a very efficient organizer. For the whole of the inter-war period he worked most diligently for the Fabians but he failed to inspire the Society or impel it towards scaling even greater heights.

14

SECTIONAL ACTIVITIES
BETWEEN THE WARS

During the First World War, the Nursery had struggled to continue lectures and social events, while its members were gradually swallowed up in the fighting forces, the civil service and other forms of war service or prison. They were all too occupied to attend lectures in London and it became impossible to raise a quorum for executive meetings. In 1917 members were asked whether the time had come to disband.[1] They voted to carry on and Margaret Postgate, the future Mrs Cole, was asked to lecture on 'National guilds', Miles Malleson on 'Socialism and the cinema' and Webb on their duty to the Labour Party. Nevertheless activity did not revive and, in 1918, a handful met and agreed to dissolve the Nursery while pledging themselves to work for the Labour Party 'or any other useful organization' and to continue to meet informally.[2]

Unexpectedly, in January 1922 *Fabian News* announced that the Nursery had been revived for the benefit of those interested in socialism after they had left 'the varsity'.[3] Though separated by only a few years from the end of the original Nursery, the new generation had an outlook markedly different from that of the founders. Survivors of the war had passed into the senior society. This new Nursery was entirely post-war in its ambition, purpose and experience. Generally too young to have been politically active before the war, they now inherited a world buzzing with talk of peace settlements, international organizations, new regimes and alliances; they also inherited a new Labour Party believing in a more democratic, post-war Britain in which to function by virtue of its new structure.

Beatrice Webb did much to inspire this resurrection. The new Nursery swept into action crying 'Young Fabians awake! – Young Fabian Essays may one day appear.' It opened with a social in January, announced plans for a revue in April, then held a debate on guild socialism which ended in their condemning it as completely impractical. Despite the upper age limit being now 35, the Nursery was allocated a section in *Fabian News* coyly headed 'The children's corner'. There in March the secretary declared: 'It has taken the Nursery two months to dispose of Guild Socialism and Douglasism, to settle the affairs of Egypt and to enrol eighty members. Next month it is to tackle Webbism and solve the problem of India.'

The young people greatly admired Gandhi, who had joined the Fabian Society when in England in April 1920. He resigned four years later for no stated reason whereas Jinnah, who had joined at about the same time while studying law in England, remained nominally a Fabian until 1938 though his subscription ceased in 1933.[4] They were less enthusiastic, indeed ambivalent, about Webb's latest book on a socialist Commonwealth of Great Britain.[5] A serious study of local government began in preparation for the week given to the subject at the summer school. Political action offered itself in the elections in December 1922 and 1923 with the constant demand for addressers of envelopes and 'knockers on doors'. Its numbers trebled through its activity during an election campaign in which fifty-six Fabian candidates stood and Webb, Attlee, Snell and seven others were returned to Westminster. The ebullient chairman and secretary retired at the end of the first year's work as both were 'seeking fame abroad' and reports in the *News* became a little more restrained. But the Nursery had been re-established on a firm footing and, between picnics, play acting, eurhythmics, dances, cabarets, reading and listening to Shaw, members turned their attention to the Fascist coup in Italy, the situation on the Ruhr, and Russia under the Bolshevik regime.

In its second year numbers rose sufficiently to allow formation of several distinct groups to study the machinery of government, finance and public speaking.[6] Impulsion was lost in mid-1925 when disillusionment about a post-war world which was neither brave nor new and disappointment with the brief life of Labour's first government took hold. Numbers dropped abruptly and there was considerable internal dissension and loss of direction. Seven of the extremely hard-working committee lost patience with the frivolous majority and broke away to form the New Fabian Group to study specific problems in agriculture, education, local government and industry, find out about the situation in Russia and gain experience in public speaking.[7] The rump of the Nursery proceeded to run a course of lectures on industrial socialism, indoctrinate new members and associates on socialist theory and practice and to produce a threepenny 'Nursling'. The New Fabian Group, which pursued a serious image, competed with 'The Cunctator', one copy of which was deposited in the Fabian Common-room and a duplicate circulated. Their weekend conferences at Old Jordan's Hostel, Beaconsfield, became an annual event. The Nursery countered with a bid for popularity by running an Easter School at Knocke in Belgium. Both sections indulged in play reading; both engaged popular speakers on socialist themes; both were given seats on the Summer School Committee. After the New Fabian Group had been running for six months the Executive gave permission for a publicity section to seek greater press coverage for the Society and to organize outside speaking engagements for members of a lecture committee.[8]

While some of the New Fabian Group were participating in the TUC campaign against the Trade Union Bill the less militant Nursery was content to devote its autumn lecture series in 1927 to a study of trade unionism, followed by a series of discussions on the chief resolutions adopted at the previous party conference.[9] The 'Nursling', after a difficult hatching, finally died while 'The Cunctator' was dropped after three or four monthly issues because contributions were so poor. A pamphlet committee produced nothing and the Nursery was too busy lecturing for the London Labour Party in the wards to try its hand at writing.[10] As numbers decreased and notices in *Fabian News* of their activities became more and more laconic, the youth sections tried by revision of their rules in late 1929 to revitalize their members but with very little success. The lethargy then settling over the Fabian Society seemed to be smothering them in spite of their struggles. The final notice of the New Fabian Group's activities appeared in March 1930, when three lectures by Herbert Agar, Maurice Reckitt and Harold Laski were advertised. Its members then transferred to the SSIP and the New Fabian Research Bureau.[11] With no competition to provide a stimulus the Nursery limped along, showing a transient interest in the Anti-War Movement, in what was happening to socialists in Austria, and in how a Fascist thought.[12] After war broke out, it could no longer continue as a separate unit and members were encouraged to join the main Society.

Some of the younger members were so disgusted by the Society's lethargy that, in 1936, they created yet another new Fabian section, designed to investigate new methods of propaganda and put them to work for the Labour Party by recruiting technicians and those in the professions.[13] This group was wholly within the Fabian Society and was called the 1936 Fabian Group. To some extent it was attempting what Wells had tried a generation before. In one of its first lectures a professional advertising man condemned the Labour Party's dull, outmoded pamphlets and posters. It also embarked on a pamphlet called 'Winning the middle classes for Labour' and a related series of lectures on Labour's appeal to the doctor, lawyer and teacher. It investigated the state of socialism in the universities and discovered that, whereas the Oxbridge approach was too idealistic, in the provincial universities students' uncertainty of finding a job after graduation was convincing them that there was something very wrong with society. The Labour Party welcomed the Group's help in canvassing for membership. Concerned about the way in which advertising media had been exploited in Europe in the last six years they began investigating. Richard Crossman gave the first lesson on Nazi propaganda methods, in which he damned the torchlight processions, use of hypnotic lighting effects and other means by which the blackshirts entrapped followers. Nevertheless, when asked to help in the Labour Party's 1938 recruitment campaign in four London constituencies, the group boasted of enlisting 240 members in Chelsea by dint of a torchlight procession and a particularly lurid attack on the housing situation in the ward.[14]

Two dances were organized for the benefit of the Labour Party Spanish Campaign and the committees for Spanish Medical Aid and Dependants' Aid. To these Ellen Wilkinson, Victor Gollancz, Attlee, Laski, Herbert Morrison and Sybil Thorndike were all persuaded to lend lustre, with a 'beautiful Spanish dancer' as an additional attraction.[15] They received great publicity but very little profit. Briefly the Nursery revived, with the young people snatching at a little gaiety before the clouds of war broke. In 1939 there were fewer conscientious objectors, Nursery members were swept into the fighting forces and its attempts to continue as a working body petered out.

The Women's Group showed a tendency to stagnate during the inter-war years. It entered the 1920s feeling that much of its former work, especially that involving collaboration with the Research Department, had been completed. Though there were plenty of members, no great campaign emerged to capture the imagination. Women over 30 had the vote and the chief task was to ensure that they were politically educated to use it; the remnant of the Suffrage Fund was available for this. Mrs Shaw, conscious of this decline withdrew her considerable financial support and forced the Group to appeal to the Executive for an official grant to pay its secretary's salary.[16]

Some members felt that the problems of working-class women ought to be left to the industrial organizations while the Women's Group concentrated on those of the middle class, including the training of domestic servants, and on the working of the new Ministry of Health and other matters covered today by consumer protection groups.[17] They still sat on committees of women's organizations entitled to submit resolutions to the annual National Labour Party's Women's Conference. In addition, the Women's Group helped with fund raising for the London Labour Party and the ILP.[18] At tea-meetings in the Fabian Hall, prostitution, infant and maternal mortality, and the falling birthrate were all discussed. Any member standing at a local election was helped by speakers, canvassers and a grant of up to £10 for election expenses. When ten stood in the 1923 general election a dinner was given in their honour. Margaret Bondfield was similarly fêted when she was chosen president of the TUC that same summer and again when she, Dorothy Jewson and Susan Lawrence became MPs. Throughout, it campaigned for the 'flapper vote' but became disenchanted with the International Women's Suffrage Alliance which, while pressing for the abolition of night-work for female manual workers, totally disregarded the needs of professional women who had to work at equally unsocial hours. National and international movements for the protection of children and the preservation of peace gained more united and consistent support from the Women's Group than from the main Society, although it was never very efficient at organizing corporate action.

An avant-garde innovation in 1927 was the group's provision of a woman lawyer for impecunious women needing legal advice.[19] For once Galton, the General Secretary, became really enthusiastic about the scheme and promised the Society's full support. A room in the office was allocated one night a week to Gwen Petersen, a solicitor experienced in that kind of advisory work, to hold a surgery and the scheme was advertised by churches, and at Party headquarters. A consultation fee of one penny was charged, threepence if a letter was involved, and Miss Petersen gave her services free. The first case to come to court cost the group 30 shillings, which was discharged by one of the committee. Thereafter appeals in *Fabian News* produced sufficient to cover their costs. The scheme was a great success but when the Labour Party itself established a Poor Man's Lawyer in Horseferry Road the Group gladly relinquished the burden of constantly raising money for it.[20]

In the mid-1930s Women's Group's work virtually ceased because the founders were ageing and the more effective younger members were immersed in work on the LCC as chairmen of sectional committees. When the great amalgamation took place in 1939 (see chapter 17) it was hoped that new, younger Fabians would join the Women's Group and a few Research Group members dutifully did so, but it took a war to provide them with some really productive activity. The inter-war years were undeniably dull within the Women's Group. It carried out worthy consolidation but there was no sparkle nor elation.

During those years, summer schools continued and survived repeated rebellions against the rules imposed by the manager. Dr C.E.M. Joad was blacklisted for staying out all night after an expedition to Dartmoor, apparently in the company of two young ladies. Others were rebuked for returning at two in the morning, 'in couples'. For fear of the school turning into 'a centre for experiments in the New Morality' all applications in the 1920s were minutely scrutinized by the committee.[21] Nude bathing and sunbathing were, however, allowed to continue. Finally, in 1938, after Joad had been welcomed back as a lecturer, the committee decreed that existing rules were indeed antediluvian and a more liberal regime was essential. Mary Hankinson took offence and refused to act as manager and even, sadly, to attend that year as a guest of the Society to mark its appreciation of her thirty years of devoted service.[22]

Every year the school had to face a hazard or drama of one kind or another. The last week of the 1920 school at Priorsfield, Godalming, was planned as an international week and invitations were sent to 120 foreign socialists, half of whom accepted. Unfortunately only seven turned up, because of the war in Poland and other crises in Europe. The following year Dr Marie Stopes came to lecture on 'Women as mothers', and the rather nervous director for the week noted in the logbook: 'Considering the subject, the lecturer and the audience, all went off fairly well – as only one passage in the discussion could be described as obscure'.[23] The proprietor of a school booked for 1925 suddenly cancelled the agreement at the end of April on realizing that the Society was a socialist body.[24] Makeshift arrangements were made for the school to be held in a different place each week.

Ballroom dancing classes run by Blanco White rivalled country dancing in popularity and eventually superseded it, to Harry Snell's disgust.[25] Amber Blanco White and her husband were a great social asset and helped improvise a jazz band one year. In succeeding years amateur musicians did their best to co-ordinate attendance at the school and brought their instruments with them. The Old Gang's charisma could still attract large audiences. In 1935, for example, Webb enthralled a young, left-wing audience by his account of the USSR. When the school was held at

Frensham it was possible for parties to go to tea with either the Webbs at Passfield Corner or with David Lloyd George, who escorted them at breakneck speed round his farm, expounding on agriculture all the way and revealing, when questioned, that he neither knew what turnips were nor why he grew them. At the age of 80 Edward Pease, too, held the school captive with reminiscences of the early Society.[26]

When the political lethargy which had engulfed the Fabian Society after the Labour Party split in 1931 showed some sign of lifting Webb proposed a rapprochement with the New Fabian Research Bureau by offering its members twenty or thirty places in the 1935 summer school. Three years later, with amalgamation under discussion between their respective officers, the Society invited the Bureau to organize one week of the school. With the aid of Hugh Gaitskell's eloquent, persuasive and well-informed lecture on Labour's fiscal policy this ruse succeeded and the summer school remained an important and immensely useful feature of the Society after the two organizations joined forces in 1939.

Each of these sectional activities played its part in holding the Fabian Society together for twenty years while its philosophical development and creative vitality were at a very low ebb. The Nursery ensured that a succession of young people were imbued with Fabian socialism, learned about Fabian methods and brought their critical faculties to bear upon both. The Women's Group supported women entering political life, whether simply as voters or as practising councillors, trade union officers or Members of Parliament. Above all, it induced women to observe political, social and economic affairs, make up their own minds about what ought to be done and, whenever possible, to act. The prime contribution of the summer school to the political life of the society lay not in the subjects and theories dissected and put together again in argument year after year; the unique benefaction was the fellowship engendered among members living and playing together while discussing the tenets of their faith. People sought refreshment there year after year, keeping themselves in touch with the Society's roots and their loyalty to the Labour Party inviolate.

15
FABIANS
AND GOVERNMENT

Britain entered the 1920s no longer the undisputed world leader in industry; Germany and America had been challenging that supremacy since the turn of the century. By losing the war Germany had temporarily lost ground in the race. Payment of reparations urgently compelled it to get back into competition, although the collapse of its economy first caused havoc in Europe. America had sufficient natural resources to be a net seller and so, for a few years, it appeared to be a land of unlimited opportunities, until like Britain it found itself overproducing, as a result of contraction of markets in the rest of the world. British heavy industry received its first blow when Dreadnoughts were no longer needed. Private buyers could not provide a sufficiently large home market for the expanded motor industry. Inevitably the European nations' reaction to war was to build self-sufficiency into their reconstruction design; the demand for British-made vehicles and machinery which had caused a brief post-war boom vanished as soon as they could produce their own. Even British coal was not imported to the same extent because new European factories were more economic in its use and some were exploiting oil and hydroelectricity.

Such was the scene when Labour first came to power. Much of the vast capitalist wealth which socialists had planned to redistribute to the working classes had already been redistributed in a manner totally unforeseen when socialist theories had been evolved. The Labour Party first took office at the end of a four-year decline in trade, when recession and demobilization had pushed unemployment to 2 million in Britain, and France was occupying the Rhineland in order to squeeze reparations from a strike-devastated and incapable Germany.

For four decades the Fabian Society had been far more interested in obtaining social reconstruction by persuading others to accept and implement its ideas, generated during years of research and cogitation, than in thrusting the Labour Party into power. Socialist legislation looked easier when the party was not responsible for finding the money to administer it, or for solving the day-to-day problems of government.

Themes for autumn lectures are a reliable indication of the prevailing trends of Fabian thought. In 1919, 'New phases of socialism' covered the need for rehabilitation in India, Ireland and Russia, as well as the not very urgent demands at home for nationalization of industry and guild socialism, and the two succeeding series concentrated on the post-war problems. Unfortunately, lecturers neglected the specific questions facing Labour MPs.

At the beginning of 1922, the Executive Committee realized that the next general election might be called much earlier than expected. The lecture committee thus decided that the Labour Party should be made to face its own weaknesses by an autumn series on 'Can Labour govern?': problems of national defence, the Empire, the relationship between the state and industry, foreign affairs, and finances were analysed. Shaw closed the series with 'Can anyone govern?' His audience was soon to find out whether Labour could.

At each lecture the chairman appealed for contributions to the Parliamentary Fund and £1400 was promised in time for the election in December 1922.[1] Fifty-six Fabians stood: ten were successful, fewer than hoped, of whom three were members of the Executive – Attlee, Snell and Webb. Still, the Parliamentary Labour Party was almost doubled. Analysis of the poll showed that Fabians had contested too many rural seats in view of their essentially urban image and outlook. Not all those whom the Society claimed as victors succeeded on their Fabian appeal; Ben Tillett's strongest support came from the trade unions. Nevertheless, the result was heralded as a victory to crown the fortieth anniversary of the Society's foundation.

In summer 1923, an emissary of the Liberals opened negotiations with the General Secretary on some form of Parliamentary collaboration.[2] No pact was made. The Parliamentary Labour Party of 143 was weakening the effective power of its adversaries without attempting to force through any constructive legislation. So successful was it that the government asked for a dissolution after less than a year and the Society again found itself in need of funds to subsidize Fabian candidates. Donations poured in, enabling one in three of the Fabians who stood to be returned to Parliament – a proportion not quite as good as the general Labour result, where nearly half the candidates were elected, but reasonably satisfactory.

According to Webb's own, retrospective memorandum on the Labour government of 1924, no one really believed the party might be called on to take office until the day after the poll. In his chairman's address to the party conference the previous June, Webb had estimated that the Labour Party would need two-thirds of the vote at a general election before it would be asked to form a government.[3] He reckoned that could not possibly be achieved until 1926. In December 1923 the Labour Party did not even hold a full third of the seats in the Commons, but after discussions with the Party Executive and the TUC General Council, the Fabian group realized that, however unprepared the Parliamentary Labour Party might feel, the advantage of being recognized as the official opposition, won at the previous election, could not now be abandoned by a refusal to take office. A warning from a socialist ambassador to Webb that George V had told him that in the event of a Government defeat he would certainly send for MacDonald drove the Labour leader home to Lossiemouth to construct his cabinet list in peace, although, because of the fine balance between the Parties, the Conservative leader would remain Prime Minister until openly defeated in the House of Commons. MacDonald eventually became Prime Minister on 24 January 1924.

Webb had persuaded the inner group to leave selection of a cabinet entirely to MacDonald, though he could not resist reminding him of the statutory requirement that one or more Secretary of State be in the House of Lords.[4] Although MacDonald had harboured a certain antagonism towards Webb for years, even before he resigned from the Society, he still needed him and several other Fabians in the Government. Of the twenty-two Fabians elected, five were made cabinet Ministers and four others put in charge of minor departments. Only Henderson and Haldane had had previous cabinet experience. MacDonald shrewdly consulted Haldane on his choice of Ministers but was rather gauche in his relations with Henderson, the obvious alternative as party leader.[5] Webb was treated more considerately, though MacDonald, possibly at Haldane's persuasion, made him accept the prestigious Board of Trade instead of the younger Ministry of Labour, where he would have relished the opportunity to tackle the unemployment problem. Fortunately, Margaret Bondfield, whose experience in the industrial field had become well known to Fabians through her work in the Women's Group, was appointed Parliamentary Secretary at the Ministry of Labour, to handle the position of women in industry.[6] Webb had suggested to MacDonald that she ought to become the first woman Minister. In every way Webb co-operated with the Minister of Labour, Tom Shaw, even chairing the special committee on unemployment and housing. They were both frustratred in their attempt to solve the unemployment problem by lack of funds and, they thought, over-cautious officials. Webb left office a disappointed man, having made no great socialist innovations at the Board of Trade where the work with facts and figures was well attuned to his particular talents.[7] Undoubtedly, Webb's most useful contribution to the first Labour government was his vast command of information; in cabinet he lacked decision and political aggression.

Fabians now applied themselves to constitutional problems and study of local authorities' powers. Harold Laski proved a most prolific writer, explaining the subtleties of the King's and Prime Minister's relative responsibilities in dissolving a minority government and the complicated problem of the second chamber when the rank and file were still clamouring for abolition of the House of Lords. Machinery of government was his prime academic interest at this time and his expertise soon dominated the content of Fabian tracts, building up the Parliamentary Labour Party's confidence in its own ability to govern. Two other political scientists, Herman Finer and W.A. Robson, tackled the implications of proportional representation and compulsory voting.

Within three months of the election Laski produced a tract explaining how a party might govern with only a minority of seats, by depending on the goodwill of other parties to get its Bills enacted.[8] After describing the difficulties and necessarily short tenure of a minority government, Laski stated that the balance of parties then invalidated the theory that it was not in the power of the monarch to refuse dissolution without favouring the alternative party and destroying the political disinterestedness of the Crown. His warning that frequent elections were undesirable because the administration would have no opportunity to carry through a determined policy finally destroyed the former Fabian principle of annual parliaments proposed in the Newcastle Programme. MacDonald undoubtedly read this tract, which quoted his recent statement in the *New Leader*: 'I should on no account leave to the Monarch the dangerous and invidious task of safeguarding the nation against too frequent dissolutions', and which demolished his proposition that Parliament ought to fix a minimum period for its own existence.[9] Laski's argument may well have contributed to MacDonald's decision to ask for dissolution of the first Labour government in October 1924. Four dicta by Laski appear to have swayed MacDonald's actions and relations with the King in 1931:

It appears essential to vest the ultimate right of dissolution in the Prime Minister. Its exercise must be within the limits of his discretion. He must be able to appeal to the Crown for the power to dissolve in the certainty that the Crown will grant his appeal.

The right of the Crown is an advisory right only; the centre of power is the leader of the party in office. It is his duty to consult, and, obviously, where he is dealing with a monarch who has long been at the centre of affairs, who has come to have, by virtue of experience, almost an intuitive sense of the impact of policy, he will be wise to obey the advice he receives with greater care than any other to which he has access.

The Prime Minister may threaten to dissolve; but no Prime Minister will dissolve unless he has a substantial issue or some solid achievement upon which to go to the country.

No Prime Minister will wantonly thrust an election upon the country if he can avoid it with honour.[10]

The first Labour government was not a success. Most Ministers entered office with no idea of how their departments functioned or what their own powers and responsibilities were within them. It was not an easy government to control since competition and jealousies broke out within it and without. In some instances, civil servants dominated their principals. Nevertheless, of Bills introduced in its nine months, about 50 per cent more than average, seventy-nine received the Royal Assent. Since that was the usual number of Acts passed in that length of time, Labour's lack of experience did not unduly frustrate the business of parliament. Some Ministers, in fact, managed to earn the good-will and support of their permanent officials by their very eagerness to learn and work hard; they learned much in a very short time.[11] But no amount of hard work could keep Labour in power for long without a clear majority. When MacDonald asked for the dissolution, he commissioned Webb to draft the King's speech in less than twenty-four hours, to prevent the parliamentary election clashing with the local ones scheduled for November. Thus ended the Labour Party's 'scouting expedition in the world of administration – a testing of men and measures before they are actually called upon to exercise majority power'.[12] At the dissolution twenty-five Fabians were in the House of Commons. Eighty-one stood in the October election, of whom eighteen were successful, a drop which accurately reflected general Labour losses.[13]

Webb's lecture in November, entitled 'Fabianism justified', claimed that people joined the Society 'to assist in every way the permeation of all types of English minds by Fabian doctrines, without advertisement or ostentation'.[14] Permeation was the only immediate possibility. The Conservative Party would clearly stay in office for some time and so Fabians returned to the routine business of obtaining nomination for constituencies, nursing them, raising funds and formulating constructive policies and recognizable goals against the next general election. Tract No. 5, *Facts for Fabians*, was refurbished under Hugh Dalton's supervision. A small committee was set up to consider republishing Tract No. 70, *Report on Fabian Policy*, to which MacDonald had objected fiercely when he was new to the Society. All this was comparatively dull and the Society's impetus and popularity diminished. Many were disappointed that so few socialist measures had been implemented during Labour's first taste of power. Recruits fell to a mere quarter of their former level while the usual number of losses were sustained. Fresh inspiration was desperately needed.

The ILP welcomed a period in opposition to rethink its socialism. Brailsford, Hobson, Wise and Creech Jones, instructed to prepare a manifesto on *The Living Wage*, submitted their first version for criticism to Beatrice Webb, who complacently reckoned that she was being used as a 'foolometer'.[15] As a major part of the ILP's 'Socialism in our time' programme in 1926 it was regarded by Fabians as far from practicable.

Meanwhile, the New Fabian Group, persuaded by the Executive to consider financial policy,[16] began exploring the fresh economic theories simmering in Cambridge and the LSE. Workers undergoing hardships partly caused by France's action against Germany began to protest. A strike by the Miners' Federation culminated in the General Strike. The Society could do little more than offer sympathy through the Women's Group which held drawing-room meetings to enable women in comfortable circumstances to learn of the background to the strike from two miners' wives from South Wales. Its constitution prevented collective political action, though individual members were free to play whatever role they thought fit. Fabians helped to organize relief for strikers and their families, maintain milk supplies for mothers and babies, and keep communications open between different parts of the country, even though the Society did not believe in the potency of one big strike. Douglas Cole's rooms in Oxford became a hub of strike activity and some of his students drove his wife between Oxford and London, bearing messages to and from those who knew what was happening at the centre.[17]

In response to a demand by members to be told the Fabian position in the ideological confusion, Laski and Galton drafted a resolution supporting the fight by the Miners' Federation and protesting against the Government's curtailment of negotiations at a point when, it was believed, a settlement was in sight.[18] Galton, inundated by members' queries, was instructed to tell each enquirer that the Society, being unrepresented on the Miners' Federation or the TUC General Councils, had played no part in the General Strike, had not even expressed an opinion in favour of it, that being inconsistent with all its declarations of policy and contrary to the Fabian Basis. He pointed out that the Labour Party, debarred from intervention in an industrial dispute and confined to political action by its constitution, had none the less been doing its utmost to find some method by which the strike and the miners' dispute could be brought to a just settlement. The original draft of this letter ended with a rather emotional appeal to Fabians to give assistance to all those who were suffering hardship as a result of the confrontation, but this was excised by the Executive.

Membership fell noticeably in the next few months. The officers were loath to admit that any full members had resigned because of the Executive's refusal to give a clear lead over the strike, but they had to acknowledge that many associates had withdrawn their subscriptions over the issue. There followed a gradual decline in numbers, audiences at the autumn lectures shrank and the consequent drop in income inhibited many research projects.

Despite its own dullness the Fabian Society now tried to enliven the Labour Party's programme. A committee consisting of Laski, Snell, Tawney, Dalton and, of course, Webb was asked to persuade the National Executive Committee to present its manifesto as a literary document prefaced by a statement of the party's aims and objectives, rather than as a bleak list of demands. If it were confined to a limited number of points based on the principles of *Labour and the New Social Order*, and expressed in a manner that implied a great deal more, the Society was prepared to produce a series of tracts to exemplify the Labour Party's intentions.[19] The outlook was hardly inspiring for either the party or the Society.

Fortunately, a new project now appeared to enable the Society to continue its work for the Labour movement. In 1923 the party had organized a conference for exchange of views on local government between councillors, prospective candidates and local authority officers.[20] Participants asked for a journal to continue this work but as the party had no funds available, it turned to the Society, which undertook to finance and run a monthly, *Local Government News*, for two years, until the party was in a position to take it over. Room was made in the office for W.A. Robson, their former local government expert, to edit it, and the first penny number appeared in January 1924. It soon achieved a circulation of over 2000 and the original eight pages had to be expanded to twelve. The office was beseiged by enquiries from councillors, and former tracts on housing, rates and taxes were in constant demand.[21] Robson, who wrote nearly all the journal, produced a new tract on the district auditor and Herbert Samuels another on county councils.[22] At the end of the two years the Labour Party still could not afford to take over and so the Fabians struggled on, devoting the income from a trust fund left by a former member, Henry Atkinson.[23] When the magazine's failure seemed inevitable in 1928 Noel Buxton gave £200 to tide it over for another year.[24] To create a sounder financial base the Local Government Bureau was formed to give anyone in local administration the magazine and any relevant tracts, a means of exchanging information, opinions and news of developments in the several authorities, and even a possible medium for conferences and collective action to push through progressive measures – all for 5 shillings a year.[25] Many ruses were employed to keep the magazine and Bureau running, even sharing the *Political Quarterly*'s office (Robson being then joint editor with Kingsley Martin). Publication of the journal ceased only when Robson's academic work reached such proportions that he felt he had to resign his editorship and direction of the Bureau. Its work was then absorbed by the Fabian office and its separate existence ceased.[26]

During 1928 the Society acquired and moved into 11 Dartmouth Street, its ultimate home. Shaw made this possible, by lending £2500, as a 5 per cent loan to be secured by a mortgage, towards the purchase price of £3150.[27] Organization in the new office was not completed in time for the promised pre-election tracts to be produced and the customary appeal for the Parliamentary Fund raised less than £800. Nevertheless, Labour was returned to office, and, while the interest of electors could still be held, a series of pamphlets emerged to clarify Labour's foreign policy and attitude towards the League of Nations, its fiscal, agricultural and imperial policies and the implications of the Local Government Act of 1929.[28] It seemed as though the fresh impetus had arrived.

Meanwhile Cole had returned to the fold. After severing his connection with the Labour Research Department in 1924, because of communist domination of its work, he had been without a formal position within the Labour movement, though contributing with tremendous influence to its literature. In 1928 he agreed to lecture on his brand of socialism to the summer school at Cirencester Agricultural College.[29] His period of withdrawal had given him time to rethink his faith and, according to the school's director, the lecture

> was a frank recantation of his earlier, impracticable and theoretical opinions and gave a reasoned, workmanlike account of constructive proposals for immediate party aims . . . of the kind which can be carried into effect when we obtain a majority and which meanwhile can be preached to the electorate.

Soon after he was persuaded to rejoin the Society, which regarded his membership as essential; but he was highly critical of its inertia and weariness. His view of the 'faults of the Fabian' led to the next major development in its structural history.

The full extent of the lethargy was temporarily masked by Labour's return to power in 1929, when forty-seven of the ninety-nine Fabians who stood were elected, a high return for a membership of less than 2000. Eight of the nineteen Fabians in the government had major cabinet posts. Margaret Bondfield was appointed Minister of Labour, thus becoming the first woman to hold cabinet rank, while Susan Lawrence, as Parliamentary Secretary, supported another Fabian, Arthur Greenwood, in the Ministry of Health. Webb joined his brother-in-law, Lord Parmoor, in the Upper House, taking the title of Passfield and holding the offices of Secretary of State for the Colonies and the Dominions. He relinquished the latter department to J.H. Thomas after a year, when pressure of work became too great in the build-up towards ratification of the Statute of Westminster which recast Britain's relations with the Empire. Webb would gladly have retired in 1930 but the Prime Minister was anxious to retain him as an undramatic head of the Colonial Office to publish the highly controversial Palestine White Paper, prepared by the previous government. Though he was extremely gentle and patient with pressure groups while there, he could never understand why they became so worked up about colonial and Mandatory affairs.[30] Unfortunately, the White Paper was even more explosive than anticipated and the rest of the cabinet failed to give Webb the right degree of support. A Committee of Ministers took Palestinian affairs out of his hands and virtually placed them in those of the Foreign Office – a situation reflected in 1947–8 during the negotiations over the relinquishment of the Mandate, when Ernest Bevin was Foreign Minister and Creech Jones Secretary of State for the Colonies. Thus, although Webb issued an important memorandum on the paramountcy of native interests in East Africa, another instructing local governments to give official support to trade unions in the colonies, though he set up the Joint Committee of both Houses, which, in investigating the Hilton-Young and Wilson reports, summoned natives of the territiories concerned to give their evidence in person, and unified the colonial services, he himself saw little return for his work but controversy and recrimination. It was left to the Prime Minister's son, Malcolm MacDonald, during the second National government when he too directed colonial affairs, to build on the foundation Webb had laid.

MPs were not the only Fabians consulted by the Prime Minister during the second Labour government: Cole and Professor R.H. Tawney served with the Liberal John Maynard Keynes on the Economics Advisory Council to the cabinet. They were asked to determine the chief causes of Britain's industrial condition, how to revive trade, develop markets, increase exports and improve employment prospects; also to define Britain's policy on tariffs, bulk purchasing mechanisms and market expansion in trading with the rest of the Empire.[31] The disorientation of the cabinet and the Society's failure to propose constructive remedies for the world economic crisis, retreating instead into abstract studies of Fabianism and social philosophy, stirred Cole to personal though comparatively circumspect rebellion against the remnants of the Old Gang who still, despite themselves, exerted a disproportionate influence.[32]

He gathered a group of equally troubled friends and launched a new research group to seek practical and long-term solutions to the economic and administrative problems that were bewildering the Labour politicians. Both the Fabian Executive and the Prime Minister approved of his intention to produce socialist inspired reports on existing conditions.[33] This group became the New Fabian Research Bureau. Before it could possibly have any effect on party politics or cabinet action MacDonald substituted the National government for the Labour one.[34]

Fabians differed in their judgement of MacDonald's method for dealing with the economic and political crisis. All those in the cabinet resigned and went into opposition, but the Attorney-General, Sir William Jowitt, a recent member, and junior Ministers Lord de la Warr and G.M. Gillet remained in their posts. Forty-three of the fifty Fabian MPs went into opposition, like most of the Parliamentary Labour Party.[35] When MacDonald appealed to the country on 27 October eighty-six Fabians stood for election as Labour candidates; all but Clement Attlee, Sir Stafford Cripps, George Lansbury and Tom Williams were defeated, yet all six who stood as National Labour candidates were successful.

Webb retired from office for the second time frustrated and exhausted. A draft letter written some time in summer 1931 shows that, out of pure exhaustion, he had earlier broached the subject to MacDonald:[36]

> I feel that I must remind you, now that you will necessarily be considering Cabinet changes, of my wish to be relieved from office. The past two years have taken a good deal out of me; and at the age of 72 I really cannot continue without risk of a breakdown.
>
> I need not say how much I have enjoyed working with you in the job you gave me, in spite of the succession of difficulties with which I have had to cope. It has been a time of absorbing interest to me, and I only regret that I have been unable to be of greater assistance in the counsels of the Cabinet.
>
> I should like to go immediately, but I realize some of your difficulties, and I am also anxious not to create the least impression of differences over policy. It is for this reason that I only ask you to include my dropping out among the shifts that must presently be inevitable. At the latest I feel that I must be free to go away for a long rest in the Autumn; I assume that your other changes cannot well be postponed beyond October, if indeed so long as that.

Webb's frustration and disappointment grew during the constitutional crisis. The irritation verging on scorn from Harold Laski, and Webb's criticisms helped to foster the belief that Ramsay MacDonald had betrayed the Labour Party. Nearly half a century was to pass before David Marquand produced a less impassioned assessment.

Webb first gave vent to his bitterness at the failure of the second Labour government in an article, 'What happened in 1931: A record', published in the *Political Quarterly* in January 1932.[37] He accused MacDonald of smashing the Labour Party, not only by his actions during the sixty-three days when only he knew the full story of what was happening, but even by failing earlier to mix socially with his colleagues, thus creating a bond of personal loyalty, and of wishing to reduce to impotence the troublesome members of his own side. Webb had experienced comparable irritation himself at Fabians declaiming against his own policies at the Colonial Office. Leonard Woolf, Leonard Barnes, Charles Roden Buxton, McGregor Ross and Norman Leys had had no qualms about censuring his restraint in an office which they considered the stronghold of reaction. He should have had some sympathy for the leader of the Parliamentary Labour Party. The only vestige of sympathy Webb revealed was for Snowden, whose disastrous budget was excused on the grounds of ill health. MacDonald he could not forgive, because he believed that he had deliberately chosen to lead a National government in order to 'ditch' the 3 million unemployed, cease paying unemployment benefits and thus balance the budget. To Webb in his seventies, after a lifetime spent in investigating the causes of unemployment and seeking means of preventing it and of combating destitution when there was no work, this was, indeed, the ultimate betrayal. His anger blinded him to the fact that formerly he had been just as willing to make use of those in other political camps in order to achieve what he thought needed to be done, justifying the act with the name of permeation. He fulminated against MacDonald's calling a general election after the immediate crisis had been averted, as he was in honour bound to do. Webb accused MacDonald of employing a number of underhand devices, such as the Post Office Savings scare, to cause a landslide victory over his former party. In the final assessment, however, the shock of Labour's defeat was presented as a blessing in disguise, a catalyst for amalgamating the diverse elements of the party. Webb had, admittedly, gone into the first Labour government thinking it a 'great lark', though doubtful of what it could achieve; he emerged from the second declaring that the Labour Party had been thrust prematurely into responsibility and that its true milieu was in opposition. He foretold that the tasks ahead would be education, attracting members to the party, detailed construction of a progressive policy, continuous publication of socialist propaganda and re-establishment of friendly relations within the party: tasks for which the Fabian Society was specifically designed but did not have the vigour in the 1930s.

As Webb's article reached the public a booklet by Harold Laski, *The Crisis and the Constitution: 1931 and After*, was being set up at the Hogarth Press.[38] Laski there speculated that the idea of a coalition had probably been in MacDonald's mind for some time and that his former colleagues might reasonably feel they had been tricked 'by the employment of a weapon devised for quite a different purpose'. Contrary to his former advocacy of the Prime Minister's essential power over choice of a dissolution, he here argued that the decision next time ought to be a collective cabinet decision. MacDonald was accused of secretiveness, desertion of the Party, of transforming the House of Commons from a policy-making to a policy-accepting assembly, above all of having no faith in the power of socialist legislation. Laski insisted that Labour should not take power again without a workable majority. The lessons learned during the two periods of office and the final debacle became the theme of his lecture to the Society in October that year. His views reinforced the sense of desolation and disorientation among Fabians and in the ranks of the Labour Party.

Laski was not alone in his estimation of the faults revealed in the British constitutional structure. A number of his contemporaries were highly critical of the parliamentary structure, the relationship between Crown and Parliament, between the Prime Minister and cabinet, and between the cabinet and the majority parliamentary party. Many Fabians could see within the framework of the Society no means of constructing a workable reform programme with any chance of adoption by practical politicians. The Fabian tortoise had not sufficient innovative vigour to overcome its carapace of tradition, which weighed it down with out-of-date methods of work and thought. Those who decided to stay in the Fabian Society made a number of attempts in the next seven years to reinvigorate its work, as the last chapter demonstrated. For others Cole's New Fabian Research Bureau with its activist, political twin, the Society for Socialist Information and Propaganda, seemed viable alternatives.

16
THE SSIP AND
THE SOCIALIST LEAGUE

In the 1920s and 1930s Dartmouth Street was not the hub of Fabians'
activity as Clements Inn had been in the nineteenth century. At Westminster and in Whitehall a great struggle was taking place to re-establish
the country's economy by curbing public spending to convince foreign
creditors that further loans to Britain would be ultimately redeemable. In
the universities new economic theories were being hatched which would
unseat those which had held sway for some decades. Many academics then
discussing these theories with Keynes were indeed Fabians: Cole, Dalton,
Durbin, Gaitskell and Meade. That the debate was primarily carried on
outside the Fabian Society was to some extent due to lack of imaginative
energy in publication policy and in the office in particular. Although
interest was still evinced at meetings in Keynesian theories and the other
academic variations, the Society was not being run with its former fervour
and so it lost its position at the forefront of debate. The events leading to
publication of the fifth edition of the original *Fabian Essays in Socialism*
illustrates the lack of drive.

Shaw suggested in 1931 that the Fabian Society should publish a volume
of essays on the constitutional machinery required by socialists to run the
state, written by men of under 50, such as Cole, Kingsley Martin, Laski,
Robson and Tawney.[1] They were all, by then, involved in similar studies
independent of the Society and had lost faith in its ability to promote such a
work. Egged on by Beatrice Webb, who thought such a book of essays
might be the way to get Labour back into power in five years time, Galton
eventually consulted Laski and Robson, who were most deflating, and so
the Old Gang reverted to an established money-spinner – a fifth edition of

the original *Essays* with an even newer preface by Shaw.[2]

Several younger Fabians became seriously worried about the situation in Britain during Labour's second period in office and communicated their anxieties to their friends – economists from the LSE and Oxbridge, younger people influential in the trade union movement and some of the more open-minded and slightly rebellious MPs. At Easton Lodge (owned by Lady Warwick, the mistress of Edward VII who had been converted to socialism by Robert Blatchford) they met for spartan weekends, effervesced with radical ideas and dreamed up a series of conferences. At these, papers by experts were debated for a couple of days at a time by all those with a professional interest in the reform of Parliament, imperial questions (towards which the Labour Ministers seemed to have a particularly uninspired ideological approach), banking and finance, international affairs (where the practice of international accountability seemed to be faltering and disarmament policy rejected), and local government (where socialization was not proceeding fast enough). Meetings of a different kind were also planned, to attract university students, women in the Labour movement and the younger, more progressive trade union officials.[3]

The enthusiasts sought a way to extend their influence even further. Their first idea was to found a newspaper, for which purpose £400 a year was immediately offered by D.N. Pritt, and G.R. Mitchison was instructed as treasurer to set up a fund-raising scheme.[4] They first thought of offering to buy the financially distressed *Clarion*. Ernest Bevin produced a mock-up of the paper, costed the project, and was delegated to discuss the project with Davies of the *Clarion*. Others were moving just as fast. By the end of February a skeletal organization began to take shape and provisional articles of association were drawn up for a company called Tribune Publications, with Bevin, Cole and Mitchison as directors.[5] The paper was to sport a coloured cover with the name 'Tribune' and cost threepence. For about a year great hopes were entertained, but then the idea was dropped as unviable.

Even before their first full conference the group began talking of founding a new society. Douglas Cole favoured two separate societies, one to concentrate on research, perhaps in association with the Fabian society, the other on political activity, chiefly propaganda. There was much discussion in university commonrooms and meetings of all kinds of socialists. Cole drew into his orbit Arthur Pugh of the TUC. Arthur Henderson became so enthusiastic that he offered to host a dinner in the House of Commons to broach the subject of the still nameless society to people likely to be interested.[6] Ramsay MacDonald accorded his acquiescence if not ardent support, while his son Malcolm, a bright, young MP, joined them for a few months until the events of 1931 forced a judicious severance.[7] Pugh warned Cole not to poach on the preserves of either the Labour Party's or the TUC's research departments. Of that there was little danger for Cole intended his new creation to tackle problems of no interest to them.

The first recorded conference was held from 28 February to 2 March 1930, to discuss the reform of Parliament and local government.[8] Ernest Bevin, disgruntled by the inefficient way Labour Ministers were running their departments, was discovered to hold unexpectedly strong views on cabinet structure and so was invited to expound upon them at the conference, seconded by Colin Clark.[9] Bevin envisaged a cabinet of only nine – MacDonald then had twenty – with the Ministers themselves concentrating on policy, relieved of the chore of administration by under-secretaries of higher rank and powers than the existing junior ministers, and the Prime Minister supervising directors of statistics, research and economics and the law officers, empowered to override any Ministerial obstruction. It was a very close-knit scheme, bearing some resemblance to the 'overlord' plan suggested in the 1940s, and offered much scope for discussion – exactly what the Cole entourage delighted in. It excited considerable interest and some very hard opposition. Attlee and Dalton were led to re-examine their own ideas on the subject and each produced a memorandum, some months later. Bevin and Cole also led a debate on the economy campaign introduced by the Government and on unemployment insurance in general. Cole was then chairman of the Government's Economic Advisory Committee's subcommittee investigating the way the national insurance scheme was working.

While this conference was still at the planning stage rumours circulated that a nefarious plot against the Labour Government was being hatched at Easton Lodge. To crush these rumours Bevin and Cole were compelled to issue a statement in the *Daily Herald* on 17 February 1931 explaining that they were doing no more than investigating the problems the Labour movement must face in the future.

The provisional committee used this weekend to 'hammer out' the constitution of the projected research society. Cole told the gathering that he thought the Fabian Society was willing to distribute publications for such a society without exercising control over its programme or their contents.[10]

The Executive Committee had already approved the new venture in principle, but before confirming use of the Fabian name it required fuller details of the society's structure and plans.[11] Approval was more easily obtained for a research body than for a propagandist one and so the scheme of two, virtually independent societies was confirmed. Attlee was soon chosen chairman of the research society, Lloyd vice-chairman, Mitchison treasurer and Cole honorary secretary.[12] Demarcation lines between the two organizations were worked out and, at the next conference in mid-May, the governing body of the Society for Socialist Information and Propaganda was selected, with Bevin as chairman, W.R. Blair, Pritt and Cole as vice-chairmen. Margaret Cole, Beales and Mitchison were honorary secretaries and treasurer.

The society's awkward name was immediately abbreviated to SSIP, pronounced Zip, thus endowing it with a zestful image. At this point E.A. Radice was appointed secretary for both societies, at £400 a year (the amount Pritt was willing to donate) but with only three months' employment guaranteed. Cole announced that the New Fabian Research Bureau had already embarked on its work and that four pamphlets would soon be ready for circulation to members, on Russian trade, disarmament, departmental reform and unemployment insurance. SSIP's plans for a series of lectures in London that autumn were already crystallizing. Cole had drawn up a list of thirty-six speakers and subjects for the Labour Forum series, designed to appeal to trade unionists.

His antipathy for parliamentary politics pervaded the constitution of both new societies. Neither was to be affiliated to the Labour Party, though the Bureau hoped to benefit indirectly from the Fabian Society's formal affiliation.[13] Discussion could then be completely free; although conclusions might benefit the Labour Party, they could not compromise it. However, SSIP deliberately set out to influence the grassroots of the union and Labour movements. A network of branches throughout the country was envisaged, firmly controlled from the centre, to obviate undue influence from extremists. Head office would have to sanction and control any research by the branches and all publications and statements.[14]

By a flood of lightweight pamphlets on topical subjects, in eye-catching red and white covers, SSIP planned to attract attention and prepare the ground for the more serious publications from the Research Bureau. Cole swiftly produced a series of six study guides on the gold standard and banking, capitalism and the principles of socialism.[15] He also wrote the first of the Bureau's pamphlets, *The Essentials of Socialism*, and a tract for the Fabian Society on socialist propaganda, both published in 1932.[16] The range of Cole's work during 1931 was amazing, especially in view of his diabetes. He was writing, acting as an economic adviser to the Labour government, pursuing an academic life at Oxford, setting up two new societies, attending frequent conferences and committee meetings, including those of the Fabian Society Executive.

Some Fabians who had previously not made much of an impression now began to emerge as leading personalities in the new structure. Three younger economists, Colin Clark of Cambridge, Evan Durbin and Hugh Gaitskell, both from the Cole stable at Oxford and then lecturing in the University of London, put their talents at the disposal of the Bureau. Sir Stafford Cripps offered to help raise the £2000 needed for the first couple of years' work, making large donations himself, as did the other rising young socialist lawyer, Pritt.

In some ways organization was very informal. Although while the Bureau was allowed to accept donations from those who were not members of the Labour Party, SSIP could not, yet SSIP soon became the better endowed of the two. The Coles' London address served for SSIP, that of the Bureau was 11 Dartmouth Street, until both bodies rented adjoining rooms in Abingdon Street and shared the services of Miss Jeeves.[17]

Easton Lodge conferences increased in frequency and size. Sessions were highly confidential and no minutes were circulated afterwards, lest frank discussion be inhibited, but full notes were kept of the debate for use in preparing pamphlets.

Even before SSIP announced its existence at Transport House on 28 June, an application came from John Parker, another Oxford economics and politics graduate then working on the government's Manpower Survey in Liverpool, to be permitted to start a branch there. Similar branches were soon to emerge in Birmingham and Manchester. Sixty-nine people joined SSIP that June and several London districts asked to be allowed to form study groups. SSIP rapidly published a pamphlet on Anglo-Soviet trade, which the Prime Minister's Economics Advisory Committee was anxious to promote, and another providing *Facts and Figures for Labour Speakers*.[18] Four others based on conference conclusions were nearing publication and a circular was drafted aiming to recruit members, guide formation of new branches and dispel all doubts about their intention to support and assist the Labour Government's interests and policies. As the government's difficulties mounted so did enthusiasm for SSIP.

Suddenly SSIP's confidence was shaken by the national crisis following the run on the pound in August and a manifesto had to be drafted explaining to new members where it stood. Educational work planned for the early autumn was replaced by electioneering, for which a speakers' panel was swiftly recruited. An election manifesto, *For Those Over 21*

Only, written by Cole and signed by Pritt and Bevin, announced that since the capitalist system was demonstrably breaking down, haste had to be made to replace it with a new social order by taking control of national finance, reorganizing basic industries as public services with planned production and price control, organizing bulk purchase and international barter and confiscating the wealth of the exploiting classes.[19] Radice wrote twice to the Labour Party's research secretary placing the services of SSIP entirely at the party's disposal, an offer which it was little inclined to accept.[20]

Fifty SSIP members stood at the election; only Attlee and Cripps were successful. Bevin analysed the immediate post-election situation at a conference at Digswell Park in mid-November, at which defeated candidates reported their experiences and views on electors' attitudes.[21] Dismay at the result could only be dispersed by determined action. SSIP publication was resumed. Bevin and Cole jointly produced a booklet on *The Crisis*, which was published by the *New Statesman* and very widely read.[22] Joint discussion groups with local Labour Party and trade union branches were formed to resolve points of socialist policy and a programme to stimulate rethinking among members of the party.

Despite lingering Labour Party suspicion, an audience of 150 attended Cole's lecture on the world crisis on 28 November 1931 and three succeeding talks with titles strongly reminiscent of the early Fabian series: 'The way out in home industry', 'The way out in foreign trade' and 'The banks and the crisis'. London membership was only 412 at that time.[23] In the rest of the country there were less than 150 members, even though thirteen branches from Cornwall to Cupar had sprung up. At Transport House, weekly Labour Forum lectures catered for this interest and a monthly bulletin, *SSIP News*, kept the branches informed of each others' work.[24] Cole's wide-ranging list of speakers were not all members of the Labour Party; John Maynard Keynes took his turn with Ernest Bevin, George Lansbury, A.L. Rowse, Frank Wise, John Middleton Murry, Frank Horrabin, Sir Stafford Cripps and Clement Attlee.

A full post-mortem of the disastrous October election, with analysis of the full membership's views on causes of defeat obtained by a postal referendum, revealed that most completely rejected the gradualism and attempt to build a socialist state within a capitalist regime which the remnants of the Old Gang advocated, and demanded more drastic measures.[25] They felt that the Labour Party, lacking a constructive economic policy and still relying on *Labour and the Nation*, had offered the electorate nothing. Like the Fabian Society a couple of years before, they now demanded a short, clear-cut Labour policy statement confined to a few points, with a coherent plan of action. Like the Fabians, SSIP offered to exemplify each point through a pamphlet. Imperative policy points were abolition of the House of Lords by dint of flooding it with new peers, nationalization of the Bank of England, national planning and development to revitalize industry and cut the unemployment figures and a clearly defined monetary policy to combat inflation.

With the Labour Party back in opposition, SSIP theorists were able to indulge in the luxury of devising far-reaching schemes of reform.[26] Outrage at MacDonald and regret at not sacking him earlier was to some extent assuaged by new proposals for choosing and controlling the party leader. It was agreed that the Parliamentary Labour Party was the best judge of a leader and prospective Prime Minister, advised by an NEC forbidden to nominate but allowed to blackball its choice. They even suggested that the PLP should vet the Prime Minister's choice of cabinet, and that he should be required to consult that cabinet before seeking a dissolution or dismissing one of its members.

Cole created the myth that the rest of the world would become hostile to Britain if a Labour government were elected again. He argued that fiduciary measures such as abandoning the gold standard would have to be introduced to prevent foreign financiers ruining Britain's economy. (The National government had to do that in any case within one month of assuming office.) The thorny question of compensation for nationalization was persistently evaded and the question of tariffs shelved with the excuse that the effects of the Ottawa Agreement had to be seen before decisions were made. On the other hand, nationalization of the joint stock banks was fervently advocated.

The chief practical use of the Easter conference had been expansion of plans for propaganda.[27] Study circles in each constituency and monthly propaganda meetings by every local Labour Party were their aims. Dalton, sure that Labour's National Executive Committee would welcome action by SSIP, promised to persuade head office to accept its help to produce brighter literature. Individual members were urged to increase their output of books and pamphlets. Head office was expected to link SSIP with the local Labour Parties and to arrange joint meetings with trade unions. An autumn and winter programme for the Labour Forum, with a series of Friday evening lectures and conferences on Russia, was constructed, regardless of the fact that these would compete directly with the Fabian autumn lectures, then declining in popularity but still a source of revenue to the Society.[28] To ensure that the Labour Forum would be even more popular in its second year, the entrance fee for non-members was to be reduced to threepence.

At this point, spring 1932, John Parker, who had often been consulted on matters of branch organization, expected to take over the management of both SSIP and the New Fabian Research Bureau. Radice had offered his resignation from March in anticipation of being appointed to an academic post at Oxford. Parker had been offered the secretaryship and had accepted. Both young men were disappointed. Radice remained secretary of the two bodies and Parker, having resigned from his Liverpool post, returned to his family home in Bristol where he helped build up yet another local SSIP branch and set it on a course of research while he searched for employment. The matter was sorted out later in the year when Radice departed for America and Parker eventually entered into his true Fabian vocation in London.[29]

A section of SSIP had taken to meeting with a few other members of the Labour Party in George Lansbury's room in the House of Commons on Fridays to consider the causes of Labour's inadequacy. Though Herbert Morrison refused to join the Friday Club, Attlee, Cole, Cripps, Dalton, Laski, Pugh and Tawney all contributed to the discussions, which resulted in the memorandum entitled 'A Labour programme of action', intended to replace the outdated *Labour and the Nation*.[30] Lansbury arranged for it to be placed before the policy committee of the NEC but refused to circulate it to the Parliamentary Labour Party because of the objections that might be raised against some points. Bevin, indeed, complained to Cole about the patronizing attitude towards the trade unions and a thin crack appeared in their collaboration.

Redrafting the memorandum was cut short by developments within the ILP which involved Cole and his colleagues in an attempt to form another political party out of the unhappy remnants of the old. This involvement swiftly brought Cole's organization to an end. At the beginning of July 1931 he wrote to the other members of the SSIP executive that if the ILP disaffiliated from the Labour Party at its Bradford conference on 30 July, as seemed likely, the remnant, forming an individual socialist society still capable of working within the Labour Party, might usurp their own function as its propagandists. Jealous of their power to influence the Labour Party, dedicated to trying to direct the Labour movement along lines of their choosing, his executive asked him to draft immediately an appeal to all branches of the ILP for use if, at the party conference at Bradford, it decided to disaffiliate. This was, in effect, to be a bid to take over the 'loyal' remnant of the ILP. Cole warned the committee that if they were to do this the whole structure of the Society for Socialist Inquiry and Propaganda would have to change.[31] Only a few branches had been found in the provinces, but these were very active; Liverpool had produced two pamphlets of its own, Cornwall a report on the tin-mining industry which had been referred to the Research Bureau as being the kind of work more suited to its form of publication, the Research Series, and Bristol was deep in research.[32]

Although Cole and Bevin disagreed over the principle of running Labour parliamentary candidates a draft appeal was ratified by the committee at the conference at Digswell Park when Laski explained the 'Plan of action for Labour' to members.[33] The conference sanctioned a proposal by the executive that when the result of the Bradford meeting was known the SSIP should formally invite members of the National ILP Affiliationist Committee and other prominent members of that party favouring combining with the Labour Party to join SSIP, which would in turn consider affiliation.

Difficulty in finding members of SSIP to sign Cole's appeal in August – Bevin and Creech Jones were on a Workers' Travel Association cruise – delayed distribution until the situation had changed so much it became irrelevant. The ILP Affiliationist Committee in London, of which Frank Horrabin was the chairman and Frank Wise, Brailsford and Creech Jones leading members, had recognized the need for a new socialist organization which, though it would do work similar to that of SSIP, would have a greater appeal outside the middle class and be able to absorb several small socialist protest groups which had sprung up outside London. The Coles went to see Bevin on the way to Scotland to sound out the Scottish ILP. They devised a scheme to usher in the new organization, which was to be called, nostalgically, the Socialist League, at a meeting in October, immediately before the Labour Party's conference in Leicester.[34]

On his return from holiday Bevin approved the idea of amalgamation of socialist bodies but reminded Radice, who was on the joint committee, that the interests of the Social Democratic Federation, of which he himself was a member of over thirty years standing, should be consulted.[35] He was most disturbed when Radice told him that the SDF took the line that everyone else should join the Federation and that it therefore refused to collaborate in founding the League.

Eventually the ILP section forced the others on the joint committee to recognize Frank Wise as chairman of the League and to accept four only of the ten seats on the national executive, to be filled by Cole, William Mellor, Postgate and Pugh.[36] The SSIP managed to place Margaret Cole, Radice and Mitchison in key positions as officers. Bevin felt betrayed particularly since in the earlier discussion, Mitchison, the Coles, and Arthur Pugh had all agreed with him not to accept Wise as chairman, because he was labelling SSIP members intellectuals while presenting himself as the representative of the 'horny-handed'.[37] Bevin believed, probably rightly, that his own strong, steady hand was needed at the helm to make the League a success. He was so hurt that he refused a compensatory seat on the NFRB committee and thereafter was wary in his dealings with the Cole group.

Ordinary SSIP members, too, were annoyed at their representatives' willingness to give in to the ILP demands. Many SSIP members boycotted the Leicester meeting because of affronts offered by the organizing committee.[38] The Socialist League was, therefore, founded with a scant handful of the SSIP leaders assisting and still hopeful that the new association of socialists might achieve more on behalf of the Labour Party than they were able to do.

Back in London after the conference the executive committee met to work out the details of a general meeting at which it was to report on transactions at Leicester and take a vote on federation. A report by John Parker, who had been sent to sound opinion in Birmingham and Liverpool, had already indicated that the provinces did not approve. Cole had discovered that Scotland was antagonistic and there were mixed feelings in London. Each of the SSIP executive, including Bevin, handed Cole a letter of resignation for use at a general meeting, to facilitate dissolution of the society if members so decided.[39] Gaitskell and Evan Durbin were utterly opposed to the society becoming embroiled in a political quasi-party. They submitted two amendments to the executive's chief proposal to forbid joining the League unless clauses permitting membership of non-Labour Party members and the nomination and financing of candidates at elections were excised from its constitution.[40] Both former pupils of Cole, they remained unflinching on those very matters about which he had declared himself adamant when founding SSIP and on every one of which he had given way in the negotiations. Durbin proposed a merger with the New Fabian Research Bureau whose less spectacular growth was based on much firmer foundations. In effect that took place, though SSIP was dissolved and members transferred their loyalty as individuals. The flexible financial administration now facilitated reallocation of funds to the Research Bureau. Reaction against what was happening in the League gave a considerable boost to the Bureau's work and the slightly increased membership became more fully dedicated.

Considerable damage had been wrought in the process. Cole eventually had to admit to himself that flirtation with the League had been a mistake. After just a few months he resigned from it on realizing that, just like the Labour Research Department, it was being taken over by elements far more red than he was. With patent relief he found he could once more concentrate on the New Fabian Research Bureau's programme of work.

Thus ended the flight of most of the radicals from the Fabian nest, although, until they rebuilt and enlarged it, they were not able to settle down as fully fledged Fabians. Stafford Cripps and Pritt stayed on with the Socialist League, outside the Labour Party, but most roosted happily in the New Fabian Research Bureau.

17

THE RESEARCH BUREAU
AND THE SOCIETY

The New Fabian Research Bureau was designed for stability. People known and respected in the Labour movement, Haldane, Wells, Julian Huxley and Beatrice Webb, were invited to form a Council to advise on its management and assured that research on policy matters would neither overlap with that of any other body nor commit the Labour Party to its conclusions.[1] Seeking no trade union or Labour affiliation, its members would act as individuals. Cole promised that the Council would seldom meet; all he wanted was the prestige of their names.

As the Fabian Society was obviously the most fruitful source of members Radice, after consulting Galton, sent a letter to all Fabians, explaining that the Bureau's aim was to investigate and give its opinion on different lines of policy, not espouse any particular one. It would explore and criticize, but even its own members would not be committed to controversial conclusions.[2] Until March 1933 a statement of its aims and purpose printed inside the cover of its pamphlets stated that it was working in conjunction with the Fabian Society though having an independent membership and constitution. Members would not need to belong to the Labour Party; any non-aligned person wishing to share the work could be admitted as a non-voting associate.

As Beatrice Webb had done for the Fabian Research Department twenty years earlier, Cole drew up an impressive curriculum and *modus operandi* for the Bureau, which was printed and circulated for the guidance of research workers.[3] There were three main committees to control working parties dealing with specific subjects. An Economic Research Committee supervised eight working parties, which divided between them every

173

foreseeable problem connected with nationalization of the productive and distributive industries and control of national finance. New members were asked to volunteer for a group and state their relevant interests and qualifications; Cole advised each working party, in reviewing its particular subject, to bear in mind four themes: the basic definition of socialization, control by government or Parliament, provision of capital and timing of compensation. Preliminary reports were expected at the earliest possible opportunity. Considerable dissension developed between Cole and the other economists, Beales and Gaitskell, over assumptions regarding nationalization. Cole wanted it taken as an article of faith; they thought it had to be justified before inclusion in a statement of socialist aims.[4]

At Easton Lodge in May 1931 a Bureau Committee for International Affairs was formed and presented with a plan of research into the basis of internationalism, international economic relations and the prospects for a planned world economy, together with a survey of existing international agreements.[5] This committee functioned for the next nine years and eventually its members formed the nucleus of the Fabian International Bureau. Some of them, like Leonard Woolf, had been involved in the earlier work on international accountability under Beatrice Webb's patronage. Its work was launched at a conference later that month at which Eric Lauterpacht, of Cambridge, read a paper on arbitration in international affairs, and at which a number of new issues for study were presented, such as a long-term study of disarmament involving an estimate of a 'justifiable police force armament'.[6] Disarmament and its enforcement were then central to Arthur Henderson's foreign policy and his under-secretary, Hugh Dalton, was one of the most vocal at Bureau conferences. Woolf was, inevitably, a large contributor to this particular debate. The International Affairs Committee's scheme of work was less complicated than that of the Economic Committee.

A third major committee, the Political Committee, was destined to work on the constitutional and administrative problems then dominating the Easton Lodge gatherings. Ten working parties were thought necessary to examine the machinery of government, parliamentary and cabinet responsibilities and powers, the House of Lords and the relationship between central and local government.

This immense schedule was prepared in time for the inaugural meeting on 29 May in Transport House. After long, carping debate, it was adopted in its original form, and the working parties settled down to write their preliminary reports. Naturally, as the work progressed, the plan's intricate structure was modified, but on the whole it functioned well for the first five years, and kept everyone busy. Leonard Woolf, who had learned years before to cultivate highly individual political theories within an apparently rigid framework, became chairman of the International Committee. Gaitskell took charge of the economic studies as Cole's assistant secretary and combined with Evan Durbin and Colin Clark to produce some distinctive theories; Harold Laski, though in America at the time, was designated chairman of the Political Committee.

Relationships with other bodies next became a prime concern. Gaitskell proposed that at each executive meeting of the Bureau Radice should present a report of SSIP's activities and vice versa. The Haldane Club, eager to collaborate, was pleased to be asked to act as the Bureau's 'legal committee', since it had been formed specifically to proffer legal and technical advice to organizations of the Labour Party, trade unions and co-operative societies.[7] Though the Coles thought Galton a stick-in-the-mud, he was made a member of the Political Committee and joined a small group examining the railway situation in the light of the recently published Weir Report.[8] For nearly twenty years he had been secretary of the Railway Nationalization Society which then rented one of the rooms in 11 Dartmouth Street; it was therefore unthinkable to ignore him and his experience.[9] The greatest care was always taken not to annoy the research department at Transport House. A proposal that a consultative committee on research might be set up jointly with the Socialist League was consequently very short-lived.[10] The Bureau executive committee was most embarassed to discover six months after Ramsat MacDonald had been expelled from the Labour Party that he was still nominally a member of the Council. Horrified, it instructed Radice and Cole to settle the matter.

The Webbs planned to visit Russia in May 1932 and persuaded Cole that an expert delegation from the Bureau ought to go to observe the economy.[11] A subcommittee for examining ways and means persuaded the *Daily Herald* to commission a series of articles from the travellers, for which £120 was paid in advance. Margaret Cole and several others spent about six weeks in Russia trying to be as objective as possible; illness prevented Cole from joining them. In the event, the *Daily Herald* was unable to print the commissioned articles and Gollancz eventually published their work as a 5 shilling book.[12]

John Parker, as general secretary, made an effort to develop provincial groups. The strongest SSIP branches had transferred their allegiance to the Bureau and now intensified their researches. Cole laid plans for specialist groups in Oxford and Cambridge to tackle the practical applications of economic theories, in Manchester to review ways to expand the cotton industry, and in Geneva to observe developments in the League of Nations; all to be linked by a bulletin or quarterly journal publishing the results of their work.[13] He also wanted to recruit young people active in the Labour movement, on the staffs of universities, in the co-operative movement or employed by local authorities, to act as local correspondents in the large towns and cities, to spread news of the Bureau's work and to send back information on local developments. As soon as the academic year began the Cambridge group was asked to prepare a report on the national financial situation and suggest remedies for the problems likely to face an incoming socialist government.[14] Meanwhile the Haldane Club was studying nationalization and preparing an opinion on the legal forms of wartime regulation of industry by the state and their 'applicability to the problems of a socialist government'.[15] Leonard Woolf's committee worked on treaty revision and international control of raw materials as means of preventing war, because those countries stripped of colonies by the Treaty of Versailles were then complaining of being deprived of access to primary products.

When the Bureau offered to help reshape Labour Party policy for the next election it was told to collaborate with the various subcommittees of its Policy Committee. Laski had already been invited to prepare a paper on the procedure for abolishing the House of Lords and had asked A.L. Rowse to assist him.[16] While Rowse presented a reasoned case against abolition, other Bureau members wanted 600 peers to be created at the next election and Stafford Cripps favoured challenging the existing upper chamber in the first fortnight of the next Labour Government. In 1935 the Haldane Club was asked to draft an enabling Bill.[17]

As each working party reached a stage in its research where it could produce some original ideas and a cogent argument, the subject was thrown open for consideration by the full membership, just as in the early days of the Fabian Society. One such conference on the House of Lords was cancelled in 1936 and replaced by a post-mortem on the recent Labour electoral defeat, entitled 'Winning the election'. Discussions at conferences on colonial trusteeship or foreign policy exerted an identifiable influence on the memoranda presented to the Labour Party Advisory Committees on Imperial and International Affairs, partly because of Leonard Woolf's influential position on both. Vast amounts of background literature, official party statements and newspaper cuttings were collected to assist the research and were extensively used. Individual industries and services were studied intensively with a view to nationalization and surviving working papers record the early thoughts of several politicians and trade union leaders who influenced the third Labour Government's actions.

When the Bureau turned its critical attention to the work of the LCC and London Labour Party it greatly incensed that pre-eminent cockney, Herbert Morrison, who had been wary of the SSIP and the Bureau from the very beginning. Gaitskell modified Cole's original scheme as the work progressed, and when Evan Durbin produced a second five-year plan the roles of several working parties were changed. But most subjects listed in the beginning were at least attempted and study of the structure of local government had been conceived as an adjunct to that of central government from the very beginning. Morrison, however, felt their inquiries were an unwarranted intrusion and almost a personal affront, since he had led the Labour candidates to an impressive majority in the LCC elections of 1934. It remained his kingdom until 1945.

In the 1930s Douglas Cole wrote on average three books a year, some with his wife or brother-in-law. He also edited one a year – William Cobbett's *Rural Rides* and *Letters*, the first volume of Karl Marx's *Capital* and William Morris's *Stories in Verse and Prose*. For holiday relaxation he and Margaret wrote detective stories. In addition, he turned out 117 pamphlets or articles for the Fabians, the *New Statesman*, the *Political Quarterly*, the *Fortnightly Review* and a host of other publications.[18] He would have liked others to be similarly prolific. By the end of 1937 forty-two pamphlets in the Bureau's Research Series had been published, of which he had written three. The Fabian Society produced only ten tracts in that time. The overall impression produced by the early Research Series was that government was a far more professional affair than the Labour movement had previously conceived it to be, and that a really efficient research and policy-making organization was essential if the party were ever to carry through effective legislation on a return to office.

The Fabian Society produced only three tracts in 1938. The Bureau had exhausted the impetus of its first five-year plan of research and virtually completed a second wave of studies. By the Munich crisis it had embarked on more protracted investigations employing three research workers, Polly Hill, Christopher Mayhew and Charles Smith, financed by a grant from Lord Pakenham.[19] A number of storms, chiefly financial, had been weathered by then. For the first three years membership had been under 150 and, apart from a few generous contributions the majority of subscriptions were between 10 shillings and £1 a year. Pamphlets had achieved a certain reputation and membership very nearly doubled as a consequence by 1935; a few overseas members were scattered throughout the Dominions and British dependencies, Europe and America.[20] Income was still far below needs and so the committee changed the rules to permit subscribing bodies; twenty-two joined immediately, including twelve trade unions and a handful of trade councils and local Labour Parties, though lack of interest of these last bodies remained a disappointment. Even so 1935 was a year of financial hardship. The New Fabian *Quarterly Journal* had been created in March 1934 to provide twenty pages of facts and figures, short topical articles and progress reports on the Bureau's research. It now had to be halved because it was proving too expensive in spite of its popularity. An appeal to members resulted in enough special donations for 10 per cent cuts in salaries to be revoked at the end of the year, though Darling, who had earlier been given notice, left for America, taking a lot of Bureau papers with him.[21] His place was filled by John Cripps, who offered to work for a year without pay. Others, like Jane Rendel and Lewis Clive, slaved at research programmes and prepared publications for a mere £1 a week expenses.

These ardent optimists undertook increasing work and in March 1936 they moved to 37 Great James Street, where there was room for future expansion. In the Fifth Annual Report the executive committee recorded six books published as well as twenty-seven pamphlets, and sixty members who had stood as Labour candidates in the general election. The target for membership was then 1000, of whom the Bureau had enrolled just over 400. As world trade improved people began to look beyond their immediate financial worries, interest in politics revived and 212 new members enrolled. Income from various sources, including royalties on their books, rose to £1243 and the Bureau was able to take over a second floor of offices in 1937. Activities expanded in several directions, though again only through the work of volunteers, for whom constant appeals were made. Two dinners were held, at which Jan Masaryk spoke on the situation in Czechoslovakia and Walter Nash on New Zealand's Labour government. An earlier scheme to visit Germany had fallen through for lack of support. Instead, a party of thirty visited Sweden to study its political structure and social conditions. They found the Swedish government most co-operative. A very well-attended conference on its findings was later held in Oxford, and was followed by a small book bearing the same title, *This Socialist Sweden?*.[22]

While the Fabian Society was becalmed it looked hard at what the Bureau was producing on particular points of policy and concluded that an important task remained, to produce in a new series of essays a reinterpretation of the fundamental principles of British socialism in the light of current events.[23] Publicity about the Fabian Golden Jubilee brought a

1   Edward R. Pease in 1913,
first General Secretary

2   Ian Martin,
present General Secretary

3 Sidney Webb by Edward Swinson, 1934

4   Beatrice Webb in the gardens of Passfield Corner, 1941

5   Annie Besant, English Theosophist

6　G.B. Shaw and H.G. Wells

7　'Six Socialists' by H.G. Wells

8 Passmore Edwards Hall, The London School of Economics and Political Science

9 Election handbill for
Graham Wallas, 1894

10   G.B. Shaw and W.S. Sanders at the hustings, Portsmouth, 1910

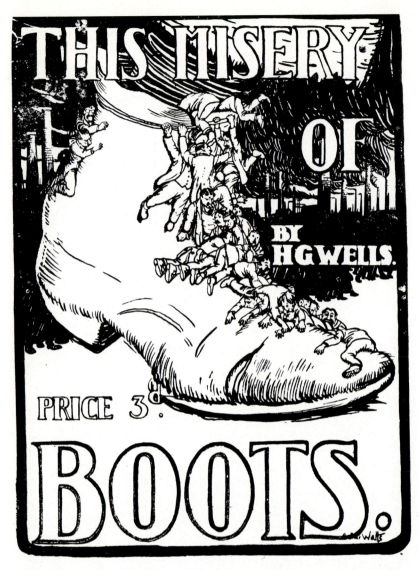

11 *This Misery of Boots* – H.G. Wells's first pamphlet for the Fabian Society, 1905

FABIAN WOMEN'S GROUP

Fabian Tract No. 162.

FAMILY LIFE

on a

POUND A WEEK

———

By Mrs. Pember Reeves.

PRICE TWOPENCE.

12   *Family Life on a Pound a Week* by Mrs Maud Pember Reeves, 1912

13 The young
Leonard Woolf

14 R.H. Tawney
by Vicky

15   G.D.H. and Margaret Cole, *The Bystander*, 20 April 1938

16   Fabian Summer School, Kiplin, Yorkshire, 1926

17   Fabian Summer School, Wiston House, Sussex, 1953 – study groups on the lawns

18 Fabian Easter School, Beatrice Webb House, Surrey, 1953. Left to right: James Callaghan, Bill Rodgers, Tony Crosland, Hugh Dalton, Hilary Crosland and Audrey Callaghan

19 Arthur Creech Jones invested with the robes of a Yoruba chief at the Africans' reception in Lagos, March 1944

20　New Year School, Beatrice Webb House, Surrey, 1964. Left to right: Tom Ponsonby, Peter Townsend, Claus Moser and Shirley Williams

21　Labour Party leadership debate, Central Hall, Westminster, July 1983, organized by the Fabian Society for BBC's *Newsnight*. Left to right: Roy Hattersley, Eric Heffer, Phillip Whitehead (chairman), Neil Kinnock and Peter Shore

22 Centenary New Year School, Oxford, January 1984 – Roy Hattersley and Phillip Whitehead

23 Centenary Summer School, Beatrice Webb House, Surrey, June 1984 – Ian Martin and Peter Townsend at the scoreboard of the Fabian Society v. *New Statesman* cricket match

24 The Fabian Window, ordered by G.B. Shaw in 1910 and designed by Caroline Townshend

small rise in numbers and subscriptions during the year, while bookings for the summer school increased; even so, it was not an impressive revival. In February 1935 the Executive considered closer collaboration with the Bureau and tentatively offered to give it one week of the summer-school programme.[24] The Bureau declined because it was trying to mount an investigation of Nazi Germany similar to its Russian expedition, including a parallel volume of essays.

Galton then parried a proposal by Webb to merge the two bodies, fearing he would be put out to grass if a more dynamic administration were introduced. The Executive yielded to his wishes because he had served the Society with utter devotion never missing a single committee meeting and cheerfully submitting to a cut in salary with extra work when others were dismissed. A couple of years later, however, the Society looked for a second time at the prospect of amalgamation. Its own position had deteriorated, the Bureau's had noticeably improved. Forty-two research pamphlets and eight books had not only attracted gratifying attention, but, read in conjunction, provided a quite impressive socialist programme and survey of policy. The *New Fabian Quarterly Journal* was rivalling the *New Statesman* as an outlet for Labour's views on international and imperial affairs; the Fabian Society was certainly publishing nothing in that line.

As the Fabian Society's effectiveness declined so did its reluctance to contemplate amalgamation with the Bureau. Its retrenchments in 1937 led Margaret Cole to state that soon nothing would be left but the office and Galton, and that if the Bureau waited patiently everything the Society had, its prestige and publishing facilities, would eventually fall into its lap.[25] To strengthen the Bureau's bargaining power a recruitment campaign was launched and reports appeared in the *Journal* of its rapid approach to 800 members. Emil Davies, the treasurer, struggled hard to get the Society out of the red before any serious talks took place. At the beginning of the year there had finally been £1 in the bank after all bills were paid.[26]

On 10 January 1938 the officers of the Bureau finally plumped for amalgamation, fully aware that they would have to adopt the name Fabian Society in the end for the sake of two large legacies which were not transferable to any other named body, and that full affiliation to the Labour Party was inescapable because the Society had devoted too much time and skill to forging a good, working relationship, in which its ideas bore fruit, to jettison it at this point.[27] Yet Galton, fighting a rearguard battle, was still only willing to discuss with Parker further collaboration and adopted several ruses to retain the initiative.

Three or four years later Galton recorded in an autobiography his own reactions to the initial proposals. It is difficult not to sympathize with him for he undoubtedly dreamed of carrying on for as long as Edward Pease. He paid tribute to the good work done by the Bureau and admitted that, in view of the possibility of war, to join forces made sense for the two societies. Sadly, since he recognized that it would involve his own retirement, he felt it was impossible to resist the change. Understanding his reluctance to depart the Bureau representatives, while brooking no doubts that he would have to go, did what they could to cushion him from too sharp a severance.

It took many months of negotiation to settle the terms of merger, partly because the Bureau executive insisted on provision being made for associate membership for persons not affiliated to the Labour Party and that the mandatory signing of the Basis should be dropped. Cole, having won his point over signing the Basis had then objected to adopting the Fabian Society's name because it looked like a Fabian takeover.[28] Emil Davies allayed his fears, emphasizing the Society's lack of drive and its new-found solvency (thanks to a few wealthy backers).[29] The new rules and terms of amalgamation were approved by the Bureau's executive in July: the Fabians took longer to find the right moment.[30] In September the Executive agreed in principle to amalgamate but took another month to approve the much revised rules and the temporary set of rules devised to bridge the gap until the new Fabian Society could emerge from its chrysalis at the first annual general meeting of the joint body.[31]

Ratification of the governing bodies' decision by their members was still necessary and obtaining it was a ponderous affair. The Fabian Society had prepared the way for acceptance by reporting on the Bureau's activities in *Fabian News* towards the end of 1938, giving a favourable account of its summer-school week.[32] The time-honoured ritual was observed of distributing a copy of the new rules with the *News* and summoning members to a meeting on 8 December to vote on the amalgamation. They were warned that a 75 per cent majority was necessary to carry it through and that the vote would be invalid unless a minimum of fifty members attended. On 8 December, eighty-two gathered in the Livingstone Hall, Blanco White explained the rules and Emil Davies recounted the full story of the negotiations and the reasons for amalgamating. A long ritual discussion ensued between many familiar personalities, Mary Hankinson, Amber Blanco White, W.A. Robson, Cole, Hubert Humphreys and the former General Secretary, W. Stephen Sanders. Seventy-eight voted for amalgamation, none opposed, four abstained.

The Bureau's approval was sought on 25 November. Hugh Gaitskell,

Evan Durbin and Leonard Woolf were uneasy about details in the second rule dealing with status of members and their relationship to the Labour Party, but conceded that careful rewording later could meet their objections. Amalgamation was accepted and all was set for a joint co-ordinating committee to finalize the new structure.[33]

Cole wanted to reassure Bureau members that the merger would not destroy the principles upon which it had been founded and so issued a letter as chairman elect of the joint society.[34] He promised that though affiliated to the Labour Party:

> by a self-denying ordinance necessary for the preservation of its objectivity of research and catholicity of membership, it [would] refrain from advancing at Labour Party Conferences any proposition of its own, and [would] aim rather at informing and influencing Labour and Socialist opinion by means of its publications and discussions than at directly sponsoring any particular project.

Claiming, doubtfully, that amalgamation had always been in the minds of the Bureau's founders, he pointed out that this transformation would produce more members, more income and greater prestige. He finally justified adoption of the Fabian name by admitting that a lot of income would have been sacrificed by choosing any other.

Beatrice Webb played her part in reconciling Fabians to the new order by condescending to assume the new office of president and issuing a presidential message which, after summarizing the Society's history, propounded the view that when new bodies emerged and took over some Fabian functions, as the Labour Party had, members helped them to get started and moved on to something new.[35] She directed members to adopt a new attitude to the promotion of socialism, abandon political action and give priority to research because without knowledge socialists could neither cure the two supreme domestic evils, unemployment and the falling birth-rate, nor deal with the disastrous situation in Europe. She applauded the self-denying ordinance. Although she could see that it would be many years before the Labour Party could hope to return to power she did not actually say so here. Instead she prophesied that:

> as research entails attracting intellectuals interested in discovery, [Fabians would] inevitably have a conflict of opinion about immediate policy between those who are to the right and those who are to the left in the labour movement, and those who are neither one nor the other.[36]

That being so, sponsorship of any policy at Labour Party conferences was undesirable. Her powers of persuasion had not faded with the passing years though she was now over 80. Her support of the merger added the final scruple to make it acceptable to both sides. Galton was certainly convinced by Beatrice Webb's argument and adopted it as his own, even though like many other members he disagreed with and was considerably embarrassed by her current enthusiasm for all things Russian. His memoirs assert that, though development of the political side of the Society's work and promotion of candidates had been rewarding before 1931, if the Society was to continue it must, without abandoning the Labour Party, undergo a complete change of tactics and revert to research. Still active and energetic at nearly 72 (in his own opinion though certainly not in others'), he could not stomach reversing the Society's trend for the last two decades and so, with a great wrench, he retired. Edward Pease, too, resigned from his office of honorary secretary at the end of the year. Sidney Webb had been too frail since his severe illness early in 1938 to take any active part in the Society and Shaw had withdrawn some time ago. Beatrice Webb held the presidency just long enough to ensure continuance of the Fabian Society in its new guise and then, in June 1941, withdrew, full of years and honour. Thus one era ended and another began.

18

THE COLONIAL AND
INTERNATIONAL BUREAUX

For the Fabian and New Fabian Research Bureau, as it was ponderously named for the first six months, a formidable amount of work was scheduled for 1939, much of it directed towards methods of socializing selected branches of industry. Lord Pakenham's grant supported three research assistants. Christopher Mayhew's examination of ideas for a national investment board caused a stir among those interested in fiscal policy.[1] Charles Smith's food policy to abolish malnutrition and combat deficiencies in supply and distribution was published in 1940 as *Britain's Food Supplies in War and Peace*. Keynes's niece, Polly Hill, briefed to seek new machinery for dealing with the unemployed and establishing a health service, family allowances and wage regulation, produced another book, *The Unemployment Services*. The International Section completed pamphlets on trusteeship, Ceylon and colonial facts and figures, and Filson made a study of London's success with direct labour and bulk-purchase of supplies. Energy and enthusiasm ran so high that most working parties were able to dissolve within the transitional six months, and a new work schedule was designed which placed Cole, Durbin and Gaitskell in charge of all economic subjects.[2] By July, in defiance of the clouds massing over Europe, the Society was confidently planning a programme designed to recruit new members and support the Labour Party.

Meanwhile a Rules Committee struggled yet again to produce a more generally acceptable Basis than the one Cole offered, with rules defining the role of the local societies. The book-box scheme ceased and books were sold or went on new shelves in the commonroom, now turned into the research room, the realm of Durbin and his new research assistant, Richard

Padley.[3] By June the amalgamation was complete, honorary officers had been confirmed in their positions, Lord Addison elected the first honorary member of the new society, and subcommittees reduced to three, for finance and general purposes, for research, and for tracts and propaganda. Cole chaired two of these and Margaret Cole, as honorary secretary, served on all three. At last they had achieved, and controlled, their desired twofold structure for research and propaganda in a single society.

The first instruction of the Tracts and Propaganda Committee was that Amber White should ask H.G. Wells to revise *This Misery of Boots* for reissue as a probable money-spinner. Material from local branches of the Research Bureau would be used up in 'Facts' for Cardiff and Manchester and a questionnaire sent out in the autumn to discover members' talents and enable the staff to compile a speakers' list. The Fabian structure was essentially the same under its new coat of paint.

The solitary tract by Brailsford on India and the seven Research Series pamphlets published in 1939 were not exactly products of the reborn Society.[4] The most original was *Labour in the West Indies* by W. Arthur Lewis, the young West Indian economist then resident in London.[5] In it he showed why the few MPs interested in colonial affairs, who were impatiently awaiting the report of the Royal Commission on the West Indies, were so incensed about Parliament's and Whitehall's neglect of the Caribbean peoples. Fabian anxiety over developments in Europe produced the book *Hitler's Route to Bagdad*, a series of territorial studies edited by Leonard Woolf and illustrated by the noted cartographer and cartoonist, Frank Horrabin. It was inspired by the best-selling pamphlet, *German and Czech: A Threat to European Peace*, which tried to satisfy public need for a kind of 'Facts on South-East Europe'.[6] Chapters on Yugoslavia, Rumania, Bulgaria, Greece and Turkey underwent repeated revisions as the political situation changed.

Many Fabians cut short their holidays that August and returned to the capital, some even deserting the last week of the summer school. The day after Chamberlain announced that Britain was at war with Germany all the Executive in London converged on Dartmouth Street to determine the Society's role. They decided not to evacuate the office but to safeguard the staff as much as possible and try to complete whatever of the work in hand had not become irrelevant, while buying stocks of paper as a defence against future shortages. Except for John Parker who, as an MP, was exempt from military service, the whole staff was liable to be drafted into the fighting forces or transferred to war work of some kind at any time. Indeed, Christopher Mayhew, a member of the Territorial Army, had already received orders to report for duty. Fortunately they were spared one anxiety: during the holiday John Parker and the assistant general secretary, his brother-in-law Billy Hughes, had despatched copies of all Fabian publications and all important manuscripts and publishers' agreements to a relative's house in Derbyshire, far enough from London to escape bombing.

The Research Committee drew up an entirely new programme, beginning with a definition of the Society's war aims and proposing to observe and criticize wartime legislation, including the emergency Orders in Council which might so easily erode citizens' rights. Help was offered to the Labour Party in all its research, and co-operation planned with the Haldane Society, PEP and the Union for Democratic Control. The current issues of *Fabian News* and the *Fabian Quarterly* were scrapped and rewritten. Cole instantly drafted a new leading article for the *News* on the role of the Society in wartime.[7] Margaret Cole wrote one for the *Quarterly* on government control over the individual and the national economy.[8] She sent out a circular asking for volunteers to carry on the work of the Society and her husband dashed off a pamphlet describing the way the ordinary citizen could safeguard democracy during wartime, outlining the tasks ahead for individual Fabians and the appropriate Fabian attitude during the emergency. Cole emphasized the need for 'clear thinking, determined action and the will to hold together even when we differ upon secondary issues. While men's minds are keyed up by suspense, the chance is ours to organize and redirect the democratic forces.'[9]

Cole's rallying call in *Fabian News* was a rather more explicit essay on the way the newly elected fellow of Nuffield College viewed the Society's purpose. Of prime importance was the formulation of a peace settlement capable of avoiding 'the calamity of a second Versailles and a second abortive League of Nations' while procuring the happiness of all, victors and vanquished. New policies for controlling raw materials and overseas investment and establishing worldwide monetary stability were imperative – policies such as Gaitskell, Durbin and Clark had been modelling in memoranda for the NFRB. He insisted that Fabians had to solve the increasing problems of colonial administration and devise a practical formula for a powerful and acceptable international peace-keeping authority. Careful scrutiny of legislation might enable them to prevent socialist measures introduced in response to the demands of war from persisting as a kind of 'bastard socialism'. The third vital Fabian duty was, as always, to keep people informed of their rights and duties for which a larger active membership was needed. Cole's final trumpet note was that the Fabian

Society was the one socialist body able to remain sufficiently independent to work out the right safeguards for democracy.

The Executive was confident it knew what it was fighting against in this war because of what was happening to socialist friends in Europe. Creech Jones and his Workers' Travel Association had leapt into action early in the year to transport several hundred by train and ship from Prague to Hays Wharf, London, with the last 440 being airlifted from under the German invaders' noses.[10] The year since the Munich crisis had been very educative. Even former pacifists had become convinced that this was a good fight for Fabians. But they had to make sure of what they were fighting *for*. Like the Fabians, the Labour Party was unprepared for the new situation and had invited John Parker to contribute Fabian expertise to its International Subcommittee of the NEC. In an attempt to resolve all confusion a conference was summoned on 14–15 October, entitled 'War – for what?', to coincide with publication of Cole's tract, *The War on the Home Front*. Participants agreed that they wanted a good peace settlement with provision for a free Poland and Czechoslovakia, a truly democratic Germany, universal exclusion of communism, self-government for all those colonies ready for it and the rest placed under an international authority. But no one suggested how all this was to be achieved. Cole's two essays were of far more practical value to the Fabian Society in determining its war aims.

The International Section was the first part of the Society to reorganize, forming a War Aims Committee. Rita Hinden, recently recruited to assist Leonard Woolf in drawing up a colonial version of 'Facts and Figures', was made joint secretary with Margaret Cole. Philip Noel Baker was co-opted to ensure the closest links with those parts of the Labour Party engaged in similar work. Exploratory talks with the editor of the *New Statesman*, the Union of Democratic Control, the League of Nations Union and the Royal Institute of International Affairs were held to define respective spheres of interest. The Fabians elected to scrutinize the League of Nations, the colonies and post-war economic reconstruction. By the end of the year three independent studies had been started by the War Aims Committee.[11] One of these, by Rita Hinden, with the advice and support of Margery Perham, Leonard Barnes, Julian Huxley and Creech Jones, was published in 1942 as *Plan for Africa*. It laid down most of the principles of Fabian colonial policy developed in the first five years of Fabian involvement with colonial affairs.

Activity surged through the Society. The Local Government Section collated material for a book on evacuation problems by Margaret Cole and

Richard Padley.[12] On the international side memoranda received from a number of socialist refugees who had gravitated to Dartmouth Street dealt with the changes in their countries since 1920. Creech Jones, Leonard Woolf and Rita Hinden drew up an ambitious scheme of work on colonial problems while Haden Guest began noting the effect on the colonial empire of blockade policies. The Ethical Union provided funds for Polly Hill to investigate the effects of evacuation and wartime shortages on Aylesbury, a reception area, work taken over when she was drafted into the civil service by Peggy Jay.[13] A War Economics Committee formed under Evan Durbin to study measures of economic control made necessary by the war donated its working papers to the XYZ Club which had already begun a similar investigation.

Early in the new year the International Section, to avoid overlap with Labour Party researches, branched out into activities other than research connected with Anglo-French co-operation.[14] Konni Zilliacus, Tawney, Robson and Henri Haucke of the French Ministry of Information were all roped in to draw up a scheme including a new monthly bulletin. But at this time the Fabian office was so short of paper that it could only mimeograph essential memoranda and as few copies of each as possible. Therefore an old device was revived for the first issue of this new venture: the Fabians asked the editor of the *New Statesman* to publish *France and Britain* as a supplement on 29 June, an unfortunate date because the army in France had by then capitulated and British forces had been lifted from Dunkirk. Nevertheless the Anglo-French Co-operation Committee went ahead with its plans and the *New Statesman* printed four articles on the importance of defeating the Nazis, the causes of France's collapse, the prospects facing the French people and the economic value of the French colonies to the Allies. Once again Cole was responsible for the leading article, Philip Noel Baker, Dick Mitchison and an unnamed French contributor provided the others. By the time the next issue was due the Workers' Educational Association had agreed to print *France and Britain* every other month as a supplement to *The Highway*. The authorities would not condone this expedient for long and the Society, even without an extra ration of paper, had to issue it as a separate publication under its own imprint. All the original programme of closer co-operation and exchange of information with socialists in France was obliterated by the German conquest, but plenty made their way to London and with their help plans emerged for producing a history of the development of ideas on Anglo-French union since 1815. Helped by a refugee, Rita Hinden began preparing an outline of work on the position of the French colonies and the way in which Britain might help them. This was passed on to the editorial board for inclusion piecemeal in the bulletin, which in March 1941 was able to stand on its own feet. In the face of considerable administrative difficulties, *France and Britain* continued to be produced, a little irregularly, until August 1945.

Money as well as paper was short in 1940, but this problem was solved by grants for research from the Sarah Hall Trust created to publicize the work and principles of Robert Owen.[15] From 1940 the Sarah Hall Trust regularly contributed to the domestic research of the Fabians on specific projects, such as paving the way for acceptance of the Beveridge Plan with explanatory literature.[16]

Dr Rita Hinden, who claimed she knew nothing of the colonies until she returned to England from Palestine in 1938 and was guided to work on Africa for the Fabians, had found that initial research very difficult because of scarcity of reliable source material.[17] A discussion with Margaret Cole and Leonard Woolf led to the resolution to set up a bureau for the collection and use of information, both of them insisting that it could only work if Arthur Creech Jones acted as its chairman. Ever since he had entered Parliament he had tried to educate the public as well as politicians on colonial problems. He longed for some such organization and had helped to found three bodies to assist colonial peoples: the Friends of Africa, the Colonial Affairs Committee of the TUC, and the West Indies Committee. He was delighted with the Fabian project, and immediately got to work on it, bringing along to Dartmouth Street any of his papers that might be of use and offering to call a meeting of MPs so that Rita Hinden could explain the purpose of the Bureau and ask for parliamentary assistance.[18]

All four enthusiasts were members of the International Section's committee, and had no difficulty in convincing it of the need for a new department for colonial affairs. Within a month they, with the General Secretary, had devised a means of financing it.[19] Creech Jones had captured the interest of Lord Faringdon and persuaded him to donate £50; £150 more came from a remnant of the grant made for the aborted Anglo-French research. A whole year of Rita Hinden's time was thus pre-empted and plans were formed to raise a special fund to extend the work.

The first meeting of the Fabian Colonial Bureau took place on 26 October 1940, with Creech Jones in the chair.[20] Wilfred Benson of the ILO and Professor William Macmillan, who had helped reveal the neglected state of the West Indies and the African colonies in two books published in 1938, joined Parker, Dr Hinden and Margaret Cole.[21] They formed a consultative committee, with Margery Perham, Sir Drummond Shiels, W. Arthur Lewis, Frank Horrabin, Leonard Woolf and, a later addition, Julian Huxley. Creech Jones volunteered to enlist a panel of MPs to ask Questions in Parliament. Publicity was sought from the London correspondent of the *Manchester Guardian* and Reuter's overseas correspondent, both of whom were thought to be sympathetic. Areas defined for investigation were: the marketing and storage of primary products, especially cocoa, the purchasing price of which the British government had drastically reduced in West Africa in spite of a rising market; possible links between economies in colonial social services and the offer of war gifts from the budgetary reserves of those dependencies; facts on the effects of conscription in Africa for the Native Labour Corps during the First World War (because it was feared that the recent Kenya Defence (Native Personnel) Regulations might have the same results); and the extent to which the recommendations of the Royal Commission on the West Indies had been carried out.

At first there was a certain hostility in the Colonial Office to the new Bureau. Dr Hinden nearly abandoned the project but Creech Jones persuaded her to continue, believing that, if the Colonial Office saw that they were determined to persist and really wanted their facts to be accurate and their comments constructive, the officials would become more amenable about supplying information and more friendly towards the Bureau; and so it proved.[22] Eventually, their sincerity and patent goodwill towards the colonies thawed the Colonial Office and a relationship, friendly as well as businesslike, was established. As meetings of the advisory committee were difficult to arrange under wartime travelling conditions monthly reports on work were sent to each member for comment. The Bureau was given permission by the University of London to use its Colonial Department's library in the Institute of Education, which had an admirable collection of press cuttings.[23] Volunteers with access to colonial newspapers sent relevant extracts. The Public Relations Officer at the Colonial Office began sending it all relevant Ministry of Information News Bulletins. To avoid overlapping with other agencies interested in the colonies, Creech Jones asked the British and Foreign Anti-Slavery Society, the West Indies Committee, PEP and the League for Coloured Peoples to add members to the Bureau's Advisory Committee. The Parliamentary Panel grew apace while Creech Jones personally consulted the experts in the Colonial Office on all manner of problems. As an MP he had direct access to the Secretary of State.

After the Advisory Committee was asked to use personal influence with the press, the *Daily Herald* accepted some notes on the effect in Jamaica of the British ban on banana imports. The editor of the *Manchester Guardian* was very willing to publish articles and snippets of information supplied by the Bureau, while the *New Statesman* immediately printed an article by Rita Hinden on the political significance of the Delhi Conference.

By the time the second monthly report was issued the Bureau was able to list ten different topics upon which Questions had been asked in Parliament for which it had provided the inspiration and background material. Creech Jones was pressing for continued publication of the invaluable series of reports on the colonial territories introduced by Malcolm MacDonald in the last two years of his Ministry and now threatened by wartime economy measures and the difficulties of compilation. More and more newspapers and periodicals were willing to take material from the Bureau: *Picture Post* actually asked for its help when compiling a feature on the Empire, and the *Economist* even offered payment for articles. Cole's admonition to keep a watch on legislation led to the Bureau bringing pressure to bear on the government regarding the virtual suspension of the 1940 Colonial Development and Welfare Act, passed while the small boats were bringing the men back from the Dunkirk beaches.

The Bureau also sought contacts with individuals and organizations in the colonies, in order to get first-hand information. Again Creech Jones was able to supply a list of his correspondents in Africa and the West Indies, and the Advisory Committee produced other names.[24] Soon the Colonial Bureau's post equalled that of all the Society's other sections put together. Apart from dealing with the topics presented daily for its attention, it decided that some major research projects should be undertaken. The first was the way in which the Colonial Legislative Councils worked; MPs having little knowledge of them and the Bureau finding itself unable to help, some very badly worded parliamentary questions were tabled at first, eliciting useless replies.

At the beginning of 1941, Frank Horrabin offered the Colonial Bureau his eight-page journal, *Empire*, with a guarantee against loss in the first year – just what it needed to present its work to the public in a regular, consolidated fashion.[25] An editorial board of Creech Jones, Margaret Cole, Margery Perham and Horrabin undertook to advise Rita Hinden on editing a bi-monthly report on work in progress accompanied by some stimulating short articles and series of informative paragraphs on the colonies and Parliament. Additional restrictions on newsprint dashed all hope of expanding *Empire* but the Bureau's means of communicating broadened dramatically as it became better known. The BBC asked it to participate in a series of broadcasts aimed at Germany on the Labour attitude towards colonial policy (an official attempt to counter the propaganda of the mid-1930s when Germany was demanding the right to colonial territories). Friendly relations with the Empire Section of the BBC resulted in frequent educational broadcasts by Creech Jones on *Calling the West Indies* or *Calling West Africa*. This exercise was as useful to the British government as it was to the Labour Party and the Bureau. The Empire Section of the Ministry of Information regularly supplied the Bureau with press releases and other forms of information and the British Council also took an interest in it.

It soon became obvious that some means of increasing its income had to be found. The Advisory Committee and the Executive decided that membership should be thrown open to the public. For an annual subscription of 7/6d members might receive *Empire*, two Bureau pamphlets a year 'to a value not exceeding 1/-', regular reports on its work, notices of conferences and meetings on colonial subjects sponsored by the Society, and they would also be allowed access to the research material in the office.[26] Even before completing its first six months of work the Bureau had supplied speakers for conferences held by other organizations and received invitations to join their committees. Above all it had become the clearing-house for information on the Colonial Empire long coveted by its chairman, and was of inestimable value to him in his parliamentary work. Its information was of course available to all MPs, whatever their party. The Bureau had to walk a tightrope between not poaching on work being done by the Colonial Office or by Nuffield College in a semi-official capacity and acquiring sufficient knowledge to be able to express a valid opinion when the time came.[27] Both institutions were then investigating indirect rule (specifically Margery Perham's sphere of interest) and the production and marketing of raw materials in the colonies. Rita Hinden, keeping a record of the subjects dealt with by the Bureau, was able to remind Creech Jones or any of the panel of MPs whenever a subject was due to be followed up in the House. *Empire* provided him with a second string to his bow for airing his views on a special subject; it doubled the impact of his speeches in the House.

The Bureau's first opportunity publicly to define its attitude towards the colonial Empire was the weekend conference held at St Peter's Hall, Oxford, in July 1941, on 'The colonies, the war and the future'.[28] Professor Macmillan, Rita Hinden, Sir Alan Pim and Margaret Wrong addressed sessions on the obstacles to establishing a sound colonial economy produced by 'hostile nature' and the conditions of war, and the benefits bestowed by educating the colonial peoples, especially their leaders. In his chairman's introduction to the conference Creech Jones presented, in effect, a declaration of policy. Describing the colonies as Britain's neglected estates he spoke of the government's and the public's responsibility to ensure that in future they were justly treated. Because little had been done to implement the Colonial Development and Welfare Act it was incumbent upon Fabians interested in colonial affairs to insist on its good intentions being fulfilled and that money voted by Parliament be spent for the benefit of the colonial peoples not for that of white entrepreneurs. The Bureau had, in a single year, adopted a strong policy line that it was the right of all peoples to benefit from the natural resources of their own territories, that colonial economies should not be geared to the profit of the white settlers and that since advance towards self-government was only achieved by forcing the British Government's hand it ought to do just that. Rejecting Shaw's concept of international control of colonies Creech Jones asserted that Britain had an obligation to her dependencies and could not cast them off completely even under the guise of granting independence. On the other hand representative government, considered as a first step towards responsible government, could not be granted too soon because all colonial peoples had a right to voice their own desires and requirements. This now became the basic Fabian colonial policy, the foundation upon which all work for the colonies would be built. All who worked for the Bureau were utterly convinced of the value of what they were doing. An exhilaration permeated all they did, even after Malaya's unforeseen capitulation to the Japanese invader had increased the guilt felt on account of past neglect in the colonies. In March 1942 the Bureau held a second conference, in London, to consider the lessons to be learned from the disaster and the apparent refusal of the multiracial population there to join the British troops in the fighting.[29] Conclusions reached were that too little had been spent by Britain on research and on developing the colonies, that the British government was reluctant to grant responsibility to the colonial peoples, that initiative was being stifled in the administrative officers and in the people. A note was sent to the NEC suggesting that it was time the imperial section of the Labour Party's interim report on policy *The Old World and the New Society*, was drastically revised in accordance with Fabian views.[30] The Colonial Bureau thereafter consistently ignored the Society's self-denying ordinance with regard to policy statements.

At this point the Bureau's officers began advocating a Colonial Charter, on the lines of the Atlantic Charter just signed by the Prime Minister who had refused to extend its terms to the colonial Empire. The idea had first been mooted by Lord Hailey to the Anti-Slavery Society, which now collaborated with the Bureau's advisory committee. Three Bureau sub-committees were appointed to study the implication of a Charter laying down principles of social and political development and guaranteeing civil rights to colonial peoples. Their work resulted in three important Fabian publications: *Labour in the Colonies*, which advocated labour departments in each of the colonies and revision of industrial and trade union legislation;[31] *Downing Street and the Colonies*, which tackled the problems of constitutional relationships between Britain and her colonies and the need to redesign recruitment into the Colonial Service;[32] and *Co-operation in the Colonies*, which took longer to complete, there not being the same urgency in the subject.[33]

Throughout summer 1942 Rita Hinden, Creech Jones and C.W.W. Greenidge, the Anti-Slavery Society's secretary, exchanged memoranda on the form the Charter should take.[34] Enthusiasm for it mounted and Creech Jones, speaking at a conference on it in November, vehemently attacked Churchill for his pugnacious reply to the President of the United States that 'We mean to hold our own'. Creech Jones claimed that the Empire conferred no inherent rights on Britain and that the government must, in the future, yield to the colonies' desire for independence.[35] In future Britain would have to conform to principles laid down by an international authority and participate in the world economic organizations needed after the war. Submission to world opinion on colonial administration was obviously different from Shaw's internationalization of the colonies. This ardent championship of an explicit charter was later withdrawn following the realization by Creech Jones when attending a meeting of the Institute of Pacific Relations in Canada that nations without experience of colonial responsibility might dictate unacceptable provisions to Britain and destroy the good work already being done.

During the Bureau's third year, the West Indies Committee was absorbed by the Bureau and became a subcommittee following the death of David Adams, its chairman. It continued raising West Indian questions in Parliament and directly with the Colonial Office, tackling such matters as the transfer of the Jamaican telephone system to a commercial company and the vital need for direct West Indian representation on the Anglo-American Caribbean Commission.[36]

The research committee's members were considered, within the Labour movement and elsewhere, experts on colonial constitutions and labour legislation in the colonies. Whenever the Labour Party Advisory Committee on Imperial Affairs was formulating policy on any subject, it sought the Bureau's opinion formally as well as that of its members on the committee. Gradually more and more of the Bureau committee had been co-opted; Leonard Woolf had been its secretary almost from its conception, and on the death of Sir John Maynard in December 1943 Creech Jones was appointed its chairman. The Fabian Colonial Bureau thus, unofficially, became the research organization for the creation of a Labour colonial policy.

To celebrate the Society's diamond jubilee a volume of *Fabian Colonial Essays* was compiled, though not actually published until 1945.[37] This was the first work to compare with the original *Fabian Essays in Socialism*, thus a symbol of the Society's revival. The colonial essays made no attempt to bring the contributors together in order to formulate an agreed approach. The 1889 *Essays* had evolved from a co-ordinated series of lectures and were edited by a playwright with a sure sense of impact. As editor of this volume Rita Hinden aimed simply to ensure that the authors covered a broad spectrum of the problems to be solved after the war. In the Introduction Creech Jones defined the nature of socialist responsibility towards the dependencies. The final essay, an article by the editor reprinted from the *Fabian Quarterly Journal*, explained the role of the Bureau as the agency by which socialists could discharge that responsibility.

When *Fabian Colonial Essays* were written the Bureau had about 800 members, half having joined in a package deal offered by the main Society whereby those paying the highest rate of subscription received the publications of both Bureaux as well as all pamphlets on domestic issues. The other 400 or so were people who found the Bureau useful but either did not wish to join the Society or were ineligible because of other political affiliations. Among these were many people from the colonies resident in Britain as students, workers or exiles, who frequently visited the office to find help in their personal problems or give information on their own countries. Rita Hinden's and Marjorie Nicholson's warmth and understanding during such interviews secured a whole network of friendship with people in the colonies who trusted the Bureau to have their interests at heart. In this way Hastings Banda and Jomo Kenyatta joined and used the Bureau; Norman Manley, Nnamdi Azikiwe and Sir Stewart Gore-Browne, principally correspondents, also dropped in whenever they had occasion to visit London. While the staff hoped to gain knowledge from them, they in turn hoped to engage the services of the Bureau and to influence its opinions. Officers of the Colonial Service with progressive views while 'beachcombing' also took to dropping in at Dartmouth Street to grumble about wartime restrictions and reactionary views at home which prevented them from introducing the reforms they desired. They harangued the staff about what their charges needed, argued with them, criticized the Bureau's theories and sharpened their wits on Fabian ideas. Sometimes they were inveigled into addressing popular lunch-time meetings of members. Almost always they kept in touch with the Bureau after returning to their own territories. Thus the wartime history of the Colonial Empire drifted into the files of the Colonial Bureau.

Some of what was learned in his manner found its way on to the pages of *Empire* , which was one of the principal means by which the Bureau could reach out to the people in the colonies. Naturally, whenever requested, and even when it was not, advice was sent to individuals, unions or co-operatives in a ceaseless flow of letters to the colonies. Inevitably there were long delays; nevertheless the system worked. *Empire* was used to spread the fruits of research to the colonies, to assure the colonial peoples that their problems, hardships, needs and desires were being kept before the eyes of Parliament and the British government by reports of parliamentary questions, delegations to Ministers or visiting Colonial Governors. British readers were supplied with accounts of the most recent developments in the colonies, stringent criticisms of governmental action or lack of action, statements on what ought to be done about wartime detainees, food distribution, industrial development, international relations, expansion of higher education and so forth; also with homilies on the principles that ought to govern future British colonial policy.

As soon as the Colonial Bureau was seen to be a valuable adjunct a proposal was made to create an international one in its image.[38] Already the Executive possessed a consultative panel of European socialists; it now wanted a team of MPs to deal with international problems in Parliament. A donation of £200 was made for a six-month experiment, with Doreen Warriner as honorary secretary, Delphine Chitty employed as her assistant and a working committee of twelve, drawn from the International Section's committee. It was to study, provide facilities for research by others and stimulate discussion on a socialist basis. Foreign contacts were limited while Europe and so much of Africa and Asia remained in the grasp of the Axis, but direct exchange of views with socialist exiles in Britain, special lectures and conferences were expected to produce agreement on post-war reconstruction and Europe's relations with the USA and USSR. A weekly International Affairs Discussion Group with about seventy members was immediately absorbed. Study groups set up to produce a book on

European reconstruction, edited by Leonard Woolf, soon ran into difficulties because of wide divergence of views between its authors.[39] The book was abandoned and individual chapters redesigned as pamphlets. The discussion had, however, proved useful in clarifying the argument for another book, *When Hostilities Cease*, which was the outcome of a conference on relief and rehabilitation held in December 1942 at St Hilda's College, Oxford.[40]

The Bureau having proved its worth in the first six months, a guiding committee was added to the advisory panel and Konni Zilliacus redesigned the study groups to tackle separately relations with Germany, America, Russia, and France. The last of these was just the editorial committee of *France and Britain* and did little beyond keeping that going. Evan Durbin became chairman of an international economic reconstruction group to continue the research begun by the New Fabian Research Bureau on bulk-purchase, international banking, foreign exchange control and trading agreements.[41]

Almost immediately after the International Bureau's inaugural meeting in the Caxton Hall, which did not take place until 24 January 1942, Philip Noel Baker, its chairman, said he would have to resign because the pressure of his work as a member of the wartime Coalition government was too great.[42] John Parker persuaded him to remain the nominal chairman because a change just then might damage the Bureau's credibility. Leonard Woolf meantime consented to act as the working chairman. Noel Baker continued to serve the interests of both the Society and the Labour Party by including Fabian recommendations in the party's official policy statement on international reconstruction.

Following the inaugural meeting when membership was thrown open to individuals numbers rose to 400, including representatives from twelve countries. Because the prime intention was to encourage discussion between European and British socialists the Bureau placed far greater emphasis on conferences and demonstrations than did the Colonial Bureau. May Day International Reunions were held annually in London, attracting audiences of about 700 and the attention of the BBC. For 1943 the programme bore the warning that: 'A rehearsal will be held at 3 p.m. of The Internationale, since the singing of it at the end of the Programme is to be recorded' – a wise precaution because few knew the words.[43]

In 1941 and 1942 Londoners spent most evenings in air-raid shelters. Those on duty in makeshift ARP or ambulance unit quarters, with time on their hands between raids, needed something to ward off the nightly tedium. Soon the Bureau's panel of speakers was in great demand to present short talks on the current situation and the probable post-war scene. Weekly meetings were organized to brief the speakers on the Bureau's most vital concern, post-war relief and rehabilitation. The BBC used recordings of parts of the St Hilda's conference for home and overseas broadcasts, especially those beamed to the fighting forces and to Europe. To capture the interest of Americans and instruct them in the problems Europe would have to face after the war, 1000 copies of *France and Britain* were sent to an agent for distribution in the United States. Groundwork for this propaganda was done by the study groups through a whole series of conferences held in uncomfortable wartime conditions, some involving the main Society, others only the Bureau. At these the tricky problems of reparations, displaced persons and the status of racial minorities were analysed at great length. Brailsford's Penguin paperback, *Our Settlement with Germany*, was written partly as the result of one such conference. A series of public lectures was also arranged to precede the presentation of the resolution on reconstruction by the NEC Policy Committee at the 1943 Party Conference. Several Fabian memoranda were submitted to the Advisory Committee on International Affairs on Britain's post-war attitude towards ex-enemy states and the need for medical and other voluntary relief organizations to be granted immediate ingress to countries on their liberation.[44]

Bureau publications were distinguished from other Research Series pamphlets by yellow, blue or striped covers, instead of the usual plain red. Rousing titles were chosen by the International Bureau, such as *Help Germany to Revolt*.[45] Some European socialists, like Dr Paolo Treves, found in the *Fabian Quarterly* a medium for publicizing their own views and little known facts about their countries.[46] With heavy workloads, war service and a rapidly changing map of Europe members of the Bureau tended increasingly to make use of the *Quarterly*. One or two of their articles could be found within the pages of every issue. In that way it was possible to kindle such enthusiasm for the post-war international scene that, late in 1944, conferences on the post-war settlement were held in eight different towns.

By that time the tide of war had turned and it was possible to look forward to the end with some certainty. French, Belgian and Dutch friends wound up their affairs in Britain and prepared to return home to shoulder the tasks of reconstruction. Accordingly, in October a farewell gathering was held, when letters bearing good wishes and signed by members representing twelve different countries were handed to those present and despatched to those already departed. Some had been members of the short-lived International Youth Forum, sponsored by Lord Faringdon to encourage contact between the younger exiles. Lectures and schools for American servicemen stationed in Britain had also been organized, as Bureau members, fearing that American money might be used to suppress socialism in Europe after the war, wanted to educate the young servicemen in the principles of Fabian socialism.

In that last year of the war Creech Jones, as chairman of the Parliamentary Labour Party's newly formed International Committee, employed the same technique as he had used on behalf of the Colonial Bureau to rouse the interest of MPs in international problems and to get a concerted programme of Parliamentary Questions put to Ministers in order to extract, piecemeal, government policy statements.[47] Through him, as an MP, the services of the International Bureau were continuously placed at the disposal of the Parliamentary Labour Party, while the influence of the chairman, Leonard Woolf, was exerted in the party's Advisory Committee.

When the war in Europe at last came to an end, in May 1945, the International Bureau discovered with some surprise that, while absorbed in the problems of post-war reconstruction in Europe, the kind of international settlement envisaged by the rest of the United Nations and the Labour Party's policy statement on the Atlantic Charter, it had lost sight of its duty to spread socialist theories. Nothing could be done about that until after the general election. With Labour's victory many of its most active members were drawn into the government. It was then time for the International Bureau to rethink its aims and attitudes and seek a new role in the post-war world.

In contrast, the Colonial Bureau was well assured of its post-war aims, which were not directed to imposing socialism upon the rest of the Empire but to fulfilling obligations and responsibilities identified during the last four years.

By the time Labour came to power in summer 1945 colonial policy, which the party had for so many years treated in a very cursory manner, had been studied, debated, elaborated, criticized and honed down to desirable goals by the Fabian Colonial Bureau. The prime goal consisted of granting to each colony the greatest extent of self-government of which it was capable: representative government, which some territories possessed already; responsible government, towards which some were moving fast; finally, complete autonomy. It was hoped that all who achieved the last would appreciate the advantage of mutual support and choose to remain as independent states within the British Commonwealth. The Fabians now understood that purely constitutional reform would produce a very unstable structure unless each country achieved a viable economy, run by a population sufficiently educated to handle the machinery of democratic government and to assume responsibility for public services developed to such an adequate level before independence that they would not later present insoluble problems of maintenance. No one realized then just how little time remained to prepare the individual territories for independence. Not only members of the Bureau but also those who served in the Colonial Office, the Crown Agents and the Treasury believed that the gradualist approach, punctuated by the occasional leap in the dark, would achieve most of the desired aims. They all placed their faith in a redesigned Colonial Service, embodying trade unionists, technical experts of all kinds, men with industrial and business experience, to augment the administrative, educational, health, veterinary and forestry services to provide this necessary preparation for devolution of power. A redesigned Colonial Service was expected so to utilize the funds decreed by the Colonial Development and Welfare Act that the former Empire would become productive, gain self-confidence while progressively assuming responsibility and, under the protective benevolence of the United Nations, be transformed from a British liability to an asset to the whole post-war world. There was neither enough time nor international trust for this to be achieved.

Disillusionment also lay in wait for the International Bureau, which hoped that the friendships formed during the war would eliminate national self-interest as the guiding principle of world politics and substitute post-war international co-operation, so that Britain and France, with the rest of the European countries at their back, could play an effective role in the balance of the Great Powers. Knowing that the map of Europe would be redrawn by the peace settlement, the leaders of the Bureau could do no more than hope that those practical measures for international co-operation to achieve reconstruction, constantly discussed by them and their socialist guests during the previous two or three years, would indeed build a friendly Europe and eradicate the bitterness of inter-war grievances. No one then foresaw a Cold War, a Berlin Wall, a Korean War and the formation of antagonistic blocs within the General Assembly of the United Nations Organization.

19

THE HOME FRONT

The two Bureaux had spent the war trying to disseminate information on their areas of interest. Domestically, far more groundwork by way of research, clarification of ideas, speculation on ways and means and publicity had already been done by 1939 to construct a route to social regeneration, although there was no guarantee that its work would be used. However, Fabian opportunists, led by the Coles, were convinced that the war should be accepted not only as a challenge but as a substitute for the revolution formerly assumed to be the precondition for creating a Utopia. An opportunity to follow his Fabian bent under government and university auspices was offered to Cole and he seized it, dragging the Fabian Society along with him.

There was, of course, considerable fumbling at the beginning. For the first three months of the war its officers merely cruised along a familiar route offering Labour leaders pamphlets on local government, financial policy, economic organization and political and social development, until they had exhausted the fuel in their tanks.[1] At the beginning of 1940, however, the Executive was virtually remanned because of resignations from many who had been scooped up to work for the government. Richard Crossman, Creech Jones, Molly Bolton, Ernest Davies and Mary Sutherland were co-opted in their stead, the pattern of work changed and the Coles took a more determined hold on the Society's management.

At this point Douglas, in Oxford, had to work to a large extent through Margaret. Her first mission was to wake up the Women's Group and mobilize it for an investigation into the fast-changing relationship between family and state. From February 1940 group meetings, suspended because of the difficulty of finding some safe place to meet, were resumed. The annual general meeting was announced, the annual dinner revived, to honour women doing notable war-work. The speakers' panel was brought up to date in the hope of influencing and educating co-operative associations and women's groups within the local Labour Parties. Because of wartime duties and worries few women responded to requests to speak, or to the questionnaire sent out to discover what such groups and the trade unions wanted the Fabian women to work on.[2] Nevertheless lunch-time meetings and a conference were arranged so that busy women might obtain some mental refreshment by considering the role of women in the 'new order'. Subjects discussed ranged over marriage and women's economic independence, children's allowances and provision for maternity and for children under five. The fact that Fabians were still discussing these matters raised thirty years earlier is itself revealing. Little had happened to improve the separate economic position of women in that time, though a certain progress was traced in provisions for their and their children's physical well-being. The Group's minutes imply that members were not very interested in its activities. The war brought too many other problems, too many fears to cope with.

After several false starts the Group resumed a study initiated during the First World War on the emergency decisions and new practices in industry and elsewhere which would have a profound effect on women's post-war employment and rehabilitation. A joint committee requested by a conference of thirty-one women's organizations was set up to examine developments in women's employment, including union agreements. Members of five professional associations, eight trade unions and the TUC sat on this Fabian committee and two part-time workers were hired to handle the paper-work and analyse the committee's findings. Unfortunately the TUC became reluctant to allow the committee facilities for studying the wage structure of manual workers and so the investigation could not be as comprehensive as originally planned. Despite this drawback a useful report was produced on women in the professions, the civil service, teaching, nursing, medicine and local authorities; it was debated by the committee and submitted as evidence to the Royal Commission on Equal Pay. No trace of all this paper-work remains in the Fabian archive; it must have been sent for recycling during the big salvage drive in 1944 which removed a considerable amount of the Society's accumulation of routine material. Before it disappeared Margaret Cole used it to produce a Fabian tract.[3] No other major project was undertaken, although Violet Creech Jones produced a useful pamphlet on nursery education and several individual members of the Women's Group contributed to the book on the social lessons learned from evacuating children from London to the country.[4] At the behest of the Ethical Union and with the moral support of the Group Doreen Idle produced a monograph on how the social structure and life-style of one borough, West Ham, had been changed by the bombing; it contains many observations on social criteria for town planning which are being presented as entirely new discoveries today.[5] Towards the end of the war, members began to feel that the need for a separate group for women had disappeared. Once again a war had propelled women considerably further towards the achievement of equality with men. They began to feel that their work should be conducted, in future, within the main Society, and that it was counter-productive to act as a splinter group. Although, for reasons of sentimentality and companionship, the Women's Group continued until 1948 it was doing little but meet for dinner, and so it dissolved.

Meanwhile a different development, with Cole at its centre, engaged the Fabian men. In spring 1940, while old members of the Research Bureau were taking heart at the government's use of their earlier work on malnutrition and food distribution, Ernest Bevin appealed to his former collaborator, Douglas Cole, to work with William Beveridge on the official Manpower Survey. This sparked off a Cole research project running parallel to the Fabian Society. Douglas and Margaret swiftly roped in friends and acquaintances, many of them Fabians in universities and adult education bodies, in schools and local authorities, to gather statistics on manpower needs and supply. Andrew Filson became Cole's assistant at the Ministry of Labour, while John Parker, Billy Hughes and the research secretary were all allocated sections of London from which to collect statistics.[6] The authorities knew that in fact their greatest difficulty would be not unemployment but mobilizing a sufficiently large supply of workers to satisfy industry. Cole laid down guidelines for the inquiry and organized collation of the returns, all at top speed because Beveridge had to produce a report for Parliament to act on in September. Cole, like Webb in former days, could not bear to see a good working organization disintegrate if it might be diverted to other uses. He therefore persuaded the Hebdomadal Council of Oxford University that the machinery of the Manpower Survey should be converted to preparing the ground for post-war reconstruction by the government, and that it should be supervised by committees with a base at Nuffield College, of which he was then sub-warden. Cole convinced the cabinet, Treasury and other government departments that urgent social and economic reconstruction after the war would require far more reliable information on probable conditions, resources and, above all, desirable goals, than had been available after the First World War, and that his machinery could produce it. Arthur Greenwood, as Minister without Portfolio responsible for the Department of Reconstruction, obtained from the Treasury £5000 in February 1941 for the Nuffield College Social Reconstruction Survey. For this domestic survey and a parallel research programme on the colonial Empire, under Margery Perham's control, the university authorities made the college a grant of £10,000. Cole was once more in his element. As Director he was able to identify subjects for research, and assign them to suitable academics. The starting-point was always the information requirements of a particular Ministry, but responsibility for breaking down such requirements into manageable sections was delegated to Cole and the relevant committee in Oxford.

To ensure co-ordination, a Wartime Research Committee was created, consisting of academics readily available for frequent meetings in Oxford, nearly all of whom were serving on the interactive committees responsible for different aspects of the investigation. Academics of all levels were mobilized for Cole's grand new scheme of research into the redistribution of industry and population caused by the war, the effects of this on local government and the social and education services, and their long-term implications for restoration or reconstruction in peacetime. Changes in Europe's industry resulting from German occupation would undoubtedly affect post-war British industry. The University's Institute of Statistics and the research and propaganda branch of the Institute of International Affairs which had taken refuge in Balliol College were therefore enrolled for a third survey to collect information on Europe, forecast Britain's capacity to meet post-war European needs and to work with the international agencies that would have to be created to organize trade, investment and finance. The Wartime Research Committee did its best to co-ordinate and control the domestic, international and colonial projects and keep them aligned to the purpose for which they had been instituted. It was a virtually impossible task despite the fact that Cole was employing the same structure of diverse studies linked by conferences which had operated so well with the New Fabian Research Bureau. Two series of weekend conferences were held, one to assemble local investigators and work out lines of inquiry and the format for their reports, the other to bring together some investigators, civil servants and other experts on specific subjects to review material collected and pool experience and ideas on a particular problem. Afterwards memoranda were drafted, circulated for criticism and after revision sent to the client Ministry. Names of leading Fabians peppered the attendance lists. Often, however, government departments wanted the information before it had gone through this sifting, and were then disappointed with the raw information presented in a variety of forms. Conditions of war militated against efficient, purposeful production.

At first Cole had difficulty in obtaining access to official information for his investigators, a difficulty that was never wholly overcome. Many officials remained unconvinced of the Survey's post-war use because they could not prognosticate the facilities upon which they could call. These doubts influenced the Treasury when, some months after the major government reshuffle in 1942, a dispute arose between the Government Reconstruction Secretariat and the Survey over the right to publish or even circulate its reports and memoranda, which the former considered to be official documents. The Treasury refused to renew the general grant and stipulated that any Ministry commissioning an investigation must finance it from departmental revenue. Much of the work had to be wound up at speed, and individual investigations into many industries curtailed, though the Scottish Office, the Board of Trade and Ministry of Works and Planning, remembering the depressed areas of the 1930s, issued a new mandate to the Survey to complete the studies on location of industry in these regions. Frequent disruptions caused by the conscription of research assistants and by secondment of senior investigators to government departments compounded these difficulties. Cole himself spent much of his time in the Paymaster General's office engaged in Webbian socialism – drawing up post-war policy recommendations for the reorganization of water, gas and electricity supplies. An attempt to find out what the ordinary man would need and desire in peacetime, by getting adult education bodies to run study groups and classes geared to the work of the Survey, failed to produce results and reflected badly on it.

At the height of its activity, problems of overwork, faulty communications, co-ordination and presentation arose and repeatedly 'interim reports' had to be handed to a Ministry in the hope that a fully considered one might follow in a couple of months. By mid-1943 tailoring the research to government demands and funding became impossible. Access to confidential papers had been withdrawn and the steering committee was told by the Board of Trade that all future reconstruction work would be official and the Survey's lot would be to prepare material for writing up in the department. A clean break was preferred and Nuffield College made itself responsible for finishing off the work in hand and, publishing anything suitable. Accordingly the London office was closed, staff was reduced, the various divisions of research were amalgamated and eventually absorbed into the normal work of the college, when it was granted full status and the Hebdomadal Council relaxed its control. Several reports of conferences were later published by the Oxford University Press. After preparing one of these, *Employment Policy and Organisation of Industry after the War*, Cole, worn down by events, was granted sick leave in June 1943 and withdrew to Dartington Hall. A.D. Lindsay, a Fabian colleague from early days in Oxford and now Master of Balliol, acted as temporary sub-warden and director of the Survey while it was running down. Guiding committees for research into education, social services, local government and industry were reconstructed under the guidance of several who had played a large part in the Survey, Thomas Balogh, R.C.K. Ensor, Michael Fogarty and G.D.N. Worswick. Thus, though Cole resigned his directorship of the Survey in January 1944 and his fellowship at the end of the same term, the shadow of the Fabian Society still hovered over Nuffield College.

Yet any claim that the Fabian Society created Nuffield College or dictated, then or later, what its work should be would grossly misrepresent the relationship between the two in the 1940s. When the College was created economics, administration and sociology were deemed to form the main part of its studies, with an interchange between the business world, industry, officials of central and local government and academics. A number of academics attracted to work in this field were also attracted by the Fabian Society. Gravitating towards the college, they became involved in the Survey, but when it was wound up their studies continued within the college and developed along individual lines. The Fabian Society has always paid considerable attention to the results of those studies, which have remained highly relevant to its own concerns, and there have always been Fabian members of the college, as there are of social studies faculties throughout the country. Warm tribute was paid to Cole at the termination of the Social Reconstruction Survey that he had never tried to impose his political predilections on the work nor its members.[7]

The Society's research had, inevitably, run parallel to that of the Survey, having been concerned first of all with elucidating the arguments which led up to the *Report on Social Insurance and Allied Services* of 1942 by William Beveridge, and then with a study on the control of industry. From the first emerged a book on social security embodying the Society's evidence presented to the Beveridge Committee, which used a great deal of the material garnered during the previous decade on social needs and deficiencies, and the conclusions reached on viable solutions and remedies. The other study produced a compilation of the expert Economics Committee's views on wartime control and its implications for the post-war world.[8] With the third book in hand at the end of 1942, *War over West Ham*, they provided a complete picture of the social condition of Britain at that time with a sober, but optimistic view of what could be done to change it by the introduction of socialist measures.[9] Meanwhile Research Series pamphlets visibly benefited from involvement of individual Fabians in investigations for the Survey. One of the first tasks of 1943 was to enquire of Sir William Beveridge whether he was setting up any organization to promote his *Report*, since some civil servants and members of the government were less enthusiastic about the principle of social insurance after its publication than they had been while it was being drafted. Beveridge preferred to leave lobbying to others and so the Society prepared to collaborate with the Labour Party and the TUC in educating public opinion, by supplying public speakers, articles for the press, pamphlets on related questions and briefs for MPs. For six months a Fabian Social Security Committee exerted every effort to promote the report's recommendations and to launch the all-party Beveridge Social Security League.

In mid-1943 G.R. Mitchison had become chairman of an Advisory Home Research Committee to co-ordinate the work of an Industrial Group, the Women's Group and various subcommittees tackling domestic problems in a rather haphazard way.[10] A triple structure for research was thus completed, covering all home, international and colonial research.

Frank Horrabin, six months after giving *Empire* to the Colonial Bureau, offered his and Julius Lewin's publishing company, Palm and Pine Ltd, to the Society.[11] Creech Jones soon joined Horrabin and his wife Winifred, and Leonard Barnes as a director of the company. *Empire* consistently ran at a loss which had to be made good by donations from the directors. When the Executive accepted the gift, Margaret Cole, Emil Davies and John Parker each bought fifteen shares and completed the complement of seven directors. On acquiring its own publishing company the question of whether the Society could produce a monthly journal arose; for the first of many times the Executive reluctantly concluded it was not a viable proposition. In December the company's name was changed to Fabian Publications Ltd. The Society thus gained protection from any libel claim, potentially a great asset though never realized.

At the end of 1942 Cole resumed control and redefined the policy and scope of the Fabian Society.[12] He concluded that most of its contemporary work was neither true research nor propaganda, being more a matter of finding an expert, persuading him to write a paper on his speciality and publicizing this knowledge and the conclusions to be drawn from it. Time had come for a new programme to be worked out. Cole advised a loose liaison with other sections of the Labour movement to avoid overlapping. To tighten up research the secretaries of the three departments formed a Staff Consultative Committee which met every two months to report on progress but took no initiative as regards the subjects of research.[13] Rita Hinden criticized the home department for not combining political action and research and suggested it adopt an adviser like Creech Jones.

The Home Research Committee concentrated on studying the implications of full employment, completing a book by several authors on industrial controls (later rejected by the Coles as being in too much need of revision before it was fit to publish), and preparing a series of amendments to the Education Bill, most of which, it later claimed, reached the Order Paper of the House of Commons.[14] Under its more efficient regime pamphlets poured out in 1944 and 1945; anything else worth publishing found its way into the *Quarterly Journal*, providing a comprehensive, contemporary view of Fabian predilections. Margaret Cole produced a synopsis with a strong historical bias for a second volume of *Fabian Essays in Socialism* to mark the Society's diamond jubilee. When the Home Research Committee rejected it, she tried to turn it into a pamphlet on the history of the Society. The subject grew as she thought about it and eventually it emerged as *The Story of Fabian Socialism*.[15] A synopsis by Cole for a new volume of essays was rejected as too personally biased. In March 1945 the Research Planning Committee, judging education and industry to have had enough attention, began looking at fields neglected in the past five years: foreign trade, currency and investment, international political relations and domestic politics and administration. Now, with the war nearly over and the prospect of a general election in the near future bringing back party politics, constitutional and political problems once more attracted the Fabians.

Politics had not been entirely neglected during the truce between the parties under which by-elections were avoided by filling any vacant parliamentary seat with a member of the same party that had won it in the 1935 election. A new Socialist Propaganda Committee in the early 1940s re-created local societies and political education in the provinces.

At the amalgamation the Fabian Society had only nine local societies, which merely paid affiliation fees and received a ration of literature. They disappeared in 1939. A decision that wherever possible local groups should be encouraged only brought two into existence. Yet in the next annual report eleven active societies were listed. The oldest one, Liverpool, had recovered after suspending activities at the beginning of the war and news was received of a vigorous society in South Australia, the Victorian Fabian Society, which is even more active today.

This, then, was the pattern at the end of the phoney war when London Fabians, dispersed in the provinces, began to feel deprived of political and social activities. Since wartime disruption focused attention on social and economic problems, some base for discussing ways of re-creating society after the war was obviously needed. Fabians all over the country wanted some guidance from Dartmouth Street on what to do and so they were encouraged to monitor BBC foreign language broadcasts and tell the General Secretary what they thought of them. They were also given the customary exhortation to spread socialist views through the local press and in local discussion groups.[16] But at the 1941 summer school, students clamoured for clear and continuous direction on the best way to work for socialism. Inspired by Russia becoming one of the Allies, they wanted to revive the high, ethical enthusiasm of Blatchford and Hardie and to carry it to those outside the Labour movement. Cole promised to do something and within weeks invited the Labour, trade union and co-operative movements to a conference in London to consider forming a new organization for socialist propaganda.[17] He did not envisage a specifically Fabian body but a more general organization geared to sending out propagandists to speak to small groups about socialist principles and the way they could be applied, first to winning the war and then to building a socialist commonwealth exploiting and controlling science, technology and industry to the full. Leading Fabians, trade unionists and Labour Party members met in private the day before his conference and persuaded him that his scheme would work only if set up under the auspices of, not in competition with, the Fabian Society. The delegates accepted this idea and the Fabian Executive instructed the Coles, Victor Gollancz, who had been the chief instigator of the demand for action at the summer school, and a few others to make a feasibility report. In his memorandum on the new organization Cole offered to donate the royalties of his latest book to its work. Other donations flowed in and, within three months of the summer school's first demand, a new Committee for Socialist Propaganda was in residence in Dartmouth Street, under the general control of the Executive and, moreover, with the blessing of the Labour Party.

The original plan was very ambitious, demanding one committee for finance and administration and another for controlling methods of propaganda. Cole always tended to think big but this time he had to compromise, and the result was very different from what he had first imagined. Nevertheless, considering the restrictions of wartime, a great deal was achieved. Speakers were briefed in classes and by notes for visits to discussion groups in army and air-force camps as well as groups of civilians in factories or private houses. Still obsessed with the idea that the greatest defect in socialist literature was a lack of short, simple pamphlets to explain socialism to different sections of society in their own language, Cole set about writing the *Fabian Letter Series*. It was in this that the detective-story writing side of Cole came to the surface. In *A Letter to a Soldier*, assuming the guise of a soldier of some two years standing, he wrote as to a friend he had made when they were both recruits, sleeping, washing, eating and parading together, to have 'another shot at' turning him into a socialist and at persuading him of the value of planning in the post-war world. *A Letter to an Industrial Manager* reads very much like a proposal for a merger from one businessman to another. This was the sort of publicity and propaganda that Cole had wanted to distribute through SSIP but had not quite achieved; now the time was right, and others began to add to the Letter series.

Communal living and enforced dependence on strangers for protection and support impelled young people towards socialism in those dangerous years. Fabian undergraduates were clamouring for a new university socialist federation of some kind to canvass universities where no socialist club existed, provide advice on propaganda, allocate subjects for research and organize vacation work-parties in the war industries or trade unions. They also demanded Fabian weekend schools where they might learn leadership and modern methods of propaganda. Plans were made to raise £350 for a University Socialist Union.[18] Harold Laski, the Fabian chairman, favoured the scheme and led the guiding committee of Fabians and six representatives from academic institutions. He wrote a very handsomely printed leaflet on the aims and objects of the union entitled 'Student manifesto'. Although university societies were formed, no organization to train undergraduates materialized.

Publication was actually the most difficult part of the Socialist Propaganda Committee's programme. All forms of publishing were beset by three intractable problems: shortage of staff, paper and transport. A 'Socialist news commentary' planned for distribution to the fighting forces would only be feasible if a failing periodical could be taken over by the Committee, at no cost to itself, because of the government prohibition on new journalistic enterprises. Publishers were wary of handling the committee's literature because for Fabians to attract a buying public, costs and profits had to be cut to an absolute minimum, though Victor Gollancz was willing to help over booklets and more substantial material. The idea of the 'Commentary' was reluctantly abandoned.

When Gwynn Llewellyn Jones, the Fabian Society's organizing secretary, was appointed secretary to the Propaganda Committee, in summer 1942, Dorothy Fox became his assistant, embarking on more than thirty years of service to the Fabian Society beyond London. Their task was to encourage the formation of local societies and by the end of the year sixty new ones had been established, membership increased impressively, though it still averaged little more than five per parliamentary constituency.

In July 1942 the Colonial Bureau learned that a Nigerian Labour Study Circle had become a Fabian Society where Europeans and Africans could meet for discussion. Its first conference was attended by trade union representatives from the civil service, technical and teaching professions, for it was very much a society of the African educated élite.[19] When Creech Jones visited Nigeria as a member of the Elliot Commission on Higher Education in West Africa, in 1944, one of his many private engagements was a visit to speak to this local society. He was greeted with great acclaim, listened to with almost embarrassing respect and photographed with a group of the founding members. This Society helped to organize a reception for him in the Oko Awo recreation ground at Lagos, at which thirty-two organizations who knew of his work in Parliament for Nigerians were to be represented. He was wholly unprepared, however, to meet 1500 Nigerians of all races, tribes, religious persuasions and forms of dress. It was an everwhelming event which gave him inspiration and encouragement to continue his work of promoting the welfare of the colonies despite rebuffs and criticisms. At the time he overcame his emotion to deliver a speech calling for co-operation among the people themselves and with the government and other agencies to exterminate ignorance, illiteracy and superstition, which stood in the way of the good health and good education without which democratic self-government would be impossible. Then he strode about in the chieftain's robes which were presented to him during the meeting, looking like a Welsh druid. Similar unforeseen demonstrations of enthusiasm occurred at several places as he travelled with the Commission through Nigeria.

John Parker, meanwhile, was corresponding with John Rossiter, an Englishman who had lived in Cape Town for more than twenty years, about a suitable constitution for an all-white South African Society.[20] Parker, of course, advised him to leave any specific reference to colour out of the constitution, so that non-whites would be able to join later. He put him in touch with members of an earlier society in the Cape. The new one started with thirty members and attracted audiences of double that number to monthly meetings to hear Margaret Ballinger speak on the native question and Dr E.R. Roux on social planning and the scientist. It created another branch in Stellenbosch and tried to found consumer co-operatives.

Autumn chill cooled the fervour of the Socialist Propaganda Committee a little and more moderate ambitions prevailed. Margaret Cole complained that it had failed to become the large-scale propagandist organization anticipated, the full committee of 'big Names' practically never met, and its work was being done by a mere handful.[21] Since the Committee was so unwieldy, the administration was formally handed over to a Guiding Committee. The *Directive*, a mimeographed monthly bulletin, gave guidance on how to run a local society and what to discuss in it.

As local societies multiplied they discovered a need to keep in touch with each other and with the central office. Relations had hitherto been left vague so that they might evolve naturally. A convention was held on 6 December 1941 to discuss a formula which would accommodate local fears of central domination, and central fears of local extremism. Jim Callaghan of Llandudno, Jack Diamond of Central London and Gwyneth Morgan of Cardiff, with an equal number of the Executive, were appointed to produce a revision of the rules and lay down guidelines for the future relationship between London and the provinces. Within a year the matter was settled to everyone's satisfaction.

The Coles had already tried, independently, to discover what the ordinary member wanted of the Society by inviting all the London conveners and local secretaries to their home to talk over difficulties and needs.[22] In the office Dorothy Fox was receiving reports from the provinces which revealed that the new societies could have anything from a dozen to 150 members. Those revived after a number of dormant years usually attracted about fifty. Some of the Scottish societies had kept going throughout the bleak 1930s; they were the most independent, ignoring the self-denying ordinance against sending regular policy statements to local Labour Parties. Callaghan and Diamond produced a spate of new ideas and helped draft model rules of procedure and a model constitution for the local societies before the former had to depart on naval service. Transformation of the Socialist Propaganda Committee from a more or less autonomous body into a regular Fabian subcommittee was partly due to their counsel; they wanted no more of Cole's breakaway groups. Each month officers and other members of the Executive visited new societies to inspect and encourage; Oliver Gollancz replaced Llewellyn Jones, and the committee was renamed the Methods of Propaganda Committee.

Propaganda produced was not very impressive. A publicity folder advanced the argument that lack of socialism was hampering production in the war industries, because control was still in the hands of great combines which were afraid of jeopardizing their post-war profits by all-out effort at that time. The first pamphlet, *Take Over the War Industries*, used the same theme, vaguely implying that victory depended on converting men to socialism immediately.[23] More convincing was the argument that a secure peace and a social system properly deploying science and technology could ensure plenty for all; socialism alone could achieve this, therefore socialists should work to establish it now. Great stress was laid on what individuals could do by preparing themselves to talk 'sound, practical sense' to fellow workers, neighbours and friends, and by forming discussion groups and persuading organizations to which they belonged to hold meetings to examine how socialism related to the war effort and to the problems to be faced after the war. Much thought was given to means of reaching out to new, untapped groups, such as popular-song writers and novelists, and persuading them to inject into their work a more serious, socialist content, thus influencing the minds of the masses, but only journalists were actually approached by the Committee.

The self-denying ordinance still enforced by the central committee annoyed many because societies affiliated to local Labour Parties found it very difficult to advance Fabian views without submitting formal resolutions. The Executive advocated formal affiliation of the local Fabian society to its own Labour Party but thought that no more was required than permeation by way of discussion groups.[24] Fabian activists for Labour in their neighbourhoods disagreed. Eventually, with the Sheffield Society acting as their spokesman, they made the Executive realize that, as in 1893, local societies interpreted their role as very different from that of the parent body. It gave way and henceforth local societies were allowed to submit resolutions to their local parties on matters of purely local concern but not on international or national policy, lest some societies might hold views very different from the Fabian Society as a whole and those sectional views might be presented to the Labour Party as Fabian policy.[25]

By April 1944 membership of the local societies had risen to 1314, all of whom wanted to do recognizable practical work for the Labour Party. Above all they wanted to prepare themselves to handle the electoral machinery as soon as the wartime truce on party campaigning was revoked. To satisfy this demand conferences on electioneering were arranged in Yorkshire and Gloucestershire. Memoranda were produced by Jack Diamond on public speaking and how to run indoor and outdoor public meetings. These, with others on modern publicity methods, became the first local societies' handbook. The Guiding Committee was renamed Local Societies Committee and was to remain so for the next forty years. Arthur Skeffington was its chairman for twenty-six years and Dorothy Fox its secretary until 1974.

Through the local societies the Fabian Society was able to keep socialism alive throughout the war, hold together a nucleus of Labour supporters of gradualist persuasion, and help them to form a network of politically active men and women which could swiftly become an electioneering organization once the wartime prohibition on direct canvassing agreed by all parties was lifted. When the country was abruptly plunged into a general election in May 1945, these people had already created a climate of opinion in which the goals of social reconstruction were judged to be reasonable and desirable. They knew enough about running meetings to appear capable of running the country. By means of the publicity they had given to the Beveridge Report they had dispelled opposition to reform of the social services on moderate socialist lines, indeed they had created a demand for it. Thus much that had been recommended in the Social Reconstruction Survey's reports as published by the Oxford University Press and as exemplified in the pamphlets of the Fabian Society had been accepted. A statistical assessment of how far this contributed to the Labour victory in July 1945 is probably impossible, yet it cannot be denied that it had a decided influence. The Local Societies Committee certainly thought it would when, in June, it staged a conference at Godstone, Surrey, called 'Winning the election'.

20

THIRD TIME LUCKY

Labour leaders had known since 1931 that only a large majority in the House of Commons would enable a third Labour Government to achieve anything. This was exactly what they obtained on 5 July 1945. All the research and discussion of policy in the Fabian Society and its interaction with the party policy committees over the last fourteen years had helped the new government to know what it wanted to do. Some immediate policies were ready, some targets had been fixed. So many eminent Labour politicians had held governmental posts during the wartime Coalition that few of Attlee's Ministers were unfamiliar with the administration or the extent of a Minister's powers; some had served in both MacDonald's governments as well as the wartime Coalition. This time Ministers had far more confidence in their own ability; they were convinced that, with their clear mandate, many of the reforms desired, discussed and planned for years would be carried through. Fabians believed that society might take a big leap towards regeneration.

Of the 230 Fabians in the Parliamentary Labour Party thirty-seven were in the new government, headed by a Prime Minister who had chaired the New Fabian Research Bureau in the dark years. These were the very men who had been deliberating on the details of implementing socialist measures and they appreciated that the wartime administration had done some of the preparatory work for them. The Fabian viewpoint had been permeating government departments by way of experts seconded to work in the Ministries, the reports of the Nuffield Survey which had found their way into the official files, the fruits of pre-war Fabian research and discussion which had been placed at their disposal when provision for equitable food distribution, protection of the nation's health, control of industry and labour and influence over public opinion was called for.

Both Westminster and Whitehall knew that only far-reaching reforms in the administrative structure and its methods would make government possible. The outline of Bevin's memorandum on cabinet structure, honed down by Attlee's and Dalton's revisions, could still be traced in both the Lord President's Committee for co-ordinating the work of departments dealing with economic affairs and the several committees appointed for specific economic problems, and in Bevin's own less formal supervisory responsibility for some colonial and commonwealth matters. As the Society watched legislation being prepared for nationalizing the Bank of England, the coal industry, civil aviation, public transport, gas, and iron and steel, and for creating a National Health Service and comprehensive national insurance scheme, it rejoiced that so much past effort, so much tedious argument over every obstacle and hypothetical solution, was at last bearing fruit. Not only were many of the people who had hammered out policy on these matters in Fabian and Research Bureau conferences, committees and pamphlets the Ministers responsible for convincing before mobilizing their civil servants into drafting the legislation and then steering it through cabinet and Parliament, many of their junior Ministers were also Fabians, and so they all knew what they were talking about. Moreover, as the government made increasing use of advisory committees, opportunities arose for Fabian experts to participate in policy guidance at a different level. Thus, to take only two examples, Hugh Dalton, Sir Stafford Cripps, Hugh Gaitskell and Douglas Jay dominated the Exchequer and the Ministry for Economic Affairs, while Creech Jones in the Colonial Office was supported by Fabian Under-Secretaries and Ministers of State and co-opted Rita Hinden and other Colonial Bureau members whose knowledge and judgement he valued on to advisory committees on labour and economic development.

Of course, not all the government was of Fabian origin, not all the changes wrought were inspired by them or even approved by them, and many of their measures were modified in cabinet. It is not here possible to assess the specifically Fabian contribution to the work of the 1945–51 Labour government; that comprises a large, complicated, independent study. Our present concern is how the Labour Party's third term of office affected the Fabian Society. The consequences of power were not quite what members had expected.

At the outset Cole, suspicious of the tendency to over-exuberance and over-confidence, issued a chairman's warning that Fabians' attitude towards government would have to change.[1] It would not do for the Society to be constantly preaching to the Labour government and protesting when government actions did not meet with its unalloyed approval. Fabians would have to exercise conscious restraint if they were not to obstruct the new government's work. Because some of the most influential Fabians were now debarred by their official responsibilities, a new generation of thinkers was needed, together with a complete revision of research plans. Constructive recommendations and explanations of why reforms took so long to implement now became the Fabian style, while tracts on local government were revised and reprinted at the party's request. While still dubious about its role under the new regime and waiting to see how the new masters comported themselves, the Fabian Executive decided on a spring clean.

The International Bureau was the first section to review its position, mainly because the end of hostilities rather than the election victory compelled a new pattern of work. At first it was thought the main emphasis should be on fostering international relations among socialists. The advisory committee saw its role as developing ties with and between continental socialists. In research, international agreements concerning transport in Europe and the use of natural resources, such as the waters of the Danube, offered an interesting field.[2] In the first years of the peace the Bureau produced several pamphlets on reconstruction in Germany and Yugoslavia, and the rehabilitation of the ILO as a power in Europe.[3] Interest in *France and Britain* could no longer be sustained once the Free French returned home; the Bureau lost the valuable financial contribution to its cost from the French Government in Exile and so publication ceased.

The Colonial Bureau enthused about how much more could be done once the influx of novice Labour MPs had been recruited to its service. Because colonial affairs were to some degree bi-partisan and undoubtedly a specialist subject, it felt its work was not so much changed as expanded. It prided itself on being: 'in a key position as the only organization attached to the Labour Party which is specially devoted to colonial affairs',[4] and despite Cole, reserved the right to criticize the government's actions whenever they did not give complete satisfaction. Creech Jones and Rita Hinden had summed up the attitude expected of post-war governments towards dependent territories in *Colonies and International Conscience*.[5] Constitutional reforms in the colonies could now be accelerated through joint action by Whitehall and local administrations. Representative government could be introduced as a prelude to responsible government. The Bureau's role, therefore, was to keep an eye on legislation and other developments, do a little prodding here and there and by timely warnings prevent British officials, new governments and rising politicians from tumbling into the pitfalls that Fabians had foreseen. Since more sure and swift communication with people on the spot was now possible, fresh methods of tackling research might be employed. Rita Hinden and Marjorie Nicholson asked putative experts in several dependent territories to contribute individual sections to a book discussing whether transplantation of Britain's form of government to the colonies was desirable.[6] Briefer, less factual and more controversial pamphlets were planned to make the British public more aware of those parts of the Commonwealth then moving towards independence.[7] The first to appear was *Palestine Controversy*, in which an Arab and a Jew explained the views of their respective peoples on the future of their country.[8]

In 1945, however, the future of the Indian sub-continent had to be considered and the Fabian Society launched an Indian Affairs Group that December in the hope of influencing Parliament and educating public opinion.[9] Rita Hinden compiled a scheme for the group's structure and work. Lord Faringdon, as he had done so often for the two Bureaux, put up most of the money for founding it, assisted by another stalwart of the Colonial Bureau, Lord Listowel. A projected conference on the problems attending British withdrawal from India had to be cancelled at the last moment, when Attlee decided to send out a Cabinet Mission of Inquiry led by Sir Stafford Cripps, because public discussion of Indian independence sponsored by one section of the Labour movement, before the official body had reported on its investigations, would have been injudicious. Reg Sorensen, on the committee of the Indian Affairs Group, and Woodrow Wyatt, its secretary, went with the Parliamentary Delegation to India immediately before the Cabinet Mission, and Wyatt stayed on in India as personal assistant to Cripps. Instead of exerting pressure on the government, the Indian Affairs Group assisted with research for six projected pamphlets only one of which, on sterling balances, was completed.[10] Lack of funds curbed the group's activities and when India achieved independence in 1947 it disbanded, and responsibility for studying Indian affairs was transferred to the International Bureau.[11] An attempt to set up a Dominions Bureau failed within a few weeks.

In domestic matters the Fabian Executive decided that it was time to re-examine its basic philosophy. As a prolegomenon to research it considered reissuing *Fabian Essays in Socialism*, perhaps as a paperback in order to reach the generation of uncommitted but interested ex-servicemen and women. With the same market in mind, a subcommittee was appointed to revise and update *Facts for Socialists*.[12] Once those were in print, together with some pamphlets in preparation, including a few on government proposals for the control of industry, the Executive Committee would be ready to survey what the Labour government had so far achieved, and identify which gaps in its programme to tackle next.[13] By the end of 1946 the immediate post-war surge in publication had died down, most study groups and subcommittees had been wound up and it was time to start afresh.[14]

Meanwhile many changes had taken place in Dartmouth Street. John Parker, on becoming Under-Secretary in the Dominions Office, was named honorary joint secretary with Margaret Cole, who had to bear the brunt of the work and day-to-day decision making until Billy Hughes was released from the army and acted as General Secretary for a few months. Creech Jones relinquished chairmanship of the Colonial Bureau to Frank Horrabin on being appointed Under-Secretary of State for the Colonies. The Bureau and its colonial contacts strongly believed that Attlee should have put him in charge of the Colonial Office immediately, but George Hall had a prior claim to the post as Under-Secretary during the Coalition. Even though the Bureau staff knew that their former chairman was fast learning ministerial responsibility, disappointment persisted and when Hall made his first formal policy speech in a Commons Supply Debate, they criticized it in *Empire*, treating him in much the same way as they had treated Oliver Stanley.[15] The workload of the Bureau rapidly increased as colonial activists began pressing for government action more to their liking and so Marjorie Nicholson was appointed full-time assistant secretary after helping for some time on a less formal basis.

The secretaries of the other departments departed for posts in the Labour Party administration and so the Executive appointed Bosworth Monck, a good organizer, as the new General Secretary. Monck had been working in the cabinet office and later stood as candidate for Pembroke. He immediately produced a breakdown of staff duties and instituted a procedure for dealing with committee papers which has changed very little in nearly four decades. Membership of the national society then stood at 4170, that of the local societies at nearly 3000, having increased by a third in a single year; expected annual income was £8500 yet a deficit of £1250 was expected that year unless an energetic membership drive took place. Monck designed several schemes for recruiting from several individual professions, industry, the trade unions and students, and arranged a propaganda rally in the Albert Hall where the main attraction, a Guards band, was ultimately forbidden to perform for a political organization.

Despite such setbacks, numbers and income continued to rise at an unspectacular rate.

Undaunted, Monck next turned his attention to the way the chairman of the Executive was chosen and questioned the usefulness of the honorary secretaries.[16] He saw Douglas and Margaret Cole and John Parker as a new Old Gang, inhibiting his every move. In a note to the Executive, he welcomed certain individuals invigorating particular sections of the Society's work, but objected to some exerting general control over the Society. On the whole the Executive took this sign of rebellion very calmly, merely observing that honorary secretaries had been very useful in the past. Cole, however, resigned from the chair within a week of the note being submitted, John Parker was created vice-chairman – a new office – and Margaret Cole was confirmed as honorary secretary with a right to be consulted on all establishment matters while Monck reigned supreme in the office. He was allowed a fairly free hand because everyone realized that central organization had become very slack, but the Executive indignantly rejected a programme he put forward for a second Labour term in government.[17] The Executive Committee had always decided such matters of policy and was shocked that its General Secretary should seize the initiative, even one selected for his drive. Monck had been tactless and had gone too far too fast, yet he was not wholly to be blamed. As he saw the situation, all the circumstances – the departure of key staff and officers, and influential members, completion of long-standing work and the emergence of a new, potentially influential relationship with government – had provided an unequalled opportunity to reshape the Society and make a completely fresh start. The Executive, shocked and dubious, but not entirely hostile, decided that Harold Laski was the right man to control this rather unexpected development and asked him to become chairman immediately on co-option to their number.

Staff reaction to the General Secretary's ideas was rather different. Rita Hinden managed to work harmoniously with Monck because she knew exactly what she wanted in the Colonial Bureau. Others appreciated his insistence on better pay and equipment and a brighter environment. A new Staff Consultative Committee ironed out most problems and presented an opportunity for airing their views on the Society's activity.[18] Their work was harder but much more interesting.

Throughout 1946 a moratorium had been laid on publication of tracts. The *Fabian Quarterly Journal* had served the Society well for a decade and was popular, but it looked a little tired and so was redesigned. To make publishing less of a drain on resources Fabian Publications Ltd was reconstructed for fuller exploitation under John Parker's chairmanship, with Monck an *ex officio* secretary and several people involved in publishing invited to join the board. Ian Mikardo, who was associated with a firm of financial advisers, was a welcome addition.

Laski presented a new scheme of work to the Executive comparable to the pioneering research undertaken by Woolf thirty years before.[19] He envisaged three major publications: a restatement of socialist philosophy, a book on reform of machinery of government, and another on the application of socialism to international questions. Parallel to this a series of smaller books on individual socialist countries, a history of socialism in England and some biographical studies were contemplated. In the long run these promised to be profitable but the Society needed money immediately to undertake this new work. Morgan Phillips, Secretary of the Labour Party, had offered £500 for research into nationalization of either the insurance or the chemical industries, wholesale and retail distribution or the place of the arts in the community. Monck regarded such contract work as not only a way out of financial difficulties but also the sort of research the Fabians ought to be doing. He, therefore, flatly opposed Laski's scheme, against most of the Executive, led by Robson and Woolf, who argued that the Society should aim at educating the élite of the Labour movement, and not become involved in the ephemeral concerns or hackwork of the Labour Party. Polarization came to a head over expenditure on the unsuccessful recruitment campaigns. Monck pointed out that if officers had collected all the subscriptions due in 1944 and 1945 (mostly from those in the services or otherwise away from home and therefore not hunted down through delicacy) the Society would not be in its present financial predicament, that he had retrieved a considerable sum by tracking down royalties long overdue, and that the membership rise showed every prospect of continuing. Margaret Cole alone supported Monck, maintaining that the large overdraft was not the result of his expansionist ideas but had been sanctioned before his appointment.[20]

The Fabian Executive was accustomed to view internal dissension as a sign of vitality. Opposition from the principal paid officer was an entirely new phenomenon; it was ungentlemanly. Laski therefore informed him in January 1947 that it was proposing to terminate his engagement.[21] One or two Executive members appreciated what Monck had tried to do and, at their insistence, he was co-opted on to the Executive.

Out of fifty-three applicants for the post of general secretary, the choice fell on Andrew Filson, secretary to the Parliamentary Labour Party, a former pupil and research assistant of Cole, and already known to the

Executive. He was faced with paying off the overdraft and debts of nearly £2000, reducing a staff of twenty-seven full-time and five part-time workers and cutting down the sixty-seven research projects then in hand to a manageable number. The new treasurer, Ian Mikardo, and his partner Leo Gossman, prepared a report on the Society's finances, the staff volunteered to make some economies, the subscription rate was raised by 25 per cent and Laski agreed to send special begging letters to selected eminent members.[22] A Revenue Campaign Council was set up to enlist the help of local societies.[23] The immediate result was a drop in membership and funds: many who had joined at the height of election and victory fever had become lukewarm and refused to pay the increased subscription. A recruitment appeal to members to enrol one new member each produced only 123 recruits. The resulting membership was probably more suited to its task, but it looked as though the Society might well die of starvation and overwork. Some research was still possible because of grants from the Dartmouth Street Trust which had been set up in 1942 as a charitable body to receive covenanted donations. Its declared purpose was: 'the promotion of studies in political, economic and social sciences and cognate educational subjects, and for the promotion of education and dissemination of knowledge in such sciences and subjects'. Its benefactions were wholly devoted to the Fabian Society's research projects. In fact lack of money for research, the need to change tactics once Fabians found themselves on the side of the governing party, and the need to rebuild its own structure and review its purpose and aims resulted in a low output by the Fabian Society for the first two years of Labour government.

Although everyone had agreed in principle that economies had to be made and had produced endless ideas for minor ones, Andrew Filson ran into strong opposition when he launched a plan for major cuts. Rita Hinden fought against a proposal to double subscriptions to the Bureaux on the grounds that this would weigh most heavily on members in the colonies and colonial students in Britain; instead she agreed to a fractional increase and made up the deficiency by charging extra for the Colonial Controversy series of pamphlets.[24] Her own and Marjorie Nicholson's journalistic fees were paid into Bureau funds and they each took a cut in salary, even though they were paid well below the Labour Research Department rates. The Labour Party, grateful for the way in which publication of *Empire* absolved its own Imperial Affairs Committee from producing a periodical, contributed £300 annually towards its cost and the Co-operative Movement continued to support the work on *Co-operation in the Colonies*.

Arthur Skeffington, chairman of the Local Societies Committee, protested loudly when an economy of £500 was demanded from it.[25] Policy had been to spend on the local societies in the first years of the Labour government in order to create informed socialist support for Labour MPs and candidates as widely as possible and to encourage collaboration with local Labour Parties. Candidates were frequently asked to act as conveners when a new Fabian Society was needed in a constituency. Labour MPs were expected to speak to Fabian societies in their constituencies and reinvigorate them if necessary. Many future MPs first encountered the Labour Party through the local or university Fabian society. In return, local societies generally proved an asset to Labour MPs, keeping them in touch with their constituents' needs and opinions on government measures and helping to counter ill-informed criticisms of legislation and programmes. Dorothy Fox and her assistants were continuously engaged in finding speakers for the societies, encouraging them to build up their numbers and persuade members to become national members as well, thus entitled to vote in the annual election, asking secretaries to double their affiliation fees, and analysing the societies' annual reports and those made by Executive speakers after visits. Naturally Skeffington objected to cuts in the Local Societies office, where there was constant complaint of understaffing. He sought ways to offload economies on to the main administration while Dorothy Fox tried to convince the Executive that the department should actually expand in order to become a much more valuable section of the Society for the Labour Party.

Meanwhile the nation was enduring Sir Stafford Cripps's austerity regime, the beginning of the cold war in Europe, an appalling winter with fuel shortages, and petrol and food rationing. Gradually Filson managed to kedge the Fabian Society off the rocks, taking one bold decision at a time. Declaring that the Fabians had nothing new to say he guillotined Laski's proposed second volume of *Essays*. To relieve the office of much routine labour and expense the local societies were placed under regional and area committees and given considerable independence. Similarly the Colonial Bureau was made responsible for its own funding, except for a small annual grant from the Executive, in exchange for an even greater degree of autonomy than it already assumed in its separate Carteret Street office.

It was the Colonial Bureau which first realized that the Fabian Society, the Labour Party, the country and the world were getting out of phase with one another. The Colonial Bureau enjoyed a direct and amiable relationship with the Colonial Office, its advice was always considered if not always followed. Although Fabian gradualism was well attuned to the pace of the

Colonial Office, change in the outside world was accelerating and Fabian doctrine and method lost favour. Warnings of probable future dissension had actually been sensed by Creech Jones and Margery Perham during the war when they had lectured in America for the British Information Services and had had interviews with officials in the Department of State. They had discovered the temperature in the United States unexpectedly chilly and the levels of knowledge and understanding surprisingly low.

Margery Perham was the more accustomed to encountering foreign prejudice against British imperialism. During her studies of native administration, she travelled round the world comparing methods in colonies ruled by Britain and other western countries. In particular, she travelled extensively in Africa, getting to know the African peoples and colonial officers and their institutions at the most basic level. She was also lecturing and teaching the cadets taking the post-graduate course at Oxford and Cambridge for the Colonial Service, and met the criticisms of numerous Rhodes Scholars and visiting academics from the Americas, South Africa and the rest of the Commonwealth. Creech Jones, on the other hand, though he had read the same blue books and official reports, though he shared many friends among liberal academics and former officials whose main concern was the welfare and progress of the colonial peoples, had not visited a British colony until 1944 when he served on the Elliot Commission on Higher Education in West Africa. He had learned on a lecture tour of America during the war that there was a danger of critics of imperialism, other than the colonized peoples, banding together to force Britain to 'liberate' the dependent peoples prematurely, leaving them vulnerable to external attack or damaging influences and far worse off than in pre-colonial days. These two close friends became even more determined that as many British colonies as could benefit by independence should attain self-government at the earliest feasible moment, and in the meantime should be administered in the most enlightened way. It was easy for them to establish this as Fabian policy because she was an acknowledged expert in her academic field and his indefatigable enquiries in Westminster and Whitehall which had led to a quasi-Webbian mastery of a multitude of facts, were justly appreciated and many in the Bureau were already more than half convinced. In the wider Labour movement there were few who shared the Bureau's interest in the colonies. Of those few a handful rejected the Fabian philosophy and conclusions; labouring under feelings of guilt at the very fact of Empire they wished to be divested of its burden as quickly as possible.

Although until the 1945 election Creech Jones had continued to probe for information and offer his ideas on policy by all the means open to a Member of Parliament, officials in the Colonial Office had come to realize that he was an essentially constructive critic. Thus, when he was appointed Under-Secretary of State in August 1945, most of them welcomed his knowledge and understanding of their problems and aims. They knew that he had a wide acquaintanceship throughout the Commonwealth countries and had heard most of the requests and complaints that had passed over their desks in recent years and a good deal of the background to each. His promotion when George Hall was moved to the Admiralty was welcome to them. The Fabian Colonial Bureau reaped the benefit of this amicable relationship and when Andrew Cohen was made head of the African section he represented another ear open to its recommendations. Thus, during the Attlee government, many of the policies devised by Fabians during the 1940s were adopted, partly because administrators and officials had simultaneously been reaching the same conclusions. Colonies deemed ready for self-government, such as Ceylon and Burma, were granted independence within the Commonwealth or without, as they themselves pleased, and others were granted either representative or responsible government as soon as was feasible. The transition from indirect rule to local government was set in train by a dispatch sent to all governors in 1947, the Colonial Development and Welfare Act of 1950 increased and extended Britain's financial commitment to the dependencies, trade unionists were sent out to the colonies to advise on industrial legislation and assist in the foundation of unions, the Colonial Service was enlarged and diversified as swiftly as men could be trained under the new Devonshire courses.

Yet in 1947 complaints from the colonies began to flow in to the Bureau that the government was not fulfilling the high hopes of political reform encouraged by the Fabians. Because its first chairman was then the Minister responsible for the colonies, some of the most vocal agitators blamed him personally for the slow pace of economic and social development, delay in industrial legislation and, above all, because independence had not been granted immediately hostilities ceased. Gradualism was not a virtue appreciated by colonial peoples. When, in 1946, Creech Jones addressed a meeting in London on colonial policy, a mere two months after his appointment as Secretary of State, he tried to explain that creating nations, developing economies and reconstructing societies had to be tackled very slowly in order to obtain stability. This speech was later published with a summary of all the official reports and white papers on colonial affairs from September 1945 to February 1947, as the third of the Colonial Controversy series.[26] To institute desired reforms two things were required, of which Britain was very short: money and trained staff. In spite of great efforts to supply both, many nationalists felt that progress was too slow, turned from the Bureau and embraced other, more extreme movements demanding colonial independence. Nevertheless, a number of West Indians, Africans and Asians, who later became heads of state, were proud to be members of the Bureau and valued the assistance, advice and even instruction it gave them. When, in June 1948, Creech Jones again spoke on colonial policy at a public meeting in Caxton Hall, a small group of Africans heckled him throughout. Alienation from the Bureau persisted as the colonial peoples watched the bloodshed following independence in India, the relinquishment of the Mandate in Palestine and the outbreak of civil war in Malaya. Resentment in Kenya over white settlement escalated and Africans lost confidence in Britain as they watched the government's humiliating failure with the Gambian egg project and the groundnut scheme in East Africa. Disillusionment and disappointment were not universal, but there was not the same unquestioning acceptance of what the Fabian Society recommended as there had been during the war.

The Bureau's Advisory Committee and staff still believed in their work, particularly as the Secretary of State willingly discussed general aspects of colonial policy with them and facilitated consultation of his officials by Fabian deputations. Rita Hinden was appointed to the Ministry's Colonial Economic and Development Council and its Colonial Labour Advisory Committee, as well as to the Labour Party's Advisory Committee on Imperial Affairs and the TUC's Colonial Affairs Committee. She therefore appreciated how much was being done officially and how impossible it was to move more quickly when Britain itself was dependent on foreign aid from America and was facing the prospect of a cold war becoming a conflagration. Yet she found it impossible to convince many of those who wrote to her.

As far as domestic matters were concerned politicians were far too busy legislating to create new policy. Trade unionists were fully engaged in working out industrial relations and negotiating machinery suited to the unfamiliar situation of full employment in time of peace. Industrialists were engrossed in the struggle to revive the export trade after years of home consumption only and simultaneously supply the country with machinery and other consumer goods. Short-handed teachers and educationalists were finding their feet within the structure created by the Education Act of 1944. The medical profession was adjusting to the National Health Service. Everyone was so busy making the system work that they had no time to look ahead. In 1948 the Fabian Executive suddenly realized the danger of a political vacuum in a couple of years' time, because the Labour Party had no policy beyond its immediate programme. Aware that Fabians should plan for 1950 when the next general election was due, the Society bounced back, full of energy and optimism.

Ian Mikardo made a preliminary survey assuming that everything laid down in *Let Us Face the Future* would be accomplished by 1950.[27] Consolidation of the social reforms and administrative machinery, selective extensions of nationalization, creation of original state enterprises and, to safeguard sources of raw materials and build up future markets, a long-term development plan for African dependencies in which collaboration by other African and European states would be encouraged seemed worthy targets for the Labour Party over the next twenty years. Unfortunately it was not a vote-catching programme, nor did it immediately inspire a fresh programme of research.

At the summer school H.D. Hughes, lecturing on 'The outlook for 1950', warned that Labour could not expect another easy election victory because it would be fighting on its record against the accumulated criticisms of the Tory Party.[28] 'Bad economic weather' before the election would reduce Labour's chance of winning. A very real danger of apathy existed. Shortages during the austerity period would be blamed on the government. The Labour Party had lost the 1945 image of a giant-killer. A vigorous party was therefore essential.

Various practical measures were taken to help the party's 'Labour believes in Britain' campaign. Local societies were sent a discussion guide and questionnaires to sound out the average member's views on nationalization.[29] The autumn lectures and a linked series of tracts called 'The challenge of 1950' examined the probable extensions to nationalization and relative values of public control and private enterprise in industry, also the difficulty of establishing any kind of workers' control. Fabians now realized that they were not as committed to total nationalization as the majority in the Labour Party and that before proceeding further with it there were far more serious problems to solve than had been foreseen.[30] Cole analysed the draft manifesto, *Labour Believes in Britain*, in a pamphlet issued at the same time.[31] As a 'friendly critic' he told the Labour Party that it needed to let what it had already achieved settle into good working order and that it could not afford a further radical programme while national production remained low. Industrial consolidation would have to be the theme for the next few years while the economy was given every opportunity to revive. In his view, priorities were abolition of the House of Lords and reform of parliamentary and administrative machinery, matters which the government had had to neglect while concentrating on economic and social matters. He also recommended a very serious reconsideration of the way publicly owned industry was being run, because it was inefficient and unproductive. He was aware that this would not be a very popular programme, but neither was the Labour Party's. The identification of planning with socialism merely augured management by a new élite of professionals and experts divorced from worker's interests. Cole begged the policy makers to think again.

The intellectual leaders of the Society knew they should be forging ahead with a completely new interpretation of socialism. They convened a conference of the inner circle of non-government Fabian thinkers, which turned out to be the first of a series. Non-Fabian Labour members probably regarded it as the Fabians 'up to their fun' again, because their discussion had no chance of influencing the poll in less than a year's time.

At first they were held at Buscot Park, the stately Oxfordshire home of Gavin, Lord Faringdon, who almost made a career out of acting host to the Fabian Society and priming the pump for new projects. His London flat was equally at its disposal when an elegant background was required for entertaining foreign and commonwealth visitors or Fabians up from the provinces to attend the annual general meeting. A considerate as well as generous host, he issued instructions on which trains to take in order that the local taxi might convey his guests from the local station, two trains only because the taxi driver would probably not have enough petrol for repeated journeys.[32] The select few were reminded to bring two 'points' each for their bread ration, together with some fat, sugar, tea, soap and a towel, for without a catering licence he could not feed even a small conference in those days of austerity when food was even scarcer than it had been during the war.

The motive of the first conference was summarized by Cole as a loss of conviction that unqualified socialism was a source of good, or would even serve as a means to an end. Socialism in Britain was not acting as midwife to a nation of saints or even of joyful, satisfied workers. Controls accepted at first as inevitable in order to provide fair shares for all were now resented as the expected rewards in housing, food, clothing and generally better conditions seemed to be even further out of reach. External economic pressures such as had led to devaluation of the pound combined with a shortage of experienced, imaginative management, had delayed full development of the nationalized industries so that benefits were not apparent and the country's support had drained away with its morale. In other words, the people who had voted for Labour in 1945, expecting a brave new world, had been deprived and regulated too long to respond to any more demands for sacrifice and co-operation, and were unlikely to allow the Labour Party a second term to prove itself unless guaranteed a far brighter future. As Cole observed: 'It is no use for socialists to expect the mass of the people to behave more virtuously than their imaginative perceptions allow them to'.[33] Socialism was supposed to cater for the needs of the people. If it was failing to do so or was unable to do so without outstripping the nation's capacity, something must be fundamentally wrong with either the principle or its execution. Cole inferred that the measures introduced by the Labour government were 'bastard socialism', something that looked like it but was not sound at the core.

This first conference at Buscot Park in July 1949 raised more problems than it solved concerning the respective roles of public and private enterprise, the extent and type of taxation required to pay for the social services, the reforms needed in the machinery of government and how to develop an 'active democracy' ready to participate fully in shaping the country's future. A second Buscot conference was opened in January by Tony Crosland with a dissertation on 'Happiness in the welfare state' in which he aired a number of ideas worked out more fully in his seminal work, *The Future of Socialism*. Like the book when it was published in 1956, this paper aroused considerable controversy and set the tone for the whole conference. After it the group decided to circulate amongst themselves loose-leaf notebooks in which further observations could be entered and commented upon.[34] There were at least four of these notebooks, covering price control policies, industrial democracy, investment policy and the British socialist way of life including the use of leisure and the promotion of individual freedom and happiness through the reform of obsolete laws on, for example, divorce, licensing and the censorship of plays.

Although they continued to be referred to as Buscot conferences, rather than by their true title 'Problems ahead', this was the last to be held in the house near Faringdon. The Fabians felt unable to ask for hospitality there after Crosland accidentally broke a priceless vase. Subsequent conferences in this series were mounted in Oxford colleges.

In the February 1950 election, Labour received roughly 1.25 million more votes than before, while the Conservative vote increased by twice that amount. This combined with the long-overdue rationalization of constituency boundaries since the 1945 election, meant that Labour was returned to office but with an overall majority of only six. Since it was most unlikely that the new government would be able to stay the full five-year course, pressure was on the Buscot group to produce its projected second volume of *Fabian Essays* in time to invigorate support for the party and so produce a larger majority. Its format was discussed at a conference in University College in June.

Cole had again been elected chairman of the Society when Laski retired to write a long-planned study of political thought. Cole produced a synopsis which covered the content of their discussions so comprehensively that the resulting volume would have been enormous.[35] In October, again in Oxford, Crosland and Crossman were instructed to draw up a new synopsis for a book defining socialist principles in the current and future world situation, reinterpreting both Fabianism and Marxism, reviewing what Fabians wanted to achieve and the instruments by which it might be accomplished.

Webb and Cole had totally disparate personalities, sharing only a tremendous capacity for work, yet in the middle period of the Society's history Cole exercised much the same pervasive influence as Webb in the early years. Just as Webb's theories on trade unionism and the Poor Law had a direct bearing on the Society's work in the early part of the century, so Cole's views in mid-century were the original inspiration for this second volume of essays. Now, however, his influence was past its peak. He had set up or inspired a couple of projects in Oxford for doing preparatory research on taxation and nationalization policies and served on another which began to examine how far a planned economy eroded parliamentary control over the machinery of government, none of which found a specific place in *New Fabian Essays*.[36] As the younger men whittled away at his plan for the essays, Cole lost heart and resigned from the 'Problems ahead' committee which had ignored the political problems he felt so imprtant.[37] Richard Crossman, who managed to retain his seat in the House when so many of his colleagues, including Crosland, were defeated, assumed responsibility for editing them, though this was not officially admitted until Cole resigned the chairmanship of the Society in May 1951.[38]

The essays were not ready to send to the publisher at the scheduled date, April 1951. They struggled to get the book published before Attlee felt compelled to appeal to the nation in the hope of increasing Labour's majority. An October deadline was set, but that was the month chosen for the election when all Fabians were involved in the fight. *New Fabian Essays* was finally published in 1952, in a dust-cover designed by Sir Francis Meynell, shortly after Aneurin Bevan's *In Place of Fear* was issued. Inevitably comparisons were made. Two of the essayists were supporters of Bevan – Crossman and Mikardo – the rest favoured Gaitskell; thus the broad spectrum of Fabian political opinion was represented in the work. By October over 5000 copies had been sold and it continued to sell steadily, though not spectacularly, for many years, with a little boom before each election. Yet the general conclusion, shared by the authors themselves, was that they had not succeeded in re-stating socialism. Plans were therefore made for a second volume, which never materialized. Crosland continued to struggle with the problem not only in *The Future of Socialism* but also in numerous articles for socialist periodicals and the press, in *The Conservative Enemy* and in *Socialism Now*, which, published twenty years later, presented a selection of the latest revisions of his thoughts on socialism. His views were challenged throughout, most prominently by Richard Crossman's replies in the same journals; they encountered considerable opposition from sections of the Labour Party, an opposition which appears to be diminishing today.

New Fabian Essays was none the less a considerable achievement. It would have been difficult under any conditions to have matched the political impact of the first volume. In 1952 the climate of opinion was such that no dynamic philosophy of socialism could emerge to galvanize a Labour movement exhausted by what it had already done to regenerate society, in an unfavourable international context. The essayists were hobbled by the need to furnish their theories on socialism with practical solutions immediately applicable to the evils of the day. The irresponsibility of the early Fabians had vanished once Labour had experienced a term of real parliamentary power. But no one had discovered how to solve contemporary problems. They were only just beginning to find out how far practical socialism had strayed from its original intentions, how far it had been mistaken in the past, how far re-evaluation could remedy past mistakes and correct wrong assumptions. *New Fabian Essays* was a brave attempt to make such a reassessment. Expectations had been too high and so disappointment was inevitable.

21

OPPOSITION AGAIN

Disappointment at the Labour Party's defeat in 1951 was profound. Yet some Fabians believed that greater steps in creating socialist policy were taken when Labour was in opposition. In a pre-election warning of possible defeat John Parker had reminded members that Fabian ideas of the fifteen years from 1930 often emerged years later as NEC policy recommendations to party conference.[1] What Fabians could do once they could do again. No one, except perhaps Richard Crossman, expected Labour to be in the wilderness for the next thirteen years.[2] Determined to promote practical, long-term objectives for the next election manifesto, based on the reduction of inequalities within a mixed economy, the Society set out to identify the late government's mistakes, those achievements which could not carry on under their own momentum, and the major gaps in policy.

William Rodgers was appointed assistant general secretary just in time to hold the fort while Donald Chapman was winning the Birmingham constituency once briefly nursed by Cole. Chapman had taken over from Andrew Filson as General Secretary in 1949, after running the Home Research Department, and had been at the centre of the 'Problems ahead' debate. Naturally he did not wish to resign just when that debate was about to bear fruit, and therefore continued to serve on a half-time basis. Bill Rodgers therefore took on more responsibility than he anticipated. Fortunately the Society was unusually solvent, no major crisis loomed and the two young officers agreed on their prime duty to enrol a new generation of members.

By now most of the Webbs' contemporaries and closest collaborators had vanished. In 1949 and 1950 alone Katherine Bruce Glasier, Marjory Pease, Harold Laski, Shaw and Emil Davies, the devoted treasurer for so many years, all died. In 1952 the Webbs' early research assistant, Frank Galton, died, and so did Beatrice's nephew, Sir Stafford Cripps, who had just become the second president of the Society. Cole accepted an invitation to become his successor. Though he stipulated that he should remain 'inactive', he made his influence felt, not least by eliminating loyal toasts at celebratory dinners.[3] Younger politicians now on the Executive, Anthony Crosland, Richard Crossman, Hugh Gaitskell, Roy Jenkins, Ian Mikardo and Harold Wilson, were aware of how the relationship between the Society and its public had changed in the past six years. They knew that a public benefiting from a welfare state could not have the same attitude towards socialism as there had been in the nineteenth century. Moreover, whatever the Society said in future would be judged in the light of what Labour had done in office.

To all appearances the Society was set for another phase of blooming, as Margaret Cole termed it. There was nearly £2000 for research from the Sarah Hall and Dartmouth Street Trusts and from the Transport and General Workers' Union, a growing membership, and 117 local societies. Unfortunately, many new recruits who had joined in protest at Labour's defeat lost interest by the time their second subscription was due. Nearly a hundred vanished in 1953. Autumn lecture attendance dropped by a third, bookshop sales halved and all Fabian functions that winter lost money. Publicity had been good and the central office had made great efforts to stage popular events, therefore the decline was interpreted as a general loss of confidence in Labour, partly due to the rift widening between Gaitskell and Aneurin Bevan. Half-way through the life of the Conservative government the Labour Party could display little fight, few new ideas, little determination to follow them up and, as a fully employed population reached out towards affluence at last, fewer pricks against which to kick. Even the Colonial Bureau's independent income fell, activities had to be drastically curtailed and many routine tasks abandoned by a depleted staff. Control over action in Westminster weakened and the Bureau became far less influential there and in Whitehall. The top-heavy Advisory Committee was pared down to a Working Committee led by Creech Jones, back again in the saddle though Lord Faringdon remained the Bureau's chairman.[4] Its many eminent academics and three retired Colonial Ministers who had been co-opted in 1952 were asked to transform themselves into a panel whose members could be consulted individually, at need.

Immediately after the 1951 election Marjorie Nicholson told the Executive that the Bureau's fight for political progress, economic develop- ment, the social services, trade unions and co-operatives had virtually been won though not by socialists alone.[5] The needs of the dependent peoples were very different at mid-century. The time had come to rethink aims and means of achievement. A beginning had been made at a conference in September 1950, entitled 'Challenge to Labour in the colonies', at which Jim Griffiths, Rita Hinden and Creech Jones had tried to point the way ahead.[6] In the 1950s much energy and concern for dependent peoples which might previously have been pre-empted by the Bureau was absorbed by the Movement for Colonial Freedom or the Africa Bureau, organiz- ations which worked in fields contiguous and sometimes identical with the Bureau's, though with a different emphasis on direct political or human- itarian action.

Colonial politicians were gaining in confidence and expertise. The painstaking letters of advice on the nuts and bolts of union organization dispatched by Rita Hinden and Creech Jones in the early 1940s were now replaced by two-way correspondence debating the finer points of constitutional law or parliamentary strategy. The secretary spent more time now putting colonial correspondents in touch with experts in the United Kingdom than, as formerly, setting the Bureau staff to hunt out the information themselves and transmitting, sometimes translating, it to her African or West Indian contacts. For instance, in 1952 two new Nigerian Ministers asked her to arrange a meeting in Dartmouth Street for them to discuss the problems they were facing at home with economists and Bureau experts on West Africa.[7] Need for greater professionalism distanced the Bureau from its members in the colonies.

The greatest Commonwealth crisis the Bureau faced in these years was the Conservative project for a Central African Federation. While Creech Jones had been in office he had been urged by Southern Rhodesians and by Roy Welensky from Northern Rhodesia to amalgamate the two territories with the protectorate of Nyasaland. This demand had been presented to the British government in various guises during the last thirty years, sometimes involving East African territories. A Fabian deputation had visited Jim Griffiths, when he was known to be under the same pressure, to strengthen his resistance. In 1952 the Reverend Michael Scott gathered a group of friends, including Creech Jones, Professor Arthur Lewis, Rita Hinden and Margery Perham, and created the Africa Bureau 'to advise and support Africans who wished to oppose by constitutional means political decisions affecting their lives and futures imposed by alien governments'. Many Fabians were instrumental in its work or subscribed to its funds yet it was essentially a non-party organization.

The closest liaison was maintained between the two Bureaux, with most of the leading Fabian colonialists acting as advisers on their special subjects. Creech Jones, now out of Parliament, produced the Africa Bureau's first pamphlet, *Africa Challenge: The Fallacy of Federation*, a strong, reasoned condemnation of the intention to impose on a black protectorate and mainly black colony a constitutional alliance desired only by the white minority in Southern Rhodesia and a few in Northern Rhodesia. The new Bureau's methods mirrored the Fabian Society's and made possible collaboration over a study group, press conferences for both the official representatives in London for talks with the British government and the unofficial spokesmen of various African groups, and meetings with MPs and concerned bodies. A joint delegation went to the Colonial Office to discuss the Conservative government's *Draft Federal Scheme*.[8] The Anti-Slavery Society was also drawn into this collaboration. Year after year Fabian opposition to Federation continued. In 1955–6, nine meetings were called at which African visitors to London spoke against Federation.

Fabian members of the Africa Bureau were also responsible for secretly engineering a meeting between Seretse Khama, the Mochuana chief exiled because of the difficulties caused by his marriage to an English girl, and his uncle, the former regent Tshekedi Khama by smuggling them out of London by separate routes before the newspapers heard, and leaving them alone to achieve a reconciliation. This paved the way for settlement of the constitutional problem, restoration of both men to their proper positions in Bechuanaland and for the eventual appointment of Seretse as President of the independent Botswana[9].

Several noted Africans were members of the Colonial Bureau at this time: Julius Nyerere, Dr Hastings Banda, Jomo Kenyatta, Dr J.B. Danquah, Nnamdi Azikiwe whose name is on the list of members to this day, and Kenneth Kaunda. They all fed the Bureau continuously with personal views on current problems and events in Africa. Tom Mboya, who joined while an undergraduate at Oxford, in 1952 helped write a pamphlet with a foreword by Margery Perham, *East African Future*, which was for a time banned in East Africa, and later produced for the Bureau *The Kenya Question: An African Answer*.[10]

Federation of the West Indies, on the other hand, was welcomed by the Fabians. Creech Jones had called the first West Indian conference on the subject at Montego Bay in 1947. The Bureau published, in 1952, a pamphlet to encourage the West Indians to accept the proposition as a challenge to proceed towards communal independence and dominion status in the near future.[11] Six years later, in order to explain the situation in the West Indies to the British public and elucidate the problems for the West Indians themselves, encouraging them to make the rather weak, infant federal government viable, John Hatch, the Commonwealth Officer of the Labour Party, produced a tract full of facts gathered during a recent tour of the West Indies, which urged them to *Dwell Together in Unity*. On this the Bureau lost a lot of money because large numbers ordered for sale in the Caribbean islands were never paid for.

Rawle Farley and Colin Hughes kept the Bureau up to date with developments in the West Indies where, as university lecturers, they had ample opportunity to observe and analyse. Norman Manley, Prime Minister of Jamaica and a corresponding member from the beginning, regularly wrote to the honorary secretary and the secretary, as did Sir Grantley Adams, the first Federal Prime Minister, Dr Eric Williams, Prime Minister of Trinidad, and Cheddi Jagan of British Guiana.

The Bureau wanted to carry out a thorough reassessment of its position and philosophy in the 1950s. The Labour government's actions since 1945 had to be evaluated: it had, after all, issued the controversial banishment order against Seretse Khama and relinquished the Palestine Mandate in circumstances leading to bloodshed and alienation. The Bureau also wanted to establish whether the Conservative administration, in reversing some of the Labour government's measures, was reacting according to its own political philosophy, or whether some apparently retrogressive action was simply intended to slow down the rate of change in order to build a firmer political structure. Then it would have to decide whether Fabian aims and policies were relevant to current requirements in Africa, the Caribbean and South-East Asia. In April 1954, therefore, Creech Jones was asked to edit a second volume of *Colonial Essays*, on the theme of the collapse of colonialism and a constructive, alternative policy which would take into account the influence of the Trusteeship and Security Councils and the effect of resolutions passed by the United Nations General Assembly on the world-wide attitude towards colonialism.[12] His original plan was to open with a combined analysis by himself and Rita Hinden of the nature of imperialism and the modern socialist concept of it, relating that to the policy and actions of the recent Labour government. Richard Crossman, Marjorie Nicholson, Thomas Balogh, Arthur Lewis, Margery Perham, Margaret Reed, Kenneth Robinson and Wilfred Benson were asked to contribute essays on all aspects of colonial policy.[13] This synopsis was presented to the Executive just as Creech Jones re-entered the House of Commons, having won the by-election at Wakefield.

The next couple of years were the worst possible time for producing a major restatement of colonial policy. First Marjorie Nicholson decided that she could deploy her particular expertise to greater effect in the colonial section of the TUC. Thereupon the Fabian Executive, which was experiencing one of its periodic financial crises, relinquished the Carteret Street lease and squeezed the Bureau into a room in Dartmouth Street. Lady Selwyn-Clark became secretary in the time she could spare from her work at County Hall. Eirene White averted a threat to cut down *Empire*, renamed *Venture*, to a quarterly magazine by volunteering to act as unpaid editor until the crisis passed. Meanwhile a general election distracted both essayists and editor.

Desire for major policy restatements was not confined to the Colonial Bureau in 1954, the year the Society completed its three score years and ten. Edward Pease, at 97, was too frail to attend any celebration but sent a telegram of congratulation to the Society. At a private ceremony, held at his home and attended by about forty older members, he was presented with a specially bound volume of *New Fabian Essays* and a signed copy of Attlee's memoirs, *As It Happened*. Pease died the day after the Society's seventy-first birthday.

Rejuvenation was the theme of the seventieth anniversary, with Attlee speaking a little drily of the continuing importance of the Society's work, Professor Tawney, who had been a Fabian for half the Society's life, asserting that Fabian empiricism would ultimately obtain the ends they all desired, Cole rallying the Society as the 'thinking machine of British Socialism' to ask the right questions about current problems and cease trying to find new answers to those that no longer obtained, and Hugh Gaitskell joyfully helping to roll up the Caxton Hall carpet so that he and other limber Fabians could round off the reception with an impromptu dance.[14] Rejuvenation in this case took the form of a desire to publish essays. Creech Jones had already said he was willing. Hugh Gaitskell now offered to mastermind the longed-for second volume of *New Fabian Essays*, while Harold Wilson undertook to edit a volume of *International Essays*. Collaboration between the editors and the three groups of essayists was essential, of course, some being expected to contribute to more than one collection. One difficulty was that Balogh and Nicholas Kaldor each refused to produced an essay until he knew what the other had written. For all three books the 1955 general election proved a great hindrance, with the writers temporarily focusing on such close objectives that they were prevented from adjusting their sight to the more distant horizon. These three volumes were, naturally, the product of the more mature Fabians. To excite the interest of those under thirty-five an essay-competition was arranged in the autumn on the theme of 'Why I am a socialist'.[15]

At the general election on 26 May 1955, more than a third of the Labour candidates were Fabians, and 116 of those 220 were successful. The proportion of Fabians elected was 12 per cent higher than that of Labour non-Fabians and John Parker held on to his majority of over 25,000. *Fabian News* was able to report that all four of the Labour committee examining party organization were Fabians, including the current chairman, Harold Wilson, and Arthur Skeffington who, as chairman of the Local Societies Committee, had a finger on the pulse of Labour in the constituencies. Thirteen members of the eighteen-strong Labour Parliamentary Committee were Fabians, including the party leaders in both Houses, as were seven of the eight Labour delegates to the Council of Europe's Consultative Assembly and the substitute delegate, Roy Jenkins. Unaided, Fabians could form a quorum in the House of Commons Select Committee on Estimates and, predictably, ten of the twelve Labour members on the Executive Committee of the United Kingdom branch of the Commonwealth Parliamentary Association were Fabians. There were thus plenty of authoritative outlets for Fabian views provided the Society had something constructive to say about the new problems facing the country.

Nevertheless, Labour had been defeated for the second time and the number of local societies dropped to ninety-three with a 10 per cent loss of members. Were the rank and file losing heart or were they so beguiled by the affluence now replacing the austerity of the 1940s that they were losing their convictions? The 90 per cent who stayed now appointed their own research secretaries to direct independent projects and send in material requested by Dartmouth Street on problems of old age and the allocation of council houses.[16] Labour was fast losing not only votes but party members at this time and, except for two fairly short revivals in 1957 and 1963–4, the decline in individual membership has continued ever since.[17] The Fabian Society's influence is most directly felt by this individual membership which embraces the middle-class section of the party, as the recruitment campaign launched in the mid-1950s illustrated. Canvassing the divisional Labour parties and Labour candidates yielded only twelve recruits in 1956–7, whereas tea meetings in the universities of Oxford, Cambridge and London and at the annual NALSO conference, hosted by Bill Rodgers and younger members of the Executive, brought in a hundred new members. An appeal in the *New Statesman*, signed by Attlee, evoked the best response of all; 170 people actually joined though many more uncommitted socialists took the trouble to enquire into the Society's work and were probably netted when the appeal was repeated in succeeding years.[18] University tea-meetings, held annually since 1954, had done much to reduce the average age of the membership and an under-thirties summer school was held in 1956.

Lethargy induced by affluence was not the sole reason for a decline in active individual membership of the party. The ideological conflict between Bevanites and Gaitskellites left many confused about where their sympathies lay. Both Bevan and Gaitskell had supporters on the Executive, and though the Fabian Society has always prided itself on being able to accommodate the full spectrum of political views within the Labour movement (a claim frequently challenged by its critics who place it on the right of the party), it reverberated at times to the clashes between the two. Inevitably some of the struggle between the two factions was played out within the Society, even though it is maintained that partisans who cut each other dead in the Palace of Westminster would sit on the same Fabian committee and discuss its business without acrimony.

The struggle came into the open after a resolution was presented at the annual general meeting of 1955 requesting a special committee to review the rules for election and co-option to the Executive and methods of appointing honorary officers and subcommittees.[19] It was claimed that ordinary members felt excluded from the Society's work and decision making, believed that it was pointless voting for a new Executive when defeated candidates were immediately co-opted; they suspected that the Society was run by a self-perpetuating, invulnerable clique. The Executive had always reserved the right to co-opt to its number any member who could make a particular, expert contribution to research. Nominees for election were normally of such kind and, being relatively unknown to the main body of electors, often received too few votes to qualify for an elected seat. When co-opted later it appeared that the Executive was ignoring the wishes of the Society and packing its ranks with those whom the members rejected. If a certain line of research had been under way for some time the same people might be repeatedly co-opted, hence the charge of self-perpetuation. For six months a special committee battled with this problem without coming to a conclusion even when it invited comments and suggestions from the full membership. No fault was found with the selection of standing committees but co-options rankled. The committee exceeded its mandate by examining the relationship of the local societies with the national body and advised an administrative structure based on the party's regional divisions: an attempt to tighten the bonds between the party and the Society at a very sensitive period.[20] A Bevanite member of this committee who thought its enquiry had been too superficial, Ian Mikardo, presented a minority report to the 1956 general meeting advocating division of the whole national Society into branches, thus abolishing the distinction between it and the local societies. Arthur Skeffington led an opposing faction of local society representatives and Gaitskell supporters in a debate which became very heated, continuing for five hours and producing so many alternative plans that Mikardo eventually asked for a special meeting to debate the matter to conclusion. The Executive refused and referred the matter back to the local societies, with additional solutions for them to consider in three regional meetings. By now they were not feeling quite as cut off from the mainstream of Fabian thought because series of lectures were being given annually in Cardiff, Gloucester, Grimsby and Leeds. Moreover, a separate inquiry chaired by Eirene White had confirmed the conclusion reached many years before that though provincial societies might comprise or produce a different kind of Fabian from those based in London, the former being more representative of the general Labour movement and the latter closer to the Parliamentary Labour Party, all were fundamental parts of the same movement. The national society therefore had become reconciled to the fact that local societies, though an expense, were not only desirable but essential to it as a means of disseminating Fabianism. In the end a good case was made for encouraging local members to become national ones and for doubling the affiliation fees – to satisfy one side – and for building up the conferences on local society research, held annually at St Antony's College in Oxford, as a means of keeping members' interest alive in the details of Fabian work and fostering their ability to carry it out on their own account.[21]

Gerald Kaufman, who had recently been assistant general secretary, tried the following year to get both co-options and election to the Executive abolished, but his scheme was far too radical for the majority of members who rejected it decisively at the general meeting. Even a move for annual general meetings to be held outside London on alternate years was utterly squashed. When it came to the point, the average member did not really want the Fabian Society changed in any radical manner, and so reformers among the leaders had to adapt their tools in the time-honoured, gradualist fashion, to do the work that had to be done.

Publication of essays turned out to be impossible in 1956. After succeeding Attlee as leader of the party in January, Gaitskell became immersed in the conflict with Bevan and the dispute in Conference over Clause Four of the constitution and unilateral nuclear disarmament. The Executive relieved him of his editorial responsibility and asked Roy Jenkins to see how many of the completed essays could be published individually as pamphlets.[22] Gaitskell's own essay was readily adapted and published as the 300th Fabian Tract, *Socialism and Nationalisation,* and launched at the reception in the House of Commons to celebrate the twenty-fifth anniversary of the New Fabian Research Bureau's birth.

So much in the colonial field then demanded political action that little time could be spared for wide consideration of policy. The colonial essays, too, came to a standstill in 1956. Franchise legislation in Central Africa, the land rights of those dispossessed by the Kariba Dam, South Africa's repeated pressure for incorporation of the High Commission Territories, constitutional developments in Malaya and Singapore and in the West Indies, and problems concerning the Colonial Development Corporation all clamoured for attention and discussion. By mid-year Rita Hinden decided to withdraw from the honorary secretaryship which imposed a heavy burden of work. Devoted as all the officers were to the cause of the colonial peoples, none had surpassed her in unflagging energy, sympathy and desire to serve; yet now she felt that her office had been 'more a title than a reality for some time, and as such it serves no purpose except to give [her] a perpetually uneasy conscience that [she was] not fulfilling [her] duty'.[23] The Bureau could ill afford to lose her unequalled experience, therefore it persuaded her to become a member of the Working Committee where she still epitomized the Bureau.

Notwithstanding ceaseless political activity the Bureau had lost confidence. Parliamentary Questions declined in number and effectiveness, lobbying of MPs brought far less result, partly due to slackening of direction, partly to loss of staff. Attendance at private meetings in the House of Commons to hear the views of colonial visitors or of members returning from Commonwealth missions dwindled sadly.

Ill fortune dogged the essays to the very end. Work was resumed on them and they were eventually sent to the Hogarth Press in October 1957, only to be rejected on the grounds that the book would be a commercial flop. Eirene White and Bill Rodgers rallied round the disconsolate editor and between them they whipped it into a guise more acceptable to the publishers. Unfortunately, its date of issue coincided with a newspaper strike, which removed any hope of reviews in the daily and provincial papers. Still the first edition sold out in less than three months.[24] What the public thought about it when it appeared cannot now be traced. Throughout all the revision and reshaping Creech Jones had stuck to his original purpose of explaining what the Labour Party had attempted to do between 1945 and 1951. Admitting that some mistakes had been made, he maintained that the Labour government's colonial work had been constructive, satisfying and 'remarkably consistent with its philosophy'.[25] Rita Hinden, having traced in her essay the history of the dichotomy in socialist thought on empire, reached the conclusion that British socialists were at last learning 'that an evil is not undone simply by withdrawing from the scene of the crime; there is still a debt to history waiting to be discharged'.[26]

This was what Fabian thinkers on colonialism from Shaw, through Leonard Woolf and Charles Roden Buxton to Creech Jones, had been saying consistently for the last fifty years. Other essayists had tackled the implications of the worldwide growth of nationalism since 1945, the effect of the decline of the sterling area and Britain's changing role in Europe on economic and political relations with the less developed Commonwealth countries, the impact of western civilization on social development and the irrelevance of western educational methods and materials in many countries of a different culture. Wilfred Benson, who had been a strong member of the Bureau even while working abroad for the ILO and the United Nations, traced the growing UN involvement in trusteeship and non-self-governing territories, and the changes since 1945 in international institutions created to handle the world's problems. Eirene White's summing up contained three warnings: first, that it was a mistake to think that all under-privileged coloured people were socialists or even that socialism meant the same thing the world over; second, that once the snowball of political independence was set in motion it rapidly became an avalanche which overwhelmed all attempts at gradualism; third, that the revived interest of the United States in world affairs added an incalculable factor to policy formation. The essays' general import was that while much remained to be done in an increasingly complex world, Britain's achievement in the colonies was better than was willingly admitted and her responsibility still obtained.

Harold Wilson, who encountered just as much frustration over editing as Gaitskell, handed over the *International Essays* to Tom McKitterick, who had succeeded Leonard Woolf as director of the Bureau in 1952, and Kenneth Younger, a former junior Minister in the Foreign Office. When the essays eventually appeared in 1957 they made no attempt to present a blueprint for foreign policy, but aimed at stimulating thought and discussion within the Labour movement. The authors agreed that the dominant problem for the remainder of the twentieth century would be that which had overshadowed policy discussions ever since the beginning of the Berlin airlift – how to ensure peaceful coexistence of the Communist and non-Communist blocs. One solution offered was to balance military vigilance against Communist aggression and attempts at expansion with, in less fraught times, a reduction in the level of defence commitments. This would permit more attention to be given to stemming the advance of Communist influence in those underdeveloped countries attracted by totalitarianism by providing self-government and aid through international agencies, at the same time fostering economic advance in the developed countries so that they could support the agencies financially. Britain particularly needed economic growth, according to Thomas Balogh, to re-establish her bargaining power and influence on and through the United States. John Strachey, who believed that ultimate abolition of nuclear war was the only policy which could possibly give Britain real security, nevertheless advocated an interim defence policy consisting of: '(a) the creation of a really effective nuclear deterrent and (b) the maintenance of conventional forces for local war and Commonwealth peace purposes only'.[27] The inflammatory mixture of poverty and nationalism in Middle Eastern countries, whose oil was the vital strategic pawn in the game of international diplomacy, was analysed at length in an essay completed before Britain became involved in the Suez war. Warning was also given of countries in the Far East becoming pawns in western power politics if Britain could not persuade the wealthy countries, principally the United States, to support long-term development in Asia. Patrick Gordon Walker, with past experience in the Commonwealth Office, begged for a non-party approach to both foreign and Commonwealth policy, and expressed the belief that by forgetting its imperial past, Britain could become an even greater force for peace and international understanding than the United Nations. The Fabian role, individual and collective, in all this was pointed out by Denis Healey: 'educating public opinion on the need for international co-operation and . . . encouraging the moral qualities required to sustain it'.[28]

This volume of essays was a brave attempt to record the Fabian range of views on Britain's place in the world order, her duties, obligations and responsibilities towards the maintenance of world peace and prosperity. Even as the essayists were writing the kaleidoscope turned. In the aftermath of the Suez crisis they suspected that they should attempt a re-evaluation of Britain's international commitments but the idea was aborted by yet another general election.

Time and again the International Bureau tried to establish closer relations with socialists in other European countries and with the Soviet Union. One group studying the problem of coexistence with the eastern bloc thought the best way to do this in 1955 was to pay a visit to the USSR. For nearly a year Bill Rodgers wrote letters to the ambassador in London – which were acknowledged but not answered – and telephoned to cultural and trade attachés, only to be blocked by amiable answers which seemed to promise much while meaning very little. Further efforts met with no greater success. The Webbs' enthusiastic account of Russia in the 1930s had done nothing to pave the way to Moscow for Fabians a quarter of a century later. Even a diplomatic approach by Christopher Mayhew in 1956 could not persuade the embassy to name any Russian visitors to Britain who might speak at Fabian meetings. Although individual European socialists still maintained an interest in the Society and friendship with its leading members, no proposal to collaborate ever got off the ground.

When autumn lectures in 1957 on 'Realities of foreign policy' caused a stir, Anthony Wedgwood Benn scrutinized the Bureau's work and produced a report on how to make it more vital. It could have been entitled 'Faults of the Fabian Part II'.[29] As he saw it, public opinion mattered to statesmen more than ever in an age of mass communication. Views hostile to Britain bandied on the floor of the United Nations General Assembly soon girdled the world. This made it particularly vital that the major topics of foreign policy should be publicly debated in Britain and the Fabian International Bureau could provide an ideal forum for foreign statesmen to put their arguments. Benn suggested inviting representatives from Russia, China, Poland, the United States and Africa to discuss publicly and privately colonialism, disarmament, political liberty, racial discrimination and similar subjects. Such a scheme was quite beyond the capability of a mere branch of the Society which had recently axed one of its major activities in order to save £120. Independent funding being essential, he planned to persuade the BBC or independent television to broadcast and televise the public debates, thereby covering the cost and at the same time stimulating wide interest in Fabian aims and activities. Unfortunately, both the BBC and ITA rejected the scheme and it was watered down to inviting speakers from embassies in London to take part in debates sponsored by the Bureau and the Central London Fabian Society, always the most active of the local societies.[30] Audiences of well over a hundred attended a debate on settlement in Europe and listened to Professor Arthur Schlessinger's views on the state of American liberalism. Denis Healey was then chairman of the Bureau, but Benn's reputation within the Society rose so sharply as a result of this initiative that he topped the poll in the Executive election, having served on it for a mere year.

Although the Conservatives won the 1959 election, support for Labour grew sufficiently to initiate recovery from three disastrous election results in a row. Within the Labour movement came recognition that the Fabian Society, having delivered several major reinterpretations of socialism, again had a valuable contribution to policy formulation. The Society responded and for the first time in ten years membership rose without any vigorous recruitment drive. A rise in pamphlet sales helped to bring its income within reach of its expenditure. Local societies perked up and held day schools. The Scottish Region mounted a summer school, which was an outstanding success. At the party conference in Scarborough a brains trust for local society delegates attracted a record attendance. Audiences at provincial lecture courses on foreign and party policy rose fivefold. Those who had been worrying about the Society's future for the last three years regained their confidence and set to work.

To mark the seventy-fifth anniversary Clement Attlee, Douglas Cole, Hugh Gaitskell, Jim Griffiths and all Fabians of over fifty years' standing were invited as guests of honour to a reception on 16 February 1959.[31] Cole died before he could keep the engagement and the large memorial meeting in his honour, held only five days before, naturally cast a shadow on the celebrations. Though this was a time for Fabian nostalgia the Executive was firmly resolved not to cling to the past but to look to the future, which belonged to the young. One of the younger members of the Executive, Brian Abel-Smith, joined Bill Rodgers and Tony Benn in a plea for a less dreary Fabian image. They each offered a different solution to the problem of how to attract new blood. Abel-Smith was impressed by the success of the Universities' and Left Review Club, which, though too far left for most Fabians, offered dangerous competition. He urged the Executive to meet the challenge with more attractive and controversial literature (because his students at the LSE condemned Fabian pamphlets as forbidding in appearance, turgid in style and dull in content) and meetings in pleasant surroundings, preferably with a coffee bar where they could stay on afterwards to talk. Bill Rodgers had discovered when sifting through the archives that three-quarters of all Fabians had been under 30 when they joined, and that the main loss of members came after the first year. He was vitally concerned with keeping new members interested until they had passed that dangerous stage. The small number at the heart of the Society would continue to construct the policies and use their influence on friends in high places, but a society which was patently ageing and

declining in numbers would impress no one. Benn agreed with much of
what the General Secretary had said but denounced the Society as stuck in
a rut. His guiding principle was Cole's dictum on the Fabian Ancients:

> Their names will be forever associated with what we do, and we shall be
> able to do it better for having their record behind us. But we do not
> propose to live on the legacy they have left us. We are doing our own job
> in our own way.[32]

He claimed that there should be more than 2800 members on the books
and questioned the propriety of Fabians allowing themselves to become
part of the Labour 'Establishment'. Part of their function should be to rock
the boat in order to reveal any leaks above the water-line. Bill Rodgers,
supported by Tony Crosland, believed that patient, social engineering was
the Society's most effective field. Benn, in contrast, wanted it to investigate
the major questions of the day – the H-bomb, disarmament, the
development of Communist societies and the anti-colonial movement.

After considering these three views the Executive asked its most recently
co-opted member, Shirley Williams, to find out whether the committee of
the Universities and Left Review Club would contemplate any form of co-
operation. Tony Benn now suggested public debates with the Bow Group,
the Conservative equivalent of the Society, and autumn lectures on the
next twenty-five years by speakers who would still be under 65 in 1984.
Revision of rules to bring declared Fabian objects up to date, a membership drive concentrating on the universities and the sixth forms, and much
closer collaboration with the Labour Party and TUC over publications
were all put on the programme for this jubilee year. With sights on a 1964
election rather than one in autumn 1959, the Home Research Committee
appointed three groups to draw up long-term research programmes on the
social services, industry and the economy, to be used as a basis of discussion
with the political and industrial branches of the Labour movement.

A long overdue addition to the Society's declaration of aims and
purposes was achieved as a result of Benn's proposed revision of the rules.
It was the first fundamental insertion since the equal citizenship clause
more than fifty years before, though there had been several tinkerings with
the rules in between. When his recommendation that two sentences should
be inserted in Rule 2 was put to the vote they were accepted with almost
unanimous acclaim.[33] Those two sentences were: 'It also aims at the
implementation of the Charter of the United Nations and the Universal
Declaration of Human Rights. It seeks the creation of effective international institutions to uphold and enforce world peace.'

The Society's financial position forced it to discontinue the *Fabian Journal* which had performed a valuable service for a third of the Society's life but ran at a loss.[34] *Venture* survived because it had become more or less viable with the help of a Labour Party subsidy.

Only the slightest check to Fabian progress was caused by the general election of October 1959. There had not been enough time to complete the renovation of the Society or for the effect of some of the changes already made to filter through to the general public, and so Labour's loss of nineteen seats and the decline in its share of the total vote did not depress the Fabian Executive, but made it even more determined to prepare the party for victory in five years' time. Since nothing was found to be wrong with Labour's programme, it decided to devote two years to burnishing the Fabian image and the following three to working on the party's policy and presentation.

Pursuing the search for younger members, Shirley Williams and Brian Abel-Smith were delegated to investigate setting up an Under-30s Committee, more like the Local Societies' Committee than the old Nursery. Bill Rodgers arranged a meeting to discuss the form and intent of the proposed new branch. Agreement was reached that it should have a separate constitution, endowing it with a large degree of autonomy, although the main Society would exert a certain control over its actions. Its aim would be to recruit young people not only to the Fabian Society but to the Labour movement generally, and to co-operate with the Young Socialists. In addition to publishing three pamphlets a year, under the Fabian imprint, it would organize its own related conferences and arrange study trips to European countries. All young Fabians would be eligible to join at no additional subscription and non-Fabians might become associates. At this point, Bill Rodgers resigned from the General Secretaryship, leaving the new vehicle for socialist education in the safe hands of his successor, Shirley Williams, and his assistant, Dick Leonard. Shirley Williams undertook to remain in the post for three years to see the redesigning of the Society through to completion. Brian Abel-Smith was selected to represent the Executive on the management committee of the new body. Partly due to Dick Leonard's tactful management, the Young Fabian Group had a firm basis by the time it was officially recognized in May 1960. Accompanying the announcement of its birth was a statement of its determination to be more adventurous than the parent body, to avoid commitment to any one brand of socialism and to provide a 'forum for different points of view within the Left'.[35]

During his last few months as General Secretary, Bill Rodgers had sent out a questionnaire to one-ninth of the Society's members as a basis for a series of articles on the modern Fabian. He had discovered that the typical Fabian was '44 years of age, married, lives in London or the Home Counties and is professionally engaged in education or management'.[36] In fact, 57 per cent still lived in or near London, only 19 per cent were women, an equal percentage were engaged in industry or business management, about 30 per cent were teachers, university lecturers or students, while only 2 per cent were in non-professional occupations. Half the members had given as their reason for joining the Society that they were socialists, about a quarter that they thought it worth supporting, a large section that they liked Fabian attitudes and almost as many that they could thus satisfy their interest without commitment. Yet it appeared that half of those who answered had taken no part in Fabian activities, they were merely paying their subscriptions and receiving the literature, having entered the Society on principle they were 'too busy' to play an active role. On the eve of his departure Bill Rodgers's third article opened with a subdued analysis of how little the Fabian Society seemed to have influenced the Labour Party in the nine years that he had been at Dartmouth Street, how powerless it had been to prevent the Party's decline. After warning that the prospect of another Labour government was continuing to recede, he did his utmost to inspire the Society to use its energy and talent to revive the party. He believed that by arousing public concern about what was still wrong with society and drawing people of good will and radical instincts into the Labour Party, Fabians might still be able to stiffen its backbone. He reaffirmed his faith that the real contribution of the Fabian Society was its method and approach: 'the objective study of facts, however unpalatable; intellectual honesty in the face of prejudice and pressure; frank speaking when the timid and calculating prefer silence and equivocation',[37] and that its strength lay in renouncing collective commitment except broadly to socialism.

On translation to the Executive Rodgers was asked to write a pamphlet on the post-war work and influence of the Society.[38] He rejected the idea because Margaret Cole's book, *The Story of Fabian Socialism*, was almost ready for publication. His farewell coincided with an appeal to members by Jack Diamond, the treasurer, for £5000 to lift the Society out of the red and provide it with the sinews of war.

In the month of his departure *Fabian News* reported the death at 99, in St Louis, Missouri, of the last of the Society's founders, Percival Chubb.[39] The following month the birth of the Young Fabian Group was announced. These two events marked the beginning of a new phase in the life of the Society. Billy Hughes, the chairman in 1960, had appealed for a redefinition of socialism in his New Year message.[40] Spring lectures with the theme 'Forward to 1964' attempted to do this as well as explore why the Labour Party was failing to appeal to the people. The opening lecture by Tony Crosland begged for less wrangling within the party and greater concentration on positive policies,[41] a cry repeated many times in the next two decades. During the summer, while *Socialist Commentary* edited by Rita Hinden was also examining the reasons for Labour's repeated defeats, Fabian schools reviewed 'Socialism and the complacent society' and 'Socialism in action' in a determined attempt to reconnoitre the way ahead. That autumn the Fabian offensive was launched to put Labour back in power in 1964.

Their first efforts to counter mid-century political apathy were not as successful as the officers had hoped, mainly because the roots of dissension within the party were so deep that Fabians could see no immediate way to eradicate them. Not the 1950s struggle between personalities but the fundamental, political dichotomy of Labour was splitting the movement, a dichotomy which surfaced fully only after the party had achieved its original social goals and had to reselect aims and purposes. Moreover, Fabians and others had begun to realize that what had been set in motion in 1945–51 had not been an incontrovertible success. Poverty, deprivation, ignorance, greed, envy and sloth still existed and thwarted the moral regeneration anticipated by the early Fabians as the outcome of economic and social reforms. Modern Fabians, deeply disturbed by this revelation, could not evince the conviction necessary to influence the Labour movement.

A more immediately identifiable cause for their failure at this time was lack of money. Only £3000 of the requested £5000 had been raised, some of which had to be spent on repairs urgently required in Dartmouth Street. The annual general meeting confirmed a rise in subscriptions proposed by the Executive; as always, this led to a fall in membership, though new members proved their enthusiasm by paying at the top rate to receive all publications. Fabian pamphlets were given more attention in the press and sales rose, partly because of the series called 'Socialism in the sixties', an examination of the remaining social evils and the remedies which might be applied to them and become a comprehensive policy for Labour. The series, which embraced all the tracts published between 1956 and 1964 which were not produced by the Bureaux, was initiated by a reprint of Hugh Gaitskell's tract on nationalization.[42] One of them, *Casualties of the Welfare State*, became a best-seller in Fabian terms.

The Young Fabian Group wished to play a role parallel to that of the main Society in 'resocializing' the Labour Party's programme. Its lectures, discussion meetings, weekend schools and study groups in the early 1960s all reflected this desire. Young Fabians believed they had a fresh viewpoint to offer and their first pamphlet was a critical review of the provisions for non-student youth in Britain presented in a highly autobiographical manner.[43] A committee of inquiry chaired by Lady Albemarle had made recommendations for the youth service which were unacceptable to the Young Fabian writer, Ray Gosling, then secretary of a self-programming youth-club in Leicester, financed by a limited liability company with a pop-star, a racing driver and the founder of a chain of holiday camps as directors. They objected to the patronizing attitude of the report, and called for a demonstration of trust by the older generation towards the younger – like the trust given to the Young Fabians by the parent society. No obstacle was put in the way of their publishing views very different from those of the elder Fabians, or encouraging affiliated groups in the provinces; they responded by acting responsibly.[44] Their second pamphlet, the product of a study group during the 'great defence debate' in the country as a whole, discussed the morality and practicality of NATO's dependence on nuclear weapons and advocated a policy of neutralism.[45]

The Young Fabians were deeply concerned about the effect decisions being made by their elders would have on their own future. They demanded the right to job satisfaction for all and protection against manipulation by the press. Many projects were embarked on with enthusiasm but not completed, a result of too many ideas. They had no counterpart to Shaw and Wells, though they listened avidly to the views of Hugh Gaitskell, Richard Crossman, Tony Crosland and Peter Shore on socialism. Winter months were devoted to study groups on the public-school system, the arts or the co-operative movement.[46] Yet, like their predecessors in the Nursery, they had a great deal of fun. Parties at their schools continued into the early hours, they swam at midnight or sang songs by camp-fires.[47]

While the Labour Party prepared to make another bid to govern the country, the numbers of Young Fabians grew rapidly, almost doubling each year. By the election they held distinct views on how the structure of the party could be improved, the changes they would like to see in education, transport in the crowded cities, Britain's oil sanctions against Rhodesia and the new Britain they wanted.

As the Young Fabian Group flourished, the Commonwealth Bureau declined. In May 1960 a subcommittee was instructed to consider its reorganization.[48] Creech Jones, again chairman of the Bureau, was then nearly 70 and, though nominally Labour spokesman for the rapidly diminishing number of colonies, had been virtually superseded in this role by Jim Callaghan. With his health failing, he could never again serve as Minister. Hilda Selwyn-Clarke was still secretary, with Margaret Roberts, soon to become Margaret Legum, as her very energetic assistant. After nine months of consultation the committee concluded that if the Bureau were to cover both Commonwealth affairs and the problems of the underdeveloped nations, the natural extension of its work, extra staff and money would have to be found.[49] Future work was difficult to plan because of the number of subjects which impinged on the preserves of the International Bureau. In 1961, therefore, a joint committee of both Bureaux was appointed to 'set the Commonwealth in its international perspective', review overlapping interests and generally redefine their respective roles. Hilda Selwyn-Clarke had withdrawn to the position of adviser to the Bureau because of ill health by the time the committee reported and Margaret Legum took responsibility for both Bureaux, with John Syson, the editor of *Venture*, taking over during her annual travel leave.

Complete amalgamation was, at first, resisted – nominally because no one in the Commonwealth Bureau had sufficient international expertise to make such a scheme work, in reality because of the Commonwealth's traditional assumption of superiority. While a joint working group was set up as a compromise, the Commonwealth Bureau tried hard to prove its independent vitality and viability, but when Margaret Legum announced that she too, intended to retire, Faringdon paved the way for true amalgamation by contributing a generous amount towards the staff's salaries for the first year. Rita Hinden's fears that the Bureau's traditional work for the dependent peoples would disappear if the merger took place were assuaged by creating a large subcommittee to deal exclusively with those matters:

> which could be advanced by political action within the British Parliamentary framework, and on which socialist opinion was reasonably united, e.g. colonial policy, certain aspects of British Commonwealth policy, United Nations questions and our contributions to the needs of the developing world where expertise and experience of the subcommittee would be invaluable.[50]

The amalgamation took place in 1962. Creech Jones resigned the chair and, with Faringdon, Rita Hinden and Hilda Selwyn-Clarke, joined the committee of the International and Commonwealth Bureau under the leadership of Tony Benn. Dick Taverne chaired the subcommittee, Creech Jones served on it until failing health forced him to curtail his non-parliamentary commitments in October 1963. He died in October 1964.

Benn was elected chairman of the combined Bureaux in February 1963, with Faringdon as vice-chairman. Inspired by his desire to revitalize that aspect of the Society's work great efforts were once more made to change the style and scope of *Venture*.[51] Fabians were beginning to write for two new journals on social and political issues, *New Society* and *Aspect*; *Venture* was the only bait to entice them back. Moreover, the Movement for Colonial Freedom was planning a parallel journal called *World Panorama*, the Africa Bureau was producing *Africa Digest* and the Labour Party's *Commonwealth Digest* had gained a circulation of over 800. All were competing for the same readers and the Fabians were determined that the Society's voice should be heard. Help came from the party, which contemplated minimizing its financial risk by allowing *Venture* to absorb the *Digest* in return for an additional, small subsidy. Faringdon was also willing to subsidize an enlarged *Venture* for a limited period.

Pamphlets were still being produced, though none emerged from the Commonwealth section's study groups on British Guiana, Aden, the future of the Commonwealth, and financial and technical aid; their outlet was *Venture*. Reg Sorensen had published a tract on Aden only two years before.[52] A solitary tract on South Africa following its expulsion from the Commonwealth and one Research Series pamphlet on Rwanda were all that appeared between the merger and Labour's return to power in 1964. The International Section, however, was prolific during the early 1960s on the two major themes of defence and the consequences of Britain joining the EEC, on which issue Fabian opinion was divided. By that time the Fabians felt they had said all they could on the general principles of Commonwealth and international relationships, that they had cleared up misapprehensions about what the Labour Party had done in the past and indicated the direction to be taken in the future by means of the two books of essays.

Tremendous efforts were made by Shirley Williams and her assistant to increase membership, because huge tasks faced the Society and could not be tackled unless the workload and the financial burden were more widely spread. Trade unions were canvassed for fresh affiliations and increased donations. University and public libraries were invited to take out subscriptions for Fabian publications. Tom Ponsonby cultivated student organizations and helped Fabian societies in the universities. Like her predecessor, Shirley Williams was always a welcome visitor to local societies while Dorothy Fox and Arthur Skeffington continued to provide continuous encouragement to the provinces, in person as well as by letter. Fabian work was publicized in several novel ways. The General Secretary accepted invitations to take part in popular radio programmes on current affairs and offered an imaginative project to the organizers of the Festival of Labour in London, in 1962. Unfortunately the organizers whittled the scheme down to a two-day exhibition of the Society's work in their arcade for affiliated bodies in Battersea Park, but allowed a luncheon party in the House of Commons based on the theme of bridging the gap between politicians and scientists to go ahead.[53]

The publication of Margaret Cole's history did more than anything else to prove to the public that the Fabian Society was still very much alive. Scholars' interest was greatly stimulated by this labour of love which entertained while it instructed. After she had finished consulting the archive she persuaded the Executive to open negotiations for depositing all records not in current use in her husband's former college, Nuffield, alongside his books and personal papers.[54] They were transferred to the college in 1966, just before the Cole Room was created out of the basement in which they had been stored in Dartmouth Street. The Colonial Bureau papers were more appropriately deposited in Rhodes House Library, where they joined those of Creech Jones, donated by his wife to the Oxford Colonial Records Project inspired and instituted by his close friend, Dame Margery Perham. Both collections are in constant demand by historians and political scientists. To parallel *The Story of Fabian Socialism*, the sixth edition of the original *Fabian Essays in Socialism* was published, with a new introduction by Professor Asa Briggs, all four earlier prefaces and the postscript added by Bernard Shaw in 1948. This completed the reassertion of Fabian principles and the Society's continued devotion to them which had been put to the test when the electorate turned from socialist aims in 1950–1.

The intervening years had been spent enquiring into how much could be preserved of the Fabian ethos while the world changed around it. The conclusion was that much that had seemed right originally was still valid, although there might need to be a certain amount of retailoring for the more mature body. A new Nursery was in existence, the Kraus Reprint Corporation had negotiated to reproduce the whole of the *Fabian Quarterly* and was exploring the American market for reprints of all the Tracts and Research Series pamphlets, while another company was seeking to microfilm all of them up to 1950.[55] Growth of social studies on both sides of the Atlantic in the second half of the century made this an attractive proposition.

On retiring from the Executive in 1963, Margaret Cole agreed to become the fourth Fabian President. So many members of long standing applied for tickets to the dinner celebrating her elevation that the room originally booked in the House of Commons proved too small and the event had to be transferred to a restaurant.[56]

The opportunity for the electorate to end Labour's thirteen years in opposition was fast approaching. Policy preparation was the main Fabian preoccupation for this election. It had used the period of opposition well. With three new volumes of essays, sixty Tracts and eighty-eight Research Series pamphlets, the publications of individuals such as Crosland's *The Future of Socialism*, Clegg's *Industrial Democracy and Nationalization* and Michael Shanks's *Lessons of Public Enterprise* and many others, the Society felt it had done its best to educate the Labour Party in both the theory and the practical application of socialism. Of course, the party was not relying exclusively on Fabian research and recommendations for its 1964 programme; several other research bodies had grown up within the Labour movement in the last fifteen or twenty years, but the Society still had a great deal to offer.

22

FRIENDLY CRITICS

The mid-1960s saw an upsurge of optimism that was not wholly warranted. The pace of cultural change from 1964 to 1984 was possibly swifter than at any time in the last two centuries. A whole generation which had passed through state schools established by the 1944 Education Act and higher education establishments supported by state grants now took for granted the right to protest whenever it disagreed with decisions taken by others. The whole population had fast become accustomed to the idea that it had a right to social services and full employment. It demanded protection from injustice and provision of equality, whatever that last term meant. None of this created solidarity. 'I'm all right, Jack' had long been a catch-phrase and the 'angry young man' stood alone. While older slogans might still echo, a Labour government was no longer expected to fight capitalism for it was felt that all had become capitalists then. Instead it was required to milk any stray wealth that remained and exploit the country's resources to the full in order to provide continuous economic growth to meet the desires of the electorate while keeping taxation to the minimum. The consumer society had been created and few at first saw its perils. Towards the 1970s those few rapidly multiplied, and some deliberately turned their backs on 'civilization' as it was presented to them, calling it a plastic society, and sought personal salvation in a more primitive existence, evangelism, solitary adventuring or following a guru. There were 'flower people', hippies and communes. Others blatantly over-consumed, disregarding the resultant penalties – the cities silting up with too many cars, loss of respect for property leading to loss of regard for persons, air pollution, water pollution, even pollution by noise. In the full flush of consumerism those below the poverty line were swept under the deep-pile carpet. Comparability in wage levels appeared to be the generally recognized symbol of equality. Obversely, as the plethora of playthings began to pall, a caring society emerged. People began to realize that their new society was not the desired regeneration. They appeared to have acquired problems even greater than those solved. Groups sprang up to help individuals such as the battered wife or the single parent. Existing organizations to assist children in poverty, the homeless young, the aged, the illiterate, the alcoholic, the suicidal, were recognized as essential. Concern was shown about racial and sexual discrimination, political prisoners, and the needs of the Third World. Self-help, mutual aid and altruism bloomed together.

Fabians had, of course, long provided an outstanding example of the caring society. They were concerned about all those causes adopted by individual groups, they were in the traditional manner found on their committees. However, the collective Fabian approach and methods of dealing with a particular problem often differed from the groups', partly as a consequence of far longer acquaintance with it. Accordingly, it was essential to make the Society's views instantly recognizable and continuously heard. As soon as the precarious Labour government of 1964 was installed the new General Secretary, Tom Ponsonby, set out to meet this challenge. He built up a new team of writers, rationalized office routine so that his small and virtually untried staff was able to tackle a large increase in duties and encouraged the more adventurous editorial policy for *Venture* sparked off by a controversial article which fiercely attacked the Wilson cabinet's policy over Vietnam. The Executive at this point doubled its insurance cover against libel. For the first time a designer was called in, to create a cover for Young Fabian pamphlets, and give Fabian publications the professional appearance needed in this age of the media.[1] The plea of Wells more than half a century before was at last being met.

Absorption of the National Council of Labour Colleges by the TUC's educational branch now provided the Society with an opportunity to expand its publications. The TUC had no use for the publishing or trading side of the work of the National Council of Labour Colleges, and its magazine *Plebs* was offered to several bodies, including the Labour Party and the Fabian Society. The Fabian Executive wanted a domestic magazine to counterbalance the international *Venture*, and eventually agreed to run *Plebs* for two years provided its former directors would contribute £5000 in instalments from the sale of the former college property in Hampstead. The package dropped into the General Secretary's lap was a strange one and caused him many a headache. J.P.M. Millar still had several months of his contract as editor to work out and so no clean break could be made in editorial policy in April 1965 when it was handed over. The name had to be retained because of the need to hang on to the subscriptions of the old-fashioned socialist readers for whom the magazine had a nostalgic attraction. But some change had to be made so that *Plebs* would pay for itself after an initial subsidy from the TUC ceased. The Fabians wanted to make a fresh appeal to trade union and Labour Party activists, particularly those in local government, and to the young technocrats who might appreciate the educational bias. In the end a compromise was chosen. *Plebs* assumed some of the functions of the old *Local Government News* and the *Fabian Journal*, without achieving the distinction of the latter. It also provided background material linked with the TUC educational courses and an outlet for any Young Fabian study group material not substantial enough for pamphlets. Geoffrey Cannon, the designer, refurbished it so that it bore a strong resemblance to all the other Fabian literature, Dick Leonard struggled manfully at the head of an editorial committee to turn it into a magazine with impact, 90 per cent of its original subscribers remained loyal to it, yet it continued to be an encumbrance, not an asset. Intensive efforts were made to build up a new clientele in constituency Labour Parties, Young Socialist branches and Trades Councils.[2] Only by continuous pushing could its circulation be maintained and more money was needed than advertising space produced. When contributions from the NCLC ceased it would undoubtedly founder.

A merger with *Venture*, in order to produce an entirely new journal, was rejected for fear of losing the large orders from the unions. Besides, as the only British publication devoted solely to the affairs of the emergent nations, *Venture*, in its existing form, was important to the Labour movement. Among personal subscribers it numbered four Prime Ministers, one former Prime Minister and several other Ministers of former colonial territories; Commonwealth ministries and universities also received it, and it was widely quoted by Commonwealth legislatures, the United Nations, and the British Parliament.

Bill Rodgers made a plea for less but higher-quality publication, more closely aligned with the traditional role of the Society. Tracts and Research Series pamphlets were critical but not as constructively so as in the past. Moreover, a residual anxiety still haunted leading Fabians that the principles of socialism had still not been adequately stated in contemporary terms. The Young Fabians were planning their first book of essays, demanding more power to the people.[3] Their elders had a guilty suspicion that they ought to make a major, philosophical statement for which they were not prepared. Britain was in the throes of the financial crisis which led to devaluation of the pound in 1967. Sources for the large borrowing necessary to operate the deficit economy upon which the welfare state rested had become more difficult to find. Immigration from the Commonwealth unexpectedly escalated so that legislation was required to regulate social and industrial relationships which had formerly depended on the goodwill of the people. Increase in the population was only one of the many reasons why, at a time when unemployment was extraordinarily low and more married women were working than ever before (as far as statistics could prove), Britain could not produce and market enough goods to support the existing social services, much less improve and expand them as the people demanded. National confidence in Britain diminished. De Gaulle's repeated refusal to let Britain join the Common Market, developments in the Commonwealth with international implications, the continuing defiance of Rhodesia, the condemnation by other nations of Britain as an imperial power when the benefits of empire had vanished, together with the intractable situation in Ireland, eroded Britain's confidence. All problems began to appear insoluble. In the face of such insecurity the Fabian Society needed to draw on all its reserves of confidence and sense of direction in order to discover the new route to social regeneration.

Individual Fabians may have possessed these qualities but were forced to bide their time for collective action while the office was being transformed. So many alterations were needed to strengthen the building and to comply with local fire regulations that it was decided to take this opportunity to completely redesign its interior, making it more comfortable and efficient and a more valuable property. To install modern heating and ventilation, redivide the offices and create, in the Cole Room, the longed-for meeting-place complete with coffee-bar, the largest ever appeal for funds was made in 1965. To make room the archives were shipped to Oxford and the library was sold to the University of Hull. More than eighteen months of turmoil followed, until the alterations were completed in time for the annual general meeting of 1967. Instead of the usual invitation to a prestigious speaker to address the meeting, members were invited to visit Dartmouth Street in small groups, see what had been achieved and admire the Cole Room.

Somehow, through all this, pamphlets were published and distributed with *Fabian News* – not as many as usual but a good number. The regular functions still took place, schools being held at Christmas, Easter and in the summer though conferences had lapsed. The Local Societies Committee pursued its business as usual and a couple of study groups managed to study educational problems and discrimination against women. But the society felt an imperative need for more positive action. Therefore, soon after the 1966 election increased Labour's overall majority by ninety-two, the Executive held several extraordinary meetings to consider the Society's role over the next five years and concluded that it should be the Labour Party's friendly critic.[4] There was some anxiety lest the Society become a rallying point for all the discontents within the Labour movement. Bill Rodgers was particularly concerned about this because he knew, as Under-Secretary in the Ministry of Economic Affairs, that the tough economic situation facing the country would severely curb expansion of social reforms. Accordingly a scheme was devised whereby Ministers would be invited, one by one, to meet small sections of the Executive to talk about their problems and suggest lines of work for the Fabians, discuss their departments' work with groups of experts and preside over seminars at which they would present papers.

Douglas Houghton, the Minister without Portfolio, was the first guest speaker. An expert on pensions and insurance, he advised the Home Research Department to set up study groups on disablement benefits and industrial injuries, child poverty, fatherless families and family incomes, discriminatory benefits and the Ministry of Social Security's function as a welfare agency.[5] The industrial insurance group, in abeyance since 1961, was reconvened and work began on several neglected aspects of poverty and social deprivation. Peter Townsend, the Fabian chairman, started off the autumn lectures with an attack on the government's half-hearted approach to the reconstruction of health and welfare services and the poverty of large and fatherless families, and its failure to live up to professed socialist and egalitarian principles. Richard Titmuss was another outspoken critic of the government and the uncaring, affluent society. Richard Crossman, then Lord President of the Council, gave a final summing-up of the series, which was 'a really rumbustious reply' to the other lecturers' fierce attack on the government 'for failing to abolish poverty'.[6] An old-style, hard-hitting debate ensued which continued into the New Year School on the theme of 'Labour's hot potatoes'. All four lectures were printed as tracts and reissued within months in book form as *Socialism and Affluence*.[7] While outsiders might view this as a disloyal attack, the Fabians regarded it as 'a dialogue between the Labour Government and its thoughtful friends outside, in industry, the social services, the universities and elsewhere', and expected Ministers to 'listen even when the candour of friends speaking in a good cause becomes hurtful to them'.[8]

Not that there was such a clear-cut distinction in this instance, since more than half the Executive were members of the government. The government seemed to be exploiting the Society's ability to arouse public feeling in favour of social reforms it wanted to introduce, as is shown by Crossman's appointment as Minister of Health and Social Security in November 1968. Even though very few of the improvements demanded by the friendly critics could be introduced before the government's defeat in 1970, the fresh approach to social insurance and social security, designed to ensure that those needing help received it as their right and not as charity, marked the end of the old Poor Law mentality.

Friendly criticism needed to be persistent but, for the most part, undramatic, academically searching and constructive. The *Fabian Journal* had been the ideal medium for that kind of writing, but whenever a new version of it was discussed, the claims of pamphlets always triumphed because they produced revenue. The old journal had never sold more than 120 copies; any pamphlet at this time had an immediate sale of about 1000 or considerably more if the subject was of lasting interest. Growth of social studies in the universities and colleges of higher education favoured pamphlet sales; interest in a new journal was expected to be too ephemeral to extract regular orders from library and faculty committees. *Plebs* ran into very heavy weather in 1968: circulation had dropped to a third of what it had been and advertising income plumetted.[9] Consequently, *Plebs* disappeared in 1969 after Robert Maxwell's attempt to transform it into a new publication altogether, 'The Trade Unionist', had foundered.[10]

Familiar people, too, were moving further back on the Fabian stage. A direct link with the New Fabian Research Bureau's domestic research programme was snapped when Billy Hughes, originally its assistant secretary, retired after twenty years as chairman of the Home Research Department.[11] Searching for a new approach to domestic research the Executive Committee appointed four steering committees to initiate new projects, such as study groups to shadow each of the major government departments. The International and Commonwealth Bureau, assisted by the Young Fabians, assumed responsibility for all work connected with the EEC, a heavy one because the Labour Party had no intention of producing any literature on the subject. Fabian views on the Common Market were as diverse, though not as inflamed, as they had been on the Boer War, therefore a conscious effort was made to present every shade of opinion to the public. The young Fabians took the opportunity of study weekends in

Germany, Sweden and France to investigate the way things were organized on the continent in the legislatures and trade unions as part of their study of what integration with Europe would imply. Various formats for presenting these views were envisaged. The steering committees finally decided on a second volume of *International Essays* to be edited by George Cunningham, helped by an advisory committee, a third volume of *Fabian Essays in Socialism* to pick up the philosophical struggle where the second volume had fallen short, and a collection of essays on industry; in addition two other books laying down policy lines for education and the social services were expected to emerge from the ministerial interview scheme. By such substantial statements of principle it was hoped to point the Labour movement in the right direction for the 1970s.[12]

David Owen and Robert McFarland now weighed in, saying that redefinition of Fabian aims and purposes was long overdue, that extremely talented and distinguished people were not being used effectively and arguing that because there were now so many pressure groups at work the influence and permeative power of the Society had become a myth.[13] Young Fabians were also most insistent that they and the senior Society needed to collaborate with other groups concerned about specific problems.[14] They were disappointed with the government's record since 1964 and wanted to identify social needs and make a series of policy recommendations establishing priorities and alternative programmes for the 1970s. Just like the Nursery before them, a large section now called for deliberate declarations of collective policy on specific issues by the Society. They all ignored one very important point: the Fabian Society had invaded every level of educational establishment in the country and had thoroughly permeated what had come to be known as the media. Wherever social sciences were being studied Fabians were teaching and extending the borders of the science, whenever political questions and current affairs were discussed, Fabian broadcasters, journalists and lecturers were found in the forefront of the discussion. The Fabians were fulfilling their own particular role in an extrapolation of what Webb and Wallas had directed the local societies to do in the 1890s. Thus, although there were vociferous demands for new methods in Fabian work, the means that answered best in the dissemination of Fabianism were merely adaptations of the way in which the Society had always operated, because that had been based on a sound system and was admirably suited to the talents attracted by its philosophy.

Some changes had taken place of their own accord during the transition to the 1970s. Summer schools had declined. The former four weeks a year for over 200 people had shrunk now to one week of family school in Wales, attracting about thirty adults and half the number of accompanying children, and one overseas school also of about thirty. Day schools, on the other hand, had become very popular, but weekend schools had almost vanished except for those run by the regions or the Central London Fabian Society, always very active. Systematic and continuous recruitment ever since Tom Ponsonby had become General Secretary had produced a steady rise in membership which looked like continuing for some time. This large membership had become preoccupied with the moral aspects of socialist policies. A reversion to the original Fabian predilection brought about by the knowledge that socialist measures had not brought the expected relief from poverty and social deprivation for all, though many had undeniably benefited, that the cost of the system was mounting, and that international problems were constantly increasing. The Executive had to consider the Fabian contribution to the 1970 election manifesto and look ahead to the issues likely to arise in the last quarter of the century.[15] Not that the Fabian leaders suffered from the delusion that the Society was the only body to exert an influence on Labour's policy – the Tribune Group, for instance, was exerting considerable leverage to shift it to the left. Shirley Williams made a strong case for introducing into Labour's political debate such questions as the validity of economic growth, the moral approach to scientific research and development and the doubtful acceptability of ever-increasing expenditure on the social services.[16] The autumn lecture series, 'Socialism in a dangerous world', reflected this reversion to the moral aspects of socialist policies.

Though the Labour government was defeated in June 1970, the Fabian Society emerged triumphant in the autumn. Its popularity took the Executive and the General Secretary by surprise. Offsetting a loss of members the previous year there was now a gain of over 1000, which meant numbers were higher than at any time since 1947 – over 4000. Shirley Williams topped the poll which some read as an indication that members approved of her approach to the next decade. She continued to top the poll for the next three years. There was little time for self-congratulation at this sudden rise in Fabian fortunes. As at the end of the 1945–51 government, several ex-Ministers were invited to discuss the way forward with sections of the Executive and members who were experts in relevant fields of study or public service. This time government advisers were also invited to give their opinions on what had gone wrong. There was profound disappointment throughout the Labour movement that the last Labour government had achieved so few of its aims. Fabians, at least, realized that the government's attempts had been frustrated by the increasing size and complexity of the problems. Therefore they faced the next decade with their heads up and a fresh plan of campaign. Seminars were held on the proper attitude for the Labour Party towards the problems raised by international companies, the place of voluntary participation in running the social services and positive discrimination in many fields.[17] Conferences and weekend schools concentrated on 'Priorities for the seventies' and, like the pamphlet series 'Socialism in the seventies', reviewed the policy issues recently neglected by the party. Many of these dealt with the failure of perfectly good legislative measures to produce the intended social reform, a topic then of great concern to the series editor, Brian Lapping, and to Brian Abel-Smith and Peter Townsend.[18] Public interest in what sections of the Labour Party were saying naturally subsided after the election and yet twice as many of these tracts were sold as in any previous year. Tony Benn described the phenomenon as a socialist renaissance.[19]

Twice the usual number now joined the Society; the Young Fabian Group doubled in size between 1970 and 1972. In a mere three months, after a recruiting advertisement in the *New Statesman*, 650 new members were enrolled. Tom Ponsonby was at the heart of this revival, buoyantly presenting nearly every Executive Committee meeting with a fresh memorandum on how to exploit the energy and enthusiasm of the new members, how to boost their numbers to 10,000 so that there would be ample funds to produce the two pamphlets a month which would make the Fabian Society the ginger group of the Labour Party. The large influx of young people new to the Fabian ethic made less difference than expected to the Society's thought and methods. Although more attention was now being paid to the interests of minorities and to the gap between the developed and the underdeveloped nations, although the Young Fabians produced two pamphlets which attracted considerable attention from the press – *Strangers Within* on the position of immigrants in Britain, and *Womanpower* on that of women – young people began to drift away.[20] They were primarily disappointed that the Fabian method of influencing the Labour Party was not through direct resolutions to Conference which always received a lot of media publicity and discussion, but through recommendations and memoranda to the Labour Party's various committees and to trade union inquiry commissions.

A change was taking place, too, in the local societies which wanted their relationship with the corresponding local and regional bodies of the Labour Party reviewed and realigned.[21] They asked that the role of the Local Societies Committee be reconsidered because it had been completely inundated by the amount of work entailed in administering the hundred, rapidly growing societies. After twenty-five years continuous service as chairman of the Committee, Arthur Skeffington decided to retire, feeling unable to satisfy the current pressure for local societies to increase their influence on the local Labour Parties. Tom Ponsonby had to take up this challenge. There was a considerable danger that without closer links with the parent body, the local societies might become less Fabian and more militant, causing either friction between the party and the Society at all levels or a decline in local societies as members found more attractive affiliations. He persuaded the Executive to raise the capitation fee to a more realistic level and spend the increased funds on developing the local societies and giving positive encouragement to their research into local problems. It was at this point that the world economic situation began to bite into the plans of the Fabian Society. The process was gradual. Lack of money and inflation meant less work could be undertaken, and less publicity could be given to what was completed. Frustration grew as the Executive had to ask for sacrifices by both staff and members in return for decreasing achievement.

The Dartmouth Street and Sarah Hall Trusts were then providing almost all the funds for the Society's main research; occasionally a bequest financed a particular piece of work. Administration costs had been greatly increased by the decision to make salary scales comparable with those of Transport House. In emergencies, members of the staff have occasionally elected to renounce promotion or salary increases, and in recent years the expedients of reducing hours worked or voluntary wage cuts have curbed escalation of the annual deficit, while research continues to be financed either by the self-sacrifice of individual members or by the trusts and similar, outside institutions. Hubert Humphreys, who died in 1969, left the Fabians a one-fifteenth share in his house in Birmingham, which helped towards propaganda pamphlets as he had wished, but the £2500 did not go as far as was hoped because of inflation.

Financial difficulties mounted but the Fabians were again enjoying themselves with Labour in opposition. They felt creative, problems were attacked with vigour, dialogue with the leaders of the Parliamentary Party was constructive and once more they were free to take a wider view of the economic, social and political situation. Increasingly, opportunities for collaboration with political groups outside Britain were sought. In 1971 a spring conference at Wiston House in Sussex discussed Britain's place in Europe and European political organization with the German and French equivalents of the Fabian Society, the Friedrich Ebert Stiftung and the

Centre National d'Etudes et de Promotion and L'Office Universitaire de Recherche Socialiste.[22] Fabians knew Wiston House well, having sent delegates there to official conferences on questions of common European concern in the 1960s.[23] The Society was next invited to collaborate with the Club di Roma and the review *Proteus*, in arranging a conference in Italy on the environmental implications of technological advance.[24] Meanwhile Young Fabians organized their own four-day visit to Brussels.

Peter Hall thought, in 1972, that the Society ought to use its newly acquired knowledge to formulate an agenda for the next Labour Government.[25] The Conservative government had reached mid-term and if the Society was to have any influence on the next election programme the Labour Party needed at least two years to digest Fabian ideas. In his New Year greeting from the chair, he announced the creation of special 'task forces' to correspond with each of the main governmental departments, to study their deficiencies, requirements, capabilities and powers of implementation. Designed to involve Fabians at all levels they had a broader range of members, reported regularly to the whole Society through the pages of *Fabian News*, appealed for comments and generally operated in a much more democratic way than previous working parties. It was hoped thus to abolish the annual complaint that the only views expressed by the Society were those of the Executive and the main body in London, and the only action taken that initiated by them. Young Fabians instantly responded to the challenge and volunteered for work on whichever of the groups appealed to them – within a year their executive committee was boasting that they had dominated the discussion in the task forces.

The amount of paper used was prodigious. Before the next Labour Party conference their aim was to produce a statement called the 'Radical agenda' which would define principles of policy for the party and lay down practical goals for the next Labour government. This would be presented in pamphlet form for consideration by delegates at Conference, after which, in the autumn lecture series, shadow ministers would be asked for comments. Conclusions would then be reconsidered in plenty of time for a possible election in 1974. The International and Commonwealth Bureau alone branched out into seven different task forces, covering such topics as the law of the sea and areas of residual responsibility such as the Falkland Islands, Gibraltar and Hong Kong. A greater degree of democracy in the work was introduced by the invitation to all members to send in written evidence and recommendations on each subject; progress reports were published each month in *Fabian News* – the modern-day equivalent of submitting tracts for criticism at members' meetings before publication.

Task-force conveners drew up a questionnaire aimed at finding out from ex-Ministers what they thought of the kind of machinery with which they had had to work. This struck the Executive as highly impertinent, since it included questions about Ministers' pre-office qualifications for their particular offices, whether they had carried out the aims with which they had assumed office and, moreover, whether they remained valid. In a similar spirit, the International and Commonwealth Bureau insisted on drawing up a dossier of recommendations to hand to an incoming Labour Foreign Secretary against which he could measure advice from official quarters. *Venture* had performed this task for the Bureau in the past; now transformed into *Third World* under John Hatch's editorship, its design and function were entirely different from those of *Empire* when it had stood alone in the field. *Third World* now had to compete with the output of the Africa Bureau, which catered for those with a political but not necessarily socialist concern, and the literature of the missionary societies, Oxfam, Christian Aid, Unesco and Unicef, which met the needs of philanthropic interests.

The great 'Radical agenda' project fell rather flat in the end. Ten of the task force preliminary reports commenting on different aspects of party policy documents were combined in *Towards a Radical Agenda* in time for the party conference, where it sold reasonably well.[26] Some of the task forces had then continued with their allotted task to produce full-scale, more considered reports, but a number gave up the struggle. Fabians could not hide their chagrin at the Society's failure to 'address itself centrally to the critical relationship between spending programmes and available resources'.[27] The Society had never, in fact, produced a solution to the fundamental problem of the cost of socialism, how to pay for reform after the initial capital charge had been defrayed. A committee asked to draw up a fully costed alternative budget had failed. The Society, which always expected to be able to answer questions that everyone else found impossible, was surprised when it, too, was defeated.

Some Young Fabians had developed in the task forces a taste for policy formulation. In 1973 they made themselves responsible for reviving *Plebs* claiming that they could make the periodical contribute constructively to the socialist debate.[28] Each issue was designed to have a main theme and to carry regular features on parliamentary and provincial affairs, aid and development, foreign policy and a review of the arts. *Plebs* was now offered as a medium for debate directed at policy making instead of mere comment.[29] The third number, in ten brief articles on different fields of policy, threw the ball into the scrum in the hope that the main Society would clear it. Denis Healey was persuaded to spell out the rules of play in an article on 'The next Labour government: Cost and priorities' for a special autumn issue to be sold at the 1973 party conference.

Fabians were now very pessimistic about Labour's chance of success at the next election. The party was certainly not presenting a very convincing image of an alternative government. Members were urging the Executive to take the lead but, try as it might, it could produce no great breakthrough in socialist thought, no inspiring new aims and purpose for itself or the party. The Society had plenty to say on a great number of individual matters of concern and its ideas were permeating the media, but what was said did not build up to a single, recognizable philosophy. It had become enmeshed in the coils of its own friendly criticism. Richard Titmuss, revered as the most clear-sighted analyst of the moral values involved in policy making, died early in 1973. Fabians could still derive inspiration from his book, *The Gift Relationship*, and his two tracts, *The Irresponsible Society* and *Choice and the Welfare State*, but he had not been a manipulator or a whip cracker like the Webbs or Shaw.[30] His legacy to the Society was a stringent assessment of modern socialist aims and actions, at a time when Fabian socialism had become buried under a mound of Fabian socialistic measures. Anthony Crosland, too, was greatly respected, but his influence on the Society was nearer that of Wallas than of Webb and a combination of Webb and Shaw was now needed.

As this became evident members began to drift away from the Society. Attendance at autumn lectures fell so low in 1972 that there were grave doubts about holding them again. Lately they had produced no pamphlets and as an evening's entertainment the autumn lecture was now said to be a bore.[31] Good though *Third World* was it now cost more to produce with each passing month. As the Society sank deeper into the red the Executive decided not to observe its ninetieth anniversary but to begin planning centenary celebrations as early as 1980. The Fabians responded by reverting to the springs of their own existence and seeking inspiration from the lives of earlier, generative socialists. In *Radicals, Reformers and Socialists* six of the former biographical tracts were republished, presenting Fabians with a chance to compare their own interpretation of socialism with that of Thomas Paine, Robert Owen, Francis Place, William Lovett, and Sidney and Beatrice Webb.

Fabians recognized that the mounting confrontation between industry and government would not be dissipated by mere substitution of a Labour for a Conservative government. Neither was armed with a remedy for what was happening. Meanwhile, workers' confidence and security was draining away in the period of the three-day week and being replaced by an aggressive self-protection.

This situation inevitably placed the Labour Party back in office in 1974, some months earlier than the Executive had anticipated. The customary list of Fabians in the government was a proud one.[32] Seven former chairmen, one of them the Prime Minister, the current chairman Frank Judd, four former chairmen of major committees, two former general secretaries and an assistant general secretary all held government posts. The authors of twenty-six Fabian pamphlets now sat on the government benches. This was permeation indeed and hopes ran high for the introduction of a radical programme on the lines of the agenda recently proffered. The new blood to take their place in the continuing critical and constructive work of the Society was not as promising as in the past, though the Young Fabians contributed valiantly in the study groups and pamphlet committees. National membership still dropped monthly and the general picture of what was happening in the local societies was not at all clear.

While inevitable gaps in committees were filled and work realigned the major preoccupation in the Executive was how to keep afloat with inflation rising to over 25 per cent. A second and third volume of biographical studies promised to be lucrative.[33] Luncheons hosted by Fabian Ministers and other public figures were gratifyingly successful in obtaining instant gifts and covenanted donations for the Dartmouth Street Trust; a generous legacy from Blanche Colebrook in 1975 put the Society back on its feet. *Third World* was sacrificed to production of International and Commonwealth Bureau pamphlets, which seemed more effective just then. Stringent economies were made in the office, and the subscription rate was again raised. All these measures saved the Society from foundering but were unable to ensure continued buoyancy. The Executive embarked on a full-scale investigation of what had gone wrong since the beginning of the decade when the Society had been, apparently, riding the crest of the wave. Decline in numbers was attributed not only to lack of funds to invest in recruitment drives, but also to the mistaken claim in earlier campaigns that the Fabian Society was the Labour Party's ginger group. Young recruits, beguiled by the boast, had rapidly become disillusioned and departed. During the life of the 1974 Labour government, Young Fabian numbers dropped by 60 per cent. A more accurate assessment of the Society's function was now made: that it provided a position for debate within the Labour movement which lay half-way between academic treatment of political themes and that of the party meeting. Margaret Cole criticized

Fabian publications for being too 'ingrowing' and the product of writers writing for each other's enjoyment. She demanded more literature with popular appeal. Others on the Executive wanted a higher philosophical content in the literature because for many years attempts to discuss what the Society meant by socialism had been unsuccessful.

The officers and the Executive slaved throughout 1976 to reverse the Society's dangerous decline. An impressive appeal for new members and £200,000 was launched by Sir Harold Wilson in midsummer, shortly after he had handed over the premiership to Jim Callaghan. In the appeal brochure the claim was made that:

> The Fabian Society is the most influential, and productive independent research group, measured by the number of its ideas which have been put into action. Since before it played a crucial role in the formation of the Labour Party, the Fabian Society has produced books, pamphlets and magazines which have been essential reading for ministers, civil servants, journalists, students and politicians of all parties, here and abroad. Many of these documents have become fundamental research material, having influenced legislation bringing benefits to all sections of society.[34]

This claim was a reasoned, just assessment of the Society's modern role, but it did not have the ring of 'to help on the reconstruction of society'. When the General Secretary, on taking his seat in the House of Lords and as chairman of both the Greater London Council and the London Tourist Board, left Dartmouth Street in September, more than half the money required had been promised. The following month, in her first report to the Executive as full General Secretary, Dianne Hayter had to announce that in the past year national membership had dropped by 544, and stood at only 4100. Local society numbers were also down, with under 2000 members in just over eighty societies, and about half of those came into the national count. Twice the number of people were leaving each month as were joining and the Society was only two-thirds the size it had been in 1970.

Although everyone in the Executive was itching to do something really effective to brighten the political scene, 1977 had to be dedicated to regaining strength. Publication continued at a low rate, part of it friendly criticism, such as Lisanne Radice's proposals for reform of the House of Commons and Dianne Hayter's suggested methods for democratizing the Labour Party.[35] Neither of these pamphlets produced the shocked outcry that would have arisen in the infancy of the Fabian Society. Both the

House of Lords and the Labour Party had long become immune to shafts of the Fabians. Even Crosland's tract which defined socialism as 'a set of values, of aspirations, of principles which socialists wish to see embodied in the organisation of society' now caused little stir.[36] Pressure groups working outside a party framework and the political action of the trade unions were causing so much clamour that the collective Fabian voice was being drowned, though those of individual Fabians still rang loud and clear from the universities, from newspapers and political journals, from radio and television. Thus a relatively small number continued to produce solid Fabian work without imprinting it with the Fabian logo too blatantly.

Two quintessentially Fabian politicians died in the 1970s: Richard Crossman in 1974 and Anthony Crosland in 1977. The Society sorely missed their distinctive, powerful and contrasting contributions to Fabian thought. They were as important to its life as Webb, Wallas and Shaw, whether sparring in the pages of *Economica*, or planning the Society's future in Executive meetings, hammering out socialist philosophy in Buscot conferences or collaborating over production of *New Fabian Essays*. Each had prodded others into thinking along new lines; Crossman by rousing others to vocal opposition, Crosland by a lively presentation of a constantly developing personal philosophy. Crossman's diaries give some impression of his brand of Fabianism. A commemorative volume of essays dedicated to Antony Crosland, and intended to extend his work, was published just as doubts and arguments about the future of the Party and of democratic socialism was reaching a crucial point.[37] There are strong signs that his ideas are having an increasing influence on the Fabian Society's views of the principles of future Labour policy.

While still acting as friendly critics of the Labour government by, for example, sending delegations to Ministers when it was thought not enough was being done to establish industrial democracy, any exhilaration Fabians might feel from good work well done was dampened by growing concern about the future of social democracy. Need for contact with progressive groups abroad became increasingly important; it was a policy to which the General Secretary was completely dedicated. The possibility had already been investigated by Brian Lapping while attending the establishment of an association for a Social Democratic Europe in Bergisch Gladbach in 1976. He thought that European social democrats would respond well to a Fabian initiative if it were made in a 'suitably gentle and well-prepared Fabian way'.[38] A Fabian initiative in the year prior to election of the first Euro-MPs was obviously important because of the influence the EEC would exert over domestic as well as foreign policy and the Society had a duty to speak out on European matters; so tracts and research pamphlets were produced investigating and explaining such matters as Eurocommunism or regional policy.[39]

Waning popularity was not confined to the Fabian Society in these years. Labour was losing support as it approached the end of its constitutional term even faster than a party in office expects in its fourth year. Lack of a powerful, constructive policy to fend off the worst effects of worldwide economic imbalance was painfully obvious to all. The party was intolerably divided over the general direction it should take. In an attempt to clarify the issue the Social Policy Committee began work on a book exploring the reasons why an equal society had not been established, why unemployment was rising, and why the cost of the social services was proving too high, despite the liberalizing measures introduced and the attempts made to bring about economic equality when Labour had been in office since the second world war.[40] Many of the assumptions and views current in the 1930s were again being aired. Forecasting a Labour defeat at the next election, Fabians wanted to discover the deeper reasons, provide a remedy, point the way forward and help the party recover. In *Labour and Equality*, not published until 1980, after Labour had been rejected by the electors, they revealed how little the recent government had achieved of its stated intent to redistribute wealth, income and resources to benefit the poorer elements of society. Unable to reach a common conclusion as to why, they were left with the forlorn hope that their efforts had contributed to the debate on how to make a Labour government really effective. Sadly the editors observed that, 'Labour in government seems to become more conservative even as Tory Governments become more radical or at least daring'.[41]

While the book was in preparation the research committees and Young Fabian executive met to pick priorities for the 1980s and the latter came up with a very popular pamphlet which assessed what Labour had done and restated what its aims should be; it was called *Why vote Labour*.[42] Shying at what was happening in the Labour movement and the Society in particular they had already called for:

> a complete renewal of the Society such as took place in the 1930s with the founding of the New Fabian Bureau, in which self-imposed blinkers can be cast away and due priority given to unfashionable ideas which may develop into an alternative way forward.[43]

Before long an event took place which caused as much pain and anguish to the whole of the Fabian Society as the triple birth of the SSIP, the

NFRB and the Socialist League half a century earlier. As then, the upheaval occurred at a time when the Labour Party was seriously fragmented, impotent against world economic forces, disoriented, losing the confidence of the industrial side of the movement and was left with a membership of about a quarter of a million which hardly qualified it to be considered representative of the country as a whole. As before, members of the Society who had been most deeply involved in Fabian work were instrumental in bringing about this change.

Before that took place Fabians united in mourning the death of one of its great figures, Margaret Cole. At the memorial meeting on 15 July 1980, held in a committee room of the House of Commons, John Parker, John Saville, Peggy Jay, Shirley Williams and Brian Abel-Smith all spoke of what she had meant to them as a leader in the Society, as a sharp critic of its faults and as a chronicler of its deeds. Tales were told of her appearing as a gypsy in one of the summer-school reviews, of the terror she inspired in young members' hearts when she rebuked them for inaccurate or loose statements, of the broadcast by a former office girl in Dartmouth Street who had declared that at their first encounter she thought she had been hired by a witch.

At the local societies' tea soon after, there was much talk of the way Fabians were being ousted from their local Labour Parties by the tactics of more militant members, who shouted them down whenever they rose to speak or filibustered them. Shirley Williams had recently received such treatment when addressing a public meeting arranged by a local Fabian society. There was an uneasy buzzing in the hive.

In November a second ceremony commemorating a great Fabian was held: a plaque was unveiled on the wall of 21 Mecklenburgh Square, the home of R.H. Tawney. John Parker was then invited to become the fifth president of the Society, a choice which not only paid tribute to his own contribution to Fabian life and work over fifty years but also indicated members' desire for reassurance of Fabian stability and the continued value of Fabian principles.

The same autumn Shirley Williams, Bill Rodgers and David Owen had begun to reveal their dismay at the attitudes they encountered at the constituency level of the Labour movement and at developments in the party machinery.[44] Roy Jenkins, temporarily able to observe Britain from a distance while serving as President of the OEEC, had earlier given a broadcast lecture which implied that he thought the existing Labour Party in Britain had so far lost its way that he would not be averse to founding a new party on his return to England.

The Labour Party split into mutually suspicious, power-hungry factions, clearly incapable of uniting to form a government unless the whole structure and machinery of the party were rebuilt. Fabians were divided between those who despaired of unity ever being achieved and those who hoped that something might be salvaged from the bitter recriminations between left and right. Turning for consolation to practicalities, a Fabian study group sought to discover how far Labour's shortcoming in office could be blamed on deficiencies in the machinery of government. The Young Fabians did their best to recruit new members by contesting the prevalent identification of the Society with the right wing of the party.[45] The Executive tried to grapple the Society to the party by filling all its rightful seats on London and regional party committees, making effective use of the Fabian vote in electing the affiliated socialist organizations' representative to the NEC. Visits to China for the Young Fabians, India for the main Society, and to Gambia were set in motion. The General Secretary made great efforts to establish collaborative research with European organizations into socialist history. None of this revitalized the Society or prevented the crack in the Labour Party from widening.

In the traditional chairman's New Year message to the Society, Shirley Williams warned that 1981 would be a period of upheaval and that what was to come was still unsure. She wrote that Fabians in the past had made a major contribution to thought about the welfare state, but now the 'reservoir of socialist thinking' had been drained, Labour was bogged down in sterile debate over exhausted programmes. Therefore Fabians had a duty to 'construct a programme of Fabian thought to underwrite the democratic socialist alternative in a difficult and confused decade'.[46]

At the 1981 New Year school held at Headington, Oxford, most people were confused and unhappy about what was happening in the Labour movement. They had long been disturbed about the struggle between left and right over choice of the leader of the party. The larger number tended to favour the General Secretary's solution for satisfying all factions, that of keeping choice of the Parliamentary Party leader in the hands of his colleagues, and giving a certain amount of power to a second extra-parliamentary leader, the party chairman, chosen by a more democratic ballot of the whole of conference.[47] But there were plenty of alternative solutions to the problem advocated by others and constantly haggled over. The discussion would build up until the fringe Fabian conference scheduled to take place during the party's special conference on the leadership issue at Wembley in January. It was known that Shirley Williams and several of her closest colleagues were adamantly opposed to choice of the parliamentary leader, the prospective Prime Minister, being taken out of the hands of the Parliamentary Labour Party. As director of the school, Shirley Williams called for radical solutions to Britain's three major problems: growing poverty and inequality, disillusionment with Labour's advocacy of state enterprises, and impersonal bureaucratic provision for welfare.[48] The Executive and the subcommittees looked hard at what the Society was doing. They decided it was doing too much research, too little political education in trade union branches and similar sections of the Labour movement, and failing to produce a sufficiently strong policy statement on foreign affairs. Tentative plans were made for new work and then the blow fell.

On 4 February the chairman and the treasurer, John Roper, wrote to the Executive saying that should either of them leave the Labour Party, his office would be placed in the hands of the other Fabian officers, who would be expected to advise the Executive on appropriate action.[49] Less than a month later, on 2 March, the rest of the Executive was informed that its two chief officers had indeed left the Labour Party that day, but that they hoped they might still be able to 'play a full role' as members of the Society. Two other Executive members, John Cartwright and David Sainsbury, followed their lead. The officers requested the vice-chairman, David Lipsey, to take over as chairman, the 1980 chairman, Peter Archer, to become his second in command and Brian Abel-Smith to be treasurer for the rest of the year. It was not at all clear whether the constitution permitted Fabians who resigned from the Labour Party to remain members of the Society. The four ex-Executive members had resigned their party membership, not their socialism; therefore they would not be violating Rule 2 which states: 'The Society consists of Socialists.' Rule 4 decreed that: 'Full membership . . . shall be open to all who are willing to accept the rules and bye-laws of the Society.'

The four, who wished to remain members, had subscribed to this ruling in the past and the Executive had no reason to believe that they were no longer willing to do so. The statement on the application form, however, was differently worded; it said that full membership was open: 'to all who are eligible for individual membership of the Labour Party'. Local societies and the Bureau could allow those not eligible to join the party the status of associate member; but that was not what those forming the Social Democratic Party desired. They had always played a leading part in the work and decision making of the national Society and wished to continue to do so because they believed that their ideals were still the same as when they had joined and been accepted by the Society. Although the rules

273

specifically permitted the Executive to deny membership to any applicant for due cause, they did not decree that it had to expel someone who was already a member nor define any conditions for expulsion. The Executive had always assumed that it might expel if necessary, but even a quarter of a century earlier when a declared Communist had been nominated for the Executive election it had avoided depriving him of Society membership.[50] It now consulted a solicitor, who could give no more decisive ruling than that the rules probably did allow membership, though not of the governing body, to those ineligible to join the Labour Party.

In the Society all the ancient anguish caused by Ramsay MacDonald's action in 1931 returned. All the arguments dating from the time of the Labour Party's foundation, when Fabians were still supporting or even standing as Liberals in certain constituencies, were revived whenever the extent of Fabian commitment to the Party or to socialism in general was discussed. All Fabians were grieved at the rift which had opened up in the Society. A decision was taken to consult the full membership and, since the annual general meeting was still six months away, a postal ballot was arranged. Most Fabian Social Democrats refused to withdraw from full membership until the referendum had been held, arguing that resignation would imply that they no longer considered themselves socialists and that, as socialists they still had a right to play a full part in this particular socialist organization's work. The alternative argument was that it was impossible for members of another party to vote in the Executive elections and decide Fabian policy as long as the Society remained affiliated to the Labour Party, which it fully intended to do even though the party doubted its loyalty.[51]

In the ballot in May, the Executive requested members' approval for a change in the rules disenfranchising those who were members of parties other than the Labour Party while permitting them to receive the literature and take part in meetings, schools and conferences as associates. Both sides of the argument were amply represented. In a total vote of 2899 the majority in favour of the rule change was a mere 201.[52] As many now felt about the Labour Party, so some felt about the Society: it was no longer the one they had known and loved.

At the annual general meeting at the end of the year, resolutions were submitted asking either that the new wording of Rule 4 should be annulled or that any such change should be declared invalid since it had not commanded a two-thirds majority. The result of the ballot, however, was confirmed by 133 votes to 52. When the subject was raised at the 1982 meeting by some who still hoped to revert to the old rule, the ballot decision was, after debate, confirmed again.

In the year following the creation of the Social Democratic Party, the Fabian Society lost about 10 per cent of its members – the drop from 30 June 1980 to 30 June 1982 was 619, leaving the Society with 3138 national members. To interpret this loss as a direct transfer from the Fabian Society to the SDP would be false. Nor, on the other hand, would it be accurate to estimate that only about 600 had so changed their affiliation, since some members who had left the Fabian Society in the previous decade may also have joined the new party. A great deal of income was lost to the Fabian Society in the two years. With a threatened deficit of £40,000 on a £60,000 income there were doubts as to whether it could survive. But the Fabian Society always has survived and now, with the help of 'red angels' and 'pink cherubs' (major and minor donors) financial disaster has once more been averted. A new General Secretary, Ian Martin, has replaced Dianne Hayter, who fought gallantly for the Society through eight years of service.

While the storm in the Society was at its worst the Centenary Committee, which began to meet in 1980, was suspended. In mid-1982 it valiantly resumed its deliberations about mounting an exhibition to illustrate the Society's past and present, issuing a bronze medal and some commemorative mugs and plates, and producing several more light-hearted diversions to prove that it is still alive and ready to face another century of trying to 'help on' the reconstruction of society.

23

ONE HUNDRED YEARS OLD

Predictions that the Fabian Society could not survive the repeated disasters of the early 1980s have proved false, though for some time the Society was very sick indeed. Month after month members applied every remedy they could command, and spoke heartily of recovery while dreading the very real possibility of extinction. Each was convinced that it could not be allowed to expire because of its symbiosis with the British Labour movement. Devoted nursing brought results and, on 11 March 1984, the convalescent's hundredth year was celebrated by a retrospective exhibition in the foyer of the St Pancras public library, opened by the new Labour leader. Now the prognosis is that, with proper sustenance and the exercise of circumspection, the Fabian Society could even regain the full vigour of its youth and once more startle and sparkle.

A significant indication that the main crisis was over emerged during the Local Societies Annual Meeting held in the House of Commons on a very hot day in July 1983. To delegates fanning themselves with agenda papers the Executive announced its determination to reinstate the Fabian Society as the prime interpreter of British socialist philosophy. It postulated that at the root of the Labour Party's recent troubles lay a stubborn adherence to certain socialist tenets irrelevant to the present needs and desires of the people. Official Party ideals and motives had become outdated and policy makers were inhibited from producing solutions to present-day problems by the traditional rhetoric relating to property ownership and nationalization of industry. Therefore the Labour Party had lost the confidence of the electorate and had been soundly trounced in the recent general election. The Executive intended once again to act as the Party's best friend and critic by placing Fabian analytical and creative skills at its service. For its own part, the Executive recognized a need to revert to the aims and purposes of the founders and, as Stella Meldrum stated in her chairman's report for 1982–3, was 'concerned to recapture the ideological initiative, and to reassert the moral basis for our beliefs'.[1]

At this juncture the Labour Party made a vital decision. Michael Foot, its first leader to be elected by the new selection procedure, had retired and a new leader had to be chosen. Of the four candidates standing for election three were serving members of the Fabian Executive.[2] An ideal opportunity thus existed for the Society to demonstrate its consanguinity with the Labour Party and reaffirm its support. It invited the four candidates to produce individual statements of their socialist philosophy and their dedication to the party. These, longer and more explicit than their manifestos distributed to the unions and to party members, were precipitately published as Tract No. 489, *Labour's Choices*, by Roy Hattersley, Neil Kinnock, Peter Shore and Eric Heffer. Immediately afterwards the Society brought the four candidates together on the same platform, before a selected audience of political experts and journalists, to clarify further their respective claims to be elected leader. Because this was the only occasion on which all four would appear together the event was given national television coverage. Before the speakers the new Fabian symbol glowed bold and red. The new Labour leader was thus publicly assured of the Society's support. Neil Kinnock, who had topped the poll for the Fabian Executive election the previous year, was the successful candidate.

After this overt act of fealty to the Labour Party the Fabian Society looked forward far more cheerfully to 1984. An intensive review of the past by Fabians seeking personal reassurance and a more judicious view of the way ahead has raised many questions concerning the value of past action and the justification for embarking upon a second century of work with an unpredictable outcome. Reaffirmation of intent to recapture the ideological initiative and restate the moral basis of their beliefs apparently brings Fabians back to where the founders stood a century ago. Does this mean that they have achieved nothing? Certainly not. It merely means that the task is sisyphean. Society will always require reconstruction and there will always be a need for Fabians to 'educate, agitate and organize'.

Since the task has not been completed, has the Society helped in the reconstruction of society? The answer is a firm 'yes'. Without its research, creation of new modes of enquiry, collective effort, inspired faith, generosity in making the results of its work available to legislators and

administrators, persistence in pressing them to act on their recommendations, and without so many members undertaking the legislation and
administration themselves, many of the social improvements and reforms
of the last century would never have been achieved. Great scope exists for
detailed studies of the extent of Fabian influence in the many specific areas
of social, economic and political reform, nationally and locally, especially in
the period since 1939. Within the confines of this book it has not been
possible to do more than touch on the nature of that influence. Though the
Fabians have, undoubtedly, 'helped on' the reconstruction of society (for
Britain is very different now from what it was a hundred years ago) there is
still as much as ever to be done, since reconstruction is a never-ending
process. When one asks whether the effort was worthwhile the answer
again must be 'yes', because the present generation has inherited not only
material benefits but also a socially responsible outlook.

What has been said already proves that the Society has the capacity, the
duty even, to be useful. Not only is it the oldest socialist body in Britain, it
is also the oldest research organization allied to a political party. The
Conservative Party now has its Bow Group, the Liberal Party has Arena,
and in January 1982 the Social Democratic Party launched the Tawney
Society, openly declaring it to be the counterpart of the Fabian Society. If
imitation is indeed the highest form of flattery, the Fabian Society should
feel very flattered. From time to time these organizations benefit from
debating certain political problems with each other. For instance, at the
Fabian New Year School of 1984, in Oxford, Phillip Whitehead and
Michael Young, the latter representing the Tawney Society, led a debate
on the nature of socialism, in an attempt to resolve misunderstandings
between the two bodies.

Four questions remain to which the answers cannot be clear cut. First,
will the Society always be small? It is likely to be because its work demands
special talents and has a restricted appeal. Fabians have always been a
minor portion of the Labour movement, yet they have always exerted
considerable influence. The Society has always managed to function with
small numbers, and there is no reason why it should not continue to do so
provided it can command enough money. Second, what should be its
future role? In general, much the same as it has always been. Shaw labelled
the first essayists 'communicative learners'; to a large extent that is what
Fabians have been for a hundred years, constantly reinterpreting the real
needs of people and the ways in which political and economic circumstances can be used to meet them. Specific details of future work can only
be decided when particular needs arise. Third, whether the Society should

always be as closely linked with the Labour Party as it has now become is a question that must be left hanging in the air. The nature of the relationship has fluctuated constantly since the creation of the party; there is no real reason to believe that such fluctuation will cease. The Society can remain of use to the Labour Party only if it stays true to its own principles, aims and purposes, if it periodically reviews them to test their continuing validity and avoids the ever-present danger of degenerating into a mere talking-shop. Argument may be, as Bland said, the *raison d'être* of the Society; it must be perceptive, purposeful and productive argument.

The initiative has already been taken in reviewing those principles, aims and purposes. The tools being used are the traditional ones: the conference or school for discussion and clarification of ideas, the tract and the volume of essays for publishing the lines of argument, the conclusions reached for indicating the way ahead.

In summer 1982 the idea was first mooted that a new volume of essays would be a fitting celebration of 1984. Ben Pimlott accepted an invitation to edit them on the understanding that the discussion should not be confined to Fabian ideas but should entail examination of the wider socialist theories. Advocacy of a Fabian ideology unrelated to the other strands of philosophy woven into the fabric of British socialism was not only unreasonable and undesirable but also impossible. The volume was therefore to be called *Fabian Essays in Socialist Thought*.[3] The following year prospective authors were invited to present schemes for their contributions at a symposium, where the book's twofold structure and intent was determined. The first six essays, to form part one, would examine Fabian doctrine, work and influence in the past and assess the innate contradictions thus revealed. The second part would aim at analysing the fundamental socialist concepts of liberty, equality and fraternity in the setting of modern life and defining the way in which they should be interpreted and applied in the future. No collective view or conclusion was expected to result from this series of essays. As always, each writer's thesis would be based on his own socialist creed and visions, on his practical and academic experience and expertise. The essayists emerged from this exercise with a firmer faith in the continuing validity of those fundamental socialist concepts but with a less dogmatic certainty than had the early Fabians of the inevitable success of the socialist 'way out'. Bernard Crick has supplemented his essay on equality with a tract on the way socialist values have survived the passage of time but need to be reanimated with the more democratically critical spirit of today.[4]

Writing such essays in socialist thought has certainly clarified the writers' views of what Fabians are, why they themselves are Fabians and supporters of the Labour Party. Pimlott explains that for many Fabians 'concern about the dispossessed in the centre of the big city is the most compelling reason for working within the Labour Party'; [5] they choose the Labour Party because they believe it to be the compassionate party. Yet they are aware that the needs of the skilled worker and of the professional or middle classes must also be met if a society of equals is to be created. Equality does not mean uniformity of income, power, possessions or opportunity, but man's freedom to fulfil himself, to contribute what he can to society in his own particular way and to be respected for what he is, not for what others think he ought to be or can be manipulated into becoming in the grand scheme of a socialist state. In fact, the state is there for his use, not to act as his God. This is far from the Webbs' concept that the right institutions could produce the good society. Nevertheless, the new Fabian interpretation of liberty and equality, and the fraternal spirit with which it is imbued, have evolved directly from the motives of the founding members. They would not have taken this form without the multifarious contributions of former members to socialist thought, without the differences of opinion and concomitant soul-searching of recent years. The influence of the Webbs, Shaw, Wells, the Coles, Tawney and Crosland is still evident, but today's Fabians have embraced as their creed that: 'true socialists are concerned with judging morally the social consequences of individual actions'. [6] Still believing in radicalism that 'involves the knowledge, confidence and will to bring about great changes', [7] they define the essentially practical role of the Fabian Society in terms that its founders would have appreciated: 'to inquire, expose, inform and educate; to inspire rather than to instruct; above all to give confidence by indicating the extent of possible achievement'. [8]

So, finally, what is the Fabian Society? Sidney Webb provided an oblique answer when he said that: 'the work of the Fabian Society consists of the work of individual Fabians'. The best definition of what the Society is today is the statement on the back of recent tracts:

The Fabian Society exists to further socialist education and research. It is affiliated to the Labour Party, both nationally and locally and embraces all shades of Labour opinion within its ranks – left, right and centre. Since 1884 the Fabian Society has enrolled thoughtful socialists who are prepared to discuss the essential questions of democratic socialism and relate them to practical plans for building socialism in a changing world. Beyond this the Society has no collective policy. It puts forward no resolutions of a political character. The Society's members are active in their Labour parties, trade unions and co-operatives. They are representative of the labour movement, practical people concerned to study and discuss problems that matter.

APPENDIX
OFFICERS OF
THE FABIAN SOCIETY

Presidents of the Fabian Society

1939–41	Beatrice Webb
1951–52	Stafford Cripps
1952–59	G.D.H. Cole
1962–80	Margaret Cole
1980–	John Parker

Chairmen, NFRB

1931–34	C.R. Attlee
1934–37	Lord Addison
1937–39	G.D.H. Cole

Chairmen of the Fabian Society

1939–46	G.D.H. Cole
1946–48	Harold Laski
1948–50	G.D.H. Cole
1950–53	John Parker
1953–54	Austen Albu
1954–55	Harold Wilson
1955–56	Margaret Cole
1956–57	Arthur Skeffington
1957–58	Roy Jenkins
1958–59	Eirene White

1959–60	H.D. Hughes
1960–61	Lord Faringdon
1961–62	C.A.R. Crosland
1962–63	Mary Stewart
1963–64	Brian Abel-Smith
1964–65	Anthony Wedgwood Benn
1965–66	Peter Townsend
1966–67	William Rodgers
1967–68	Arthur Blenkinsop
1968–69	Peter Shore
1969–70	Thomas Balogh
1970–71	Jeremy Bray
1971–72	Peter Hall
1972–73	Anthony Lester
1973–74	Frank Judd
1974–75	Nicholas Bosanquet
1975–76	Colin Crouch
1976–77	Giles Radice
1977–78	Dick Leonard
1978–79	Phillip Whitehead
1979–80	Peter Archer
1980–81	Shirley Williams
1981 Apr	David Lipsey
1982	David Lipsey
1983	Stella Meldram
1984	Jenny Jeger

Treasurers of the Fabian Society

1884–1911	Hubert Bland
1911–36	F. Lawson Dodd
1936–47	Emil Davies
1947–50	Ian Mikardo
1950–64	John Diamond
1964–65	Michael Shanks
1965–68	Brian Abel-Smith
1968–74	Anthony Lester
1974–76	Giles Radice
1976–81	John Roper
1981–82	Brian Abel-Smith
1982–84	Nick Butler

Honorary Secretaries, NFRB

1931–35	G.D.H. Cole
1935–39	Margaret Cole

Honorary Secretaries of the Fabian Society

1884–85	Frederick Keddell
1885–90	Sydney Olivier
1890–91	E.R. Pease
1915–39	E.R. Pease
1939–53	Margaret Cole
1953–71	John Parker
1971–	none

General Secretaries, NFRB

1931–33	E.A. Radice
1933–39	John Parker

General Secretaries of the Fabian Society

1891–1913	E.R. Pease
1913–20	W.S. Sanders
1915–19	E.R. Pease (Acting)
1920–39	F.W. Galton
1939–45	John Parker
1946–47	Bosworth Monck
1947–49	Andrew Filson
1949–53	Donald Chapman
1953–60	William Rodgers
1960–63	Shirley Williams
1964–76	Tom Ponsonby
1976–82	Dianne Hayter
1982–	Ian Martin

Assistant Secretaries of the Fabian Society

1939–42	H.D. Hughes
1942	Gwynn Llywellyn Jones (Organizing Secretary)
1943	Oliver Gollancz (ditto)
1945–46	H.D. Hughes (Part-time Organizing Secretary and Acting General Secretary during gap between Parker and Monck)
1951–53	William Rodgers
1954–55	Gerald Kaufman
1955–60	Dick Leonard
1960–61	Jim Wade
1961–63	Tom Ponsonby
1964	John Syson
1964–65	Jonathan Sleigh
1965–66	Tom McNally
1966–68	Malcolm Sargeant
1968–73	Mick Cornish
1974–76	Dianne Hayter
1976–	Richard Twining

NOTES

For the key to references to the Fabian Archive see the bibliography.

1 Foundation and basis

1 Edward Pease, *History of the Fabian Society*, 2nd edn, London, 1963, p. 40.
2 C 36 Meetings minutes.
3 C 36 4 October 1883, Meetings minutes; Norman and Jeanne Mackenzie, *The First Fabians*, London, 1977, p. 24. Although Chubb's name is not recorded in the minutes, a letter in Thomas Davidson's papers proves he was there.
4 C 36 7 November 1883, Meetings minutes.
5 C 37 19 June 1886, Meetings minutes.
6 Tract No. 2, *A Manifesto*, by G.B. Shaw, 1884.
7 Mackenzie, op. cit., p 42.
8 *Fabian Essays in Socialism*, London, 1889, Preface.
9 Though published by the Fabian Society, it was not allocated a Tract number.
10 *Morning Post*, 14 March 1886.
11 C 36 19 March 1886, Meetings minutes.
12 *The Practical Socialist*, I (5), May 1886.
13 C 36 1 January 1886, Meetings minutes.
14 *The Radical*, April 1888, 'Butchered to make a Fabian holiday', by George Standring.
15 C 36 5 February 1886, Meetings minutes.
16 C 36 19 February 1886, Meetings minutes.
17 C 36 17 September 1886, Meetings minutes.
18 Tract No. 6, *The True Radical Programme*, revised by G.B. Shaw, 1887.
19 *The Practical Socialist*, I (10), October 1886.
20 C 53/2 f 9 Notices of meetings.
21 C 53/2 ff 10–14 Notices of meetings.
22 C 52/1 f 3 Rules of the Society.

23 *The Practical Socialist*, II (15), March 1887.
24 C 52/2 f 4 Rules of the Society.
25 C 53/2 f 14 Notices.

2 Practical work and propaganda

1 *Annie Besant: An Autobiography*, London, 1893, pp. 332 et seq.
2 C 36 6 January 1888, Meetings minutes.
3 B 1/1 ff 3–5 1886 Fabian Society Report on the Unemployed.
4 B 1/1 ff 10–13 November 1887, Correspondence with the Local Government Board.
5 Norman Mackenzie, *Letters of Sidney and Beatrice Webb*, vol. I, London, 1978, p. 100.
6 C 62/1 ff 6 & 10 Lecture notices.
7 C 48/1 ff 1 & 2 Annual general meeting report and committee papers.
8 Charles Booth, *Labour and Life of the People in London*, London, 1889–97.
9 C 62/1 f 14 Lecture prospectus.
10 A 6/1 ff 86–88 17 March 1890, Letter from Annie Besant to Pease.
11 A 6/1 f 89 9 May 1890, Letter from Annie Besant to Pease.
12 A 6/1 ff 90–91 27 July 1890, Letter from Annie Besant to Pease; C 3 July 1890, Minutes.
13 C 37 21 November 1890, Meetings minutes.
14 C 55/2 Item 2 List of members.
15 F 21/1 ff 1 & 2 1890, Circular letters to Fabian societies and groups.
16 C 27/1 3 January 1890, Minutes.
17 A 1/1 f 1 30 July 1891, Letter from Shaw to de Mattos.
18 M 4 1890–2 Mounted newspaper cuttings.
19 B 1/6 f 14 n.d. 'Explanatory note on the Eight Hours Bill'.
20 C 63/3 f 4 4 November 1890, Report on the Lancashire campaign.
21 Norman Mackenzie, *Letters of Sidney and Beatrice Webb*, vol. II, London, 1978, p. 204.
22 A 1/1 f 1 30 July 1891, Letter from Shaw to de Mattos.

3 Suburbs and the provinces

1 B 2/1 January 1891, Minute by Sidney Webb and Graham Wallas to the Executive.
2 C 62/1 1885–1931, Lecture notices.
3 Edward Pease, *History of the Fabian Society*, 2nd edn, London, 1963, p. 64.
4 B 2/1 1891, Comment by Shaw on Webb's and Wallas's minute.
5 F 130/2 Item 1 1890–3, East London group papers.
6 *Daily Chronicle*, 25 March 1891.
7 F 130/2 ff 1–13 1890–3, East London group papers.

8 F 130/2 Item 1.

9 B 7/6 f 8 16 January 1892, Report of the Working Men's College Group.

10 Beatrice Potter, *The Co-operative Movement in Great Britain*, London, 1891.

11 A 8/4 ff 23–68 1890–3, Runciman correspondence.

12 A 2/2 ff 2–6 [17 December] 1891, Letter from Webb to Pease.

13 Norman Mackenzie, *Letters of Sidney and Beatrice Webb*, vol. I, London, 1978, pp. 353–4.

14 A 8/4 f 37 1890, Runciman correspondence.

15 C 38 6 and 7 February 1892, Meetings minutes.

16 C 55/4 Item 1 1890–1919, Local Societies' register.

17 C 55/2 Item 1 1890, Printed list of members.

18 C 3 11 November 1890, Minutes.

19 C 37 6 February 1891, Meetings minutes.

20 A 8/2 ff 13–46 1892, W. de Mattos correspondence.

21 Lawrence Thompson, *The Enthusiasts: A Biography of John and Katherine Bruce Glasier*, London, 1971, Chapter 3.

4 Planning the campaign for Labour

1 A 7/1 ff 118–20 1892–3, W.H. Drew correspondence.

2 *The Clarion*, 1909–10, Articles by John Burgess.

3 ibid.

4 C 38 6 and 7 February 1892, Meetings minutes.

5 C 38 20 January 1893, Meetings minutes.

6 ibid.

7 C 38 3 February 1893, Meetings minutes.

8 C 4 27 January 1893, Minutes.

9 C 4 2 June 1893, Minutes.

10 C 5 June–July 1893, Minutes.

11 E 122/3 'Report on the progress of socialism in England during the two years ending July 1893', 1893.

12 *Fabian News*, III (7), August 1893.

13 *Fabian News*, III (9), November 1893.

14 C 5 22 September 1893, Minutes.

15 C 5 11 October 1893, Minutes; C 38 13 October 1893, Meetings minutes.

16 *Weekly Times*, 15 October 1893.

17 *Cheshire Evening News*, 16 October 1893.

18 A 8/2 ff 11–12 18 October 1893, Letter from H.W. Massingham to Pease.

19 Beatrice Webb, *Our Partnership*, ed Margaret Cole and Barbara Drake, London, 1948, p. 116.

20 *Pall Mall Gazette*, 4 November 1893.

21 E 116/2 1888, *Wanted a Programme: An Appeal to the Liberal Party*, by Sidney Webb, printed for private circulation by Holborn, Westminster and

London University Liberal and Radical Associations.

22 Edward Pease, *History of the Fabian Society*, 2nd edn, London, 1963, p. 112.

23 Beatrice Webb, op. cit., p. 109.

24 *The Scotsman*, 30 October 1893.

25 *Daily Chronicle*, 30 October 1893.

26 Tract No. 24, *Questions for Parliamentary Candidates*, by Sidney Webb, 1891.

27 *Pall Mall Gazette*, 2 November 1893; *The Sun*, 1 November 1893.

28 *Daily Chronicle*, 2 November 1893.

29 *Church Reformer*, November 1893.

30 *Workman's Times*, 25 November 1893.

31 A 2/4 ff 60–61 3 December 1893, Letter from Webb to Pease.

32 A 2/4 f 64 10 December 1893, Letter from Webb to Pease.

33 *Nineteenth Century*, 'Fabian Fustian', by Michael Davitt, November 1893.

5 The Hutchinson Trust

1 C 5 2 February 1894, Minutes.

2 C 5 30 March 1894, Minutes.

3 C 5 18 May 1894, Minutes.

4 C 5 1894 passim, Minutes.

5 For a copy of the relevant part of this will see: M.I. Cole (ed), *The Webbs and Their Work*, London, 1949, p. 43.

6 A 2/5 f 61 et seq. 1894, Letters from Webb to Pease.

7 D 21/1 ff 8–9 24 October 1894, Finance and General Purposes Committee papers, Opinion of Counsel.

8 Edward Pease, *History of the Fabian Society*, 2nd edn, London, 1963; M.I. Cole, op. cit.; Janet Beveridge, *An Epic of Clare Market*, London, 1960; Sir Sidney Caine, *The History of the Foundation of the London School of Economics and Political Science*, London, 1963; C. Bermant *et al.* (ed J. Abse), *My L.S.E.*, London, 1977; *Clare Market*, 1926–8, LSE; *Clare Market Review*, 1953–73, LSE; Janet Dunbar, *Mrs G.B.S.: A Biographical Portrait of C. Shaw*, London, 1963; Beatrice Webb, *Our Partnership*, ed Margaret Cole and Barbara Drake, London, 1948, and *Diaries*.

9 *Fabian News*, V (4), June 1895; V (11), January 1896.

10 *Fabian News*, V (7 and 8), September and October 1895.

11 A 8/1 ff 9–12 8–11 April 1896, Letters from J. Ramsay MacDonald to Pease.

12 C 6 17 April 1896, Minutes.

13 Beatrice Webb, *Diary*, 18 April 1896.

14 A 8/1 f 13 14 April 1896, Letter from MacDonald to Pease.

15 *Fabian News*, VI (11 and 12), January and February 1897.

16 *Fabian News*, VII (7), September 1897.

17 *Fabian News* VIII (6), August 1898.

18 Beatrice Webb, 1948, op. cit., pp. 408–10.

19 *Fabian News*, IX (5), July 1899.

20 C 7, 8 & 24 1899–1900 passim, Minutes.

21 C 24 6 June 1902, General Purposes Committee minutes.

22 A 4/7 ff 12–13 15 July 1908, Letter from Webb to Sanders.

23 A 4/9 ff 1–2 9 January 1910, Letter from Webb to Pease.

24 A 4/9 f 28 18 November 1910, Letter from Webb to Pease.

25 A 1/2 F 8 12 October 1910, Letter from Shaw to Stephen Sanders.

26 D 21/1 1894–[1904], Hutchinson Trust Papers.

27 A 3/3–5 1897–9, Letters from Webb to Pease.

28 *Fabian News*, IV (6), August 1894.

29 A 2/4 f 48 20 October 1893, Letter from Webb to Pease.

30 *Fabian News*, IV (7), September 1894.

31 *Fabian News*, IV (10), December 1894.

32 *Fabian News*, VI (7), September 1896; VII (7), September 1897.

33 A 4/1 f 29 3 November 1901, Letter from Webb to Pease.

34 A 4/1 f 46 22 November 1901, Letter from Webb to Pease.

35 C 8 23 February 1900, Minutes.

36 Tract No. 101, *The House Famine and How to Relieve It*, 1900.

37 A 4/4 f 21 30 August 1904, Letter from Webb to Pease.

6 Labour representation

1 *Fabian News*, III (11), January 1894.

2 *Fabian News*, IV (12), February 1895; C 5 27 April 1894, Minutes.

3 *Fabian News*, V (5) July 1895.

4 C 6 6 September 1895, Minutes.

5 C 7 30 April 1897, Minutes.

6 C 8 9 July 1897, Minutes.

7 *Fabian News*, VI (9), November 1896; *Fabian News*, VII (1 and 8), March and October 1897.

8 *Fabian News*, IX (2), April 1899.

9 A 3/5 ff 10–11 7 April 1899, Letter from Webb to Pease.

10 A 3/5 ff 12–13 11 April 1899, Letter from Webb to Pease.

11 Tract No. 90, *The Municipalization of the Milk Supply*, by Dr McCleary, 1899; Tract No. 91, *Municipal Pawnshops*, by C. Charrington, 1899; Tract No. 92, *Municipal Slaughterhouses*, by G. Standring, 1899; Tract No. 93, *Women as Councillors*, by G.B. Shaw, 1899; Tract No. 94, *Municipal Bakeries*, by Dr McCleary, 1899; Tract No. 95, *Municipal Hospitals*, by Dr McCleary, 1899; Tract No. 96, *Municipal Fire Insurance*, by Mrs F. MacPherson, 1900; Tract No. 97, *Municipal Steamboats*, by S.D. Shallard, 1900; Tract No. 100, *Metropolitan Borough Councils*, by H.W. Macrosty, 1900; Tract No. 101, *The House Famine and How to Relieve It*, anon., 1900; Tract No. 102, *Questions for Candidates: Metropolitan Borough Councils*, by H.W. Macrosty, 1900; Tract

No. 103, *Overcrowding in London and its Remedy*, by W.C. Steadman, 1900.

12 A 8/1 ff 43–4 29 November 1899, Letter from MacDonald to Pease.

13 *Fabian News*, IX (9), November 1899.

14 C 8 9 March 1900, Minutes.

15 C 8 May–September 1900, Minutes.

16 *Fabian News*, X (8), October 1900.

17 *Fabian News*, VIII (3), March 1899.

18 Beatrice Webb, *Our Partnership*, ed Margaret Cole and Barbara Drake, London, 1948, p. 245.

19 C 9 13 January 1905, Minutes.

20 C 9 23 October 1903, Minutes.

21 *Fabian News*, XVI (12), November 1906.

22 *Fabian News*, XVI (10), September 1906.

23 Tract No. 127, *Socialism and the Labour Party*, 1906.

7 Extending the horizon

1 C 6 15 March 1895, Minutes.

2 A 8/1 f 9 8 April 1896, Letter from MacDonald to Pease.

3 *Fabian News*, VII (1), March 1897.

4 C 7 15 July 1898, Minutes.

5 C 39 13 October 1899, Meetings minutes.

6 C 7 13 October 1899, Minutes.

7 C 7 16 October 1899, Minutes.

8 A 6/2 f 72 8 July 1891, Letter from Bland to Pease.

9 A 1/1 ff 13–14 30 October 1899, Letter from Shaw to Pease.

10 Beatrice Webb, *Our Partnership*, ed Margaret Cole and Barbara Drake, London, 1948, pp. 188–9.

11 A 7/3 ff 44–7 24 October 1899, Letter from S.G. Hobson to Pease.

12 A 8/3 ff 3–4 25 October 1899, Letter from Sydney Olivier to Pease.

13 A 1/1 f 14 17 November 1899, Letter from Shaw to Pease.

14 *Fabian News*, IX (10), December 1899.

15 Dan T. Laurence (ed), *The Collected Letters of Bernard Shaw*, vol. II, 1898–1910, London, 1972, p. 118, Letter from Shaw to Hubert Bland.

16 A 8/3 ff 10–11 14 December 1899, Letter from Olivier to Pease.

17 C 8 12 January 1900, Minutes; A 8/1 ff 45–50 23 December 1899, Letter from MacDonald to Pease.

18 C 39 23 February 1900, Meetings minutes. MacDonald thereupon departed on an American lecture tour, from which he returned just in time for the crucial meeting at which the result was announced.

19 *Daily Chronicle*, 24 February 1900.

20 *Fabian News*, X (1), March 1900.

21 Laurence, op. cit. p. 126, 30 December 1899, Letter from Shaw to Bland.

22 Laurence, op. cit., p. 149, 4 March 1900, Letter from Shaw to Charles Charrington.
23 ibid., p. 154, 13 March 1900, Letter from Shaw to Edward Rose.
24 C 54/1 ff 1–2 1900. General notices.
25 A 7/1 ff 101–2 26 March 1900, Letter from F. Lawson Dodd to Pease; *Fabian News*, X (1), March 1900.
26 A 3/6 ff 25–40 1–28 April 1900, Letters from Webb to Pease.
27 A 6/3 ff 61–2 21 August 1900, Letter from Webb to Pease.
28 Laurence, op. cit., p. 183, 4 September 1900, Letter from Shaw to Strudwick.
29 Bernard Shaw (ed), *Fabianism and the Empire: A Manifesto by the Fabian Society*, London, 1900, p. 15.
30 ibid.
31 ibid., p. 99.
32 *Fabian News*, X (8), October 1900.
33 C 8 5 October 1900, Minutes.
34 *Fabian News*, XII (2), February 1902.

8   Mr Wells and reform

1 H.G. Wells, *Experiment in Autobiography*, London, 1934, p. 247.
2 A 9/3 ff 5–8 January–February 1902, Correspondence between Wells and Pease.
3 *Fabian News*, XII (1), January 1903; H.G. Wells, *Anticipations of the Reaction of Mechanical Progress upon Human Life and Thought*, London, 1901.
4 Sydney Olivier, *Letters and Selected Writings*, ed with a Memoir by Margaret Olivier. With some impressions by Bernard Shaw, London, 1948.
5 *Fabian News*, XIII (4), April 1903; H.G. Wells, *Mankind in the Making*, London, 1903.
6 A 9/3 ff 13–14 17 March 1904, Letter from Wells to Pease.
7 C 9 25 March 1904, Minutes; A 9/3 f 15 17 March 1904, Letter from Wells to Pease.
8 C 9 27 May–10 June 1904, Minutes.
9 *Fabian News* XV (8), August 1905. L.S. Amery, one of the Webbs' bright young men recruited into the Oxford University Fabian Society had, indeed, resigned, though he left the main Society a farewell gift of £2; it was felt that unless something was done quickly others would follow.
10 A 1/1 f 20 4 July 1905, Letter from Shaw to Pease.
11 H.G. Wells, *This Misery of Boots*, reprinted with alterations from the *Independent Review*, December 1905, Fabian Society, 1907, p. 20.
12 ibid., p. 35.
13 ibid., p. 36.
14 A 9/3 f 22 25 September 1907, Letter from Wells to Pease.
15 C 9 9 and 23 February 1906, Minutes.

16 C 9 6 April 1906, Minutes.
17 Dan T. Laurence (ed), *The Collected Letters of Bernard Shaw*, vol. II, 1898–1910, London, 1972, p. 652, 14 September 1906, Letter from Shaw to Wells.
18 B 5/3 f 90 March 1906, Letters to H.G. Wells.
19 *Fabian News*, XVI (11), November 1906.
20 *Fabian News*, XVII (2), January 1907.
21 *Fabian News*, XVII (3), February 1907.
22 ibid.
23 *Fabian News*, XVII (4), March 1907.
24 *Labour Leader*, 1 March 1907, 'Mr Wells and the Fabian' by S.D. Shallard.
25 Laurence, op. cit., p. 651, 14 September 1906, Letter from Shaw to Wells. Shaw had earlier pointed out to Wells that Pease could ill afford to give up his paid work with the Fabians.
26 C 10 31 May and 20 December 1907 and 19 June 1908, Minutes.
27 *Fabian News*, XVII (6), May 1907.
28 *Fabian News*, XVII passim; C 10 May–December, Minutes.
29 A 4/6 ff 2–3 28 May 1907, Letter from Webb to Pease.
30 *Fabian News*, XIX (3), February 1908.
31 C 10 14 June–11 October 1907, Minutes.
32 *Fabian News*, XVII (8), July 1907.

9   The Nursery and the groups

1 C 9 6 April 1906, Minutes.
2 *Fabian News*, XVI (7), June 1906.
3 *Fabian News*, XVI (12), November 1906.
4 ibid. This was particularly so in the case of Amber Pember Reeves, who was accredited with being the model of Wells's novel, *Ann Veronica*, and was the mother of his son.
5 *Fabian News*, XIX (12), November 1908.
6 *Fabian News*, XVIII (11), October 1907. Frederick Keeling, H.H. Schloesser, Clifford Sharp, Amber Reeves and G. Blanco White entered the Fabian Society by way of this Union, together with Clifford Allen, Mabel Atkinson, A.L. Bacharach, H.D. Harben and Ellen Wilkinson.
7 *Fabian News*, 1906–14, passim.
8 H.G. Wells, *Anticipations of the Reaction of Mechanical Progress upon Human Life and Thought*, London, 1901, Introduction, p. xi.
9 C 45 1910, Propaganda Committee Minutes.
10 C 45 28 June 1909, Minutes.
11 *Fabian News*, 1909–10, passim.
12 *Fabian News*, 1909–19, passim.

13 Tract No. 119, *Public Control of Electric Power and Transit*, by S.G. Hobson, 1905; Tract No. 122, *Municipal Milk and Public Health*, by F. Lawson Dodd, 1905; Tract No. 125, *Municipalization by Provinces*, by W. Stephen Sanders, 1905; Tract No. 126, *The Abolition of the Poor Law Guardians*, by Edward Pease, 1906.

14 *Fabian News*, XXI (9), August 1910.

15 H 10–19 1911–12, Fabian 'Nursling', 8–17.

16 *Fabian News*, XII (12)–XXIII (2), November 1911–January 1912.

17 A 9/3 ff 32–3 12 December 1908, Letter from Wells to Haden Guest.

18 C 10 14 May 1908, Minutes; *Fabian News*, XIX (7), June 1908.

19 Frank Wallis Galton, MS autobiography, LSE.

20 C 10 25 February and 17 June 1910, Minutes; see *Evening Standard*, 24 and 30 March 1927, where Wells and Shaw protested independently that they had always maintained close sympathy in thought and feeling.

21 C 45 1909, Organizing and Propaganda Committee minutes.

22 *Fabian News*, XX (7), June 1909.

23 *Fabian News*, XX (5), April 1909.

24 C 11 12 February 1909, Minutes; *Fabian News*, XX (4), March 1909.

25 C 11 21 May 1909, Minutes.

26 *Fabian News*, XXII (2), January 1911.

27 C 11 2 December 1909, Minutes.

28 C 11 15 April 1910, Minutes; 17th Annual Report, 1909–10.

29 C 11 7 October 1910, Minutes.

30 A 4/10 ff 12–16 8–23 March 1911, Letter from Webb to Pease and Sanders.

31 ibid.

32 C 12 10 March 1911, Minutes.

33 *Fabian News*, XXII (6), May 1911; C 40 May 1911, Meetings minutes.

34 *Fabian News*, XXII (9), August 1911.

35 C 45 1911, Organizing and Propaganda Committee minutes.

36 C 52/2 f 12 Fabian Club House Rules.

37 *Labour Leader*, 8 (48), 1 December 1911; H 1 1 May 1912, Nursery minutes.

38 H 14 January 1912, Fabian 'Nursling', 12.

39 *Labour Leader*, 8 (50), 15 December 1911.

40 *Labour Leader*, 8 (49), 8 December 1911.

41 *Fabian News*, XXIII (2), January 1912.

42 *Labour Leader*, 8 (51), 22 December 1911.

43 *Labour Leader*, 8 (52), 29 December 1911.

44 *Fabian News*, XXIII (2), January 1912.

45 A 6/1 ff 2–6 7–22 December 1911, Letters from Clifford Allen to Pease.

46 A 9/1 ff 85–6 1–6 January 1911, Letters from H.H. Schloesser to Pease.

47 *Labour Leader*, 9 (3), 12 January 1912.

48 A 9/1 f 85 1 January 1912, Letter from Schloesser to Pease.

49 *Fabian News*, XXIII (3), February 1912.

50 B 7/2 f 3 1913, University Socialist Federation Annual Report; C 13 18 July 1913, Minutes.
51 A 7/2 ff 64–5 11 June 1912, Letter from Harben to Pease.
52 C 13 19 December 1913, Minutes.

10   The woman question

1 A 8/1 ff 22–5 1896, Letter from MacDonald to Pease.
2 C 38 9 February 1894, Meetings minutes.
3 C 5 15 June 1894, Minutes.
4 *Fabian News*, XVII (2), January 1907.
5 H 35/2 Item 3 1908–11, Fabian Women's Group Report of Three Years' Work.
6 See H.G. Wells's novel *Ann Veronica*, London, 1909.
7 E 111/4 *Summary of Seven Papers and Discussions upon the Disabilities of Women as Workers*, issued for private circulation only by the Fabian Women's Group, 1909.
8 *Women Workers in Seven Professions: A Survey of their Economic Conditions and Prospects*, edited for the Studies Committee of the Fabian Women's Group by Edith J. Morley, 1914.
9 H 35/2 Item 3 1908–11, Fabian Women's Group Report of Three Years' Work.
10 Maud Pember Reeves, *Round About a Pound a Week*, G. Bell & Sons, London, 1913; new edn, Virago, London, 1979.
11 *Fabian News*, XIX (12), November 1908.
12 H 35/1 1908–18, Account book.
13 *Fabian News*, XX (9), August 1909.
14 H 20 5 April 1911, Women's Group minutes.
15 H 20 passim.
16 H 31 1911–17, Suffrage Section minutes; H 35/2 ff 8–9 December 1911, *To Adult Suffragists*, Women's Group leaflet.
17 H 20 & 21 passim, Women's Group minutes.
18 Tract No. 157 (Women's Group Series No. 1), *The Working Life of Women*, by B.L. Hutchins, 1911.
19 Tract No. 158, *The Case against the Charity Organization Society*, by Emily Townsend, 1911.
20 H 35/2 Item 5 *How the National Insurance Bill Affects Women*, [1911]; Item 6 *The National Insurance Bill: A Criticism*, [1911].
21 Beatrice Webb, *The Prevention of Destitution*, London, 1911.
22 *Fabian News*, XXV (9), August 1914.
23 H 21 1913–17, Women's Group Minutes.
24 *Fabian News*, XXIV (3), February 1913.
25 H 33 [1915], Trade Union subcommittee minute book.

11   The Fabian holiday

1 G 24/10 1 July 1955, Letter from Dr Mabel Palmer to Margaret Cole, written when she was nearly 80 and living in Durban.

2 C 10 15 February 1907, Minutes; A7/1 f 115 29 September 1957, Letter from Frank Lawson Dodd to W.T. Rodgers; information supplied to the General Secretary by Dodd in 1956, when a plan was in hand to celebrate half a century of summer schools.

3 *Fabian News*, XVII (4), March 1907.

4 G 9 1907–12, Summer School Visitors' Book.

5 G 13 1907–12, Directors' log-book.

6 G 24/10 1 July 1955, Letter from Dr Mabel Palmer to Margaret Cole.

7 A 4/6 f 11 22 August 1907, Letter from Webb to Pease.

8 G 13 10 August 1910, Directors' log-book.

9 G 1 1909–10 passim, Summer School Committee minutes.

10 A 4/9 f 18 7 July 1910, Letter from Webb to Pease.

11 G 1 15 March 1911, Summer School Committee minutes.

12 G 1 1911 passim, Summer School Committee minutes.

13 E 115/1 1912, *Songs for Socialists*.

14 G 1 1912 passim, Summer School Committee minutes.

15 G 13 1912, Directors' log-book.

16 G 14 29 August 1914, Directors' log-book.

17 G 14 27 August 1916, Directors' log-book.

12   The Fabian Research Department

1 D 2 20 June 1912, Finance and General Purposes Committee minutes.

2 Sidney and Beatrice Webb, 'What syndicalism means', *The Crusade Against Destitution*, III (8), supplement, 1912.

3 B 1/9 ff 3–9 1912, Memoranda by Beatrice Webb to Fabian Society Members on the Committee of Inquiry on the Control of Industry.

4 Beatrice Webb, *The Co-operative Movement in Great Britain*, London, 1891; Sidney and Beatrice Webb, *Industrial Democracy*, 2 vols, London, 1897.

5 B 1/9 ff 1–27 1912–13, Fabian Research Department papers.

6 C 13 23 May 1913, Minutes.

7 G 48/2 19–26 July 1913, Barrow House Conference Programme.

8 *Fabian News*, XXIV (12), November 1913.

9 B 1/9 ff 28–9 1913, Memorandum by Sidney Webb on the work of the Committee of Inquiry on Insurance.

10 *Fabian News*, XXV (10), September 1914.

11 Edward Hyams, *The New Statesman: The History of the First Fifty Years, 1913–63*, London, 1963.

12 C 10 January 1908, Minutes.

13 C 13 6 June 1913, Minutes.
14 Papers of Arthur Creech Jones, Rhodes House Library, MSS Brit. Emp. s 332, ACJ 1/2 ff 194–7.
15 *Fabian News*, XXV (10), September 1914.
16 *Fabian News*, XXV (4 and 11), March and October 1914.
17 D 2 25 March 1915, Finance and General Purposes Committee minutes.
18 Norman Mackenzie, *Letters of Sidney and Beatrice Webb*, vol. III, London, 1978, p. 45 (16 December 1914, Letter from Beatrice Webb to Woolf).
19 ibid., p. 46 (21 January 1915, Letter from Sidney Webb to Woolf).
20 *Fabian News*, XXVI (7), June 1915.
21 *New Statesman*, V (118 and 119), July 10 and 17 1915.
22 Sidney Webb (ed), *How to Pay for the War: Being ideas offered to the Chancellor of the Exchequer by the Fabian Research Department*, London, 1916.
23 C 14 28 July 1916, Minutes.
24 Leonard Woolf, *International Government: Two Reports by L.S. Woolf Prepared by the Fabian Research Department, Together with a Project by a Fabian Committee for a Supernational Authority That Will Prevent War*, Fabian Society, 1916.
25 *Fabian News*, XXVII (10), September 1916.
26 C 14 12 January 1917, Minutes.
27 H. Duncan Hall, *The British Commonwealth of Nations*, London, 1920.
28 C 14 15 December 1916, Minutes.
29 Leonard Woolf, *Co-operation and the Future of Industry*, Labour Research Department, 1918.
30 Leonard Woolf, *Empire and Commerce in Africa: A Study in Economic Imperialism*, Labour Research Department, 1919; Leonard Woolf, *Economic Imperialism*, Swarthmore Press, London, 1920.
31 *Fabian News*, XXVII (10), September 1916.
32 *Fabian News*, XXVII (11)–XXVIII (6), October 1916–May 1917.
33 *Fabian News*, XXVII (12) November 1916.
34 Mackenzie, op. cit., pp. 84–5 (14 March 1917, Letter from Beatrice Webb to G.D.H. Cole).

13   Evolution not revolution

1 *Fabian News*, XXVIII (8), July 1917.
2 C 14 1 June 1917, Minutes.
3 *Fabian News*, XXVIII (9), August 1917.
4 Passfield Papers, Section IX File 1 (i) f 150 (11 June 1917, Letter from Julius West to Pease). David Marquand, *Ramsay MacDonald*, London, 1977.
5 Passfield Papers, Section IX File 1 (i) f 152 (16 June 1917, Letter from West to Pease).

6 *New Statesman*, Supplement 14 November 1914, 'Commonsense about the war', by G.B. Shaw.
7 C 14 27 July 1917, Minutes.
8 *Fabian News*, XXVIII (9), August 1917.
9 ibid.
10 Tract No. 184, *The Russian Revolution and British Democracy*, by Julius West, 1917.
11 *New Statesman*, X (24 and 25), 8 and 15 December 1917.
12 WEA Study Guide, *Great Britain After the War*, by Arnold Freeman and Sidney Webb, 1916.
13 ibid., p. 54.
14 *Memorandum on War Aims Approved by the Special Conference of the Labour Movement held at Central Hall, Westminster, London SW, on Friday December 28th 1917.*
15 *Labour and the New Social Order: A Draft Report on Reconstruction*, Labour Party, London, 1918.
16 Arthur Henderson, *The Aims of Labour*, Labour Party, London, 1918.
17 ibid., pp. 21, 61.
18 ibid., p. 16.
19 *Fabian News*, XXIX (5), April 1918.
20 Papers of Arthur Creech Jones, Rhodes House Library, MSS Brit. Emp. s 332, ACJ 1/2 ff 194-7.
21 A.F. Brockway and S. Hobhouse (eds), *English Prisons Today*, London, 1922.
22 H.N. Brailsford, J.A. Hobson, A. Creech Jones, E.F. Wise, *The Living Wage*, ILP Publications Department, London, 1926.
23 Tract No. 188, *National Finance and a Levy on Capital*, by S. Webb, 1919.
24 C 15 17 October 1919, Minutes.
25 Tract No. 189, *Urban District Councils* by C.M. Lloyd, 1920; Tract No. 193, *Housing*, by C.M. Lloyd, 1920; Tract No. 195, *The Scandal of the Poor Law*, by C.M. Lloyd, 1920; Tract No. 190, *Metropolitan Borough Councils*, by C.R. Attlee, 1920; Tract No. 191, *Borough Councils* by C.R. Attlee, 1920.
26 C 15 2 January 1920, Minutes.
27 C 15 23 May 1919, Minutes.
28 C 15 1920, passim, Minutes.

14   Sectional activities between the wars

1 H 1 27 June 1917, Nursery minutes.
2 H3 3 October 1917-18 September 1918, Nursery meetings minutes.
3 *Fabian News*, XXXIII (1), January 1922 et seq.
4 Fabian membership card. No reason was given for his resignation.
5 Sidney and Beatrice Webb, *A Constitution for the Socialist Commonwealth of Great Britain*, London, 1920.

6 H 6 8 February 1924, Nursery minutes.
7 *Fabian News*, XXXVI (10 and 11), October and November 1925.
8 *Fabian News*, XXXVII (5), May 1926.
9 *Fabian News*, XXXVIII (12), December 1927.
10 *Fabian News*, XL (1), January 1929.
11 See Chapters 17 and 18.
12 *Fabian News*, XLVII–XLIX, 1936–8, passim.
13 *Fabian News*, XLVII (2), February 1936 et seq.
14 *Fabian News*, XLVIII (1), January 1938.
15 *Fabian News*, XLIX (1 and 3), January and March 1938.
16 *Fabian News*, XXX (4), April 1919.
17 *Fabian News*, XXXIV (7), July 1923; Barbara Drake, *Women in Trade Unions*, London, 1921; *Fabian News*, XXXII (6), June 1921; H 23 1921 passim, Women's Group minutes. Maud Pember Reeves promoted the idea that the Ministry should provide free home helps to hard-pressed young mothers unable to afford the wages.
18 H 23 November 1921, Women's Group minutes.
19 H 24 1 June 1927, Women's Group minutes.
20 H 24 6 March 1929, Women's Group minutes.
21 G 2 Summer School minutes; G 14 Directors' log-book; G 24/2 November 1919, Summer School organization memoranda and comments.
22 G 3 Summer School Committee minutes.
23 G 14 Directors' log-book, passim.
24 G 3 Summer School Committee minutes.
25 G 14 Directors' log-book.
26 G 3 Summer School Committee minutes.

15   Fabians and government

1 *Fabian News*, XXXII (11), December 1922.
2 Frank Wallis Galton, MS autobiography, LSE.
3 Tract No. 207, *The Labour Party on the Threshold*, by Sidney Webb, 4 June 1923.
4 Passfield Papers, Section IV Item 18, pp. 4–5.
5 ibid., pp. 8, 13.
6 Norman Mackenzie, *Letters of Sidney and Beatrice Webb*, vol. III, London, 1978, p. 192 (17 January 1924, Letter from Webb to MacDonald).
7 M.I. Cole, *The Webbs and Their Work*, London, 1948, p. 202.
8 Tract No. 210, *The Position of Parties and the Right of Dissolution*, by Harold Laski, 1924.
9 *New Leader*, 4 January 1924.
10 Laski, op. cit., pp. 10, 11 and 15.
11 Passfield Papers, Section IV Item 18, p. 20.

12 Beatrice Webb, *Diary*, 12 December 1923.

13 C 16 21 November 1923, Minutes.

14 *Fabian News*, XXV (12), December 1924.

15 H.N. Brailsford *et al.*, *The Living Wage*, ILP, London, 1926; Passfield Papers, Section IV Item 19.

16 C 16 25 February 1926, Minutes.

17 M.I. Cole, *The Story of Fabian Socialism*, London, 1961, pp. 21–3.

18 C 16 13 May 1926, Minutes.

19 C 16 1 December 1927, Minutes.

20 J 1/3 ff 5–10 [1927] *Local Government News*, memorandum on Fabian Society responsibilities.

21 Tract No. 190, *Metropolitan Borough Councils*, by C.R. Attlee, 1920; Tract No. 191, *Borough Councils*, by C.R. Attlee, 1920; Tract No. 193, *Housing*, by C.M. Lloyd, 1920; Tract No. 194, *Taxes, Rates and Local Income Tax*, by Robert Jones, 1920.

22 Tract No. 214, *The District Auditor*, by W.A. Robson, 1925; Tract No. 218, *The County Council* by H. Samuels, 1925.

23 Mackenzie, op. cit., p. 155; C 16 22 June 1923, Minutes.

24 C 16 26 January 1928, Minutes.

25 C 17 28 November 1929, Minutes.

26 C 17 21 January 1932, Minutes.

27 C 17 April–June 1928, Minutes.

28 Tract No. 226, *The League of Nations*, by G.B. Shaw, 1929; Tract No. 227, *Labour's Foreign Policy*, by H.M. Swanwick, 1929; Tract No. 228, *Agriculture and the Labour Party*, by G.T. Garrett, 1929; Tract No. 229, *National Finance*, by F.W. Pethick-Lawrence, 1929; Tract No. 230, *Imperial Trusteeship*, by Sydney Olivier, 1929; Tract No. 231, *The Local Government Act 1929*, by S. Webb, 1929.

29 G 15 24 August 1928, Directors' log-book.

30 Sir Drummond Shiels, 'Webb as a Minister', in M.I. Cole, op. cit., p. 203.

31 Papers of Ernest Bevin, Centre for Modern Records, University of Warwick, MSS 126/EB/EA/12 and 13.

32 Tract No. 233, *Socialism and Fabianism*, by G.B. Shaw, 1930; Tract No. 234, *A Social Philosophy for Fabians*, by R. Fraser, 1930.

33 C 17 26 February 1931, Minutes; David Marquand, *Ramsay MacDonald*, London, 1977, p. 609.

34 See Chapters 17 and 18.

35 *Fabian News*, XLII (10), October 1931.

36 Passfield Papers, Section IV Item 25.

37 *Political Quarterly*, III (1), January/March 1932.

38 Harold Laski, *The Crisis and the Constitution: 1931 and After*, Hogarth Press and Fabian Society, London, 1932.

16   The SSIP and the Socialist League

1   A 4/1 ff 12–20 1928–30, Letters from Shaw to Galton.

2   A 5/3 ff 8–9 9–10 December 1930, Letter from Beatrice Webb to Galton.

3   J 2/1 f 3 19 February 1931, SSIP minutes.

4   J 9/1 ff 11–12 3 March 1931, Letter from Pritt to Cole.

5   J 2/1 ff 1–4 February–March 1931, SSIP minutes.

6   J 9/1 f 13 14 February 1931, Letter from Arthur Pugh to Cole.

7   J 9/1 ff 5–6 February–September 1931, Letters from Malcolm MacDonald to Cole.

8   J 2/3 f 1 1 February 1931, SSIP minutes.

9   Papers of Ernest Bevin, Centre for Modern Records, University of Warwick, MSS 126/EB/MC/2/13 10 February 1931, Memorandum on parliamentary reform by Ernest Bevin.

10   J 2/3 ff 3–4 1 March 1931, Conference report.

11   C 17 26 February 1931, Minutes.

12   C 17 30 April 1931, Minutes.

13   G.D.H. Cole, *A History of the Labour Party from 1914*, London, 1948, p. 282.

14   J 2/1–2 passim 1931–2, SSIP minutes.

15   J 6/3 Items 6–12, SSIP Study Guides. A seventh was produced by Michael Stewart.

16   R.S. 1, *The Essentials of Socialism*, by G.D.H. Cole, 1931. Tract No. 238, *Some Essentials of Socialist Propaganda*, by G.D.H. Cole, 1932.

17   J 6/1 ff 13–14 Lists of SSIP publications.

18   J 6/3 Item 1 *Anglo-Soviet Trade, Some Fictions and Facts*, No. 1 n.d.; Item 2 *Facts and Figures for Labour Speakers*, No. 2 n.d.

19   J 2/6 ff 1–2 *For Those over 21 Only*, by G.D.H. Cole, September 1931.

20   J 2/5 ff 1–10 2 October 1931–17 May 1932, Correspondence between E.A. Radice and Labour Party officials.

21   Noel Baker Papers, Churchill College, Cambridge, NBKR 2/11, November 1931.

22   Ernest Bevin and G.D.H. Cole, *The Crisis: What It Is: How It Arose: What to Do*, New Statesman and Nation pamphlet, London [1931].

23   J 2/1 f 21 November 1931, SSIP minutes.

24   J 2/3 ff 102–3 28 November–19 December 1931, Report on the delegate conference on the Crisis.

25   J 6/2 December 1931–September 1932, *Zip Bulletin*.

26   J 2/3 ff 136–69 16–17 April 1932, Easton Lodge conference papers.

27   ibid.

28   C 17 26 October 1932, Minutes.

29   M.I. Cole, *The Story of Fabian Socialism*, London, 1961, p. 234; John Parker, *50 Years in Politics*, London, 1982, passim.

30 Cole Papers, Nuffield College, Box 5 File 6 9 May 1932, Letter from Herbert Morrison to Cole; Bevin Papers MSS 126/EB/SS/1/15.

31 J 2/6 ff 63–5 July 1932, Letter from Cole to the SSIP Executive.

32 J 6/1 Items 1 & 2 *Housing in Liverpool: A Study of the Facts*, n.d.; R.S. No. 3, *The Nationalisation of West Country Minerals*, by A.K.H. Jenkins, 1932.

33 J 4/2 July–September 1932 passim. Cole's correspondence; J 2/3 ff 170–95 23–5 July 1932, Digswell Park conference papers.

34 J 2/6 ff 66–70 September 1932, Socialist League inaugural meeting notices; J 4/2 ff 57–61 20 September 1932, Letter from Margaret Cole to Radice.

35 J 4/3 f 7 19 September 1932, Letter from Bevin to Radice.

36 J 4/1 ff 1–15 September 1932, Socialist League constitution papers.

37 J 4/2 ff 42–3 September 1932, Letter from Cole to Radice; J 4/3 ff 46–55 August–November 1932, Letters from John Parker to Cole.

38 J 4/3 & 4 August–November 1932, Letters sent to Radice about the Socialist League inauguration.

39 J 2/5 f 12 10–11 October 1932, Letter from Ernest Bevin to Radice.

40 J 4/3 f 27 1932, Invitation to Socialist League inaugural conference.

17   The Research Bureau and the Society

1 J 7 30 March 1931, NFRB minutes.

2 J 9/1 f 21 September 1931, Cole's correspondence.

3 J 10/1 Item 1 May 1931, 'Memorandum on a plan of research into economic policy' [by G.D.H. Cole].

4 J 7 8 May 1931, NFRB minutes.

5 J 2/3 ff 60–62 8–10 May 1931, Easton Lodge conference papers.

6 J 2/3 ff 63–72 8–10 May 1931, Easton Lodge conference papers.

7 Nick Blake and Harry Rajak, *Wigs and Workers: A History of the Haldane Society of Socialist Lawyers 1930–80*, London, 1980.

8 J 7 4 May 1931, NFRB minutes.

9 Frank Wallis Galton, MS autobiography, LSE.

10 J 7 17 October–14 November 1932, NFRB minutes.

11 J 7 11 December 1931, NFRB minutes.

12 M.I. Cole, *The Story of Fabian Socialism*, London, 1961, pp. 228–9; *Twelve Studies in Soviet Russia*, for the NFRB by M.I. Cole, London, 1933.

13 J 7 16 July 1933, NFRB minutes.

14 J 7 16 October 1933, NFRB minutes.

15 J 50/1, 2 & 7 25 October 1932, 'Emergency Powers Act'–report by D.N. Pritt; 18 October 1934, 'Land acquisition' – reports by W.T. Wells and R.T.S. Chorley; n.d. 'Wartime administration as a precedent for a socialist administration' – report by the Haldane Club.

16 J 7 14 November 1933, NFRB minutes.

17 J 7 9 February 1935, NFRB minutes.

18 See 'Bibliography of the writings of G.D.H. Cole', in A.W. Wright, *G.D.H. Cole and Social Democracy*, Clarendon Press, Oxford, 1979.

19 J 8 1938, 7th annual report of the NFRB.

20 ibid.

21 The papers were deposited in the library of Stanford University, California.

22 J 16/7 11–12 December 1937, Report of the conference: *This Socialist Sweden?*.

23 C 18 February–June 1934, Minutes.

24 C 18 February 1935, Minutes.

25 J 11/1 f 7 1937, John Parker's correspondence.

26 C 18 14 January 1937, Minutes.

27 J 11/1 f 9 24 January 1938, Letter from Parker to Emil Davies.

28 J 11/1 ff 4–5 1938, Parker correspondence.

29 Cole Papers, Nuffield College, Box 5 13 July 1938, Letter from Davies to Cole.

30 J 8 25 July 1938, NFRB minutes.

31 C 19 22 September and 20 October 1938, Minutes.

32 *Fabian News*, XLIX (10), October 1938.

33 G 59/1 28–9 March 1942, Third Nuffield College Social Reconstruction Conference.

34 J 8 n.d. NFRB minutes.

35 *Fabian News*, 50 (2), February 1939.

36 ibid.

18   The Colonial and International Bureaux

1 R.S. 45, *Planned Investment*, by C.P. Mayhew, 1939.

2 C 26 1939 May, Minutes.

3 C 20 May–July 1939, Minutes.

4 Tract No. 248, *Democracy for India*, by H.N. Brailsford, 1939.

5 R.S. 44, *Labour in the West Indies*, by W. Arthur Lewis, 1939.

6 R.S. 36, *German and Czech*, by S. Duff Grant, 1937.

7 *Fabian News*, 50 (9), September–October 1939.

8 *Fabian Quarterly*, 23, Autumn 1939.

9 Tract No. 247, *The War on the Home Front*, by G.D.H. Cole, 1939.

10 Records of the Workers' Travel Association and Francis Williams, *Journey into Adventure*, London, 1960, pp. 124–6.

11 Noel Baker Papers, Churchill College, Cambridge, NBKR 2/45.

12 Margaret Cole and Richard Padley (eds), *Evacuation Survey*, London, 1942.

13 C 26 passim, Minutes.

14 C 20 24 June 1940 et seq. Minutes.

15 C 20 13 November 1939, Minutes.

16 D 8/1 1907–11, Finance and General Purposes Committee minutes.

17 Rita Hinden, interview, 1970.

18 Fabian Colonial Bureau Papers, Rhodes House Library, MSS Brit. Emp. s 365, FCB 16/3 ff 129–233 14 October 1940–26 February 1943, Correspondence between Rita Hinden and Arthur Creech Jones.

19 C 20 28 October 1940, Minutes.

20 C 26 26 October 1940, Fabian Colonial Bureau minutes.

21 W.M. Macmillan, *Africa Emergent: A Survey of Social, Political and Economic Trends in British Africa*, London, 1938; *Warning from the West Indies*, Penguin Special, Harmondsworth, 1938.

22 Rita Hinden interview, 1970.

23 C 26 passim. Fabian Colonial Bureau monthly, quarterly and annual reports and minutes.

24 FCB 16/3 ff 129–233 1940–3.

25 C 20 March 1941, Minutes.

26 FCB Periodical Report No. 4 March–April 1941.

27 FCB 16/3 f 165 30 May 1941, Letter from Rita Hinden to Creech Jones.

28 FCB 69/12 ff 1–6 18–20 July 1941, Report of the conference held at St Peter's Hall, Oxford.

29 FCB 69/12 ff 7–19 21 March 1942, Report of a conference held in the Bonnington Hotel, London, on 'The future of our colonies in the light of recent developments, particularly in the Far East'.

30 FCB 46/3 1940–2, Colonial Policy Memoranda.

31 R.S. 61, *Labour in the Colonies 1. – Some Current Problems*, report of a committee of the Fabian Colonial Bureau, 1941.

32 *Downing Street and the Colonies*, report submitted to the Fabian Colonial Bureau, 1942.

33 *Co-operation in the Colonies*, report from a special committee to the Fabian Colonial Bureau, with a preface by C.F. Strickland, London, 1948.

34 FCB Box 39 Working papers for *Co-operation in the Colonies*, dating from 1939.

35 FCB 69/12 ff 20–23 15 November 1942, 'A charter for the colonial peoples', report of a conference arranged by the Bureau in London.

36 FCB 132/4 1941–5, Fabian Colonial Bureau West Indies Committee papers.

37 Rita Hinden (ed), *Fabian Colonial Essays*, London, 1945.

38 C 20 3 March 1941, Minutes; J 52/1 ff 1–2 March 1941, International Bureau minutes.

39 J 52/1 ff 6–16 1941–2, International Bureau subcommittee minutes.

40 J 61/2 12–13 December 1942, Report of a conference on relief and rehabilitation in Europe held at St Hilda's College, Oxford, *When Hostilities Cease – Papers on Relief and Reconstruction*, by Julian Huxley and others, London, 1943.

41 J 52/1 International Bureau minutes; J 57/1 24 April 1940, Report on the activities of the International Section.

42 Noel Baker Papers, Churchill College, Cambridge, NBKR 2/57 February–

July 1942, Correspondence between Noel Baker and Parker.

43 J 58/2 f 1 1943, May Day Celebration notice.

44 C 20 passim, Minutes and quarterly report; J 52/1–3 1941–5, Minutes and annual report; 1941–5 *Fabian News* reports of the Bureau's work.

45 R.S. 62, *Help Germany to Revolt!*, by H. Monte and H. von Rau Schemplat, 1941.

46 *Fabian Quarterly*, Spring 1941, 'Italy – what next?', by Dr Paolo Treves.

47 C 20 1944 Annual report.

19   The home front

1 C 20 11 September 1939, Minutes.

2 C 26 passim, Minutes.

3 R.S. 110, *The Rate for the Job*, by Margaret Cole, 1946.

4 Margaret Cole and Richard Padley, *Evacuation Survey*, London, 1942.

5 Doreen Idle, *War over West Ham: A Study of Community Adjustment*, report prepared for the Fabian Society and the Ethical Union, London, 1943.

6 M.I. Cole, *The Life of G.D.H. Cole*, London, 1971, pp. 230–1.

7 Cole Papers, Nuffield College; Nuffield College Social Survey Papers; M.I. Cole, op. cit.

8 Sir William Beveridge, *Inter-Departmental Committee on Social Insurance and Allied Services Report*, Cmd. 6404, London, 1942.

9 W.A. Robson (ed.), *Social Security*, London, 1943.

10 C 20 26 July 1943, Minutes; K 1/2 f 6 14 September 1943, Home Research Committee minutes.

11 C 20 22 September 1941, Minutes.

12 K 1/1 ff 1–5 1943, Home Research Committee minutes.

13 K 1/1 ff 6–12 1943, Home Research Committee minutes.

14 ibid., and C 20 1943, Minutes.

15 K 1/2 ff 15–33 1943, Home Research Committee minutes.

16 *Fabian News*, 52 (2), February 1941.

17 F 1/1–10 1941–2, Socialist Propaganda Committee inaugural material and minutes.

18 F 1/7 ff 77–9 1941–4, Socialist Propaganda Committee memoranda.

19 *Fabian News*, 53 (7), July 1942.

20 A 22/2 ff 14–28 1942–3, African correspondence.

21 F 1/3 f 40 1942, Socialist Propaganda Committee minutes.

22 F 1/4 1943, Socialist Propaganda Committee minutes.

23 Fabian Special No. 1, *Take Over the War Industries*, by 'Populus' [G.D.H. Cole], 1942.

24 F 1/7 1941–4, Socialist Propaganda Committee memoranda.

25 F 1/5 1945, Socialist Propaganda Committee minutes and committee papers.

20 Third time lucky

1 *Fabian News*, 56 (8), September 1945.

2 *Fabian Quarterly*, 47, October 1945.

3 R.S. 94, *Reparations and the Future of German Industry*, by G.D.H. Cole, 1945; R.S. 98, *Reconstruction – Then and Now*, by R.S.W. Pollard, 1945; R.S. 109, *European Transport: The Way to Unity*, by M. Zaref, 1946; R.S. 113, *The World Parliament of Labour: A Study of the I.L.O.*, by R.J.P. Mortishead, 1946; R.S. 117, *Yugoslavia Rebuilds*, by Doreen Warriner, 1946.

4 63rd Annual Report, 1945–6.

5 R.S. 92, *Colonies and International Conscience*, by Rita Hinden and Arthur Creech Jones, 1945.

6 *Fabian Quarterly*, 48, December 1945; *Local Government and the Colonies*, ed Rita Hinden, London, 1950.

7 Fabian Controversy Series No. 1, *Domination or Co-operation*, Introduction, 1946.

8 R.S. 101, *Palestine Controversy: A Symposium*, 1945.

9 63rd Annual Report, 1945–6.

10 R.S. 112, *India's Sterling Balances*, by A.C. Gilpin, 1946.

11 C 27/6 May 1947, Minutes.

12 C 27/5 April 1946, Minutes.

13 R.S. 92, *Fuel and Power: A Study in Industrial Organization and Control*, by a Fabian research group, 1945; R.S. 95, *British Transport: A Study in Industrial Organization and Control*, by Ernest Davies, 1945; R.S. 103, *The British Gas Industry: Present and Future*, by J. Mitchel, 1945; R.S. 104, *Cotton: A Working Policy*, by a Fabian research group, 1945; R.S. 106, *Labour: Control and De-control*.

14 K 7–40 Boxes of research material for numerous projects.

15 *Empire*, 9 (3), August 1946.

16 C 27/5 18 June 1946, Minutes.

17 C 27/5 July 1946, Minutes.

18 D 33/1 & 2 1946–52, Staff Consultative Committee papers.

19 C 21/5 21 November 1946, Memorandum by Harold Laski.

20 C 27/6 March 1947, Minutes.

21 C 16/6 16 January 1947, Minutes.

22 C 16/6 1947 passim, Minutes.

23 65th Annual Report 1947–8.

24 D 8/3 f 145, Finance and General Purposes Committee papers.

25 D 8/3 f 172.

26 C 27/6 May 1947, Minutes.

27 R.S. 124, *The Second Five Years*, by Ian Mikardo, 1948.

28 *Fabian News*, 59 (8), September 1948.

29 F 47/2 1948 Discussion guide in preparation for a 1950 election; F 49/5 &

6 1949–50, 'Home policy' and 'Labour believes in Britain' – questionnaires.
30 Tract No. 268, *More Socialisation or Less?*, by C. Lang and D. Chapman, 1949; Tract No. 269, *Socialism and Farming*, by F.W. Bateson, 1949; Tract No. 270, *Wages Policy?*, by T.E.M. McKitterick, 1949; Tract No. 271, *Workers' Control?*, by Eirene White, 1949; Tract No. 272, *Wholesaling and Retailing*, by Henry Smith, 1949; Tract No. 274, *Next Steps in Education*, based on a report by Joan Thompson, 1949; Tract No. 275, *Holidays and the State*, by Donald Chapman, 1949.
31 Tract No. 273, *Labour's Second Term*, by G.D.H. Cole, 1949.
32 G 50/1 15–17 July 1949, Problems Ahead Group programme and papers.
33 ibid.
34 G 50/2 January–August 1950, Problems Ahead Group circulating volume.
35 E 112/5 1952 New Fabian Essays editorial papers.
36 *New Fabian Essays*, ed R.H.S. Crossman, London, 1952.
37 E 112/5 1952 New Fabian Essays correspondence.
38 C 29/1 1950 Minutes.

21 Opposition again

1 *Fabian Journal*, 5, October 1951.
2 Richard Crossman, *Backbench Diaries*, ed Janet Morgan, 1981, p. 31.
3 C 29/3 22 July 1952, Minutes; C 30/1 2 December 1952, Minutes.
4 C 30/2 May 1954, Minutes. Frank Horrabin had resigned because of ill health at the end of 1950.
5 FCB 72/1 ff 31–46 1951, Advisory Committee papers, notes by Marjorie Nicholson on Bureau organization.
6 Colonial Controversy Series No. 7, *The Way Forward*, ed Jim Griffiths, 1950.
7 69th Annual Report, 1951–2.
8 See minutes of the Africa Bureau, Rhodes House Library, MSS Afr. s 1681, Boxes 1 and 2 1952–64.
9 Africa Bureau Papers, MSS Afr. s 1681, Boxes 225–6.
10 Colonial Controversy Series No. 9, *East African Future*, by a Group, 1952; Tract No. 302, *The Kenya Question: An African Answer*, by Tom Mboya, 1956.
11 R.S. 152, *Challenge to the British Caribbean*, by Rita Hinden, Lord Listowel, Rawle Farley and Colin Hughes, 1952.
12 C 30/2 28 April 1954, Minutes.
13 C 30/2 November 1954, Minutes.
14 *Fabian News*, 65 (5 and 6), May and June 1954.
15 C 31/2 March 1957, Minutes.
16 C 30/3 2 December 1955, Minutes; F 46 & 47 1950s and 1960s, Correspondence with the local societies about research, memoranda, guides and other related papers.

17 *The Politics of the Labour Party*, ed Dennis Kavanagh, 'The decline of Labour's local party membership and electoral base 1945–79', London, 1982, pp. 111–32.

18 C 31/1 7 February 1956, Minutes.

19 73rd Annual Report, 1955–6.

20 C 31/1 July 1956, Minutes.

21 F 68/1–3 1956–60, Conference papers.

22 C 30/4 15 November 1955, Minutes.

23 C 31/1 July 1956, Minutes.

24 *Fabian News*, 71 (2), February 1970.

25 *New Fabian Colonial Essays*, ed Arthur Creech Jones, London, 1958, p. 36.

26 ibid., p. 18.

27 *Fabian International Essays*, ed T.E.M. McKitterick and Kenneth Younger, London, 1957, p. 105.

28 ibid., p. 217.

29 C 31/3 February 1958, Minutes.

30 C 31/3 31 March 1958, Minutes.

31 *Fabian News*, 70 (2 and 3), February and March 1959.

32 Tract No. 258, *The Fabian Society*, by G.D.H. Cole, 1942; C 32/1 ff 1–8 January 1959, Memoranda by Rodgers and Benn.

33 *Fabian News*, 70 (9), October 1959, 71 (1), January 1960.

34 C 32 14 December 1959, Minutes.

35 *Fabian News*, 71 (5), May 1960.

36 *Fabian News*, 71 (2), February 1960.

37 *Fabian News*, 71 (4), April 1960.

38 C 32/2 12 April 1960, Minutes.

39 *Fabian News*, 71 (4), April 1960.

40 *Fabian News*, 71 (1), January 1960.

41 Tract No. 324, *Can Labour Win?*, by C.A.R. Crosland, 1960.

42 Tract No. 300, *Socialism and Nationalisation*, by Hugh Gaitskell, 1956; Tract No. 321, *Casualties of the Welfare State*, by Audrey Harvey, 1960; Tract No. 322, *The Race against the H-bomb*, by Denis Healey, 1960; Tract No. 323, *The Irresponsible Society*, by Richard Titmuss, 1960; Tract No. 324, *Can Labour Win?*, by C.A.R. Crosland, 1960; Tract No. 325, *Labour in the Affluent Society*, by R.H.S. Crossman, 1960; Tract No. 326, *The Socialist Imagination*, by Wayland and Elizabeth Young, 1960; Tract No. 327, *Britain's Role in the Changing World*, by Kenneth Younger, 1960; Tract No. 328, *Nationalised Industries in the Mixed Economy*, by John Hughes, 1960; Tract No. 329, *Pursuit of Peace*, by John Strachey, 1960; Tract No. 331, *Socialism and Culture*, by Richard Wollheim, 1961; Tract No. 334, *The Structure of Higher Education*, by a Fabian Group, 1961; Tract No. 335, *Trade Unions in Opposition*, by J. Alexander and John Hughes, 1961; Tract No. 337, *The Existing Alternatives in Communication*, by Raymond Williams, 1962; Tract No. 339, *The Future of the*

Unions, by William McCarthy, 1962; Tract No. 340, *Redundancy in the Affluent Society*, by Geoffrey Goodman, 1962; Tract No. 342, *Education in a Class Society*, by John Vaizey, 1963; Tract No. 343, *Out of Stagnation: A Policy for Growth*, by J.R. Sargent, 1963; Tract No. 344, *The Future of Public Ownership*, by a Fabian Group, 1963; Tract No. 346, *Planning for Progress*, by Thomas Balogh, 1963; Tract No. 348, *Pension Rights and Wrongs*, by Tony Lynes, 1963; Tract No. 349, *The Meaning of Work*, by Lisl Klein, 1963; Tract No. 350, *An Incomes Policy for Labour*, by Michael Stewart and Rex Winsbury, 1963; Tract No. 356, *New Pattern for Primary Schools*, by a Fabian Group, 1964; R.S. 235, *Industrial Relations: Sweden Shows the Way*, by Jack Cooper, 1963; R.S. 236, *The Health of the Nation*, by Laurie Pavitt, 1963; R.S. 237, *New Look at Comprehensive Schools*, by Michael Armstrong and Michael Young, 1964; R.S. 242, *The Democratic Firm*, by Norman Ross, 1964; R.S. 244, *Change in the Trade Unions*, by John Hughes, 1964; R.S. 247, *A Plan for Incomes*, by a Fabian Group, 1965.

43 YF 1, *Lady Albemarle's Boys*, by Ray Gosling, 1961.

44 C 32/3 1961 passim, Minutes.

45 YF 2, *NATO or Neutrality*, by a study group, 1961.

46 H 39 1960 passim, Minutes of the Young Fabian Group.

47 *Fabian News*, 71 (7), July 1960; 72 (8), September 1961.

48 C 32/2 4 May 1960, Minutes.

49 C 32/3 2 February 1961, Minutes.

50 C 33/1 29 October 1962, Minutes.

51 C 33/2–3 1963–4, Minutes.

52 Tract No. 332, *Aden, the Protectorates and the Yemen*, by R. Sorensen, 1961.

53 C 32/3 November 1961; C 33/1 19 December 1961, Minutes; February and April 1962, General Secretary's Report and minutes; 79th Annual Report 1962–3.

54 C 32/3 13 September 1961, Minutes.

55 C 33/3 December 1964, Minutes.

56 C 33/2 July 1963; C 33/3 April 1964, Minutes.

22   Friendly critics

1 C 34/1 February–July 1965, Minutes.

2 C 34/2 May–July 1966, Minutes.

3 C 34/2 20 October 1966, Minutes.

4 Tract No. 369, *Labour's Social Plans*, by Brian Abel-Smith, 1966; Tract No. 371, *Poverty, Socialism and Labour in Power*, by Peter Townsend, 1967; Tract No. 370, *Choice and 'the Welfare State'*, by Richard Titmuss, 1967; Tract No. 375, *Socialism and Planning*, by Richard Crossman, 1967; 'Socialism and Affluence', from *Fabian Essays* by Brian Abel-Smith and others, London, 1967.

5 *Fabian News*, 78 (1), January 1967.

6 *More Power to the People: Young Fabian Essays on Democracy in Britain*, ed Brian Lapping and Giles Radice, London, 1968.

7 C 34/2 October 1966, Minutes.

8 C 34/4 March 1968 et seq., Minutes.

9 C 34/3 May 1967; C 34/4 February 1968, Minutes.

10 C 34/4 9 April 1968, Minutes.

11 C 34/3 15 February 1967, Minutes.

12 C 34/4 February 1968, Minutes. Memorandum by Tom Ponsonby.

13 C 34/4 July 1968, Minutes. Report by Owen and McFarland on 'Publicity and membership policy'.

14 C 34/5 January 1969, Minutes. Young Fabian Group paper on 'The role of the Society'.

15 C 34/5 26 January 1969, Minutes.

16 C 34/5 February 1969, Minutes. Shirley Williams's memorandum on 'Priorities for the seventies'.

17 7 June 1971, Minutes (uncatalogued).

18 G 57/2 24 April 1971, Conference on 'International companies and the Labour movement', London; G 58/1 8 April 1972, Conference on 'Participation in local social services', London; G 58/2 10 February 1973, Seminar on 'Positive discrimination', London.

19 *Fabian News*, 82–3, 1971–2.

20 Tract No. 402, *The New Politics: A Socialist Renaissance*, by Tony Benn, 1970.

21 Tract No. 407, *The Labour Party: An Organizational Study*, by Inigo Bing, based on work by the Young Fabian Group and Local Societies Committee, 1971.

22 C 35/1 July 1970, Minutes.

23 C 35/1 October 1970, Minutes.

24 *Britain and the World in the 70s*, a collection of Fabian essays, ed George Cunningham, London, 1970.

25 C 35/1 16 November 1970 et seq., Minutes.

26 YF 10, *Strangers Within* by a study group, 1965; YF 11, *Womanpower*, by Anne Glennerster, Lynn McFarland, Rosalind Steele and Frances Stewart, 1971.

27 *Fabian News*, 81 (10), November 1970.

28 April 1971, Minutes (uncatalogued).

29 October 1971, Minutes (uncatalogued).

30 *Fabian News*, 82 (3), March 1971.

31 G 62 1961–3, Wilton Park Conferences for the exchange of views on political, economic and social questions of common concern.

32 G 63 17–20 February 1972, 'Technology on trial' Conference, Rome – correspondence, report, papers submitted by participants etc.

33 *Fabian News*, 84, (1), January 1972.

34 31 January 1972, Minutes (uncatalogued).

35 6 November 1972, Minutes (uncatalogued).
36 Richard Titmuss, *The Gift Relationship: From Human Blood to Social Policy*, London, 1970; Tract No. 323, *The Irresponsible Society*, by Richard Titmuss, 1960; Tract No. 370, *Choice and 'the Welfare State'*, by Richard Titmuss, 1967.
37 January 1973, Minutes (uncatalogued).
38 *Young Fabian Plebs*, 1, March 1973.
39 90th Annual Report 1972–3; Tract No. 414, *Towards a Radical Agenda*, by ten Task Forces, 1972.
40 *Young Fabian Plebs*, 1, March 1973.
41 *Young Fabian Plebs*, 3, July/August/September 1973.
42 *Fabian News*, 86 (3), April/May 1974.
43 11 July 1974, Minutes (uncatalogued).
44 3 May 1976, Minutes (uncatalogued).
45 January 1976, International and Commonwealth Bureau minutes (uncatalogued).
46 R.S. 332, *Influencing Europe*, by Roy Manley and Helen Hastings, 1977; R.S. 334, *Transnational Corporations*, by Carl Wilms Wright, 1977; R.S. 342, *Eurocommunism* by David Scott Bell, 1979; Tract No. 449, *Electing Europe's First Parliament*, by Richard Corbett and Rod Nortawl, 1977; YF 45, *A Wider Europe*, by Geoff Harris, 1976; YF 48, *A Regional Policy for Europe*, by Mark Swift, 1978.
47 Tract No. 448, *Reforming the House of Commons*, by Lisanne Radice, 1977; Tract No. 451, *The Labour Party: Crisis and Prospects*, by Dianne Hayter, 1977.
48 11 October 1978, Minutes (uncatalogued).
49 *Labour and Equality*, ed Nick Bosanquet and Peter Townsend, London, 1980, Preface.
50 *Why Vote Labour*, by Neil Kinnock, Nick Butler and Toby Harris, NCLC Publishing Society, 1979.
51 *A Socialist Agenda*, ed David Lipsey and Dick Leonard, London, 1981.
52 95th Annual Report 1977–8.

23   One hundred years old

1 Fabian Society 100th Annual Report, 1982/3.
2 Eric Heffer was the candidate who was not a member of the Fabian Executive Committee. Tony Benn, being out of the House of Commons at that time, did not stand for the leadership.
3 Ben Pimlott (ed), *Fabian Essays in Socialist Thought*, London, 1984.
4 Tract No. 495, *Socialist Values and Time*, by Bernard Crick, 1984.
5 Pimlott, op. cit.
6 Crick, op. cit., p. 14.
7 Pimlott, op. cit.
8 ibid.

BIBLIOGRAPHY

Primary sources

Fabian Society papers in Nuffield College, Oxford, which are arranged and listed in the following sections:

A Correspondence.
B Early papers and memorials to eminent Fabians.
C Executive Committee minutes, related committee papers, other administrative papers and material concerned with lectures.
D Finance and General Purposes Committee minutes and administrative papers.
E Publications administrative papers.
F Local Societies' papers.
G Schools and Conference administrative papers and reports.
H The Nursery, the Women's Group and the Young Fabian Group papers.
J The Local Government Bureau, the Society for Socialist Inquiry and Propaganda, the New Fabian Research Bureau, the International and Commonwealth Bureau minutes and administrative papers.
K Home Research Committee administrative and research material.
L Labour Party relations, papers arising from particular activities.
M Photographs, newspaper cuttings, early membership cards and other, miscellaneous material.

Fabian Colonial Bureau papers in Rhodes House Library, Oxford, MSS Brit. Emp. s 365, which are arranged and listed in the following sixteen sections:

1 Introduction to the whole collection.
2 Files presented by Arthur Creech Jones.
3 Home correspondence.
4 Correspondence files of Arthur Creech Jones and Hilda Selwyn-Clarke.

5 Correspondence with Members of Parliament.
6 Correspondence with the Colonial Office and other Ministries.
7 Publications of the Fabian Colonial Bureau.
8 Colonial policy and development.
9 Conference and committee papers.
10 Africa, general, and West Africa.
11 South Africa and the High Commission Territories.
12 Central Africa.
13 East Africa.
14 North America and the West Indies.
15 Asia.
16 South Pacific, smaller territories, and colonies administered by countries other than Great Britain. Newspaper cuttings and photographs.

In addition the collections of papers of individuals were consulted as follows:

Clement Attlee, both at Churchill College, Cambridge, and at University College, Oxford, the latter being now deposited in the Bodleian Library, Oxford.
Ernest Bevin, both at Churchill College, Cambridge, and at the Centre for Modern Records, University of Warwick.
G.D.H. Cole, at Nuffield College, Oxford.
Hugh Dalton, British Library of Political and Economic Science, London.
Frank Wallis Galton, British Library of Political and Economic Science, London.
Victor Gollancz, at the Centre for Modern Records, University of Warwick.
Philip Noel Baker, at Churchill College, Cambridge.
Passfield Papers, at the British Library of Political and Economic Science, London.
Edward Pease, at the British Library of Political and Economic Science, London.

Newspapers and periodicals

British Labour Weekly
Clarion and The New Clarion
Commonweal
Daily Chronicle
Daily Citizen
Freedom
Fortnightly Review
Gateway
Highway
ILP News
Independent Review
Justice

New Statesman
Oxford Reformer
  (ed G.D.H. Cole)
Oxford Socialist
  (eds F.K. Griffith
  and G.D.H. Cole)
Pall Mall Gazette
Practical Socialist
St James Gazette
Socialist
Sunday Chronicle
The Times

Labour Leader
Manchester Guardian and
  The Guardian

Westminster Gazette
Workman's Times

Fabian publications

Pamphlets

1884 et seq.	Tracts
1931 et seq.	Research Series
1946–53	Colonial Controversy Series, Nos 1–10
1961 et seq.	Young Fabian Pamphlets

Periodicals

1891 et seq.	*Fabian News*
1910–12	[Fabian 'Nursling']
1924–31	*Local Government News* (with the Labour Party)
1934–6	*Quarterly Journal* of the New Fabian Research Bureau, Nos 1–10
1936–8	*New Fabian Research Bureau Quarterly*, Nos 11–20
1939–48	*Fabian Quarterly*, Nos 21–58
1939 Nov.	*Fabian International Bulletin*, No. 1 only; revived briefly 1942
1940–5	*France and Britain*
1941–9	**Empire*
1949–72	**Venture*
1972–5	**Third World*
1943–62	*Local Societies Directives/Bulletin*
1950–9	*Fabian Journal*
1961 et seq.	*Young Fabian Newsletter* (in recent years forming part of *Fabian News*)
1965–9	*Plebs*
1973–4	*Young Fabian Plebs*

* and ** The same journal with change of name.

Volumes of essays

1889	*Fabian Essays in Socialism* (first edition), edited by Bernard Shaw.
1945	*Fabian Colonial Essays*, edited by Rita Hinden.
1952	*New Fabian Essays*, edited by Richard Crossman.
1957	*Fabian International Essays*, edited by T.E.M. McKitterick and Kenneth Younger.
1959	*New Fabian Colonial Essays*, edited by Arthur Creech Jones.
1967	*Socialism and Affluence: Four Fabian Essays*, by Peter Townsend *et al.*

1968   *More Power to the People: Young Fabian Essays on Democracy in Britain*, edited by Brian Lapping and Giles Radice.

1968   *Social Services for All? Eleven Fabian Essays*, by Peter Townsend *et al.*

1970   *The Fifth Social Service: Nine Fabian Essays*, by Peter Townsend *et al.*

1970   *Britain and the World in the Seventies: A Collection of Fabian Essays*, edited by George Cunningham.

1972   *Labour and Inequality: Sixteen Fabian Essays*, edited by Peter Townsend and Nicholas Bosanquet.

1980   *Labour and Equality: A Fabian Study of Labour in Power 1974–79*, edited by Peter Townsend and Nicholas Bosanquet.

1981   *A Socialist Agenda*, edited by David Lipsey and Dick Leonard.

Occasional publications

1900   *Fabianism and the Empire*, edited by Bernard Shaw.

1912   *War against Poverty* (with the Independent Labour Party).

1941–3   Fabian Letter Series, Nos 1–8.

1942–51 Fabian Specials, Nos 1–8.

1946   Science and Social Affairs series, No. 1 only.

1947–8   Webb Memorial Lectures.

1948–63 Fabian Study and Discussion Guides.

1950–68 Fabian Occasional Papers, Nos 1–4.

1913–17 *New Statesman* Fabian supplements.

1912   *Songs for Socialists.*

In addition there have been numerous books published by the Fabian Society, the Fabian Research Department, the New Fabian Research Bureau, the Fabian Colonial Bureau and the Fabian International Bureau. Many of these are named in the Notes.

There have also been several volumes compiled from autumn lectures and from selections of tracts linked by subject.

Books, articles and pamphlets

Addison, P. (1975) *The Road to 1945*, London, Cape.

Ball, O.H. (1923) *Sidney Ball: Memories and Impressions of 'An Ideal Don'*, Oxford, Blackwell.

Barker, A.P. and Rush, M. (1970) *The Member of Parliament and his Information* (For Political and Economic Planning and the Study of Parliament Group), London, Allen & Unwin.

Beer, M. (1948) *A History of British Socialism*, London, Allen & Unwin.

Bell, D.S. (ed.) (1980) *Labour into the Eighties*, London, Croom Helm.

Bermant, C. *et al.* (1977) *My LSE*, ed. J. Abse, London, Robson Books.

Besant, A. (1885) *Autobiographical Sketches*, London, Freethought Publishing Co.

Besant, A. (1893) *An Autobiography*, London, T. Fisher Unwin & the Theosophical Publishing Co.

Besterman, T. (1934) *Mrs Annie Besant: A Modern Prophet*, London, Kegan Paul, Trench, Trubner & Co.

Beveridge, J. (1960) *An Epic of Clare Market*, London, G. Bell & Sons.

Bevin, E. and Cole, G.D.H. [1931] *The Crisis: What It Is: How It Arose: What to Do*, London, New Statesman and Nation pamphlet.

Blake, N. and Rajak, H. (1980) *Wigs and Workers: A History of the Haldane Society of Socialist Lawyers, 1930–1980*, London, Haldane Society.

Booth, C. (1892–7) *Life and Labour of the People of London*, London, Macmillan.

Boyce, G., Curran, J. and Wingate, P. (eds) (1978) *Newspaper History from the Seventeenth Century to the Present Day* (published for the Press Group of the Action Society) London.

Bradley, I. (1981) *Breaking the Mould? The Birth and Prospects of the Social Democratic Party*, Oxford, Martin Robertson.

Brailsford, H.N., Hobson, J.A., Jones, A.C. and Wise, E.F. (1926) *The Living Wage*, London, ILP Publication Department.

Braunthal, J. (1966, 1967) *History of the International, 1864–1914 & 1914–43*, trans. Henry Collins, Kenneth Mitchell and John Clark, London, Nelson.

Briggs, A. and Saville, J. (1960) *Essays in Labour History vol. I*, in memory of G.D.H. Cole by Ivor Brown, Hugh Gaitskell, Stephen K. Bailey and G.D.N. Worswick, London, Macmillan.

Brockway, A.F. (1942) *Inside the Left: Thirty Years of Platform, Press, Prison and Parliament*, London, Allen & Unwin.

Brockway, A.F. (1963) *Outside the Right: A sequel . . . with a Lost Play by G. Bernard Shaw*, London, Allen & Unwin.

Brockway, A.F. and Hobhouse, S. (1922) *English Prisons Today: Being the Report of the Prison System Enquiry Committee*, London, Labour Research Department.

Brome, V. (1958) *Six Studies in Quarrelling*, London, Cresset Press.

Bullock, A. (1960–7) *The Life and Times of Ernest Bevin, vol. I: Trade Union Leader 1881–1940; vol. II: Minister of Labour 1940–45*, London, Heinemann.

Burrows, H. and Hobson, J.A. (1908) *William Clarke*, London, Swan, Sonnenschein & Co.

Butler, D.E. (1963) *The Electoral System in Britain 1918–51*, Oxford, Clarendon Press.

Butler, D.E. and Sloman, A. (1980) *British Political Facts, 1900–1978*, London, Macmillan.

Butler, D.E. *et al.* (1952–80) *The British General Elections of 1951, 1955, 1959, 1964, 1966, 1970, 1974 Feb & Oct, 1979*, London, Macmillan.

Caine, S. (1963) *The History of the Foundation of the London School of Economics and Political Science*, London, G. Bell & Sons.

Carpenter, L.P. (1973) *G.D.H. Cole: An Intellectual Biography*, Cambridge, Mass.

Clarke, P. (1978) *Liberals and Social Democrats*, Cambridge, Cambridge University Press.

Cline, C.A. (1963) *Recruits to Labour 1914–1931*, Syracuse, NY, Syracuse University Press.

Coates, R.D. (1975) *The Labour Party and the Struggle for Socialism*, Cambridge, Cambridge University Press.

Coates, R.D. (1980) *Labour in Power? A Study of the Labour Government 1974–79*, London, Longman.

Cole, G.D.H. (1929) *The Next Ten Years in British Social and Economic Policy*, London, Macmillan.

Cole, G.D.H. (1943) 'Beatrice Webb as an economist: An obituary', *Economic Journal*, III (212), November.

Cole, G.D.H. (1948) *A History of the Labour Party from 1914*, London, Routledge & Kegan Paul.

Cole, G.D.H. (1953–60) *A History of Socialist Thought*, 5 vols, London, Macmillan.

Cole, M.I. (1945) *Beatrice Webb*, London, Longman, Green & Co.

Cole, M.I. (1961) *The Story of Fabian Socialism*, London, Heinemann.

Cole, M.I. (1971) *The Life of G.D.H. Cole*, London, Macmillan.

Cole, M.I. (ed.) (1949) *The Webbs and Their Work*, London, Frederick Muller.

Cook, C.P. and Brendan, K. (1975) *British Historical Facts, 1830–1900*, London, Macmillan.

Cook, C.P. and Taylor, I. (1980) *The Labour Party: An Introduction to Its History, Structure and Politics*, London, Longman.

Crosland, C.A.R. (1956) *The Future of Socialism*, London, Cape.

Dalton, H.D. (1935) *Practical Socialism for Britain*, London, G. Routledge & Sons.

Dowse, R.E. (1966) *Left in the Centre: the Independent Labour Party 1893–1940*, London, Longman.

Dunbar, J. (1963) *Mrs G.B.S.: A Biographical Portrait of C. Shaw*, London, Harrap.

Durbin, E.F.M. (1939) *The Politics of Democratic Socialism: An Essay on Social Policy*, London, G. Routledge & Sons.

Dubin, E.F.M. (1942) *What Have We to Defend? A Brief Critical Examination of the British Social Tradition*, London, G. Routledge & Sons.

Eatwell, R. and Wright, A. (1978) 'Labour and the lessons of 1931', *History*, 63 (207), February.

Fremantle, A. (1960) *This Little Band of Prophets, the British Fabians*, London, Allen & Unwin.

Gordon, M.R. (1969) *Conflict and Consensus in Labour's Foreign Policy, 1914–1965*, Stanford, Ca, Stanford University Press.

Graubard, S.R. (1956) *British Labour and the Russian Revolution 1917–1924*, Cambridge, Mass., Harvard University Press.

Gregory, R.G. (1962) *Sidney Webb and East Africa: Labour's Experiment with the Doctrine of Native Paramountcy*, Berkeley and Los Angeles, University of Los Angeles Press.

Gupta, P.S. (1975) *Imperialism and the British Labour Movement, 1914–1964*, London, Macmillan.

Hall, H.D. (1920) *The British Commonwealth of Nations*, London, Methuen.

[Hardie, Keir] (c. 1918) *All About the ILP: Its Origin, Its Methods, Its Policy, Its Inspiration, Its Views on the War, Peace and the Settlement*, London, ILP Publications Department.

Harrison, M. (1960) *Trade Unions and the Labour Party since 1945*, London, Allen & Unwin.

Harrison, S. (1974) *Poor Men's Guardians: A Record of the Struggles for a Democratic Newspaper Press*, 1763–1973, London, Lawrence & Wishart.

Headey, B. (1974) *British Cabinet Ministers: The Roles of Politicians in Executive Office*, London, Allen & Unwin.

Henderson, A. (1918) *The Aims of Labour*, London, Labour Party.

Henderson, P. (1967) *William Morris: His Life, Work and Friends*, London, Thames & Hudson.

Hoffman, J.D. (1964) *The Conservative Party in Opposition, 1945–51*, London, MacGibbon & Kee.

Howson, S. and Winch, D. (1977) *The Economic Advisory Council, 1930–39: A Study in Economic Advice during Depression and Recovery*, Cambridge, Cambridge University Press.

Hulse, J.W. (1970) *Revolutionists in London: A Study of Five Unorthodox Socialists*, Oxford, Clarendon Press.

Hyams, E. (1963) *The New Statesman: The History of the First Fifty Years, 1913–63*, London, Longman.

Hyndman, H.M. (1911) *Record of an Adventurous Life*, London, Macmillan.

Idle, E.D. (1943) *War over West Ham*, A report prepared for the Fabian Society and the Ethical Union, London, Faber & Faber.

Joll, J. (1955) *The Second International, 1889–1914*, London, Weidenfeld & Nicolson.

Knight, W. (1907) *Memorials of Thomas Davidson, the Wandering Scholar*, London, T. Fisher Unwin.

Kogan, David and Maurice (1982) *The Battle for the Labour Party*, London, Kogan Page.

Koss, S. (1981) *The Rise and Fall of the Political Press in Britain, vol. I: The Nineteenth Century*, London, Hamish Hamilton.

Lapping, B. (1970) *The Labour Government 1964–70*, Harmondsworth, Penguin.

Laurence, D. (1965, 1972) *Bernard Shaw, Collected Letters*, 2 vols, London, Oxford University Press.

Lindsay, J. (1975) *William Morris*, London, Constable.

LSE (1926–8) *Clare Market*.

LSE (1953–73) *Clare Market Review*.

LSE (1934) *Register 1895–1932*, edited by the Registrar of the School with an introduction by the Director (W.H. Beveridge).

McBriar, A.M. (1962) *Fabian Socialism and English Politics, 1884–1918*, Cambridge, Cambridge University Press.

McCarran, M.M.P. (1954) *Fabianism in the Political Life of Great Britain, 1919–31*, Chicago, Heritage Foundation Inc.

MacDonald, J.R. (1923) *The Story of the I.L.P. and What It Stands For*, 30th anniversary edition, London, ILP Publications Department.

Mackenzie, N. (1978) 'Socialism and society: A new view of the Webb partnership', LSE lecture, 15 May.

Mackenzie, N. (ed.) (1978) *The Letters of Sidney and Beatrice Webb*, 3 vols, London, Weidenfeld & Nicolson.

Mackenzie, N. and J. (1973) *The Time Traveller: The Life of H.G. Wells*, London, Simon & Schuster.

Mackenzie, N. and J. (1977) *The First Fabians*, London, Weidenfeld & Nicolson.

Marquand, D. (1977) *Ramsay MacDonald*, London, Cape.

Martin, W. (1967) *The New Age under Orage*, Manchester, Manchester University Press.

Marwick, A. (1964) *Clifford Allen: The Open Conspirator*, London, Oliver & Boyd.

Massingham, H.W. (1892) *The London Daily Press*, The Religious Tract Society [London].

Miliband, R. (1961) *Parliamentary Socialism: A Study in the Politics of Labour*, London, Allen & Unwin.

Millar, J.P.M. (1978/9) *The Labour College Movement*, London, NCLC Publishing Society.

Moore, D.L. (1967) *E. Nesbit: A Biography*, London, Benn.

Moore, R. (1978) *The Emergence of the Labour Party, 1880–1924*, London, Hodder & Stoughton Educational.

Morrison, H. (1964) *Government and Parliament: A Survey from the Inside*, London, Oxford University Press.

Mowat, C.L. (1955) *Britain between the Wars 1918–40*, London, Methuen.

Muggeridge, K. and Adam, R. (1967) *Beatrice Webb: A Life, 1958–1943*, London, Secker & Warburg.

Nethercot, A.H. (1961) *The First Five Lives of Annie Besant*, London, Hart Davis.

Olivier, M. (1948) *Sydney Olivier, Letters and Selected Writings*, edited with a memoir by Margaret Olivier, with some impressions by Bernard Shaw, London, Allen & Unwin.

Owen, G. (1966) 'G.D.H. Cole's historical writings', *International Review of Social History*, XI, (2).

Parker, J. (1974) 'Oxford politics in the late twenties', *Political Quarterly*.

Parker, J. (forthcoming) *Fifty Years of Politics*.

Pearson, H. (1942) *Bernard Shaw: His Life and Personality*, London, Collins.

Pease, E. (1916, 1963) *The History of the Fabian Society*, London, Cass.

Pelling, H. (1963) *A History of British Trade Unionism*, Harmondsworth, Pelican.

Pelling, H. (1970) *Britain and the Second World War*, London, Fontana.

Pelling, H. (1976) *A Short History of the Labour Party*, London, Macmillan.

Pethick-Lawrence, E. (1938) *My Part in a Changing World*, London, Gollancz.

Pierson, S. (1979) *British Socialists: The Journey from Fantasy to Politics*, London, Harvard University Press.

Pimlott, B. (1977) *Labour and the Left in the 1930s*, Cambridge, Cambridge University Press.

Pritt, D.N. (1965) *Autobiography, Part One: From Right to Left*, London, Lawrence & Wishart.

Punnett, R.M. (1973) *Front-Bench Opposition: The Role of the Leader of the Opposition, the Shadow Cabinet and Shadow Government in British Politics*, London, Heinemann.

Qualter, T.H. (1980) *Graham Wallas and the Great Society*, London, Macmillan for LSE.

Quelch, H. [1894–5] *How I Became a Socialist*, Biographical Sketches, with Portraits, of H.M. Hyndman, William Morris, Walter Crane, J. Hunter Watts, Robert Blatchford, Tom Mann, etc. London, 20th Century Press.

Sanders, W.S. (1927) *Early Socialist Days*, London, Hogarth Press.

Saul, S.B. (1969) *The Myth of the Great Depression 1873–96*, London, Macmillan.

Schults, R.L. (1974) *Crusader in Babylon: W.T. Stead and the Pall Mall Gazette*, Lincoln, Neb., University of Nebraska Press.

Scott, J.W.R. (1950) *The Story of the Pall Mall Gazette, of its First Editor Frederick Greenwood, and Its Founder George Murray Smith*, London, Oxford University Press.

Seldon, A. (1981) *Churchill's Indian Summer: The Conservative Government 1951–54*, London, Hodder & Stoughton.

Shaw, G.B. (1909) 'Mr H.G. Wells and the rest of us', *Christian Commonwealth*, 19 May.

Sinclair, K. (1965) *William Pember Reeves: New Zealand Fabian*, London, Oxford University Press.

Skidelsky, R.J.A. (1967) *Politicians and the Slump*, London, Macmillan.

Snell, H. (1938) *Men, Movements and Myself*, London, J.M. Dent & Son.

Symon, J.D. (1914) *The Press and Its Story: An Account of the Birth and Development of Journalism up to the Present Day, with the History of all the Leading Newspapers*, London, Seeley, Service & Co.

Tawney, R.H. (1946) 'Beatrice Webb 1858–1943,' *Proceedings of the British Academy* XXIX (1943). With a bibliography by Sidney Webb.

Tawney, R.H. (1964) *The Radical Tradition*, London, Allen & Unwin.

Thompson, L. (1971) *The Enthusiasts: A Biography of John and Katherine Bruce Glasier*, London, Gollancz.

Thompson, P. (1967) *Socialists, Liberals and Labour: The Struggle for London 1885–1914*, London, Routledge & Kegan Paul.

Thomson, D. (1965) *England in the Twentieth Century*, Harmondsworth, Pelican.

Titmuss, R. (1970) *The Gift Relationship: From Human Blood to Social Policy*, London, Allen & Unwin.

Wallas, G. (1898) *The Life of Francis Place, 1771–1854*, London, Longman.

Webb [Potter], B. (1891) *The Co-operative Movement in Great Britain*, London, Sonnenschein.

Webb, B. (1910) *The New Crusade against Destitution: Being an Exposition of the Minority Report of the Poor Law Commission*, Manchester, Manchester National Labour Press.

Webb, B. (1911) *The Prevention of Destitution*, London.

Webb, B. (1921) 'The co-operative movement in Great Britain and its recent developments', *International Labour Review*, IV (2), November.

Webb, B. (1926) *My Apprenticeship*, London, Longman.

Webb, B. (1948) *Our Partnership*, ed. M.I. Cole and B. Drake, London, Longman.

Webb, B. (1952 and 1956) *Diaries 1912–24 and 1924–32*, ed. M.I. Cole, London, Longman.

Webb, B. (1963) *American Diary, 1898*, ed. David A. Shannon, Madison, Wisc., University of Wisconsin Press.

Webb, S. (1908) *The Basis and Policy of Socialism*, London.

Webb, S. and B. (1897) *Industrial Democracy*, London, Longman.

Webb, S. and B. (1898) *The History of Trade Unionism*, London, Longman.

Webb, S. and B. (1909) *Royal Commission on the Poor Laws and the Relief of Distress. The Break-up of the Poor Law: Being Part of the Minority Report of the Poor Law*, London, Longman.

Webb, S. and B. (1920) *A Constitution for the Socialist Commonwealth of Great Britain*, London, Longman.

Webb, S. and B. (1942) *The Truth about Soviet Russia: With a Preface on the Webbs by Bernard Shaw*, London, Longman.

Webb, S. and B. (1965) *Australian Diary 1898*, ed. A.G. Austin, Melbourne, Pitman.

Webb, S. and B. (1973) *Publications of Sidney and Beatrice Webb: An Interim Check List*, London, LSE.

Webb, S. and B. (1975) *Methods of Social Study*, London, Longman.

Webb, S. and Cox, H. (1891) *The Eight Hours Day*, London, W. Scott.

Webb, S. and Freeman, A. (1916) *Great Britain After the War. WEA Study Guide*, London, Allen & Unwin.

Wells, H.G. (1901) *Anticipations of the Reaction of Mechanical Progress upon Human Life and Thought*, London, Chapman & Hall.

Wells, H.G. (1903) *Mankind in the Making*, London, Chapman & Hall.

Wells, H.G. (1905) 'This misery of boots,' *Independent Review*, December.

Wells, H.G. (1909) *Ann Veronica*, London, T. Fisher Unwin.

Wells, H.G. (1911) *The New Machiavelli*, London, John Lane, Bodley Head.

Wells, H.G. (1934) *An Experiment in Autobiography*, London, Gollancz.

Williams, F. (1949) *Fifty Years March: The Rise of the Labour Party*, London, Odhams Press.

Williams, F. (1952) *Ernest Bevin: Portrait of a Great Englishman*, London, Hutchinson.

Williams, F. (1954) *Magnificent Journey: The Rise of the Trade Unions*, London, Odhams Press.

Williams, P.M. (1970) *Hugh Gaitskell: A Biography*, London, Cape.

Wilson, J.H. (1971) *The Labour Government 1964–70: A Personal Record*, London, Weidenfeld & Nicolson.

Wilson, J.H. (1979) *Final Term: The Labour Government 1974–76*, London, Weidenfeld & Nicolson.

Woolf, L.S. (1916) *International Government: Two Reports by L.S. Woolf Prepared for the Fabian Research Department, Together with a Project by a Fabian Committee for a Supernational Authority that will prevent War*, London, Fabian Society.

Woolf, L.S. (1920) *Economic Imperialism*, London, Swarthmore Press.

Woolf, L.S. (1920) *Empire and Commerce in Africa: A Study in Economic Imperialism*, London, Labour Research Department.

Woolf, L.S. (1960–9) *Autobiography*, 5 vols, London, Hogarth Press.

Worswick, G.D.N. and Ady, P.H. (eds) (1952) *The British Economy 1945–1950*, Oxford, Clarendon Press.

Wright, A.W. (1976) 'From Fabianism to guild socialism: The early political thought of G.D.H. Cole', *Society for the Study of Labour History, Bulletin* 32, Spring.

Wright, A.W. (1979) *G.D.H. Cole and Social Democracy*, Oxford, Clarendon Press.

Wrigley, W.D. (1978) 'The Fabian Society and the South African war, 1899–1902', *South African Historical Journal*, 10, November.

NAME INDEX

[–] Recorded membership dates.

Abel-Smith, Brian (1926–) [–84], 244, 246, 262, 271
Adams, Grantley Herbert, kt (1898–1971), 235
Archer, Peter (1926–), 273
Alden, Percy, kt (1865–1944) [1901–44], 70
Allen, Reginald Clifford, 1st baron of Hurtwood cr. 1932 (1889–1939) [1910–23], 101–4, 139
Atkinson, Henry (d. 1922) [1893–1922], 156
Atkinson, Mabel (1876–1958) [1897–1958], 96, 110–13, 117
Attlee, Clement Richard, 1st earl (1883–1967) [1907–67], 97, 140, 143, 145, 150, 158, 164–5, 167, 214–15, 236, 238, 244
Aveling, Edward, 43
Azikiwe, Nnamdi (1904–) [–1984], 234

Baker, Philip Noel, 186–7, 196
Ball, Sidney (1857–1918) [1886–1918], 73, 91
Ballinger, Margaret (1894–), 211
Balogh, Thomas, baron of Hampstead (life peer) (1905–) [1947–], 205, 235–6, 242
Banda, Hastings Kamuzu (1905–), 194, 234
Barnes, Leonard, 159, 186, 206
Bartley, James (1850–1926) [1890s], 41–2
Beales, H.L. [1932–], 165, 174
Bebel, August (1840–1913), 9
Benn, Anthony Wedgwood (1925–) [–1984], 243–5, 251, 262
Benson, Wilfred [1943–], 188, 235, 241
Bentham, Ethel (1861–1931) [1907–31], 109–10, 112
Besant, Annie (1847–1933) [1884–9, 1919–33], 9, 11–14, 16–17, 20–3, 26
Bevan, Aneurin (1897–1960), 229–30, 232, 238, 240

Beveridge, William Henry, 1st baron of Tuggal (1879–1969) [1908–11c.], 188, 202, 205–6
Bevin, Ernest (1881–1951) [1930–2], 157, 163–5, 167, 169–71, 202, 215
Blair, William Richard (1874–1932) [1926–32], 165
Bland, Edith (1858–1924) [1884–1924], 5, 10, 25, 108, 120
Bland, Hubert (1855–1914) [1884–1914], 3, 5–7, 12–13, 20–1, 23, 25, 29, 30, 33, 38, 53, 55, 60, 65, 70, 73, 75, 78, 87, 100–1, 127, 279
Bland, Rosamund [1906–], 87, 94
Blatchford, Robert Peel Glanville (1851–1943), 42, 163, 208
Bloch, Olaf (d. 1944) [1891–9], 34–5
Bondfield, Margaret Grace (1873–1953) [1908–21], 146, 151, 157
Brailsford, Henry Noel (1873–1958) [1896–], 139, 154, 170, 184, 197
Branting, Karl Hjalmar (1860–1925), 134–5
Briggs, Asa, baron of Lewes (1921–) [–1984], 252
Brockway, Archibald Fenner, baron (1888–), 139
Brooke, Rupert (1887–1915) [1908–15], 128
Burgess, John, 42–3, 49
Buxton, Charles Roden (1875–1942), 159, 241
Buxton, Noel Edward, baron Noel-Buxton (1869–1948) [1919–], 47, 156

Callaghan, Leonard James (1912–) [1942–84], 211, 250, 268
Campbell-Bannerman, Henry, kt (1836–1908), 69

321

SUBJECT INDEX